The Spatial and Economic Transformation of Mountain Regions

T0358877

Mountain regions are subject to a unique set of economic pressures: they act as collective enterprises which have to valorize rare resources, such as spectacular landscapes. While primarily rural in nature, they often border large cities, and the development of industries such as hydroelectric power and the rapid development of tourism can bring about sweeping socio-economic change and vast demographic alterations.

The Spatial and Economic Transformation of Mountain Regions describes the socio-economic changes and spatial impacts of the last four decades, with the transformation of mountain areas held up as an example. Much of the real-world context draws on the Alps, spanning as they do the significant economies of France, Italy, Germany, Switzerland, and Austria. Chapters address academic discourse on regional development in these mountain areas and suggest alternative approaches to the liberal-productivist societal model.

This book will be essential reading for professionals, institutions, and NGOs searching for counter-models to the existing marketing approaches for peripheral areas. It will also be of interest to students of regional development, economic geography, environmental studies, and industrial economics.

Manfred Perlik is a Professor at the Centre for Development and Environment at the University of Bern, Switzerland. He is also affiliated with Laboratoire Pacte, Unité Mixte de Recherche (UMR), at the Université Grenoble Alpes, France. As an economic geographer, his focus is on urbanization in mountain areas and his recent research deals with questions of spatial justice, transformative social innovation, and new migration – chosen or forced – into mountain areas.

Routledge Advances in Regional Economics, Science and Policy

For more information about this series, please visit www.routledge.com/series/RAIRESP

The Spatial and Economic Transformation of Mountain Regions

Landscapes as Commodities

Manfred Perlik

Routledge
Taylor & Francis Group

LONDON AND NEW YORK

First published 2019 by Routledge

2 Park Square, Milton Park, Abingdon, Oxfordshire OX14 4RN
52 Vanderbilt Avenue, New York, NY 10017

Routledge is an imprint of the Taylor & Francis Group, an informa business

First issued in paperback 2020

British Library Cataloguing-in-Publication Data
A catalogue record for this book is available from the British Library

Library of Congress Cataloging-in-Publication Data
A catalog record for this book has been requested

ISBN: 978-1-138-78408-6 (hbk)
ISBN: 978-0-367-66254-7 (pbk)

Typeset in Bembo
by Apex CoVantage, LLC

To Claudia, whose thinking influenced this book so much.
Dr. Claudia Roth, social anthropologist
(1955–2012)

Contents

PART IV
The new disparities and possible alternatives 199

Figures

Tables

Plates

Abbreviations

ARE	Federal Office for Spatial Development – Office Fédéral du développement territorial (Switzerland)
ARL	Academy for Spatial Research and Planning – Akademie für Raumforschung und Landesplanung (Germany)
BBSR	Federal Institute for Research on Building, Urban Affairs and Spatial Development – Bundesinstitut für Bau-, Stadt- und Raumforschung (BBSR) (Germany)
BfS/OfS	Federal Statistical Office – Bundesamt für Statistik/Office fédéral de la Statistique (Switzerland)
disP	*The Planning Review*, Journal of ETHZ NSL, Zurich (Switzerland)
GB	*Geographica Bernensia* (Switzerland)
GH	*Geographica Helvetica*
HKH	*Hindu Kush Himalayan*
JAR-RGA	*Journal of Alpine Research/Revue de Géographie Alpine* (formerly *Revue de Géographie Alpine* or *Revue de Géographie Alpine/Journal of Alpine Research*) (France)
MRD	Mountain Research and Development (Switzerland)
NZZ	Neue Zürcher Zeitung (Switzerland)
RERU	Revue d'Economie Régionale et Urbaine (France)
SECO	State Secretariat for Economic Affairs – Secrétariat d'Etat à l'économie (Switzerland)
SNSF	Swiss National Science Foundation

Preface

This book represents the reworked contents of a habilitation thesis completed in 2012 at the Université Grenoble Alpes. The analysis, interpretation, and the political conclusions – especially the integration of the topics of regional mountain ranges in a global context – were already contained in this text, which up to now was only accessible in its French original. The main topic of this original text was the repercussions on mountain areas of the paradigmatic transformation from post-war Fordist societies to the liberal-productivist post-Fordism. These repercussions were seen in an increase of the functional polarization between metropolitan regions (mostly located in the lowlands), and the comparatively sparsely populated mountain areas, although the structural inferiority of mountain areas is obscured by a selective valorization of the commodified landscape and state transfer payments.

Six years later, we see much more clearly the consequences of the paradigmatic turn of the 1980s. It is expressed in an increasing dynamism by all social actors to grasp chances for better livelihoods. It includes the dramatic increase in global migration flows that have also affected mountain areas worldwide, as areas of emigration as well as immigration. The immigration of 'migrants by choice' in the form of amenity migration is only the most visible form. However, it is inconceivable without the flip side of 'migrants by need' (labour migration) and 'migrants by force' (refugees). The new dynamic includes the separatist tendencies of the richest regions to reap the fruits of regional competition and the revival of a nationalist interpretation of the social question among the poor. These tendencies – which are not new but have become more pronounced – made it necessary to realign the book. The focus remains on mountain areas. The general statement also remains the same: that the post-Fordist turn did not increase the options of the mountain regions; instead, it reduced them to the selective use of landscape commodities. But the conclusions are discussed differently in this book than in the French original. The reorientation affects the question of how mountain-specific development strategies and policies are still justified in this new context, without serving particular interests. In other words, where is the boundary between justified regional interests and regional egoism? Therefore, this book is in large part new, and can no longer be regarded as just the English translation of the French original.

I am aware that the book contains some redundancies. This is because each chapter tries to conduct the discussion from a different perspective, while preserving all the facts and arguments. In some cases, the redundancies are needed in the argumentation to better understand the text; in other cases, they may have expanded the text too much. Deciding what to leave out and what to expand on was always a tightrope walk. I have tried to keep the terminology as precise as possible, but in the interests of comprehensibility technical terms are omitted or synonyms are used where they are not the core of the argument. The reader should also be aware that many terms are used synonymously. This is because the authors of the underlying concepts often use different terms for similar descriptions of phenomena and their interpretation, where I see no need for a preference for one term over another. Finally, the breadth of this topic means that while the bibliography is long, it is not yet exhaustive. To limit the scope, some frequently quoted publications had to be omitted in favour of mentioning more recent research. In other cases, it appeared necessary to mention older sources to show the origin of the arguments, even if the authors are not always cited in the text.

This book covers a personal trajectory from the social sciences to physical geography and back again, and so many people influenced this work in some way that I cannot name them all to thank them. I have tried to make them visible by quoting their works. Nevertheless, those who supported me most in recent years with their ideas and help must be highlighted and acknowledged: Marie-Christine Fourny and Bernard Pecqueur from the Laboratoire Pacte of the Université Grenoble Alpes were the driving forces behind my habilitation in 2012, which forms the basis of this book. I owe them many thanks for their help. The French-Swiss jury was composed of Martin Schuler (EPFL Lausanne), Gian-Paolo Torricelli (University of Italian Switzerland, Mendrisio), Olivier Crevoisier (University of Neuchâtel), Stéphane Nahrath (University of Lausanne), and Nathalie Bertrand (IRSTEA Grenoble). Anne Roth-Huggler (Zurich), in old age, did much work on the German–French translation for the French original, which cannot be honoured enough. Claudia Roth, my companion in life, supported this work from its beginnings with creative and critical ideas and discussions until her early death in 2012. As a long-standing researcher in Burkina Faso, she opened my view on West Africa and the application of Pierre Bourdieu's concepts.

The adaptation of the original work to the needs of the changed socio-economic environment of 2018 was supported by constructive criticism from Paul Messerli (University of Bern), who was already my mentor during the work on Alpine Towns in 2001, as well as from Martin Schuler and from Thomas Kohler (CDE, University of Bern). I am grateful for further reviews from Alice Ludvig (Vienna) and Bill Slee (Aberdeen) and the inspirations of the research networks SIMRA and ForAlps dealing with social innovation and on refugees at the mountain areas. I thank Jürg Krauer and the CDE

Bern for the production of several coloured maps inside the book. Ray Rasker (Bozeman, Montana) gave me the permission to publish one of his maps and Roberto Sega (EPFL Lausanne) adapted one of the maps from his recent thesis for this book. Finally, I would like to thank friends and family members who have supported me with their discussions and ideas in recent years, especially Sylviane Sapir, Florentin Sehn, Marlies Perlik, Antonia Dufner, and Peter Kaufmann. Tina Hirschbuehl (CDE, University of Bern) accompanied the final step and edited the rough translation. Many thanks to all.

Manfred Perlik
Basel, December 2018

Part I

Space, environment, and culture as a social question

Figure 1.1 Beauty and ugliness are no fixed judgements. They vary in space and time. The beauty of a landscape depends on societal perceptions and conventions. Its use and protection evoke trade-offs and conflicts of interest between the involved stakeholders, which become global.

Photo: North side of the Matterhorn/Monte Cervino in the Monte Rosa massif of the Pennine Alps at the Swiss-Italian border. GPS: N 46° 15.507′ E 8°28.745′, 18 February 2016.

Why this book? The common thread linking mountain development and global change

There is a huge selection of literature on mountains around the world. Some of these publications cover aesthetic issues and environmental questions, or they provide overviews of history and socio-spatial development. Others focus on urban, peripheral, and development issues, but deal mainly with sectoral aspects: the socio-economic processes taking place in metropolitan areas, intra-metropolitan differentiation and segregation, the urban transformation of rural areas, or the issue of urban-rural linkages. What is missing among these books is one discussing the new relationship between metropolitan areas and mountain regions.

Mountains are important. They deliver a considerable part of the tangible and intangible resources used worldwide. Biophysical processes occurring in the mountains have an influence on the whole Earth. Mountains host 13 per cent of the world's people, most of them living in countries of the Global South; most of them poor. Mountains have characteristics that differ considerably from flat areas, making them good case studies for between-group comparisons. Thus, mountains can serve as a laboratory to show spatial transformations and disparities more clearly than other types of territory. But the aim of this book is not only to describe. Nor is it intended as applied engineering or spatial planning for a certain region. Instead, the aim of this book is to analyse the current social transformations in terms of their repercussions on mountain territories, in order to find more balanced perspectives for the interaction with the metropolitan areas of the lowlands.

The main objective of my original work in 2012 was to show the impacts on mountain areas of the paradigmatic transformation from post-war Fordist societies to liberal-productivist post-Fordism. In the liberal-productivist context, these impacts comprise a global functional and spatial division of labour, where mountain areas turn into suppliers of specialized commodities – from raw materials to leisure – for the global hubs.

Since 2012, the negative effects of this liberal-productivist turn have become clearer, showing an increased global struggle for rare resources and the claim by ever greater numbers of people to have the unfulfilled promises of a stable middle-class future met. It is linked with the return of the old nationalist trump card, which negatively influences the debate on regional development and spatial differences. For the first time in the post-Fordist period, we are again seeing signs of agglomeration disadvantages in Europe's largest cities, through a new quality of physical insecurity and violence. The discussion on new types of spatial disparities today must consider this situation.

In the first part of this book, I discuss mountain questions in the context of socio-economic theories and approaches. Starting with the relation between humans and nature, I state that biophysical (environmental) questions are socio-economic questions, as long as the access to clean, non-polluted resources is guaranteed for certain parts of a population and as long as it is possible for certain parts to flee, or migrate, to other territories. Furthermore, I posit that the increase in diversity, said to be one of the criteria of post-Fordist societies, is pseudo-diversity, as its interpretation is scale-dependent. It is therefore also a question of the varying social mobility of individuals or groups of social actors, as shown in the example of the Lesotho Highlands Water Project in Chapter 4. Furthermore, there are always two sides to the diversity coin; its flip side is disparity.

The environmental and diversity topics are crucial for mountains, as these features are more rapidly and clearly visible than in lowlands, especially in cases of environmental degradation, errors in land use, or oscillations in population and economic activity. Space is a social construction, but it is based on material preconditions that influence the region-specific development path, or trajectory, by favouring specific uses while impeding others (lock-in). With the enlargement of economic and labour markets and the induced economic growth since industrialization, these interactions with the natural basis have been relativized. However, they still exist and define the specific options and restrictions of regional development paths: While today it is possible to construct high buildings in mountain areas, no national capital city will voluntarily relocate from the lowlands to the mountains. But also non-mountain areas will still be dependent on biophysical restrictions and facilitators (ecosystem services), and the depletion of mountain resources and the consequences of an out-of-control climate may generate a huge global irritation, not as "clashing cultures" but as a culture of clashes.

Part II uses mountain research findings (both my own and external) to prove the stated interpretations on the post-Fordist regime shift, which are discussed in Part III. The post-war years in the second half of the 20th century were characterized by the emergence of the welfare state in different, nation-specific expressions. The welfare state system reflects a social compromise, especially between capital and labour, but also in terms of equal territorial opportunities and burdens. With the Fordist crisis, this compromise is broken up in favour of a welfare regime at its lowest common denominator – volunteerism and charity. Although regional differences remain, it is the general tendency that every region has to take on self-responsibility for its economic activities by technical and product innovation and the commodification of landscapes. As the metropolitan decision-making hubs are located mainly in lowland areas, the mountain areas will mainly rely on those value chains that have a lower specific value added. Although there are exceptions and counter-tendencies, and although mountain regions may be successful in the economic short term, mountain regions reinforce a structural inferiority towards the lowland metropolitan areas.

Part IV discusses possible trajectories of mountain regions. It is assumed that global mountain development will follow a similar path to that of the European Alps, albeit with a considerable time lag (hysteresis). Further mountain development is interpreted from the aspect of a continuous increase in social interactions (sociation, or *Vergesellschaftung*). It is manifested spatially in the form of ongoing urbanization.

I draw three trajectories for mountain regions. The first corresponds to current mainstream metropolitan growth, where metropolitan areas functionally integrate their hinterlands. It might make the strongest regions even stronger. As a second trajectory, a regionalist concept is presented in which cooperation is limited to the Alpine arc and does not include the peri-alpine metropolitan regions. Such a concept is widely seen as a mountain-specific counter-model to the effects of globalization. It has up to now no real foundation, and it is not clear who would really benefit from such restricted cooperation. As region-specific solutions have become popular in the last decades, we highlight severe drawbacks in the form of isolation, segregation, and a deepening territorial cleavage. What both trajectories have in common is that they claim mountain- and region-specific solutions with arguments of economic efficiency (trajectory 1) or cultural identity (trajectory 2). Both development paths therefore do not correspond to the idea of cohesive regional development.

As a solution, I propose a third trajectory. Trajectory 3 seeks to avoid polarization between metropolitan decision-making regions and monostructured leisure regions, and it rejects isolationist-regionalist identity-driven exclusion. In such a trajectory, the metropolitan regions would have to accept that mountain regions can never be as productive as lowland regions, and they would have to support them accordingly. The mountain regions, on the other hand, must increasingly draw on external knowledge from the metropolises, to be able to react critically to the demands of use brought to them from the outside. On this basis, relations between mountain areas and lowlands would have to be renegotiated.

1 Why study mountains?

Mountains as a laboratory and pertinent indicator

1.1 The specificity of mountains

This book focuses on socio-economic developments of mountain areas in a global context, and the relationship of these areas to the densely populated lowlands. It is based mainly on knowledge of recent socio-economic and spatial processes in the European Alps, the mountain range I take as a reference for development and spatial patterns in the developed countries, those of the Global North. Taking into account development processes in other important mountain ranges in developed and developing countries, I compare recent development paths and try to find common processes.

The European Alps are a 1,200-kilometre-long and 150–250-kilometre-wide mountain range formed during the Late Mesozoic to the Cenozoic (Alpine orogeny). They are part of the Alpidic belt that reaches from the Maghreb Atlas, the Cantabrian Mountains and Pyrenees, via the Carpathians to the Hindu Kush Himalayan and the Indochine mountains. The European Alps (hereafter often 'the Alps') form a large arc that divides Central Europe and Southern Europe in the middle of Europe's most prosperous area, the *Blue Banana* (Brunet, 1989), reaching from the southern United Kingdom to the north of Italy. Therefore, the Alps are exemplary of similar mountain ranges on a global scale that can be considered well-developed, and which have undergone a profound transformation from rural to urban societies. Many processes of the Alps can also be seen in other mountain areas – in developed countries as well as emerging economies – as will be shown with some examples. Assuming there is no fundamental change in global processes, it is foreseeable that these other areas will in large part follow the Alpine transformations. For this reason, we can take the European Alps as a role model for recent development processes of mountain areas worldwide.

But apart from finding solutions to local problems, why should we study mountains at all? Certain problems and assets are unique to mountains, such as exposed topographies and specific scarcities, vulnerabilities, cultures, and resources. Much research has already been conducted to describe, interpret, and treat these issues by generations of researchers in all countries of the European Alps, as well as in many other mountain regions. This gives us a broad trove to work with, allowing us to discuss overarching questions on a more general level, by proving hypotheses of these works. This will be done to show the functional and socio-economic developments of territories that have been considered peripheral for a long time. Therefore, and in particular, this book examines the change in territorial relations, and highlights the occurrence of new spatial disparities under conditions of a changed paradigm of social relations. This change began in the 1970s and was fully underway in the 1980s, with the turn from Fordist to liberal-productivist regimes of value adding and governance.

(a)   The Alps as a role model for the diverse socio-economic development of mountains

In 20th-century Europe, mountain areas were at the periphery of economic and societal development, raising only occasional interest from a larger public. The significance of mountain areas has been emphasized especially by experts in natural sciences, natural hazards, or specific mountain resources. These resources can be tangible products such as water, raw materials, or capacity as ecological buffers ('ecosystem services') – but also (and increasingly), intangible resources such as aesthetics, spectacular scenery, objects of individual emotion and perception, and symbolic values.[1] The resources of the peripheries are essential for the growing demands of an increasing number of mobile people and globalized economies. Those who treat mountains from the socio-economic point of view do this mainly out of their interest in rural development. Mountains seen as a part of global urban development is quite rare.

The Alps are at the heart of Europe, between the most prosperous European agglomerations. For a long time, they were relatively densely populated and constituted an ensemble of cultural landscapes.[2] Their different altitudinal belts were cultivated for agriculture, and their territorialization at the end of the Middle Ages served to control transport routes and to constitute transalpine empires (especially Savoie-Piedmont). Today, they are completely integrated into global circuits as areas for the production and export of food, some highly specialized manufacturing industries, and leisure and residence. But they can also be seen as being on the European periphery, if we look at large parts of unconstructible, unusable land, and its location on the border between Central and Southern Europe, without a dominant regional capital. Viewed at the intersection of the European Blue Banana and the European Sunbelt, the Alps are part of a cluster of the most important European metropolitan regions. The Alps are both the reference and the laboratory for mountain regions in the European context: They illustrate the trajectory of uneven spatial development in Europe, where the historic medieval cities became the cores of today's metropolitan areas while the hinterlands became peripheral in absolute or relative terms. But we will see that the degree of this peripherality varied over time, and was not a linear trajectory, although we see a long-term process to urban forms of settlement.

Contrary to other types of territory, mountain regions have a specific 'vertical dimension' (Mathieu, 2011), which in agrarian times had some advantages over narrow valleys and inundated floodplains. These days, under a technologi-cal regime that primarily allows long horizontal distances to be rapidly over-come, this is a critical disadvantage. But it is not only the time needed to bridge distances that distinguishes highlands from lowlands. The gradient of altitude was also the source of a huge diversity of different human practices within a very small area to survive, work, and live in a hostile environment. This diversity developed in exchange with the lowlands and created an important comple-mentarity to them. The diversity was necessary in olden times as risk-avoiding practices of 'trial and error' and 'checks and balances'. It has been devalued with the socio-economic and technological changes of the 20th century. I will come back to this topic of diversity in Chapter 3. Mountain regions are therefore a specific example of the constellation of a former favoured space that has lost its advantage during the last century. It shows qualities that are outdated for the needs of the mainstream economy, and disadvantages that impede the overcom-ing of disparities – but it has resources that have caught the interest of external economic and social actors. This is a combination of factors that makes them ideally suited for analysis of asymmetric territorial relations.

The Alps show the evolution of a large territory at the heart of Europe that has lost its influence in the 20th century due to less profitable production systems than in the lowland economies and a delayed coming into force of Fordist equalization policies. Today – as the guiding hypothesis – a selective upturn under liberal-productivist conditions is transforming the Alpine regions to fulfil the specific needs of consumption of the stronger lowlands. Discussion and analysis is needed of this new revival of city centres and metropolitan areas, and the new functional significance of mountainous regions and their future options. This significance must be examined especially in terms of the relations with the much more densely populated urban areas of the lowlands, their eco-nomic strength, and the division of institutional and political functions between these different territories.

(b) The specificity of the mountains is not their ecological fragility: the ecological question as a social question, and vice versa

Why are mountainous regions so often chosen as the subject of research? For the scientific community and NGOs engaged in environmental protection, the answer seemed – for a long time – quite simple: the exceptional fragility of the mountains exposed to anthropogenic interventions. Global biodiversity exists in large parts due to the multitude of altitudes and microclimates of mountains but it is also transforming – 'migrating' – with the anthropogenic impact (Körner, 2015). Another common argument points to the water and food resources contained in mountain areas, whose surface area occupies 20 per cent of the globe, and that metropolitan areas of the plains and their popula-tion depend largely on these resources (e.g. CDE, 2009). Thus, most arguments focus on biophysical factors of risk and danger but seem to be neglected by a majority of decision-makers around the globe. In any case, they are not taken seriously enough to change the current practices of consumption, land use, and spatial (and climatic) transformation, which have all been clearly identified. Either there is a lack of will to understand the consequences, or the argument is not as powerful as we believed.

In a globalized world, in which the business model is based on the assumption that in the interaction of free trade and technological progress, each resource can be replaced by another, the argument of exceptional fragility of a limited territory is not convincing. If we hypothetically and counterfactually accept this argument that each resource is substitutable, then the value of mountain resources is defined only by the cost of the commodities that can replace them. In other words, if the reserves of water, biodiversity, Alpine dwelling places, or near-natural landscapes are no longer available, one can try to substitute them through technological progress or high investments to compensate the lacking resources (e.g. long-distance pipelines of clear, or technically cleared, water). This hypothetical substitution is valid even if one considers the underlying business model mainly as false and unsustainable in the long run. The problem is that while major decisions operate according to the logic that all resources are replaceable, long-term limitations are not sufficiently taken into account – or only when it is too late. The environmental sciences are trying to take into account the problem of cost, using the approach of ecosystem services (MA, 2005) and calculating the value of the endangered resources. The higher the value of the exhaustion or pollution of a resource, the greater the disincentive to exploit or to pollute further. But this procedure to calculate the value is never neutral and always contestable.[3] It is contested first by those who are interested in making another calculation, be it to pursue exploitation to continue with their business activities, or to end exploitation for ecological reasons. The used parameters will be normative and a result of negotiation power.

The ecosystem services approach has the advantage of giving the impression that 'natural values' depend on societal interpretation, preferences, and appreciation, and that access to these resources plays a crucial role. In the current context of increased mobility, individuals and social groups are, in principle, able to leave inhospitable areas, albeit at high social and financial cost – and, of course, not all social actors have this possibility to the same degree. This is not meant to be a cynical discourse. From the point of view of a secure supply of resources and environmental hazards, the peculiarity of mountains thus appears to be a gradual and not an essential problem – it depends on whether society accepts to abandon the area or wants to maintain it for human working and living. Taking this argument means that the extraordinary fragility of mountain areas is a cost factor like others, but one that could lead to major global irritation and still larger crises than seen up to now. But in the logic of the mainstream economy, it can be solved by reducing it to a matter of cost. In this argument, the Alps (and the mountains in general) are no different from other regions. There are no compelling reasons to treat them as special cases, or to take the mountains as an example of new disparities because of their topography alone.

But, as already mentioned, not all individuals or social strata have the same opportunity to flee, be it for financial or political reasons, because migration costs rise exponentially with increasing difficulties, and borders are closed selectively. The question of staying or leaving is therefore a social problem, as long as environmental changes affect only parts – and not all – of the world population.

For research on the issues of equality, equivalence, or spatio-social disparities, the interest in vulnerability of Alpine landscapes, ecosystems, and the impact of anthropogenic use is therefore important. But the impact is indirect. Vulnerability can destabilize societies in the medium term, but this effect is not limited exclusively to mountain areas. As of yet we have no answer to the questions: What is the particularity of mountainous regions that justifies taking mountains as a reference for spatial development? What qualifies mountain development as a marker?

We have thus seen that ecological questions become social questions, but the opposite is also true: social questions are ecological questions. This can be seen in the strategies taken to solve the social question, whether it is followed by a strategy of productivist growth or by a strategy of lower risks and less productivity. The productivist path strives for high impact in environmental and technical innovation, high returns on investment, and a sufficient redistribution of value added. In the ideal case, it produces more wealth at the national level and thus offers the financial means to repair damaged ecosystems and societies. The path of lower risks limits the growth of available GDP and necessitates higher efforts on fair rules for bargaining between social actors. In the ideal case, it reduces the societal costs for repairs of the environment and of violent conflicts.

This raises the questions of which products are produced, where, under what working conditions, and with how much impact on the biophysical sphere. Who decides about techniques of production and the orientation of the kind of innovations that are taken (which stakeholders should be addressed, which ecosystems, and which relation between humans and biosphere)? Which decision-makers should decide about change or an end of certain technologies, and when?

One can see that ecological degradation can provoke social crises – and, vice versa, social degradation can provoke ecological crises. It depends on which aspect prevails (Lipietz, 2012). From this we can deduce which aspects should be highlighted in policy processes for counter-steering towards sustainable development.

What role does the fragile ecological setting now play? Fragile ecosystems also exist in other areas: maritime and littoral zones, soils in the belts of tropical forests, arid zones, seismic vulnerable areas, and so on. All are different, and all have their advantages and disadvantages. But we have to separate simple 'otherness' (which means the perception of the visitor) from 'specificity' (which defines the conditions for human interaction). To say one landscape is different from another is banal. It takes on its specificity only from the options and restrictions that it causes for human settlement and work. The ecological conditions play a role here, as they offer varying conditions for the interaction between humans and the biosphere. These conditions are not static, and therefore not deterministic. They change over time, within society, and with technical ability. With advanced technologies, the differences between physical conditions can be mitigated and might allow other options – if there has been investment in research, and the efforts in adopting new options are seen as worthwhile.

In short: fragile ecosystems are not exclusive to mountains, and technical progress improves accessibility and reduces restrictions on human activities, overcoming the disadvantages of steep and mountainous territories.

(c) The lacking explanatory power of culture and identity

This book does not use concepts of culture or regional identity to explain regional development in mountain areas. Why? In the same way as for the ecological question, we can see culture as a constellation of social practices that can be derived from the contested interests of social actors in a defined social field. Every social or ethnic group, and of course any individual, has an interest to live their life under the best conditions possible. Under this aspect, culture represents a strategy to explain and mitigate the troubles and efforts of every-day life that have developed over a long time and in a specific context – and to emancipate themselves from these. In this sense, we can subsume the practices of the mountain areas' social actors under the experiences they made in their everyday life in a certain territory (a given mountain region), and in their relations and socio-economic exchange with the social actors of the lowland areas. As the exposition to biophysical nature and its constraints in mountain areas resulted in specific economies and forms of living, different as well as similar practices of life and economy developed in different parts of the mountains over time.[4] The relative independence from natural constraints has led to a decrease in mountain-related similarities. Instead, the penetration of external technologies is loosening the dependence on the natural environment, and the inclusion in global markets is generating new needs and preferences also among mountain dwellers. We can speak less than ever of an independent mountain culture.

Neither will I treat in depth the notion of identity for the development of specific regional practices in mountains. Under this aspect, identity represents a strategy to maintain a certain way of life that was once chosen, which took effort and is linked with a collective memory, and which is defended against the claims of new stakeholders, irrespective of whether these claims are justified or not, and irrespective of whether they are real or only perceived.

Each culture and each identity is, in this view, a material resource, such as ecological qualities. Nonetheless, the notion of identity is useful to describe the individual behaviour of social actors and social groups. The book does not focus on this approach in explaining spatial disparities, but I will refer to it in Chapter 9 in commenting on the practices of national-oriented and identity-based solutions, which in the public discourse are proposed as simple solutions to overcome spatial and social disparities.

(d) The historic trajectory as a universal indicator for specificity

What, if not the fragile ecology, makes mountains so specific? As it is human interaction, and the potential for human perception and use that constitutes a specificity, it is the vertical dimension and the lack of exploitable space that in the past was decisive for another development in the mountains than in the lowlands. But this alone is not constitutive when we consider that technical achievements would now allow us to live and work in mountains in the same way as in existing metro-regions or in the 'smart cities' that are planned in the deserts of the Middle East.

In Europe, people have remained sceptical about offers such as 'Come to work where others go on holiday', and their reliance on mobile phones for their professional careers or their personal relationships is not so high as to tempt them to consider a permanent move to the mountains. Regional capitals are located mainly in the lowlands, and they continue to grow. The world's high-risk zones for earthquakes, Tokyo and Los Angeles/San Francisco, are still attracting people. This provides enough arguments to explain spatial patterns through the persistence of preformed structures. Although it is possible to choose other places to live, work, or invest, the lock-in of prefigured structures constitutes a trajectory that is not given up, as the costs for a complete change would be too high. As mountains once had the disadvantage of being on the periphery, they remained sparsely populated during the industrialization period. They still remain so today, expressed in lacking national or regional capitals, even though the disadvantages could now be overcome by technical means. The development paths of the lowlands and highlands diverged, with lowlands having the advantages of agglomeration economies and the political decision in favour of technologies to bridge long distances at the horizontal level. Therefore, we can summarize the specificity of mountains by the dominant geo-factors of relief, soil, and climate, but only in combination with human activity and the trajectory of history that has been explained by evolutionary economy (Arthur, 1989; Nelson and Winter, 1982). In the past, under the Fordist paradigm, it seemed that the new technologies of the time might be used to equalize the disparities (no matter the cost). Under liberal-productivist conditions, the relief, steepness, bad accessibility, etc. have again become a factor of exclusion. Once again, it is the agglomerations in the form of the new metropolitan areas that benefit most from their density, by being able to attract people for the research and implementation of new technologies.

(e) The mountains as a case study for the spatial division of labour and asymmetric governance

Mountains have been populated since the early times of humankind because of favourable conditions for pastoralism or agriculture. They were able to establish auto-sufficient economic systems and also larger empires such as the Incan societies in the Andes.

But in most cases, the differentiation of societies preceded a development path where the mountains remained rural for a long time. Industrialization seized mountains in the Global North due to local hydropower, raw materials, and a cheap workforce, but these locational advantages remained only for a short time. Mountain areas turned to peripheries while technology-based industry and business services industries developed outside the mountains. During the social and spatial compromise of the Fordist period, the regional policies of the 1970s tried to equalize territorial development. With the liberal-productivist turn, a new push for spatial differentiation can be observed. We see a new stage of spatial division of labour on a global scale – where Asia has become the workplace of the world, the countries of the South are transformed into food suppliers, and the countries of the global cities, mainly in the North, strengthen their position as headquarters. The centre–periphery discussion enters a new chapter. Mountains are specializing and trying to valorize new resources and commodities.

With their morphological, demographic, and economic differences to the lowlands, mountains make ideal between-group comparisons. They are places where the rarity of biophysical resources (environmental goods) and of prestigious resources (reputational goods or symbolic capital) are superposed, expressed by the exposition towards natural hazards, as well as by the desire for a place of high-end leisure and of residence. A rather new phenomenon is that they also become locations for poor migrants and displaced persons (Dematteis and Membretti, 2016; Perlik and Membretti, 2018). Of course, these two aspects exist in other places, too. But they are visible in this clear difference only in the mountains and can therefore generate research about practices of individuals as well as social relations between groups of stakeholders on questions of social justice (Harvey, 1973) or spatial justice (Soja, 2010). This makes mountains an ideal laboratory in which to study new patterns of spatial, territorial, and social developments. Mountain research allows us to recognize new spatial developments that may be less visible in lowland areas. This applies especially to the development of specialized zones of leisure. But the new insights also allow reflections that may contribute to further developing theoretical approaches of regional development and spatial disparities. I will discuss these theoretical approaches in more detail in Chapter 2. Finally, mountain research allows us – and this is also one of the objectives of this book – to provide some answers to the question of which possible paths might be available to peripheral regions in the future.

1.2 How to read this book

This book presents an empirical analysis of the last three decades that is intended to show the impacts of global socio-spatial changes on mountainous and less populated areas ('rural'). The common denominator is the issue of changing spatial inequality under the following general questions:

- How are spatial hierarchies changing in the transformation from Fordist to liberal-productivist paradigms under globalization?

- What are the options for people in non-metropolitan areas, especially in mountainous regions, in the framework of increasing significance of agglomeration effects and social interactions?

The mountain areas of the world are an ideal laboratory in which to analyse these questions: Mountains deliver essential resources to the lowlands, host a population that is not yet completely integrated in the circuits of global commodification, and serve as an early-warning system to the consequences of environmental spoliation. This means that we first need an answer to the following question:

- What are the specificities of mountain areas compared to the rest of the globe? What are the consequences for mountain areas of the existence (or non-existence) of this specificity?

The countries of the Alpine arc in Europe serve as the main empirical basis. I am aware that comparability with other mountain massifs is limited and, in particular, that there are considerable differences between the mountains of the Global North and the Global South. For example, the mountains of the South are to a much greater extent raw material suppliers. On the other hand, many of the current developments in the wealthy countries are being adopted by the countries of the Global South, in the framework of rising global mobility and emerging domestic middle classes, as expressed in tourist hotspots in the Himalayas (Jacquemet, 2018) or the multilocal residences in Chili (Marchant and Rojas, 2015). The theoretical framework is based on four pillars:

1 the dialectic relation between human social practices and the natural environment;
2 the significance of political economy for spatial development, territorialization, and uneven living conditions;
3 the territorial capital derived from the historic trajectory and serving as a certain but non-deterministic constant of the social relations and future options in a given territory; and
4 the national and regional regulations, as well as traded and untraded dependencies developed on the basis of the social relations that serve as a constant, but also as elements of change.

The theoretical approaches are not specific to mountains, but their application to mountain territories gives us new insights into uneven territorial development.

The book is divided into four parts, with two to four chapters each. In Part I, 'Space, environment and culture as a social question', I treat mountain topics as a chain of social questions rather than focus on environmental and biophysical problems. Social questions are interpreted as derivates of prevailing questions of power, articulated interests of social actors, and class structures, however they might be defined. (Please note that it is not the aim of the book to deliver any precise class analysis of social actors, so notions such as *class*, *strata*, *layers*, etc. are used situatively and can often be seen in this context as synonyms.) Part II, 'Devaluation and revaluation of territorial capital in mountain areas', treats the observable processes of spatial and socio-economic development in mountain areas in their relation to lowland and metropolitan areas. This part therefore contains the empirical examples, as well as most parts of the literature linked to case studies of regional development and governance in mountain areas. Part III, 'A new level of inequality', is the interpretation and discussion of the description in the previous part. It is followed by Part IV, 'The new disparities and possible alternatives'. Should we accept the presented results? Are there other perspectives? How can we solve the described problems? Of course, this discourse can only show a rather general perspective, and will not treat concrete governance and management questions. For this, the reader should look at consulting reports and results of projects on regional development, etc. The book is intended to be read as a whole, but of course it is possible for readers familiar with mountain issues to read only specific parts. There are intended redundancies, which allows for parts to be read independently.

We are well aware that books today cannot be read in a week, and that there are parts which, at the beginning, are more interesting than others. For the busy reader, therefore, it may be useful to know that Chapters 2 and 3 offer an introduction. Chapter 9 contains the conclusions in the form of three different future trajectories, each of which may create a different scenario. Chapter 10 tries to go beyond the existing logics. The chapters in between present empirical research (Chapters 4 and 5) and a discussion of the findings (Chapters 6, 7, and 8).

Notes

1 Cf. the thematic issues of *Journal of Alpine Research/ Revue de Géographie Alpine* vols. 103(3) and 104(3).
2 Human activities in the Alps were much earlier than in many European low mountain ranges. Pastoralism in the form of transhumance dates to about 6,000 years ago (Spindler, 2003).
3 See also Kolinjivadi et al., 2017.
4 For example, similar environmentally based forms of land use but different culturally based settlement patterns in two neighbouring villages in South Tyrol, as described in the classical ethnographic work of John Cole and Eric Wolf (see Section 3.5).

2 The theoretical approach to mountain research from the socio-economic point of view

This chapter presents an overview of a bundle of theories and approaches that will guide the argumentation. It is not the intention to give an in-depth presentation, but an overview of the explicit and implicit theoretical background of the book (for an in-depth reading, refer to the original literature). This chapter also makes the link from the theoretical approaches to the question of new disparities – in general, and in mountain areas.

2.1 The dialectic of the relation between human labour and nature

(a) *The double position of the human being in nature*

Spatial issues have a special relation to biophysical issues, as shown in the current discussions on environmental degradation, urban sprawl, and climate change. The discourse is often characterized either by environmental determinism (with disaster scenarios) or, conversely, by unlimited liberty of human action (relying on incentive market instruments as the most effective solution, backed by sociological concepts of action theory). Both positions have their blind spots.

The blind spot of environmental determinism is that it does not distinguish between those who benefit from a stable environment and those who benefit from a dynamic environment. If the environment is damaged, all inhabitants who have no possibility of leaving a degraded region will suffer, while those who have the necessary resources can leave. At the same time, new business opportunities open up for those social actors involved in the clean-up. The differing interests concern social groups (the owners of resources), the relations between territories (the question of scales), and the temporal perspective of sustainability (short, mid, and long term). Of course, it is true that environmental disasters (including global warming) may induce such deep irritations that they have implications for all human beings or may ruin humankind. But as long as there is a hope that all is not lost, mitigation strategies will always be taken according to conflicting interests and relations of power.

Unlimited liberty of human action implies that every expression of real life, every perception, and every tangible and intangible good in our social practice is tradable and substitutable. This is not only short-sighted, as resources are unequally allocated, but also – and this is of more importance here – because not everything is reproducible.

Both positions have in common that they must deal with the fact that human life is limited in time and that life needs the investment of human work (expressed in time) exerted on the unbuilt and built environment, and towards other humans in the form of social interactions, to organize these interventions. This finiteness of life gives all social interactions the character of a resource, regardless of whether it is consciously calculated or not.

Social sciences share the position that space is socially constructed (Lefebvre, 1974) as it is the product of relations between social actors. On the one hand, the 'human', as the antipode of 'nature', intervenes systematically in all bio-physical systems (the environment or ecosystem). Humans modify, destroy, and rebuild according to their preferences, which are shaped by the conventions of their respective contemporary society. They use the natural resources and exhaust them partially or completely, altering biodiversity and causing intended as well as unintended outcomes (from protection against floods and avalanches, to plastic waste in Arctic waters or global warming). At the same time, being dependent on biophysical processes, humans and human societies are an integral part of nature because they are subject to biophysical cycles such as birth and death. In this sense, humans cannot destroy the environment because if humankind erodes itself, other species or materials will remain. Both positions are in a dialectical relation with implications for the effects of human intervention on the biotic and abiotic environment: first, as a constituent element of nature, humankind's actions should not be automatically considered as destructive (humans cannot act in total disregard of the environment); second, as the antipode of nature in the interest of survival, humans must create, at the expense of other species, their vital and economic space. On this point, they necessarily destroy the environment like other predators or bacteria. Humans give shape to their environment, but at the same time they are exposed to it, which limits their creative force. This contradiction is impossible to overcome and finds its expression in human interventions in living nature with oscillating strategies to change or to preserve their environment. At this point the first conflicts of land use occur, which, as we know from the Bible and the Koran,[1] were violent. The first conclusion is that there is no silver bullet, but a range of options that involve winners and losers – involving all species, including humans. And the option that is finally selected depends on the relations of power in society and the strength of its most powerful social groups or classes. As I follow a purely anthropocentric point of view, the number of stakeholders to consider is restricted to humans, and therefore a little bit reduced, but the story remains complex enough. The contradictions may be mitigated but will not be solvable.

For our purposes, it is important to state that there are always several options for different development paths, and that it is a question of invested work (and the delegation of work) that a society is willing to contribute. Human intervention in nature opens up new development paths and closes others. This can be explained by the approach of evolutionary economics (Arthur, 1989; Nelson and Winter, 1982), as well as through new institutional economics (North, 1990). It is a relation of power with dominating actors that determine a societal consensus about which path is taken. Nevertheless, it always remains contested. Land use is one expression of this general conflict. It is not contested because of its finiteness, as is often proclaimed. This is not true – in fact, there is much space on the globe, and, furthermore, physical space has three dimensions. Interests always diverge over a certain use. Conflicts of use are especially provoked by the trinity of diverging opinions about the intensity of dynamic growth, the preservation of the value of former invested work, and the preservation of investment in ancient and recent cultural practice.

(b) Local conflicts of interest vis-à-vis exploitation of the environment

From the dawn of agricultural societies, human interventions in biophysical nature have led to trouble for community life and individuals. These interventions led to learning to adapt according to the principles of trial and error, which are researched in depth in environmental history (e.g. Diamond, 2005). The interventions in nature with the production of cultural landscapes changed the range of species and biodiversity, and generated use conflicts between old and new use systems, between indigenous and non-indigenous actors, and between old and young generations. Between different groups of actors, contradictions on the extent and mode of operation always remained latent, reflecting unequal access to limited resources, different interpretations of fair rules, and presumed or real asymmetries in power relations. Decisions regarding the exploitation of the built and unbuilt environment are taken (implicitly or explicitly) according to the power and social pertinence of the successful stakeholders. While conflicts in the early societies opposed agriculture and pastoralism, today it is the conflict between investment and disinvestment in a certain region, or the conflicts of interest between manufacturers and service providers. Every intervention on the built and non-built environment alters the qualities of the territory and the living conditions of its population and generates different stakeholder groups who might be winners or losers. Ethnologic approaches describe the struggle between different stakeholders to use the territory for their own interests, to lay claim on a certain field, landscape, or region, as agonistic practices. There is always a certain competition among stakeholders with different conceptions of use where they have to find a compromise between different possibilities. Stakeholders also have a wide range of options vis-à-vis nature. But they must accept certain restrictions of use and find societal rules against depletion so that the human species, in its role as 'part of nature', is not endangered. This position adopts parts of the argumentation of *cultural materialism* (Harris, 2001/1979).

(c) Conflicts of interest between local producers and external protectors of the environment

The transformation of land by human work alters the practices of its stakeholders for future development. It generates new desires. It changes the range and selection of the preferred tangible and intangible assets: which space for economy, which for residences, and which for leisure, contemplation, and wildlife? In the old agrarian societies, such decision-making was traditionally the result of competing interests between local stakeholders. In an urbanized world, land use is part of diversifying commodity chains where the value of a certain land use is evaluated by experts (the administrations of spatial planning of Fordism) or by client polls ('willingness to pay' or Internet 'likes'). The agrarian decision-makers base this on the assumption that nothing should change in the future, and that they could bank on the inherited tacit knowledge of generations. The new decision-makers base this on codified expert knowledge or mere market power. They apply their own interests and try to anticipate the needs of further generations.

Even in the case of global warming, we must ask which regions and stakeholder groups are affected negatively, and which will benefit from climate change. Whenever a decision is made on land use issues, it determines which segment of society gains an option and which segment loses: a certain city or a certain peripheral region, the stakeholders of cultural landscapes or of non-cultivated landscapes, the friends of the wolves or those of the sheep?

As already stated, ecological problems are seen as social problems as long as the consequences of ecological errors allow individuals to buy alternatives or to run away from a degraded place:

- People with sufficient knowledge, better education, skilled social mobility, and sufficient savings can leave environmentally degraded places more easily than others – those who do are known as 'economic migrants'. They have better chances of success when they have sufficient information and the financial backing of their families.
- Cities with an expired or degraded water supply may finance pipelines to have access to untouched resources far away. Bankrupt cities are forced to buy water from polluted rivers as was the case of the American city of Flint, Michigan. Countries with growing economies but polluted agricultural land may acquire fields abroad by contracting, as the fast-growing Asian countries do in Africa.
- A location with a degraded environment is not chosen for new investments: Enterprises and new inhabitants go elsewhere.

We see that there is no objective ecological value of space and landscape. Landscape protection based solely on biophysical and aesthetic values, or 'pure nature', remains fatally blind to social processes and leads to a dead end. Landscape protection fulfils its societal task when it invokes the arguments of identity, belonging, heritage, and the participation of people in a given area. These arguments are justified by their normative character. But the protagonists should also always ask which group of social actors is represented and which is not, and whether and under which normative criteria such an exclusion is justifiable.

2.2 The commodification of mountains as landscape

Commodification means that a certain good is produced for market exchange in societies where the market economy prevails over the subsistence economy. Besides its use value as a private or public good, the good is assigned a defined exchange value. This exchange value is measured according to the efforts to produce or reproduce it, which incorporates the amount of human labour. In a less precise definition, it is the scarcity of a product that defines the price, but this scarcity is derived from human labour, too. The scarcity of an unpolluted sea after an oil rig explosion is extremely high: a clean-up is costly, but certain features of the damage can still be calculated. Many goods and services – in general, the most precious ones (those linked with the aspects of life) – cannot be calculated, as they cannot be reconstructed. For example, the value of a destroyed primary rainforest can perhaps be calculated, but it is only the loss of ecological productivity (the ecosystem services) that can be measured. Replacing a degraded primary forest will not be possible as the biophysical processes cannot be sufficiently substituted by human labour. In this case, the pricing depends on the bargaining of stakeholders and the societal consensus. In all cases, it has to be assumed that a majority sees an advantage (in other words, a use value) in unpolluted waters, primary forests, and a slowing of global warming. It depends on who has the power to define whether a good should have a use value, and which calculations are accepted to determine the exchange value. This is the problem, for example, in preparing environmental audits. We can also take the famous example from American literature: Is it an imposition for Huckleberry Finn to paint Aunt Polly's fence, or is it a pleasure – enabling the right to paint to be sold as an amenity?

Suppose a consensus about the use value is given and the relations of power between different stakeholders are not as asymmetric as in the case of Huckleberry Finn. In this case, the dual character of a commodity enables the functional and geographic division of labour, and the exchange of more products of a higher quality. There is no difference between tangible and intangible products. Making territories available for the consumption of foreign guests by the commodification of landscapes enables sparsely populated regions to offer a regional product in a larger market under the conditions of a globally accepted market economy.

There are always goods that are rare and thus become contested and negotiable resources. As production progresses, scarcity is also reproduced. So, even under conditions of abundance and wealth, it is still necessary to negotiate mechanisms of regulation for access: either through the time spent on production or by trying to develop substitute products.

After all, commodification with transformation of extensively used public goods to tradable private goods, with both use value and exchange value, is a common procedure in the context of increasing division of labour and ongoing urbanization (i.e. the increase in social interaction due to densified forms of living and high mobility). An advanced society with a division of labour would be unthinkable without an exchange of commodities, as there will always be the question of the terms of exchange.

Why should the commodification of landscapes and territories therefore be a problem, especially keeping in mind that natural resources are put in danger when they are overused?

To answer, we first have to add that use value and exchange value are related, and that finding the best relation between them is a permanent struggle between societal stakeholders about the purpose of production. The individual motivation for developing and producing commodities may be closer to either the use value or the exchange value – the relation between the two qualities is important. In the first case, the purpose lies more in developing a good product; in the latter, the purpose lies more in financial accumulation. This relation varies in space and time. The variations may occur with changing preferences, changing scarcity of a product, and changing relations of power between social groups. If the use value plays the dominant role, the scarcity of a resource (i.e. the value of past and recent human labour) may be underestimated; natural resources such as biodiversity may not even be recognized; and incentives to raise productivity, production, and innovation may be missing. These are the current arguments of the mainstream economy, which decries the unproductive allocation of rare resources, including (public) environmental goods that in this logic should be priced to avoid waste. However, if the exchange value dominates, there is an increased tendency to produce externalities at the expense of weaker stakeholders or the biophysical basis – the environment. In the case of mountains, this concerns the fact that food security by the production of local products is given up in favour of more or less long-distance transport chains.

Space, with its material characteristics such as fertile ground or a flat surface to construct buildings for dwelling, becomes a commodity when it is traded or rented. If it is used mainly for personal requirements, the use value prevails. If it is the arena of economic activity, the exchange value becomes more important. In the case of declining industrial sectors, land is sometimes the only reason investors invest, betting on abandoned manufacturing and selling the land once its value has increased. The first conceptualizations of a real estate economy date from von Thünen (1826) about the ground rent in agricultural societies, and 20 years later by Engels (1845), who described the urban land market during the period of 'Manchester capitalism' as an example of housing rents, with the conclusion that spatial inequalities and absolute and relative degradation will be permanently reproduced.

Here there is a difference. In the agricultural society, the price of land was an expression of an economy of time. Selling the ground was the exception, not the rule, and it was only possible after the privatization of common land (in the UK, with the Inclosure Acts since 1773). In the city, however, buying and selling of lots develops dynamically, generating a real estate market as an economic sector with its own interests of accumulation and political power. The Inclosure Acts, as well as the foundation of cities, with its titles of private property, displaced the original inhabitants and stood at the beginning of modern capitalism (*original accumulation* by Adam Smith, or *primitive accumulation* by Karl Marx).[2]

We can therefore define space by its physical characteristics, as well as by its social construction. Space is the combination of physical properties and its actual land use, on the one hand, and social arrangements about the conditions of its ownership and the rights of exploitation, on the other. These rights are comprised of the rules of acquisition and disposal of property, the juridical system, and the power of interpretation of formal rights and informal conventions. The constellation of these elements is highly contested and changes according to the relations of power and shifts between dominating business sectors. As nearly all land has become a commodity, with different pieces of land offering different options for use, the inequality between different areas is therefore an everlasting issue, inherent to all differentiated societies, but differing according to changed relations between stakeholders and changing norms and values.

It is one of the objectives of the present work to show how mountain territories change their character to become a commodity in the form of landscapes. It is an evolution that is relatively new, and I interpret it as a qualitative leap in market economies. I see this as a striking example of how the obsolete business model of the Fordist period results in the valorizing of new features of territories and social life. The objective of this argument is to show that in the context of a transition to liberal-productivist regimes, new social fields become included in the logic of capital accumulation, resulting in new relations of use at the local level and new relations of power between mountain areas and lowland areas.

In the Fordist period, European mountain areas lagged behind the urban and industrial development in the lowlands and profited from trickle-down effects, public investments in large infrastructure projects, and public subsidies, with the result that we no longer see large-scale disparities in these regions. But these measures did not deliver lasting stability to these regions. With the post-Fordist turn, the cities recommenced being the drivers of economic and spatial development. Mountain regions lost the local basic functions that they had gained in the Fordist era. They may receive new functions as places of residence instead. This development is linked with the creation of new commodities, especially based on real estate and new services according to offer-oriented strategies based on the elaboration of unique selling propositions. This exploitation of selective amenities and rare raw materials attacks places that were predominantly appreciated and used for their use value, by strengthening the aspect of the exchange value through commercialization of aesthetic features in particular. At the same time, they also reduce open space by new construction and they open the market for an international clientele as consumers and investors. In the next section, we will see that the exchange value aspect also becomes transformed.

2.3 The production of nature on the basis of commodification

The fact that space receives the character of a commodity that is tradable[3] is not the biggest problem of the commodification of territories. What makes commodification of territories problematic is that, under the given regimes of accumulation (Fordist and even more so, post-Fordist), the production of commodities produces liquid capital that has to be reinvested and deliver increasing rates of profit. In prosperous societies, it is becoming increasingly difficult to find new placements for capital that will yield the desired rates of profit. In this context, investment in territories, landscapes, and all subjects linked with 'nature' takes on a new significance. It shifts the relation between use value and exchange value in favour of the latter. If the exchange value plays the dominant role, production loses its significance as a way of ameliorating livelihoods. There is no discussion or debate about the reason for producing, and its winners, losers, and possible damages. What counts is that there is a profit at the very end of the process. In this logic, sealing valley floors with concrete or sponsoring renaturation of the sealed valleys have the same value and are sometimes done by the same person. In our case, the necessary accumulation of capital is a strong incentive to develop investment strategies that are short term and bet on the selective exploitation of specific mountain assets such as landscapes and branded products derived from these. Other potentials are either not seen, neglected, or consciously squeezed out. Investment in territory becomes a placement strategy for rents where societal norms and values and the interest in a sustainable regional development become secondary (see Section 7.3).

In his 2007 paper about 'nature as accumulation strategy', Neil Smith brings this topic to a higher abstract level when he states that in the past, investment strategies dealt mainly with the physical aspects of nature, which he sees as a commodification mainly of the use value aspects: valorizing the potential of aesthetic qualities, amenities of calmness and healthy environment, and spectacular views, etc. Commodification of space means putting a price on the scarcity of these places for the inhabitant or visitor – their *use value* – and at the same time setting an *exchange value*, by creating a strategic asset for investors. However, the process of accumulation of capital does not end with the replication of these commodities. Based on the exploitation of these amenities, new economic sectors are developed that affect mainly the exchange value: this includes, of course, all technologies for the treatment of biophysical pollution ('cleantech') and the biotechnical production of pharmaceuticals, but also new economic sectors of knowledge creation with scientific programmes to research nature in all its forms (from natural hazards to socio-economic change in mountains), NGOs involved in conflicts between stakeholders, and so on. We can also add the production of symbolic capital by the creation of new resort towns in the mountains for new multilocal middle classes that live in second homes, creating 'Alpine gentrification' (Perlik, 2011). For these applications, the use value sometimes still has to be found. The investment in such newly created economic sectors and the growth of the corresponding new social milieus create a new level of inequality. The inequality concerns the territorial capital and the future opportunities, rather than financial prosperity. This disparity in territorial capital outweighs the former spatial cleavages in rich and poor mountain regions.

2.4 Social relations as determinants of territorial trajectories

In the reproduction of human life, the relation between humans and nature is based on the integration of the fruits of previous production that become accumulated. Spatial development is also based on earlier structures. These structures include the accumulated work of former generations in the form of arable or building land, production facilities, communication infrastructure, and the tacit knowledge linked with it. This knowledge is not restricted to codified technical know-how, but also includes tacit and informal knowledge such as social norms, values, modes of operation, agreements, or conventions. In a given region, the entire knowledge forms a huge stock of accumulated territorial capital. It is subject to changes over time: some practices will be forgotten, others will be revised and further developed, and still others will remain in the collective conscience as positive or negative experiences. The experiences and conclusions drawn vary from one region to another. The sum of these regional practices constitutes a historical trajectory, where the past not only influences the present, but also future development. However, it is not easy to understand the processes in detail: the range of opportunities is wide and reaches from mere conservation of old practices by adding at most a few external innovations, to conscious modifications or even a complete and deliberate rupture of the hitherto taken path. Therefore, the effect of previous structures has two facets: compared to former epochs, the fruits of former labour facilitate production for the present society. But this capital stock can create a state of *lock-in* that inhibits alternative practices and prevents their improvement. In a dynamically changing world, this can cause severe problems when the old options run out (e.g. in the light of exploited oil resources, climate change, or even changed individual demands) or changes become very costly (e.g. exit from nuclear power). The new idea introduced by this approach of trajectories is that it breaks with pre-described patterns of regional development. Every region and every social actor always has a certain spectrum of possible strategies from which to act, but the topographic and historic framework conditions still matter whether they are positive or negative: as a uniqueness or as an obstacle. Consequently, the social actors are able to consciously create region-specific strategies of differentiation to develop their regional production system along a development path (or trajectory) which is a keyword from the approach of *evolutionary economy* (Arthur, 1989; Grabher and Stark, 1997; Martin and Sunley, 2006; Nelson and Winter, 1982). It is near the enlarged concepts of capital of Pierre Bourdieu (1979) and to theories of organizational structure (Coleman, 1988; Grabher, 1993; Granovetter, 1973), as well as to theories on the importance of untradeable knowledge of regional stakeholders (Pecqueur, 1997; Storper, 1995). In applying the extended understanding of capital to territorial issues, we can also speak of 'territorial capital' (Camagni and Capello, 2010; OECD, 2001).

Philippe Aydalot was one of the first to recognize the paradox that regional development neither matches the classic scenario of structuralist polarization, nor the neoclassical convergence scenario generated by almighty market rules. This phenomenon was described as *retournement spatial* (spatial reversal) (Aydalot, 1984; Pecqueur, 2006). It can be interpreted in two ways: first, as an economic phenomenon in the context of new technologies and new business models, with industrial relocations and the reinforcement of existing sites that were previously economically weak, such as the 'Third Italy' (*Tre Italie*) (Bagnasco, 1977)[4] or the East–West shift in the United States (Storper and Walker, 1989). On the other hand, it can be interpreted as a political and social negotiation process, as it was designed by the regulation approach (Leborgne and Lipietz, 1992). Both approaches lead to the same interpretation: the described processes show the dynamics of ongoing uneven spatial development. This perpetuation, however, does not depend on mechanical rules, but on social action (i.e. negotiation and compromise processes by the involved social actors) – albeit based on circumstances not freely chosen (Marx, 1852) that continue to be relevant. This also means that there is no teleological linearity of spatial development, neither to socialist models nor to neoclassical convergence of territorial cleavages.

One of the characteristics of liberal-productive regimes is that regional differentiation is consciously used as a strategic goal of regional development. This differentiation strategy does not place the interests of the producers in the foreground and is also not oriented on whether the marketed regional profile is adapted to long-term economic activity in the mountain region. Instead, a marketable offer is proposed, without questioning whether this offer is useful and sustainable. This creates a new asymmetry of power between the metropolitan decision-making centres and the mountain areas – a new quality of unequal spatial development. It constitutes a new asymmetry of power and an unequal spatial development of a new type. The examples discussed in the chapters of Part II will focus on different national and regional development strategies of mountain regions under Fordist and liberal-productivist regimes. They are related to the degree of social cohesion: equality, equivalence, or ostensibly unequal chances in life – qualities which are the background of the debate on the abandonment or maintenance of declining regions with poor potential.

2.5 Post-structuralist approaches

Beyond 'the production of space', the work of Henri Lefebvre in general has regained acknowledgement in the spatial debate. For a deeper understanding, I refer to the works of Christian Schmid (2006, 2012), Neil Brenner (2000), and Stuart Elden (2004). Here, we go into this debate only insofar as it is complementary or divergent to the approaches used in this book. In this sense, we have to state that Lefebvre's work can be seen as a reflection of the Fordist crisis of the 1960s, which was not only a crisis of a fallen rate of profit, but also a crisis of the legitimation of the growth model that was followed by the social movements of May 1968 in Paris, other parts of Europe, and North America. Henri Lefebvre conceptualized a theory of space using a threefold model that deploys a three-part dialectic. The key notions are named with two terms each: perceived space (spatial practice), conceived space (representations of space), and lived space (spaces of representation).[5] We have to consider space in its French original (*espace*), which has a broader meaning than in English or German. In this way, Lefebvre uses 'space' as an abstract notion that is comprised of much more than physical space. The three dimensions affect the production of space as follows. Individuals or groups of stakeholders in a given society produce, through everyday life, practices according to the perception in a given situation and in a given physical space. This is the perceived space. The perception is closely linked with the conceptualization. The everyday practices are part of a plan to interpret or analyse the perceived situation, in order to understand the social practices and the practices of the other stakeholders. This is the conceived space. Both the perceived and the conceived space serve a search for alternatives in spatial use, in the institutional organization of society, and in the relation between accumulation of wealth and its consumption. This is the lived space. These three dimensions are intertwined in a dialectical relation. This means that the intellectual discourse thesis – antithesis – synthesis (statement, negation, negation of the negation) is applied to a given situation (e.g. spatial use). This procedure should lead to resolving the contradiction by putting the question on a higher level of understanding.

How does this theoretical concept fit with our approach, and what are, in this light, its merits? First, we have to consider that the Lefebvrian approach was the attempt to break with the mechanistic concept of French structuralism (inseparably linked with the name of Louis Althusser). In this sense, it seems justified to search for other sources of social and territorial disparities than the pure power of accumulated capital, which, at the time, was defined in a 'vulgar Marxism' rather mechanistically as material consumable goods and the technical infrastructure to produce them. Furthermore, it was more than justified to look for societal alternatives that broke with the belief in a harmonious future paradise of eternal growth. In this sense, the notion of the lived space (*espace vécu*) was an original contribution in the search for societal alternatives. Lefebvre's concept used the dialectical method. It was a strictly materialistic, use value-oriented approach. There, Lefebvre's approach undoubtedly has its merits.

May 1968 resulted in the most influential modernization of capitalist societies in the second half of the 20th century. However, the shift from Fordist to post-Fordist societies did not bring the hoped-for emancipatory transformation to a use value-oriented urban development, but a new search cycle for the placement of liquid capital. In this way, the Fordist modernization of cities (functional separation, central business districts, suburbanization) was stopped in favour of the valorization of the historic ambiance of city centres, with Disneyland-like pedestrian zones and segregated housing areas of 'new urbanism'. And the Savoian Alps changed from 1960s post-war modernity to new types of chalet-style resort towns linked with nostalgic marketing prose

(Wozniak, 2002), or, in other words, from Jacques Tati's 'Playtime' to Johanna Spyri's 'Heidi'.

In light of this development and the uninterrupted topicality of contested spaces, I see the shortcomings of Lefebvre's space-driven explanation. We can interpret this approach as a necessary step in the dispute against structuralism and economic determinism (or vulgar Marxism). However, his concept of 'the urban' as a universalist category of sociation fatally abandons the questions of capital accumulation in the context of urbanization and the problems related with an over-accumulation as basic societal drivers in capitalist societies. In this sense, I share the critique of Manuel Castells (1972) and David Harvey (1973),[6] whereby we have to define 'capital' in a much larger sense as a transformable resource that constitutes all kinds of power relations.[7] Here, we can rely on Pierre Bourdieu, with his concept of several forms of capital (financial, cultural, social, and symbolic), which are substitutional and serve to create networks, interest groups, and finally, investors at a given location (Bourdieu, 1986). We also see the application of Bourdieu's social fields for spatial questions (Savage, 2011). Bourdieu's field theory, with the forms of capital and habitus, allows for the bridging of the structure/agency problem and the reified history of society and the incorporated history of the individual. From Lefebvre, I retain the materialist and dialectic method and the strictly use value-oriented objective of the lived space for everyday life practices, as well as for concept-making. This use value orientation can be related to reflections for new regimes of accumulation beyond the liberal-productivist post-Fordism.

2.6 The approach of regulation: a tool for analyzing societal change

(a) General overview

The regulation approach is the theoretical basis of three points of view. First, this concept is a tool that allows a qualitative differentiation of distinct periods in the evolution of capitalist societies with the specific spatiality constituted in each period. With the Fordist regimes, we saw the paradigm of equal development according to the Western type ('growth and redistribution') and its Eastern bloc version of 'real existing socialism' ('levelling the difference between town and countryside'). After the paradigm shift of the 1980s in the West and the 1990s in the East, we saw the differentiation of society and space, including the increase of the social divide concerning wages and living conditions.

Second, the regulation approach shows that societal actors change the rules when these rules no longer correspond to current practices, and when the prevailing relations of power lose their legitimation in society. This departs from old structuralist mechanistic concepts of societal stages, as well as positivist descriptive explanations of simple market mechanisms for the advantages of nations and regions. It reintroduces a component of social and political practice into a debate that has become economistic. In particular, its method to distinguish between regime of accumulation and mode of regulation allows analysis of two key aspects of human existence: the production of advanced reproduction, and the ensuing question of how much in a given society should be consumed and how much should be accumulated (which includes the inherent relations of power). Subsequently, this raises the question of the redistribution of the value added (how much and to whom) – a question that affects the relations of power in a society even more.

Third, the analysis of the paradigmatic shift already implies the possibility of a change of regimes in the future.

It is this aspect of a conscious change of existing structures that is important here – apart from the schematic terminology of Fordism/post-Fordism (which serves more as a working basis). It results, in particular, in the interpretation of the long period of stability of the Fordist period in the three post-war decades, and the explanation of the fundamental paradigm change in society since its beginnings in the 1970s and mainstreaming in the 1980s. Furthermore, it raises the question of how to interpret the character and the options of these new post-Fordist regimes.

The regulation approach conceives of changes in society as a change in the relation between the stakeholders of different logics, thoughts, or options for action. This instrument can be applied to several aspects of change in the spatial pattern: the degree of a spatial division of functions; the balance (or asymmetry) of power between the different types of regions; the relation between different groups of actors, which may be attached to productivist thinking or solidarity-focused thinking. All these aspects are part of the debate on equality, equivalence, or inequality between territories.

(b) Some explanations of the terminology

The aim of this book is to analyse the substantial changes in territorial functions and the changes in relationships between territories, to show new types of spatial disparities that occurred in the 1990s. These new spatial disparities were a delayed response to fundamental institutional changes which had their origins in the early 1970s (see Section 4.6).

These changes are described as a regime shift or paradigmatic shift from the Fordist period to the liberal-productivist period (post-Fordism). The terminology was developed within the French approach of regulation in regional economy. It is not our place to give a long systematic introduction into the theoretical concept of regulation approach, but we need some clarifications about its terminology.

Fordism refers to mass production at the assembly line (of the automobile manufacturer, Ford), and was introduced into the intellectual debate by Antonio Gramsci.[8] It goes beyond the technical focus of Taylorism of the early 20th century on optimizing work efficiency. Fordism instead means a certain societal constellation of the production of added value and its redistribution to different stakeholders (i.e. standardized mass production and mass consumption), typical for the post-war period until the 1970s in Europe, North America, and Japan. Such regimes were organized by the reconciliation of the most powerful groups of stakeholders (i.e. the employers' associations, the state, and the trade unions). In the case of countries of 'real existing socialism', the organization was undertaken by the diverse fractions of the ruling power (i.e. different state sectors of industry, the state's 'trade unions', and the changing preferences of the central power). Fordism is a specific period for what was named in the first half of the 20th century by the economist and social democratic politician Rudolf Hilferding as 'organized capitalism'.[9]

After Fordism came post-Fordism, which is often simply referred to as 'neo-liberalism'. In my opinion, the term neo-liberalism is misleading, first, because 'neo-liberal' has a double meaning. One the one hand, it can mean the backwards-oriented paradigm of Manchester Capitalism. In this way, 'neo-liberal' is used as a rather general critique on capitalism which does not allow new insights. The economically liberal economists defend 'neo-liberalism' as the start of a new era of market economy after the War (in the version of the German ordo-liberalist *Freiburg school*, linked with the name of Walter Eucken). Therefore, the notion of neo-liberalism quickly generates an ideological debate which does not get to the heart of the problem: the question of who the winners and losers are, under the unleashed global paradigm of growth. On the other hand, Fordism, and even the globalized post-Fordism, both show a broad range of different national regimes that have aspects of very open market-liberal regulations and highly planned interventionist models. For example, the Fordist regimes did not include the people of the South in their trickle-down model of social compromise. But the new liberal-productivist regimes have included new groups in the welfare state model, which has not been completely abandoned. Furthermore, we see recently in Europe and North America in right-wing movements a very hybrid form of market-liberal thinking at the national level, which claims hard political intervention towards national isolation to protect its electoral basis against economic structural change. And we should not forget that the American version of Fordism was always more market-liberal than certain post-Fordist European models still show today.

So, why not stay with globalization instead of post-Fordism? Although they have much in common, we should distinguish between them. Globalization is a descriptive name for a phenomenon that describes free trade, spatial division of labour and manufacturing, and shrinking distances through the development of new transport technologies. It does not ask for reasons, origins, or constellations of social actors. In contrast, the notions of liberal-productivism or post-Fordism describe a period that is characterized by the specific societal relations that enabled and fuelled globalization. It is a category founded with the aim of explaining societal processes (for which we still have to find a precise name).

But we cannot stay with the term post-Fordism, because this term says about social relations only what they are not (or no longer), but not what they are. I take here the notion of 'liberal productivism', a term already used in the French discourse (Lipietz, 2012), which combines the characteristic of the abandoned welfare state restrictions with the old Fordist paradigm of growth. I stick to the term Fordism because this term has become widely known. The most interesting of these terms is the distinction between two periods of capitalism. Its creators, the GREMI Circle and the Paris School of Regulation, have shown that it is worth analyzing capitalist society according to different regimes characterized by different relationships between the social actors, and that these relationships can be changed through practical action. It was the bridge between radical denial and affirmative reformism. This was the basis to overcome old structuralist thinking, building a bridge to the action theories and showing a new understanding of social change which implies that societal stakeholders have scopes of action in the broad range between fundamental opposition and simple social engineering. The shift from one type of regime to another is proof that there is a chance for paradigmatic shifts, and that there are therefore options for such a shift in the future. In this practical understanding the regulation approach is indeed a reformist concept, but it is transformative and therefore more than affirmative social engineering.

Mountain regions are generally considered rural, and the insight that they are subject to urbanization is still young. The inclusion of Europe's mountain regions in urbanization already began in the Fordist period – in both the Western and Eastern bloc – with the initiation of an alignment of living conditions between urban and rural areas, and industrial structural change. These policies aim to reduce spatial disparities in the interests of territorial cohesion and to prevent regionalist movements within the nation states by avoiding excessive differences in welfare and livelihoods. The mountain parts of a country have always been important to control a territory in its integrality. These areas were therefore equipped with basic infrastructure, albeit often with a considerable time lag compared to the lowlands. And mountains were often a projection for development policies, which served as the self-assurance of a society about its own values. As mountains are doubly disadvantaged in terms of investment in infrastructure (they have topographically induced higher costs and a smaller population among whom to share these costs), the most productivist regimes will gain the highest returns by reducing investment in mountain areas. However, such disinvestment may provoke an immediate biophysical response, as mountains in combination with human use are more sensitive, due to their exposed topography. This makes mountains a strong case study to show the qualitative differences between the old Fordist productivism and the new liberal-productivism, and to postulate a new type of spatial disparity specific to post-Fordism: Liberal-productivist regimes tend to abandon certain territories when they do not show sufficient productivity.

It is one achievement of the regulation approach to have deconstructed the logic of capitalist societies in the two categories of accumulation and regulation. The ensemble of constellations constitutes a regime[10] that differs from country to country, and even between regions in one country. Accumulation means the increase of existing capital in the form of a surplus resulting from human labour in its most general form. The institutional norms, values, and rules that determine the process of accumulation are referred to as regime of accumulation, or accumulation regime. Regulation means the societal agreement (i.e. the temporary existing relations of power) that determine the redistribution of the produced surplus. The arrangement of institutional norms, values, and rules is called the mode of regulation.

The separation between accumulation and regulation, and furthermore the thinking in terms of 'regimes' and 'modes', allows the aspects of power and action to be introduced in the form of relations (in the French original: *rapports*): Social relations, i.e. the relations of social interaction, are seen as the basis of both action and structure. This thinking takes into account both asymmetries of, and common interests for, cooperation between the various groups of social actors. It represents a link between traditionally purely structural-oriented or action-oriented theoretical concepts. Thus, the focus lies less on the idealized extreme forms of social concepts (only market hierarchy or only political hierarchy), but on their interaction. There are different possible regimes and modes, and there are different combinations between a certain regime of accumulation and a certain mode of regulation. These constellations – which vary according to time and place – allow us to explain the different national developments of capitalism (Boyer, 2004). They also allow us to abandon the mechanistic and teleological thinking of the former structuralist approaches.

2.7 Theses on established knowledge in the light of theories

The four theoretical pillars are compatible and complementary. Integrally, these approaches allow us to show that it is possible to explain the new preferences for 'nature' and 'landscape' in society from a societal rather than an individual or pseudo-neutral biophysical view. This can explain the contradictive practices of middle-class residents towards nuisance, risks, or pollution in their proximate neighbourhood: they demand extensive protective measures but express no sensitivity to other more distant conflicts.[11] With the chosen approaches, we can see how growth and stagnation largely depend on societal values, constellations of actors, and mutual trust. The idea of trajectories (in the evolution economy) or 'capital' (in the broader sense of Bourdieu) represents the rather constant element where the past influences future development, while the approach of the regulation school demonstrates the feasibility of societal change. In summary, the theories presented above underpin the theses for this book:

1 Space is socially constructed, and therefore eternally subject to conflicts of interest and to various struggles for resources. Space is also a platform for the realization of all kinds of options: production, business, recreation, and living and survival in general.

The social construction of space is associated with Henri Lefebvre (1974). It now occupies a dominant, mainstream position in social science, insofar as it is opposed to biophysical determinism and biocentrism, as well as to the idea of universal aesthetic values. The thesis of social construction is thus a materialist approach to explain the development of local places as well as large territories (including the making of 'landscapes'). This does not mean that human activities run independently of biophysical endowments, but that humans always have several options to influence environmental conditions. Through their interventions, the social actors generate the cultivated landscape.

2   Past decisions constitute a specific trajectory for each region. They influence the use of territory and its future development without determining it. The trajectory allows new windows of opportunity and closes others. Without a fundamental global crisis, mountain areas will not become metropolitan areas.

This trajectory metaphor is the quintessence of evolutionary economics. For mountain regions the application of this approach means that they cannot reverse the demographic pattern that has evolved during the 20th century. As long as territorial capital of a certain territory is constituted by demographic density and institutional thickness, urban agglomerations are advantaged, and the sparsely populated mountains cannot turn this pattern by market rules. They depend on solidarity with larger entities (in most cases national states) and can only try to renegotiate the relationship between mountains and lowlands. As the urban fabric in Europe is rather established, this pattern will not change in the near future, although it would be possible by technical means.

3   In advanced market-driven societies, repeating crises of overproduction and, even more relevantly, of over-accumulation affect the use of space. This results in disinvestments and reinvestments – and a loss of confidence in society. The paradigm shift of the 1970s responded not only to a decreasing rate of profit, but also to the scarcity of key resources such as energy ('oil crisis') and the emergence of new values which turned to new resources ('ecological crisis').

The significance of disinvestments and reinvestments for regional development and impacts in the biosphere is based on the political economics applied to spatial effects – elaborated particularly by David Harvey (1982) and Neil Smith (1984) – as well as the explanation of regime changes following a societal crisis worked out by the approach of regulation. Consequently, economic decisions, as well as taking environmental problems seriously, depend on the power of definition and the creation and valorization of new resources. The most important example in mountain regions is the use of space and landscape.

4   With the post-Fordist turn, the administrative and economic restrictions for the development of large agglomerations have been erased. Only now, cities are able to play the key role as engines of socio-economic development.

But this is not yet uncontested. Urban tertiary economies rely on the production of goods and services produced in the national and global peripheries. The problems of the peripheries are imported into the cities. On some continents, mountain areas are part of the global peripheries, but in some countries throughout the world, they are part of the metropolitan peripheries where they participate in the growth of the peri-Alpine metropolitan areas.

The character of these peripheral regions changes from manufacturers of tangible goods to providers of intangible amenities, emotions, and comfort services. The mountains are partly losing their production function, as already described by Thorstein Veblen (1899), or, in economic terms, are moving away from an export-based focus to a residential economy. Other parts of the mountains become – sometimes suddenly – important as new suppliers of liquid and solid raw materials for a globalized economy. The decisive and powerful role of large cities, as analysed by Saskia Sassen (1991), is mainly based on their ability to produce economies of size and scope, and to benefit from them by developing organizational power. In addition, its strength is based on strong and continuously differentiating urban tertiary economic sectors which are strongly supported by liberal-productivist regimes of accumulation. Again, we have the relations of power, which are addressed by the regulation approach.

5   The economic transformation provokes a spatial transformation in the mountains. They become suppliers on a global scale with a new type of resource: landscapes.

This statement corresponds mainly to the regulation approach and its explanation of societal and economic changes. It can also be explained through Bourdieu's approach. Evolutionary economics are also important: we see that the paths are never completely reversible – they lead to new liberties but also new restrictions. In the debate about the use of natural resources, the relation between humans and biosphere also plays an important role.

6   It is a normative value to balance social conflicts with a minimum of friction, and to enlarge emancipative individual and collective liberties. This concerns public accessibility in cities as well as in mountain areas, and also the possibility for economic activities by the inhabitants of these places.

Territory is always contested. Minimizing frictions is based on the concept of sustainability, which can again be explained as the relation between humans and nature, or, in regulationist terms, as the search for a regime of accumulation with low risk (low impacts, low volatility) and a cohesive mode of regulation (maintaining social peace). The normative character implies that the concept is challenged, too, by competing interests between environmental protection and development or by different concepts of land use.

Notes

1 *Genesis* 4:1–16; *Surah* 5:27–31.
2 We can observe this currently in the large cities of Africa, where the ground was traditionally common land with defined exploitation rights. Decisions on recent allotments and new private owners determine future access to the city, and are often linked with nepotism.
3 We have to keep in mind that despite all these efforts to price tangible and intangible goods, the significance of these prices has to be relativized. Regional development depends to a large degree on untradeable interdependencies between regional stakeholders, where common values such as mutual understanding and trust play an important role (Pecqueur, 1997; Storper, 1995).
4 'Third Italy' is the territory that was neither the 'First Italy', the large-scale industrialized northeast of Italy (in the Milan, Turin, Genoa triangle), nor the agricultural south. 'Third Italy' is especially comprised of the regions of Veneto, Emilia-Romagna, and Tuscany, with small-scale family enterprises without a long trade union tradition.
5 In the French original: *espace perçu, espace conçu,* and *espace vécu.*
6 'Spatial forms are . . . seen not as inanimate objects within which the social process unfolds, but as things which "contain" social processes in the same manner that social processes *are* spatial' (Harvey, 1973: 10–11, emphasis in original). In other words: 'space is not an ontological category as such, but is a social dimension that both shapes and is shaped by human agency' (Ira Kaznelson in *Marxism and the City,* New York: Oxford University Press, p. 105).
7 Claudia Roth's (2018) ethnographic analyses give a good example of the necessity of resources in the form of transformable capitals to sustain the intergenerational relations in poor families in urban Burkina Faso.
8 Quaderni del Carcere. Q. 22, 1934.
9 Introduced by Rudolf Hilferding (1982/1927). It was adopted for the discourse on institutional arrangements by historians and sociologists (Lash and Urry, 1987; Offe, 1985; Wehler, 1974; see also Lipietz, 2012).
10 The notion of regime corresponds to a spatially and temporarily limited compromise between the social actors to the 'spatio-temporal fixes' of David Harvey. In using the nomenclature of the regulation approach, I stay with the notion of regime. In German, 'regime' is misunderstandable, as in the German discourse there is a certain tradition to use this word for all kinds of dictatorship; it was especially applied to characterize the former East German state. But in its origins, the notion of regime is neutral.
11 These practices have become known as 'Nimby': 'not in my back yard', a modern expression of the St Florian's principle of burning the house of one's neighbour while sparing one's own. However, since this phenomenon has gained a reputation as being an egoistic practice, consulting agencies working for real estate developers try to discredit every citizen's protest with the 'killer argument' of 'Nimby'.

3 The issue of spatial inequality in a new light

Over the centuries, the dominant territorial cleavage was the separation of town and countryside, due to differing access of the population to basic material resources, social achievements such as education and health, and opportunities in life. Seeing social cleavages as important reasons for pauperization and violent riots, the ideas of the welfare state, based on increased productivity, tried to enable mass consumption for all, through economic growth and redistribution. This Fordist model was burst in the 1980s, by a spectrum of societal stakeholders claiming more spatial, cultural, and ecological diversity, as well as economic self-responsibility and efficiency. This will be examined more closely in the following chapters. It is interesting to note that spatial questions now appear in a new light. The impacts of the welfare state and a general growth in prosperity seem to have made the spatial question obsolete. Indeed, in most of the West European mountains, there are no pockets of poverty anymore (Gloersen et al., 2004; Stucki et al., 2004). Social cleavages have become small scale and are more visible in the cities, where they are observed with much more interest than in the peripheries. Spatial disparities occur mainly as a North–South problem. Claiming here that spatial disparities have to be looked at in a new light refers to three points. First, with the paradigmatic post-Fordist change, regions become self-responsible for their development by establishing their own distinctive production systems, to reduce the expenditure of national states and to cope with global competition. This means they have to develop entrepreneurial qualities. Second, being endowed with infrastructure is no longer the major factor leading to inequality – instead, it is the functional hierarchy that has deepened. Third, inequality is the flip side of the diversity coin, which is one of the core issues of the proponents of post-Fordist development. So, a new interpretation of disparities is needed in the light of diversity, in terms of free development of the individual, economic niches, and biodiversity. It means we can no longer encounter these new disparities with the old recipes of national welfare state growth.

3.1 Prologue: the new hierarchies between cities

The developments and examples presented here include the period of the late 1960s, when Fordism-type 'Rhenish capitalism' in Germany showed its first mini-crisis (1967): This was a first indication that post-war society did not produce uninterrupted growth, and that the cyclical crises used in vulgarized Marxist textbooks were not entirely unfounded.

Economic growth continued practically unbridled until 1973. Even peripheries and new municipalities without a great history were able to benefit from the post-war upturn referred to in Europe as 'Wirtschaftswunder', 'Trentes Glorieuses', or 'Miracolo economico italiano'. In Germany, former villages or new towns such as Rüsselsheim near Frankfurt or Wolfsburg near Hannover became 'company towns' dependent on one firm with a fast-growing mass production, in these cases automobiles. The population of these towns continued to grow, while the old industries in the Ruhr region began to decline, especially due to a loss of jobs in the mining industry. Wolfsburg, which is the headquarters of the Volkswagen company, acquired new economic and social functions and grew to 125,000 inhabitants. It concentrates permanent and temporary employees from other regions, countries, and continents, and hosts new populations that come for internships, education, and training from all over the world (ARL, 2019). But this position is very fragile. Wolfsburg is not the core of a metropolitan area. When the other town, Rüsselsheim, reached 60,000 inhabitants in the 1960s, it dreamt of accommodating 120,000 people. It had even been able to build a real theatre, thanks to municipal taxes from the main company, General Motors, with its Opel plant, which was profitable at the time but has since continuously been the target of a takeover. In the late 1960s and early 1970s, the city had an active citizenship including a strong local far-left youth movement that had spread from nearby university cities. Today, the plant is still the only big company and has just been sold cheaply, after operating at a loss for more than 15 years. The commuter flows have turned towards Frankfurt, and the population has decreased. Since the 2010s, it has stabilized due to the growth of the Frankfurt metropolitan region. The former industrial flagship, Opel, which provided 42,000 jobs in 1978, now has only 18,000 employees, and is threatened with relocation every five–ten years. Wolfsburg, which is still described as a booming city, is hurt by a strategic failure of its main company, Volkswagen. Both cities are at the mercy of the companies' volatile position. Both cities depend on one single headquarters, the failure of which can run them into decline.

In contrast, some historically important cities – capitals of their regions, such as Turin, Glasgow, or Basel – which had taken an industrial development path, have survived the current de-industrialization process and transformed from being dependent on manufacturing to becoming tertiary-driven metropolitan regions with international steering functions. These cities always kept a critical mass of a diverse population with active citizens that remained loyal to the city, even in periods of decline. Furthermore, as these cities profited very early from export-based capital accumulation, they had a head start in gaining specific knowledge on reinvesting the returns in private and public goods of culture and an emerging tertiary sector of arts. Turin made this turn with the organization of the Olympic Winter Games of 2006, making the city visible as an international destination and as an organizer of large events (Dansero and

Mela, 2007). At the moment, these types of second-tier metropolises seem to be safeguarded in their territorial position, at least in Europe, where maintaining regional cohesion is a goal of European development and planning concepts.

Some medium-sized cities are trying a similar path (e.g. Neuchâtel, La Chaux-de-Fonds, Thun, or Winterthur in Switzerland; and Mainz or Darmstadt in Germany). They may stabilize some aspects of their urban position as attractive residence sites or as a location for technical jobs within a larger metropolitan area (compared to the edge cities or the hub-and-spoke model of American cities on a smaller scale) (see Gray et al., 1996). The 'rural' areas within this metropolitan structure of cities have already been transformed into decentralized residence communities, and will be described here as peri-urban.

There are places between the peri-urban fringes and the resort towns that are usually described as rural. These areas, too, are integrated into global circuits (e.g. when the Valtellina Bresaola meat producers use meat delivered in parcels from Brazil). These areas have become subject to urbanization processes, too. But there are gradual differences, as these urbanization processes are incomplete. So, in this book I will exercise caution in my use of the notion of 'rural', keeping in mind its limitation and saving it for those areas where urban integration is only rudimentary.

In 'Towns in the Alps' ('Alpenstädte') (Perlik, 2001), I outlined the dual function of cities: their *supply function* and their *network function*. The *supply function* comprised all the activities of a city to fulfil its central place function in offering goods and services for its inhabitants and those of its hinterlands, including all the administrative and bureaucratic transactions within the state. This function coincides more or less with the Christallerian model of central places theory. The *network function* refers to all the activities of value adding for export and external communication to increase international visibility and competitiveness of the city's own export-based companies. This function was developed first by the cities of far trades, such as the early cities of trans-Saharan trade (Timbuktu), or Petra (Jordan) on the Incense Route, and then later the Hanseatic cities along the Baltic and North Sea coasts. *Supply function* can also be translated as 'use value of a city to live in for everyday life activities' and *network function* as 'exchange value for the generation of added value with the exchange of goods, services, and knowledge'.

We call this process where global relations and influences become dominant *metropolization*. From a spatial point of view, this is the dominant process in post-Fordist societies. As with the term *urbanization*, metropolization does not mean only spatial density or size, but includes involvement in international networks and competition. Metropolization describes a dual process. First, the physical expansion of large agglomerations, made possible by unleashed global mobility. Second, the expansion of liberty of action of these metropolitan areas, which transform from public administrations to collective enterprises acting like private companies. In the framework of metropolization, the function of large cities changes: the relation between the supply function (exchange and administration in the sense of a central place) and the network function (export-based creation of value added) shifts in favour of the latter. This concerns mountain areas, as their fringes are often – especially in Europe – the site of large metropolitan areas. They expand towards the mountain areas especially as peri-urban dwelling zones. But all parts of the mountains play the role of specific and important assets: lakesides in the valley bottoms, hilly zones, as well as pre-Alpine and high mountain zones for a diverse spectrum of stakeholders and uses.

3.2 Space as a contested social field

We see space as a social field in the sense of Pierre Bourdieu. Social fields are contested by the differing interests and practices of the involved social actors or stakeholders (we use these terms synonymously). This insight is not new. Diverging stakeholder interests define land use and the dynamics of innovation in the production process, which again is expressed in a specific use of space. When we speak of space, we usually mean social space. We can differentiate between natural and social space. Natural space is the product of biophysical processes. Social space refers to locations, areas, or territories treated by human societies during a historic trajectory of sociation in which social actors became more and more independent from nature. We call the spatial results of this process of sociation 'urbanization'. Urbanization therefore is independent from city-building or a certain morphologic form: The product of urbanization is not necessarily a town or a city, as it also takes place in villages in the framework of emerging market economies and an increased division of labour with an increase in social interaction. When we refer to the morphological aspects of urban enlargement, we should use a notion such as 'urban development' or the like.

This has led to a controversy over whether urbanization is an independent 'ontologic' category that drives the development of society by its internal dynamic, a position that was developed by Henri Lefebvre (1970, 1972). Assuming a complete urbanization of society, this position led Lefebvre to define society as driven by urbanization. The counter-position is that of David Harvey (1973), who claimed that although urbanization influences the relation between forces of production and social actors, it is still this relation that matters. Urbanization may unleash the forces of production with an enormous jump in productivity. But it happens on the basis of appropriated human labour during the differentiation of class structures in human societies. Hierarchical structures organize the process of production and consequently the production of space. The relation of power between social actors steers the territorialization, transformation of soil, urbanization, and the relation between city and periphery.

By definition, metropolitan economies provide their needs globally. Mountains are integrated into such global circuits – and, thus, into a process of urbanization as suppliers of the global metropolitan areas, and as providers of raw materials, water, dwellings, and leisure. An interdependence develops between mountains and lowlands, with specific relations of cooperation and conflict. The relations are determined by the value of the exchanged resources, and even more generally, by the definition of what is a resource and what is a common good; and – of course – by the ability to afford and to buy the resources. In using mountain areas as places for outsourcing specific functions, for investments or divestments, metropolitan areas use their negotiation and decision-making power based on accumulated wealth. It is a conflict between the stakeholders of different spaces: those who have the power to define the conditions of production and those who do not. In fact, the urbanization hypothesis as an ontologic question leaves out this material basis, and it also leaves out the Global North–South cleavage. Seen on a global level, mountains are often in the inferior position, as are the countries of the Global South. Especially in developed countries, they have become partly urban neighbourhoods (Perlik, 2011). While they bear the problems of socio-economic change, they also profit from the purchasing power of new migrants and daytrippers. But the relations between the urban decision centres and the mountain population concerning land use are asymmetric.

Global metropolization influences the transformation of mountains and is a characteristic of post-Fordist societies. As suppliers of amenities and raw materials, also remote mountain regions have become important for the metropolitan regions. The social actors of mountain regions become integrated into a process of mutual interdependencies between metropolitan areas and periphery. These interdependencies concern common interests in exchanging complementary locational advantages, as well as conflicts about financial budgets and strategies for future regional development. The cities may have the problem that the mountain regions become unruly and no longer accept their role as mere suppliers. They may also have a severe environmental problem, as global warming may irritate the global economy deeply and provoke a major crisis. But in the end, most of the large cities will have also the means to resolve these problems due to their socio-economic weight – at least for their own territory, with little regard for the others.

3.3 The changed logics of space in the accumulation of wealth

Since the 1980s, and even more since the 1990s with the fall of the Berlin Wall, we can observe the processes of global change, a term we will use synonymously with globalization here. This is linked with new business models where vertically integrated firms lose significance in favour of vertically disintegrated units that exchange semi-finished and final products on a global level (Dosi et al., 1990; Garofoli, 1993; Piore and Sabel, 1984; Pyke et al., 1990). There is an increase in the amount of foreign direct investments. Manufacturing disinvestment is accompanied with reinvestment in more profitable sectors. Integrated firms are split and recombined with others. Industrial profiles diverge – for example, the chemical industry splits and develops bulk chemistry, specialized chemistry, pharmaceuticals, agrochemicals, and biotechnologies as their own sectors. The relocation and reorganization of industry sectors means that companies are significantly involved in territorialization, in the constitution of living and economic spaces as well as administrative units. They de-territorialize and re-territorialize at the same time. This results in a stronger concentration of decision-making power. Due to the use of cheap labour in poor and emerging countries, and new technologies, productivity for producing tangible goods is rising at an extraordinary pace. The easy access to high technology goods ('laptops for all') and an oversupply of food (up to 30 per cent wasted), both produced at low prices, allows for the broadening of the middle classes in developed and emerging countries, and also – relatively – for the wage level to be lowered. Homogeneous class relationships with common interests dissolve into a variety of groups of seemingly independent contractors and stakeholders. In the framework of downsizing the welfare state principles, employed people are at least partly urged to look after their own retirement financing, such as in the past, when freelance artisans bought houses to rent out flats as a source of income. Today, employees live in uncertainty of being fired because of productivity improvements in their own firm, while their own pension funds place their capital in firms that do the same even better. Increased wealth has put much liquid capital on the market. Banks have abandoned their old function as guarantors of the real economy (as shareholders) in turning to a business that makes its returns by transactions, mergers, and the administration of wealth. Industrial firms have changed their model of refinancing, from bank-based credits to going public.[1] The directions of technological paths depend on new forms of funding. It needs other forms to persuade investors; international visibility becomes crucial for enterprises as well as for the entrepreneurial-acting regions. It becomes a disadvantage to be peripheral to the financial markets.[2] In recent years, decisions on technology paths reinforced research on ICT and security activities. Both are technologies that have increased productivity in mobility-relevant research. Data flows and individual mobility have exploded. The changed profiles of education and jobs have increased the significance of agglomeration economies and generated a renaissance of the city as a place of production in the inflated business services industries. Work, dwelling, and leisure merge at the same place and create personal trajectories and careers. This changes demography, socio-professional milieus, and the relations between spaces. Migration flows react to this concentration: hopes and disappointment oscillate in cities much more strongly than elsewhere, but cities prove to be more resilient. The experience prevails that individuals find more and better options in agglomerated urban structures.

These new conditions fundamentally change the spatial pattern. We see the dynamics of growing metropolitan areas on a global scale, the increase of migration flows from insecure and poor regions to wealthy regions, and the measures taken by city management to ameliorate the two major problems of large cities up to now: environmental and security issues. While other peripheral parts of territories do not receive this attention – neither from the media, nor economically, financially, or politically – they lose their few remaining previous advantages compared to large cities. Small and medium-sized towns see a relative and absolute degradation. We can observe a steepening of urban hierarchies.[3] The object lesson is the development of the United Kingdom, where the tremendous process of de-industrialization was accompanied by the decline of the midland regions and the parallel rise of the business services industry in London. The Greater London area now provides more than 22 per cent of the national GDP. This polarized development is not new, but it has attained a new quality.

In the past decades, at the global level, many mountain areas have seen severe depopulation processes due to the integration of subsistence economies into market economies, demographic transformations, and the attractiveness of urban areas. In the developed countries of the Global North, these processes took place earlier, and are meanwhile being overlaid by new specialized functions of leisure and dwelling. But certain parts of mountain territories see a steady decline, prompting a public discourse over whether they should still be supported as inhabited places. This is not astonishing. Mountain territories have lost their role as integrally developed areas of geostrategic interest and importance for national economies. While the role of the national state diminishes, individual regions are encouraged to modify their value chain production systems according to their own strengths, with a clear profile and an increased self-responsibility to cope with the higher mobility of firms, capital, and individuals. This higher mobility does not mean a de-territorialization or footloose societies, as was sometimes forecast (Castells, 1996). On the contrary: with the increased mobility of people, goods, and capital, these places gain disproportional significance, and are able to attract and keep loyal citizens. We can state that each de-territorialization is linked with a re-territorialization.[4] Under the current logic of development, mountain and peripheral regions are disadvantaged – but this is not necessarily the last word on the topic.

Nevertheless, for large parts of the territories in developed countries (the Global North), the declining interest in mountain areas is not always linked with depopulation in general. One reason is that there is still a political will to strive for cohesive territorial development. Furthermore, peripheral territories have developed new functions, especially due to new tendencies of people living in several places (multilocality). The high standard of mobility and accessibility allows former out-migrants to reinstall themselves in the peripheries permanently. Another reason is the enlargement of the peri-urban space into near mountains. This changes the pattern from obvious large-scale disparities to less visible small-scale disparities.

3.4 Landscapes: the transformation of the mountain territories

Some Alpine areas underwent early industrialization with the use of water power. But a de-industrialization process set in with the Fordist crisis. While in the 1970s and 1980s local and external people had fought against industry to make them respect environmental standards, local people now saw themselves in the position of defending these mountain-specific regional production systems, to prevent them from relocating. In other parts of the Alps, the strategies of regional post-war development tried to bring industrial manufacturing into the mountain areas to absorb the agricultural workforce freed up by productivity gains in agriculture, and to raise regional productivity as a whole. This was not completely wrong – after all, family farmers in the mountains were multi-skilled, as in many regions it was always necessary to have multiple jobs besides agriculture. But it failed where there had not been a long industrial tradition, and where factories were implanted mainly to absorb cheap labour. Sometimes, the local administration was happy to get rid of manufacturing, as this opened up new options for tourist and non-tourist services. *Landscape* replaced *region* as the new buzzword.

This change from region to landscape is more than the replacement of one economic sector by another. It signals a paradigmatic change. We can translate this as a shift from the development approach of resolving regional problems in the interest of local people, to a perception approach in the interest of external visitors and investors. In the post-war period, European mountains lagged behind and were supported by national regional policies to align their productivity to that of the lowland economies, mainly through construction of infrastructure. This changed in the 1980s. First, the manufacturing was called into question, then regional policies.

The dominance of the landscape concept over the regional concept is a trigger to accomplish the integration of mountains into larger national and international markets, and to abandon mountain areas as a place of production of tangible goods. It is, of course, the result of traditional mountain products no longer being competitive. But it is also an indicator that societal preferences have changed towards intangible, aesthetically defined commodities. In this sense, the turn from producing tangibles to selling landscape qualities means an increased functional division of labour, where the mountains represent perceptions, images, and symbols, while the production of hardware is relocated elsewhere. Landscapes target other types of tourists that constitute the geographical enlargement of the clientele at the global level.

It is interesting to see the late career of this old-fashioned German term 'Landschaft', which was for a time outdated. It became dominant during the decline of mountain agriculture and manufacturing, and at the start of the stagnation phase of tourism. Now, 'landscape' is seen as a 'natural vocation' of the mountain territories, squeezing out the remaining productive activities such as agriculture and pastoralism, as well as traditional crafts and manufacturing.

The most important indicator is the reintroduction of wild flagship animals, which is not only tolerated, but actively supported by large parts of the population (against the wishes of local people). The decline of the old mountain-specific economies and the rise of aesthetic values as new marketable qualities indicates a fundamental change from a mainly production-dominated regional economy to consumptively used areas for tourism, dwelling, and leisure.

Landscape has also become a strong asset, an intangible commodity on the real estate markets where prices depend increasingly on 'hedonistic indicators' such as an unobstructed view over lakes and mountains, measured in square metres (Fahrländer Partner, 2016). According to the model of the Swiss real estate consultant Wüest & Partner in 2014, the difference in price between an apartment without a lake view and an apartment with a view of Lake Zurich can vary between 2.59 and 9.71 per cent. Other important factors are centrality, distance to the green belt, and public transport.

3.5 The paradox of the new diversity paradigm

'Diversity' has become a keyword with positive connotations. It has a double meaning. First, increased societal wealth for the old and new middle classes in many countries has led to a rise in demand for new, differentiated, tangible, and intangible goods, no matter whether the origins of this growth lie in the desire for social ascendance (having the same as others, 'material democratization') or in the curiosity to invent new goods. The paradigm of the Fordist period, 'having more of the same', has become outdated.

But diversity has also become a strategy to avoid a direct comparison with the productivity of competitors, and to secure existing regional production systems against attacks from economic competitors, by disproportional yields (increasing returns on investment) for a limited period (temporary monopoly). The sources of reference in the current literature are Paul Krugman (1991), who delivers with his 'new trade theory' and its 'new economic geography' (or rather, new geographic economy), an empirically founded theory for increasing world trade, and Richard Florida (2002), who explains the attractiveness of large cities through their cultural density and diversity. Both are based on the impetus of permanent innovation by 'creative destruction' of Joseph Schumpeter (1942). In this sense, mountain areas are told to play the card of uniqueness, as all their production systems are costlier than those in the lowlands, and they only can compete if someone is willing to pay more for the distinctive features of a product, or if they are unable to make a direct comparison with lowland products. At this point, mountain areas begin to invent emotional stories to attract new clients. In this understanding, each region has become an 'actor' that exerts self-responsibility and has to define for its specific development its own capacities and new resources to sell to a small target group.

The invention and development of new resources generates an increased diversity of goods and services worldwide. Tangible, standardized products (such as no-brand food) become relatively less important, in favour of highly diversified intangible goods (such as knowledge of a brand-new restaurant). It is the praise for diversity in all kinds of society, from biodiversity to multicultural expressions. At the same time, this praise for diversity introduces the values of distinction, an increase in hierarchies, and a growing inequality, which first only becomes accepted, and is later actively defended. As always, these developments produce winners and losers. They concern three different social fields:

- employment opportunities, wages, and economic wealth;
- individual significance, reputation, and assertiveness; and
- ability to exert social practices and existing identities, distinctions, and minority rights.[5]

An evaluation of diversity is not possible, not only because a denomination strongly depends on norms and values. Even more important is the scale dependency of such an evaluation.[6]

From the existing ethnologic literature, we have much evidence of broad cultural and economic diversity within a small scale in the mountains, with the commonality of being well adapted to environmental conditions. A classic example from the Alps is the ethnographic analysis of John Cole and Eric Wolf, who compared two South Tyrolean villages, situated a mile apart in the same valley (Val di Non/Nonstal), with a different culture in language (Italian-/ German-speaking) and settlement structure, but with similar agricultural practices and size of estates (Cole and Wolf, 1974). Igor Jelen (1996) showed in detail the cultural life of Friuli valley people, based on the requirements of local food production during the course of the year. This small-scale vertically differentiated diversity has substantially declined with the abandonment of agriculture and emancipation of nature dependence.

Diversity has reappeared with new economic functions: Now, there is an increase in diversity of products and features at the global level. At the local and regional levels, however, diversity is declining, due to the necessities of specialization. In mountain areas, it is becoming reduced by a general division into regions specialized in production and regions specialized in consumption of amenities. This coincides with the search for a clear regional profile with a view to a higher productivity. Furthermore, it was reinforced by the strategies of companies to raise productivity through a formal division between manufacturing and business services, abandonment of manufacturing shareholdings by the large banks, and restructuring of the financial sector in the 1990s (Klagge et al., 2017).

A first conclusion is that the proclaimed higher diversity in post-Fordist societies cannot be proved, and that it is an affirmative statement to justify the liberal-productivist argumentation.

Second, the loss of significance of vertical diversity has an impact on the whole territory. The multifunctional diversity of mountain areas had created a specific complementarity with the lowlands. This complementarity took the form of a territorial solidarity between the two areas, with an exchange of resources and a mitigation of mutual disadvantages. This old complementarity is still at the centre of the analysis of Davezies and Talandier (2014) for France (see Figure 4.13 in Section 4.4). But this understanding of complementarity is in decline, with the degradation of old small-scale diversity and increasing global mobility. The close relationship between the highlands and lowlands cannot be taken for granted anymore. The new specialized functions of the mountains need a global market size. This requirement breaks the former

Figure 3.1 Biophysical diversity as a resource for socio-economic innovation. Dating from the Inca Empire, this location at 3,500 metres altitude is interpreted as a prehistoric agricultural experiment station where the Inca cultivated wild vegetables and cereals by using the very differentiated microclimate at the different altitudes of the terraces. The different depth, design, and exposition with respect to wind and sun creates a temperature range of 15° C from top to bottom. The results of the experiments were used to spread the plants to optimal sites throughout the Inca Empire.

Photo: The double amphitheatre of Moray near Cusco/Peru, 25 May 2014.

symbiotic character of the highland–lowland relation on a national level. The new complementarity between mountains and lowlands is characterized by an increased self-reliance of the mountain regions, with the emergence of independent, internationally oriented value chains. At the same time, there is an increased dependency on the national and global metropolitan hubs, due to the asymmetric distribution of population and resources. Although the material situation has ameliorated for both sides, the character of the relationship between mountains and lowlands has turned to favour the latter.

3.6 How to deal with these insights: spatial inequality and territorial capital

The value system of the Fordist period was the mitigation of inequality and acceptance of reduced individuality and diversity. The new value systems of post-Fordism praise a high degree of diversity and accept increasing spatial disparities and social cleavages. In this situation, it is misleading to insist on the old Fordist paradigms of equal development. It is misleading because the Fordist welfare systems also had their shortcomings, as they provided national solutions that were based on global inequalities. The new regimes have produced a new pattern of losers and winners. So, there is no way back to the old value system on a national basis. Claiming the Fordist social compromise today means social models that are based on exclusion of the 'other', a national 'socialism' in all possible meanings that reduces solidarity by the privileged ethnic group: those who are 'in' will be forever in social security; those who are 'out' will stay out forever.

This means that the new liberal-productivist regimes have to be evaluated according to their own logic (i.e. to provide more wealth and more options for mountain regions). They have to be taken seriously as one of different possible development paths for spatial and regional development in mountains in the future. An evaluation should concern categories such as regional equality, equivalence, or difference (or disparity). But if local differences (in terms of culture, infrastructure, and income level) offer the opportunity for a region to assert its profile − where even 'non-development' might be an asset − an assessment that only invokes the 'hard' indicators such as infrastructure or the mean of the disposable income − as was the credo in Fordism − would be bound to fail.

Those actors and regions profiting from the new paradigm of diversity see the new options for mountain regions. They are often presented as a *passepartout* to resolve the problems of sparsely populated areas, regarding strategies such as regional food, rural 'soft' tourism, and other niche products − strategies that have become known in the European Union as 'best practices'.

But taking the liberal-productivist logic as a given does not prevent a challenge of the feasibility of this development path under normative reflections and concepts. These concepts have to highlight the deficiencies of the new regimes, without going back to the idealization of old Fordist regulations.

Two approaches seem to be relevant: first, the concept of sustainability (Brundtland-Report, 1987). It has its strengths where it sets normative goals for action, e.g. the United Nations Sustainable Development Goals or the claim that future generations should have at least the same decision-making opportunities as the current generation. Theoretically, however, it is difficult to justify the concept because, by definition, it must not fundamentally question the current normative positions; it presupposes that future generations have the same values as the current ones. The other approach is the concept of territorial capital (Camagni and Capello, 2010; OECD, 2001; Pecqueur, 1997). This approach uses an enlarged understanding of capital in the sense of Pierre Bourdieu applied onto the resources of a given territory, with the concept of resources encompassing both biophysical factors and the abilities of regional actors to interact and cooperate. This latter approach is more appropriate for analysis and interpretation, since it includes both the conditions of persistence and the conditions for a break of an existing development path. Applied to mountain areas, this means that the high diversity of the various producing economies (from agriculture to manufacturing to tourism) can be seen as territorial capital that should not be sacrificed in favour of landscape amenities. But it also keeps open the possibility of a break of the trajectory – namely, when the actors involved conclude that the former capital has been damaged or devalued and that a different path has to be taken.

3.7 Guiding hypotheses for the use of recent research

The general thesis of this book is that the paradigm change at the end of the 20th century changed the pattern of socio-spatial cleavages and resulted in new disparities that are probably more serious than before, because they restrict the future opportunities for peripheral and mountain regions. In more detail, this leads to the following theses and assumptions.

1   'Diversity' is an opportunity for mountain regions, but not all have the same ability to capture it.

The transition from Fordist to liberal-productivist regimes changes the territorial business model. The Fordist model was based on increasing productivity by standardized production, combined with trickle-down effects, to enable mass consumption. This made it necessary to organize an equalized social and spatial dispersion of resources. Now, this model is abandoned in favour of a regime that focuses on innovation and diversity to raise higher rates of profit by temporary surplus monopolies, a strategy that includes the creation and definition of new resources. Peripheral areas with a low population density take on new functions attributed to: 'nature', 'environment', 'aesthetic', etc. But this attribution is of limited value for the peripheries because they do not have the potential to create new functions on their own; they remain dependent on the densely populated regions with metropolitan functions, and this dependency increases. The urban areas define the new demands (new social practices, values, and services) through their population (in the sense of a 'market power'). The large cities' capacity for the definition of power and for decision-making increases in the same way as the peripheries see the loss of a permanent population and the decline of their old economic clusters. Urban diversity runs in parallel with specialization and monostructure in mountain areas.

2   Mountain regions valorize their landscapes as a new resource, but this does not improve their position in the relation of power.

With the new liberal-productivist regimes, mountain areas have lost many traditional subsidies and payments. They are told to develop their own new resources and to valorize them according to entrepreneurial criteria. The new resources of mountainous regions are landscapes that are valorized as residential and recreational amenities on global markets. As acting on global markets requires specialized knowledge, the main actors are often out of their depth and make the wrong decisions, and the dependence on external experts increases. This does not make the new peripheries poor – rather, the contrary takes place as they gain purchasing power – but they lose their influence to decide.

3   The revival of the cities enables them to integrate mountains into their metropolitan areas as a functional asset.

The paradigm shift means that the political and economic power is – once again – concentrated in the metropolitan centres. As the former Fordist model, which sought to overcome the territorial cleavage between centre and periphery, is abandoned, there is a shift from an integral development model ('equality') to a spatial model of hubs. It is these hubs which – instead of a national state – now define the relevant tendencies of social, economic, and environmental values. The hubs are in mutual competition; they act as collective entrepreneurs according to rules that are similar to the private sector, as in the business services industry. With their new power, they are able to integrate their hinterlands as suppliers of land, scenery, and other unique selling propositions linked to topography and local culture. Second-tier metropolitan areas in particular may benefit from these locally anchored assets. Mountain regions therefore are prompted to accept a territorial business model of high specialization. This might perhaps not be bad for them in the short run, but they do not really have a choice whether to accept this concept of development or not, and they may lose well-embedded knowledge and competencies.

4   The new factors of disparities do not increase the territorial capital of mountain regions.

Spatial disparities between 'rich' and 'poor' are no longer visible in the form of largely disadvantaged regions, but can only be seen on a small scale due to intertwined economic and social relations between lowland cities, peri-urban fringes, and mountain resorts. The new disparities concern new hierarchies that evolve from a new spatial division of labour: Metropolitan areas maintain their diversity in the form of multiple economic clusters with the critical mass necessary to be competitive at a global level. On the other hand, peripheral and mountainous regions become highly specialized with economic clusters that are (in general) of lower value added; they face the crucial disadvantage that their bundle of future options is reduced.

3.8 Empirical basis

We will validate the hypotheses above based on the findings of economic, regional, and spatial research in the Alps and other, mainly European, mountain ranges since 1990. This was when discussions began about urbanization processes in the Alps, and it was a time in which many studies on the national and European levels were carried out, applying a variety of different qualitative and quantitative methods.

Preconceived knowledge is based on fieldwork and new theoretical approaches to the regional economy. Where it was possible to conduct analyses based on quantitative data, we always took the municipal level (LAU2) as the spatial level of data analysis. This level of analysis delivers a spatial pattern in a fine resolution, which was necessary to analyse the new types of disparity, but with the disadvantage that only a restricted bundle of parameters exists at this level for large areas. Demographic parameters, commuters, and the number of jobs according to census classification were used. The interpretation was mainly done by comparing time series. Data protection and different national investigation methods to obtain data make it difficult to collect data and to compare one country to another, so that many qualitative efforts and a deeper regional knowledge are necessary to harmonize data. Furthermore, the theoretical approaches used and described in the chapters above are necessary to make plausible assumptions about data harmonization, and to put the data in the right context.[7] Expert interviews with regional stakeholders in the fields of economics, politics, and civil society served to better understand the process of regional and urban development. It also included participant observation to better understand the local situation during the regional consultation. Participation in European projects, especially AlpineSpace and ESPON, gave a thorough knowledge on the prevailing strategies of best practices in the European Union. Scenario techniques were used in the project 'Scenarios for the sustainable development of the built environment in Switzerland from 2005–2030', in combination with the regulation approach (Perlik et al., 2008). Finally, the expansion of mountain research to regions outside Europe served as an important source for interpreting spatial and regional processes at a global level.

Notes

1 An in-depth analysis on the development of the venture capital industry in the UK and Germany is given in Martin et al. (2003).
2 Empirical studies (Crevoisier, 1998; Martin et al., 2005) show disproportional investment in those regions that hold financial business industry clusters.
3 The most recent example is the reduction in the number of French regions (from 27 to 18) in 2016, which also meant a reduction in the number of regional capitals.
4 This statement is supported largely by a broad spectrum of different approaches: from the GREMI approach applied to urban milieus (Camagni, 1998), via the positivist empiricism of Richard Florida's (2002) 'gay and bohemian indices', to approaches that focus on the power of accumulated capital (Zeller, 2001).
5 We speak explicitly of 'social practices', which include all cultural expressions, currents, ways of life, religions, etc., with which social actors create strategies for their individual and collective well-being.
6 The question of scale and the relations of power is part of a debate that cannot be deepened here (Agnew, 1994; Brenner, 2001; Swyngedouw, 2004).

7 For example, you cannot calculate the number of people with a tertiary education without considering that the definition of 'tertiary education' differs between countries. Taking this into account gives you different characteristics of variables that are congruent with national borders. Nonetheless, such congruencies are strong indicators for identifying different national regulations as drivers for different spatial processes (i.e. for in-migration or out-migration or birth rates).

Part II

Devaluation and revaluation of territorial capital in mountain areas

Figure 4.1 High mountains have been populated for a long time. They offer a tremendous reservoir for biodiversity, food, and livelihood. It is not enough to protect them but also necessary to find ways for their fair repartition as part of spatial justice.

Photo: Mountain village in the Peruvian Andes. GPS: S 13°34.298′ W 73°52.211′, 26.05.2014.

4 Spatial and socio-economic processes in mountains

Chapter 4 provides an overview of mountain economies with their global interdependencies and presents empirical results to underpin my argumentation. I have tried to cover a broad range of mountain areas and countries, although my focus lies on Europe, especially the Alps. This chapter serves to give a more concrete picture of the ongoing processes that illustrate the interpretative chapters that follow. Some of the examples given here are repeated in the following chapters so that there are certain redundancies, but this seemed necessary to make it easier to follow the central theme.

4.1 Mountains of the world

From 2000 to 2012, mountain populations increased from 798 million to 915 million people, representing 13 per cent of the global population. This 16 per cent increase was in line with global population growth. For these data and the following, if not marked otherwise, I draw upon data of the FAO (2015) (Table 4.1). An overview of its distribution is given in Plates 1–3 in the middle of the book. This gives an indication that on a global level, mountains are not affected by large-scale depopulation. But we have to differentiate between developed countries and developing countries.[1] Ninety per cent of this population live in the countries of the Global South. Living conditions and population development go in different directions. If we look at the maps of the 'Extended Alps' (Ravazzoli et al., 2013) or the European maps of the ESPON programme, we do not see large differences between lowlands, low mountains, and high mountains. The main differences are visible, first, between national borders where different legislation, different migration flows, and different birth rates constitute the pattern. Second, we see strong growth in favour of the large cities and metropolitan regions that might affect the centres or its sub- and peri-urban fringes. We see that even some traditional out-migration areas have seen a population growth. One can conclude that mountains in Europe are no longer the pockets of poverty they still were in the 1960s, when access to the lowlands was poor and social services were lacking. The pattern of socio-spatial disparities has become small scale, which makes them less visible. Mountains

Table 4.1 Mountain area, mountain population, and vulnerable mountain people on a global scale

Mountain area and population	2000 [%]					2012 [%]				
	Africa	Latin America/ Caribbean	Asia without Japan	Oceania*	Developed countries	Africa	Latin America/ Caribbean	Asia without Japan	Oceania*	Developed countries
Area	11	15	36	1	37	11	15	36	1	37
Population	19	16	56	0.3	9	22	17	52	0.3	10
Vulnerable people	40	30	35	77	n.a.	42	31	41	69	n.a.
	Developing countries					Developing countries				
Vulnerable people	35					39				

Source: FAO, 2015: xi.

* Without Australia and New Zealand.

have gained new inhabitants who come mainly for residence purposes, and who can support retail and social services in the periphery.

Developing countries present a different picture. Here, we see an increase in the vulnerability of mountain populations towards food insecurity. In 2000, 35 per cent of the mountain population in developing countries were exposed to vulnerability; in 2012, it was 39 per cent, under conditions of a general population growth in absolute numbers in all of the four continental macro-geographical regions. According to the same FAO source, rural areas are particularly affected, with nearly 50 per cent of the rural mountain population living in insecurity; in urban areas, it is nearly 13 per cent, or one in eight persons. The share of people living in the mountains is increasing in every macrogeographical region with the exception of Asia. These changes indicate that in Africa, mountain areas are not the most problematic; in fact, the population of mountain areas has increased, from a share of 19 to 22 per cent of the total population. In South America, too, mountain areas have remained stable at least in demographic terms (16 to 17 per cent). This can be interpreted as meaning that in Africa and South America, other areas − such as deserts or the fertile lowlands − are more disadvantaged; they are contested because of land use conflicts and have thus become insecure. East Africa, southern Africa, and South America have experienced considerable urban development in mountains, and these parts have become integrated in local urban as well as in global markets, a process that favours population growth. These developments contradict the general opinion that mountains are always in generally disfavoured areas.

The FAO authors analysed the demographic changes according to six classes of altitudes. In all classes but the highest, the population increased. But in this latter category (of about 4,500 m), the population declined considerably.

The findings of the mapping of mountains under the aspect of disparities leads to the conclusion that we have to differentiate strongly between developed and developing countries. This applies especially to the scale on which disparities occur: small scale in developed countries and large scale in developing countries. It also applies to the different economic functions and dependencies: subsistence economies and sources of raw materials in developing countries; dwelling and leisure in developed countries. This gives rise to different strategies. In developing countries, the fight against poverty, the rights of minorities, and the fight against environmental degradation are the main topics on the agenda. In developed countries, it seems more important to prevent large-scale functional disparities due to a high functional division of labour.

In this book my analysis mainly focuses on the European Alps, as this is where most of the empirical work and research was conducted. My intention is to show the new disparities resulting from the regime shift from Fordism to post-Fordism, which are less visible at first sight.

4.2 Changing significance between highlands and lowlands

Mountains have been used by humans since prehistoric times for transhumant agro-pastoralism and to connect different territories for long-distance commerce. Before the construction of secure roads, mountain people had a closer connection to the settlements on the other side of passes, as by foot and mule it was easier to cross at altitude than to access the different parts of a valley that were separated by narrow canyons. In South America, the Inca Empire spread over altitude, as the high plateaus of the Andes (the *tierra helada*) are the agricultural treasure while the Peruvian coastal area has a desert climate. As a consequence of state building and trade, Cusco became its capital. Another role in favouring mountain settlements was played by climate, as it was healthier and more tolerable compared to the lowlands. In Italy, the coastal areas and wetlands suffered malaria epidemics until the beginning of the 20th century. It was a regular practice of upper-class people to spend the summer in mountain residences, pioneering multilocal living *avant la lettre*. The British colonial power made Shimla the capital of British India. These aspects relate to the role of morphology, climate, and exposition to biophysical processes that mountain economies have to cope with. Nature has never determined a single possibility of human practice, but it always played an important role in certain development paths. There exists some scientific work to prove the link between natural endowment and societal development in the past; the best known are those of Jared Diamond (2005). There are others to show how climate and the abundance of certain resources favoured certain development paths and impeded others. For example, the question of why industrialization first took place in Europe has been explained by the indirect impact of climate: The abundance of sun in the tropics allowed continuous agriculture during the year and did not encourage an investment of labour in artisanal work. In contrast, the population of the northern moderate climates only had the summer months in which to grow food, but they were able to ameliorate their agricultural productivity by using the winter months to develop tools for this purpose (Hesse, 1982, Ruppert; 1987). The northern hemisphere was rich in wood: This allowed early experiences in developing techniques to use fire, in turn opening a trajectory for early manufacturing (Ritter, 1984). As mentioned, the steep relief facilitated economic connections via the high altitudes; it also inhibited the early use of wheels (e.g. in the Andes). In all these cases, the trajectory was facilitated by natural endowment, but nevertheless it could have gone in quite a different direction. In the trajectory of Shimla and Mexico City, the mountain cities persisted, whereas in the case of Peru or Colombia, mountain towns declined during colonization in favour of coastal cities.[2]

In South America and Asia, mountain regions have partially kept their position. In Nepal, economic growth has favoured Kathmandu but not the piedmonts in the South. In the literature, we find at least three propositions to invert the supremacy of the flat city: the mythical-romantic sketches of Bruno Taut in 1919 to achieve 'Alpine architecture', the same ideas adopted by the Dutch architectural company MVRDV to draw the scenario of a completely urban Switzerland (2005), and finally the import/export flow calculations by Florian Hug (2002) to reduce energy consumption in Switzerland, a scenario of a complete inversion of urban habitats and agricultural production areas.[3]

Of course, such a development would be feasible, as now nearly everything can be constructed on nearly every type of ground (developing ropeways to bridge urban areas in the mountains is a rather new development; La Paz is a pioneer in this respect). Yet it is the technological trajectory with railways and motorways that favoured the bridging of long distances over flat ground, which in the 20th century has pushed the expansion of cities on flat topography and produced a lock-in situation: The weight of human investment in the lowland areas will be nearly impossible to invert.

4.3 Two mountain ranges

(a) The Alps: from a European periphery to a specialized supplier for the global economy

The genesis of disparities can be retraced to the separation between town and countryside based on the increased productivity of agriculture and the differentiation of class structures with artisanal specialization and the development of far trade. The development of class structures that enabled large irrigation and cultivation processes is described by Karl August Wittfogel under the name of 'hydrologic societies' and 'oriental despotism' (Wittfogel, 1957; Witzens, 2000). I follow this classical interpretation of spatial differentiation and reject the 'cities first' thesis of Jane Jacobs (1969) and Edward Soja (2000).

In mountain zones, which are areas with scarce and poor land, the question of where to erect building habitats and where to cultivate was of special interest. It was probably mostly decided in favour of the most propitious land cultivation; one tried to spare the cultivable land when choosing where to place the farmhouse. These decisions deployed the process of territorialization. In the European mountains – unlike on other continents – no real large cities emerged that would have grown as capitals, or at least regional capitals (second-tier cities) (Bairoch, 1985; Dematteis, 1975; Perlik, 2001). But there were many small cities with functions as local markets, for passing traffic and regional and ecclesiastical administration.[4] There is certainly no single reason for the lacking expansions of these towns. The small-scale topography is certainly one reason, linked with different settling periods and the distant central power. The organization of the Alpine crossing traffic was decentrally organized, a factor that Mathieu (1998) sees as an obstacle for further development, as well as the lacking food basis to feed larger towns. At the micro-level, the steep relief restricted the radius of cultivable areas, as the distances feasible for daily field work become shorter the higher the altitude, as these heights were accessible only by foot or mule (for the case of Innsbruck, see Bobek, 1928).

On the other hand, geostrategic uncertainties influence the Alps: during the Thirty Years' War in Europe one of the first continental long-distance traders, Jodok von Stockalper, laid the route for the salt trade through the Swiss Valais, resulting in enormous growth during these years in the first half of the 17th century. After the end of the war in 1648 and after his death, the town fell into oblivion again (Aerni/Egli, 1991). While Europe developed a dense network of small towns within a short distance, also in some mountain ranges such as the Alps, other continents had longer distances between towns. This is explained by the actual transport techniques in the early days of mobility and the inauguration of the first transport systems (carriages in Europe, railroad in North America), reduction of urban centres, and spatial concentration of power, unless there is a political countercurrent (Moriconi-Ebrard, 1993; Pumain, 1999).

Initially, the mountain economy benefited from its lack of accessibility, as this protected the existing agricultural and settlement structures from the higher productivity of the lowlands. Part of the population was forced regularly to out-migrate, due to the limited food base. The Alpine population brought its cattle and cheese to the peri-Alpine cities. For a long time, there was little difference in terms of the products exchanged, to the Roman era of 2,000 years ago, when the geographer Strabo described the exchange of natural products from the Ligurian mountains delivered to the expanding capital of Rome (Strabo, 1903). People who were successful in the European cities often came back in old age, reinvesting their fortune in their home towns and villages. In some cases, these investments were the roots of an early industrialization, e.g. the textile industry in Glarus, Switzerland. With the integration of the Alps into larger markets, triggered by the railway connection, the Alps lost these old advantages, but some regions were able to develop new products for national markets, such as the large-scale apple industry in South Tyrol. Furthermore, hydropower-based manufacturing evolved, as did early elite tourism, and, later, mass tourism.

In both cases, the integration of the Alps into larger entities (national states of the 19th century) reinforced territorialization. The whole territory obtained a strategic value and had to be integrally protected and developed. In this respect, there was, in the 19th and 20th centuries, much investment in the mountain regions, of course mainly for military reasons – as is still the case at the borders of the Himalayan states of India, China, or Pakistan.

With the railways, the ideas of the labour movement reached the Alps, until then marked by peasant practices, identity, and economy. The new ideas involved, in particular, the locations of junctions, freight yards, and depots, as the historian Christine Roux showed with the example of the small town of Veynes near the city of Gap in the French Alps (Roux, 1996). The railway centralized the regional development of its axes. Tourism development benefited from this; at the same time, previously segmented labour markets were merged, facilitating emigration. In the Alps, this development is enhanced by the fact that the major lines cross the mountain range (Semmering, Brenner, Gotthard, Lötschberg, Mont-Cenis) on the shortest route instead of connecting the valleys longitudinally. These Alpine-crossing railway lines preconfigured the development of the following decades in the 20th and 21st centuries: the jump in lowland transport productivity gave rise to the first wave of European industrialization and urbanization at the expense of large parts of the mountainous areas that remained unconnected. The connected parts saw a broad range of trajectories between the creation of a specialized agriculture, such as in South

Tyrol, and their role as a workforce pool for the lowlands. Furthermore, the construction of railway lines of narrow gauges modified the territorial relations within the Alps.

In the past, we saw a small-scale hierarchy on the basis of the geological configuration of a bundle of small valleys, with local centres in the upper, middle, and lower parts. The new transport system created a new hierarchy, depending on the financial capacity and the entrepreneurial initiative to invest in the new system (such as Willem Jan Holsboer in Davos in the 19th century).[5] A layout along the large longitudinal valleys might perhaps have been more favourable for the internal development and cohesion of the Alpine region (Torricelli, 1993). The fact that transport was not laid out in this way is still a major obstacle to a cohesive mountain development in the Alps.

In the first half of the 20th century, large parts of the Alps were still undergoing an out-migration process. The 1950s post-war boom reached the Alps when Europeans were able to travel, enabling the Alps to benefit from mass tourism from the start. In addition to agriculture and tourism, Alpine economies at that time depended on their locations of old industry (mainly in the Italian and French Alps and in Styria/Austria) and their politically defined functions for the respective national state: security in energy supply by large dams for hydropower, national defence by army and customs, protection of infrastructure by civil engineers, and of course, development of the school system. Mountain development in Western Europe at that time – the 1950s and 1960s – depended on the engagement of the state's activities in the interest of the whole territory (infrastructure and public services) and on the expansion of new services provided by both petty trade and national chains (construction, car repairs, retailing, branch banks). But it became apparent that the increase in productivity and growth was much stronger in the lowlands.

For decades, it became a dogma that an egalitarian endowment with infrastructure in all regions was the prerequisite for a successful national economy. In this sense, French spatial planning in general, and the Grenoble geographers Paul and Germaine Veyret in particular, placed their hopes in investments to eliminate territorial misconnection (*désenclavement*) by access to efficient transport and communication infrastructure. The penetration of the mountains by car seemed the most promising means to end isolation; the car was identified as the vehicle most adapted to the needs of the Alps (Veyret et al., 1967). Fifty years later, the opposite paradigm dominates. The ubiquity of roads could not mitigate the hierarchy between lowlands and mountains. Today, the most disfavouring factor is the lack of a dense network of public services. The vertical topography serves to disadvantage even more, as the technology to overcome distances had been developed in favour of flat areas and long distances. Mountain areas cannot compete with attributes such as accessibility; in contrast, modern transport systems such as fast-running trains, high-capacity roads, and high-capacity aircraft bridge the mountains through tunnels or airport hubs. In this sense, the critique on infrastructural equity between highlands and lowlands was, and still is, justified. The natural physical restrictions are still valid and caused the relocation of activities from the lateral to the principal valleys, and from the headwaters of the lateral valleys to the valley mouths (CS, 2009; SAB, 2010; WIFO, 2011).

We can already come to two intermediate conclusions from the contested debates about investments in transport infrastructure. First, decision-making ('who invests where') is guided by current relations of power between social actors and a question of prevailing preferences in society. This is not new. Second – and this is shown quite clearly by the way in which the Alps have been technically equipped – existing disadvantages are reproduced in an ongoing catch-up process. The claim of Alpine regions for equal conditions of infrastructure goes hand in hand with the implementation of the newest technologies in territories which are already favoured. We see parallels to Bourdieu's explanation of habitus and distinction: the powerful regions hold the necessary social capital to re-establish their advance towards the laggards. The social compromise in a society decides about the extent of the accepted advance. The nationally different types of welfare states did not overcome this hierarchy, but slowed it down. The liberal-productivist regimes organize the state according to smaller business units, the metropolitan regions. This strategy restores the original distance.

It was not only the investment in the construction of infrastructure but also the development of financial instruments to attract firms to mountain regions. At that time, specific mountain policies were generated that aimed for equal development between lowlands and mountains. However, when these policies finally became operative (in Switzerland in 1975, with the Investment Aid Act),[6] some parts of the Alps were already weakened by out-migration (e.g. parts of the Piedmont in Italy), and others had already begun to grow.

Cities that already had a certain strength profited from the lock-in factor (as in the case of Shimla and the Andean metropolises), as the historic development path made them 'too big to fail'. In the Alps, this was mainly Grenoble, which was subsequently, in the Fordist era, reinforced by national state investments with the implementation of important research institutions. Conversely, this means that, as the Alps did not generate capital cities (either national or regional, with the exception of Grenoble) in the past, this will not happen in the future, even if new technologies would make it possible. Up to now, the lock-in factor and agglomeration advantages have favoured the peri-Alpine agglomerations and other metropolitan areas. Proof of this is the fact that the zones with the highest seismic risks are not given up – they are still expanding (Los Angeles, Tokyo).

(b) The Hindu Kush Himalayan region (HKH): the interdependencies between environment, geopolitics, and globalization

The Hindu Kush Himalayan (HKH) region is comprised of the mountain ranges of Hindu Kush, Karakorum, and the Himalayas. It extends 3,500 km over all or part of eight countries from Afghanistan in the west, to Myanmar in the east. The Himalayan range alone has total snow and ice cover of 35,110 km², containing 3,735 km² of eternal snow and ice (Qin, 2002). For more details, see Table 4.2. Hills and mountains, particularly the Hindu Kush Himalayan mountain system, have always constituted highly diversified places where adaptation, mitigation, and resilience allowed people to live and to develop. Since time immemorial, the people of the Himalayas have maintained a rich cultural identity, and have maintained food security and biogenetic diversity within the parameters of their own tradition. The HKH region is the source of ten large Asian river systems that provide water, ecosystem services, and the basis for livelihoods to a population of more than 210 million people in the region. The basins of these rivers provide water to 1.3 billion people, about 20 per cent of the world's population. This makes clear that mountains cannot be seen as isolated from the lowlands, and that mutual interests, often conflicting, dominate the relations: lowland people depend on the mountain resources and are threatened by natural hazards. Mountain people want a more secure, better life, which – under the conditions of global information and higher mobility – is more and more measured by the reference system of the more prosperous lowland regions. It is clear that in a region of the world with high dynamics of global change, climate change and regional conflicts will also result in high dynamic socio-economic and demographic transformations to a large and unforeseeable extent. These transformations especially concern land use, access to material resources, terms of exchange of these commodities, as well as the desires for intangible commodities in differentiating societies. The institutional setting of property rules and governance will be crucial for the future. The consciousness about the large impact of biophysical and socio-demographic transformation in this huge mountain region triggered the foundation of an overarching transnational intergovernmental institution, the International Centre for Integrated Mountain Development (ICIMOD), a cooperation between eight countries at a hotspot of opposing geopolitical interests.

In the following, I restrict the overview about the spatial development of the HKH region to the urbanization process in a narrow sense (i.e. on agglomerations, cities, and local centres). We can distinguish between five functional urban patterns (Wang et al., 2019).

National and regional capitals (e.g. Islamabad/Pakistan; Lhasa/China)

The national and some regional capitals follow their own interests in international competition as global cities. But they are also high-end 'central places' that hold the highest functions and services in the interest and for the prestige of the whole country. They define the national standards of economic activities and the range of consumer goods. They are the only diversified places in the framework of urbanization and attract a workforce and highly qualified specialists from other parts of the country, as well as expat populations from developed countries. This means that resources of the country are disproportionally concentrated at these places. As – on a global level – mountain regions rarely hold

Table 4.2 Key figures of the Himalaya Hindu Kush region

a. HKH regional area, estimated (Total estimated area: 3,441,719 sq.km)

	Afghanistan	*Bangladesh*	*Bhutan*	*China*	*India*	*Myanmar*	*Nepal*	*Pakistan*
HKH part (sq.km)*	390,475	13,189	38,394	1,647,725	482,920	317,640	147,181	404,195
Proportion of country	60%	9%	100%	17%	14%	47%	100%	51%

Source: Sharma and Pratap, 1994.

* Estimate based on earlier definition of the HKH region, which is smaller than the area used for population estimates.

b. Population, estimated (Total estimated population: 210.53 million)

	Afghanistan	*Bangladesh*	*Bhutan*	*China*	*India*	*Myanmar*	*Nepal*	*Pakistan*
Population, in millions	28.48[2]	1.33[3]	0.71[1]	29.48[4]	72.36[5]	11.01[2]	27.8[1]	39.36[2]
Density, per sq.km	73	100	15	17	150	34	189	97

Source: ICIMOD, based on (1) Population Reference Bureau, 2007 World Population Data Sheet. (2) Estimated based on data and information from Population Reference Bureau, 2007 World Population Data Sheet and Banskota, M. 2004: 57–105. (3) Bangladesh Bureau of Statistics, 2004. (4) China Population Information and Research Centre (CPIRC). (5) Census of India, Population Projection, 2007. Available at: www.icimod.org/?q=1137 (accessed 9 March 2017).

c. HKH region and adjacent mountain areas include

Afghanistan (AF)	all provinces except Kandahar, Helmand, Nimroz, Farah, and Herat
Bangladesh (BD)	Chittagong Hill Tracts
Bhutan (BT)	whole country
China (CN)	parts of Yunnan (Diqing, Nujiang, Dali prefectures), Sichuan (Ganzi, Aba, Liangshan prefectures), Gansu (Gannan, Wuwei, Zhangye prefectures), Xinjiang (Kashigar, Kezilesu, Hetian, Altai prefectures), whole of Tibet Autonomous Region and Qinghai
India (IN)	the 11 mountain states (Arunachal Pradesh, Himachal Pradesh, Jammu and Kashmir, Uttarakhand; Assam, Manipur, Meghalaya, Mizoram, Nagaland, Sikkim, and Tripura) and Darjeeling district of West Bengal
Myanmar (MM)	the states of Kachin, Chin, Shan, and Rakkhain
Nepal (NP)	whole country
Pakistan (PK)	North Western Frontier Province (NWFP), Federally Administered Tribal Areas (FATA), Northern Areas, Ajad Jammu and Kashmir (AJK), and 12 districts of Baluchistan

Source: ICIMOD

d. Mountain ranges

Range	Countries
Gangdise Shan	CN
Hengduan Shan	CN, MM
Himalaya	BT, CN, IN, NP, PK
Hindu Kush	AF, PK
Karakoram	CN, IN, PK
Kulun Shan	CN
Nyainqentanglha Shan	CN
Pamir	AF, PK, CN
Qiantang Plateau	CN
Qilian Shan	CN
Tanggula	CN
Tien Shan	CN, Kyrgyzstan, Tajikistan

Source: ICIMOD

e. The ten major river basins of the Himalayan region

Rivers	Basin area [sq.km]	Countries	Population [in thousands]	Population density [per sq.km]
Amu Darya	534,739	AF, Tajikistan, Turkmenistan, Uzbekistan	20,855	39
Brahmaputra	651,335	CN, IN, BT, BD	118,543	182
Ganges	1,016,124	IN, Nepal, CN, BD	407,466	401
Indus	1,081,718	CN, IN, PK	178,483	165
Irrawaddy	413,710	MM	32,683	79
Mekong	805,604	CN, MM, Laos, Thailand, Cambodia, Vietnam	57,198	71
Salween	271,914	CN, MM, Thailand	5,982	22
Tarim	1,152,448	Kyrgyzstan, CN	8,067	7
Yangtze	1,722,193	CN	368,549	214
Yellow	944,970	CN	147,415	156
Total	**8,594,755**		**1,345,241**	

Source: ICIMOD, based on IUCN/IWMI, Ramsar Convention and WRI, 2003.

the functions of a capital city, they are often disadvantaged. But in the HKH region, the majority of the national capitals lie within the mountain perimeter. Only China, India, and Bangladesh have their national capitals outside a mountain range. But China invests disproportionally in Lhasa, and India has given the status of a federal state to Uttarakhand. In Nepal, the mountainous part of the country with Kathmandu is clearly more important than the plains.

New hotspots of territorialization (e.g. Gilgit/Pakistan)

These cities achieved sudden growth by chance, either by being at the centre of regional conflicts, or by becoming centres for logistics and administration. With the development of new international transport systems, old settlements and towns gain a new strategic importance that leads to the development of new settlements and agglomeration growth. The inauguration of the Karakorum Highway (1978) led to a rise in importance of the adjacent settlements, as seen by the city of Gilgit, which had 5,000 inhabitants during the early 20th century and then grew, from 18,000 (1972), then 28,000 (1981), to 57,000 (1998). Together with its rural hinterlands, its total population was 243,000 (1998), expected to number 342,000 in 2011 (Kreutzmann, 1991; UN-HABITAT, 2010). These numbers indicate clearly that this type of city gains its growth by large migration processes due to new infrastructure or insecurity and degradation in other respective parts of the country. A similar development takes place in cities and settlements that became focus points of military deployment or hubs for logistics and foreign aid. Kunduz at the foothills of the Hindu Kush had, in the 1960s, about 74,000 inhabitants; this had risen to 268,893 by 2012 (GoIRA, 2015). It is now hosting troops, translators, NGOs, and refugees, and attracts all other kinds of commercial activities linked with those.

Old urbanization with regionally controlled production systems (Shimla/India)

Shimla in Himachal Pradesh was chosen during the colonial era as the capital of British India because of its better climate. After independence, it lost its status in favour of New Delhi. But Shimla remained as a centre of wool production, and nowadays is an important tourist destination. Shimla is – at the moment – quite secured as a large city with large hinterlands, but with a significantly lower population dynamic than the other mountain centres (142,555 inhabitants in 2001, and 171,817 in 2011).

Resort towns for tourism and second homes
(e.g. Nainital/Uttarakhand; Joshimath/Uttarakhand)

The increase in global tourism and the emergence of the urban middle classes in the HKH states have led to the rise of resort towns in the mountains that valorize amenities linked with landscape and leisure activities. They offer tourist services such as accommodation, guides for trekking tours, and ropeway infrastructure – and they deliver the ambience and the prestige of (according to the clientele) an exotic or luxury destination. Some places serve as locations for second homes for members of the national middle and upper classes (e.g. in Nainital/Uttarakhand, which is highly frequented by clients from Mumbai and New Delhi, as well as from the Arab countries) (Tiwari and Joshi, 2016). The other type of resort towns are small cities near the peaks of the mountains for trekking tourists and national park visitors such as Joshimath; the snow resort in Auli nearby hosted the South Asian Winter Games in January 2011.

Local centres (e.g. Gairsain/Uttarakhand)

It was calculated that in India there are more than 500 towns in the Himalayan hills, the majority being small and medium-sized but with rather unequal dispersion. The hilly location means that the potential for expansion is restricted and accessibility is reduced (Khawas, 2007). These local centres are the principal towns of a district or sub-district (*tehsil*). This category of small towns fulfils the function of being a traditional central place (with a predominant supply function). They are centres of territorialization of the lowest level (local administration as the state's function) and places of market exchange for the rural population. They hold basic services such as schools and retailing. As roads improve and transport volume increases, the small towns, especially if they are located at the fringes close to the plain, risk experiencing a decline in their local economies. A better connection between these places and the larger cities in the lowlands may transform these centres into purely residential areas. We have to consider that temporary out-migration from the hilly zones to the lowlands is already common practice (Benz, 2014a, 2014b; Dame, 2015).

The recent urbanization processes have not only introduced a new pattern of spatial use into the mountains. They have also introduced the predominance of the market economy and powerful economic and social actors from the outside. In terms of their consequences, the socio-economic and cultural transformations are the most important.

This also means the adoption of the current urbanization model based on a large-scale functional division of labour with global metropolitan hubs as centres of political and economic decision-making, on the one hand, and mountains as spaces of leisure, on the other. This functional cleavage can be seen in Uttarakhand. It owns the majority of the territory as property. The state follows a business model to introduce professionalized tourism with the aim of attracting wealthy foreign tourists visiting the beautiful landscapes of the Nanda Devi region. The adopted concept of American National Parks sees peasants as adversaries to biological succession; the administration tries to keep agricultural and pastoral activities out of the local communities (Naitthani and Kainthola 2015). At the same time, a construction boom on river dams is set to increase the production of hydropower in responding to the increasing needs of India as an emerging country. The produced energy also serves to develop the tourist sector. Concentration of activities on resorts and keeping out peasants both constitute part of urbanization; under the aspects of sustainable development, they are highly problematic. Here, the HKH region follows global trends as in Europe or the US, albeit with considerable delay (Moss and Glorioso, 2014; Perlik, 2011). The rural economies are squeezed in favour of leisure and residences.

4.4 Mountain-specific economies

The question of whether spatial and social development is prescribed by topography or whether the same developments take place in mountain regions as well as in the lowlands has always been of particular interest in mountain research (Fourny, 2006). Authors stating dependency of economic activity on topography have often been accused of geodeterminism. This accusation has deepened as mobility has generally increased and the biophysical aspect of a site has become less important. However, the specific advantage of the development path would always remain. It contributes to the creation of social and economic innovations where there is a long experience of the division of labour: in the large cities, which, today, are located mainly in the lowlands. Meanwhile, it has become clear that the importance of the biophysical environment is growing again. The predicted vision of a footloose society has not come true. On the contrary, the importance of regional specificities, including topography, has increased: first for marketing reasons, to demonstrate uniqueness in the interest of promoting the location, then to generate targeted new marketable products such as 'landscape'. There are therefore good reasons to examine the question of the mountain area's specificity.

(a) Agriculture and food processing

The history of settlement in the mountains is linked with the possibilities of living off a territory strongly influenced by relief and climate. The development of population in mountains depends on the available resources of arable land and pastures. The oscillations of the economy were buffered by restrictions on marriages as a means of family planning and by forced migration, which was seasonal, temporary, or permanent. The power of the dominant local families was based on – and affects – different forms of capital: tacit knowledge, social networks, and reputation, but also access to tangible resources such as the exigence and exploitation of the common land.

In the agrarian era (which ended in the Alps with the connection to the railway lines in the 1870s), larger regional disparities could not develop through market mechanisms, as the territories were fragmented by local markets. But regional disparities of course existed due to the varying dependence of agricultural production on natural conditions (climate, relief), technical innovation (different periods of introduction of three-field crop rotation, potato cultivation), and different forms of 'governance' by the feudal power, and internal colonization where appropriation of the agrarian value added was a general rule. But it was arbitrary and there were no policies of balancing.

Industrialization and railway access integrated the Alpine areas partly in larger economic territories. The access to the railway line made agricultural goods commercial and comparable, which meant that mountain economies, with their small-scale practices and lower productivity, were in large parts disadvantaged and began to transform. Certain cultivations disappeared, such as cereals; others

Figure 4.2 Agriculture has the advantage that it can be practised nearly everywhere, and if done properly, the population is less likely to face hunger and impoverishment. Devaluing the investments of generations in food security by betting on comparative advantages is rather short-sighted.

Photo: Earth lynchets above Joshimath, Uttarakhand/India at 2,500 m altitude, 8 November 2011.

developed as export products that were in high demand, due to technical innovations such as conservation using inert gas by the emerging apple industry in South Tyrol. But on the whole, the Alpine societies were weakened – and not only in their agricultural sector – due to the enormous need for an unskilled workforce in the industrialized regions of Europe outside the mountains.

Nonetheless, due to specialization, increased productivity, and compensation payments, the agricultural sector remained until today. Agriculture has lost jobs and its former reputation, but it has kept its land. External influences have increased, mainly on the technical side of production and due to new (e.g. organic) demand, but in the Alps the sector has more or less kept its structure of local entrepreneurs that still have enough power to influence national policies.[7] However, this resistance today is possible only under favourable regulations (subsidies) and distinctiveness. Where attempts were made to establish highly productive agricultural mass production, such systems failed in the long run. Camila del Mármol and Ismael Vaccaro (2015) show this with the example of the Catalan Pyrenees, where it was possible to halt the agricultural decline in the 1920s by establishing a specialized mass production for the Spanish market with dairy cows. This system was still in place during the heyday of Fordism. After 1986, with the European market integration, industrial milk production ran into decline due to overproduction all over Europe and lacking competitivity in this peripheral location. We see similar structures in the French Alps, where butter is now delivered from the Normandy coast.

Food production has resisted decline where it has become transformed into a brand, using marketing concepts and labels such as 'organic' and emotional storytelling, and positioned as a high-priced luxury good for international markets. Sometimes with paradoxical effects: The success of quinoa (once a staple food in Peru, now a health food for the North American market) has transformed this staple grain into a cash crop and made it partly unaffordable for the local population.

These new trends serve to raise the value added for maintaining agriculture. In the Alps, the small-scale family model is not questioned, but the tendency is to reduce the number of farms and to enlarge the size of the single farm on the existing farmland with fewer jobs, which means a transfer of people to other sectors (tourism, leisure, personal services) or other regions. There are, on the other hand, regions that transformed into high-performing agro-industrial clusters (such as the already mentioned South Tyrolean apple industry); such regions are strong enough to maintain their specializations, but in defending their positions of power they risk blocking new initiatives of other economic and social activities.

(b) Manufacturing activities

The manufacturing industry developed in Europe in many regions at medium and higher altitudes based on a combination of several factors:

- Biophysical conditions such as relief and water, which made it possible to establish energy-intensive activities in mountain areas.
- The technologies available at the time. It was only possible to master the cataracts of smaller valleys to produce hydroenergy, and it was not yet possible to transfer electricity over long distances. The locations were thus given.
- The initiative was externally driven by engineers educated at the new technical universities outside the Alps and investors who bought licences for the use of water.
- The workforce was partly imported from other countries, and partly absorbed from the agricultural or the artisanal sector. The new sector became regionally embedded and still exists in the Italian and French Alps, although on a much reduced level. The industrialization of the Alpine valleys also brought in external ideas such as syndicates and political parties.

In certain places, the manufacturing industry was implanted only after the Second World War through external investment as a new sector to absorb the rural workforce freed by the raised productivity in agriculture, and thereby profiting from low wages. But these implantations sometimes failed due to a missing historic trajectory and due to the start of structural change towards tertiarization in the 1970s, accompanied by a loss of acceptance of industry (due to

Figure 4.3 Manufacturing skills were an essential part of Alpine societies, and they coex-
isted for a long time with other trades, even with tourism. Their abandonment
is part of a general process of de-industrialization in Europe and the countries
of the Global North. We should not be too happy about the vanishing polluters.
The Global North had much better possibilities of finding acceptable regulations
against pollution than the actors of the new locations, who have just started their
process of trial and error.

Photo: Gardone Val Trompia/Provincia di Brescia, Italy. GPS: N 45°38.958′ E 10°14.884′, 19 July 2014.

pollution and the increasing significance of tourism). In other cases, it became a
successful model of coexistence between agriculture, manufacturing, and tourism (e.g. in the Italian Alps or the canton of Valais in Switzerland).

The manufacturing industry survived in the mountains in places with
favourable political regulations (e.g. in the transformation countries in Eastern Europe) and where the regional population supported the manufacturing
industry (e.g. Styria and Voralberg in Austria). Often, strategic political decisions are decisive for the decline of entire sectors (e.g. decisions about currency
rates in Switzerland in the 1990s,[8] and more recently, in 2011 and 2015). Good
conditions exist where manufacturing industries are strongly embedded and
the regions have an industrial tradition, enabling them to adapt to the exigences
of global change with the strategies of permanent innovation, such as the cluster of watches and microtechnology in the Swiss Jura, or the industries in the
Swiss Upper Valais and the French Arve valley. The fact that the watch industry
in the French Jura failed in the 1970s shows the significance of social and political conditions for the pursuit of the economic and technological trajectory.

The Italian *distretti industriali* (industrial districts) play an important role in this debate and there is an abundance of literature on this topic (e.g. Dosi et al.,1990; Garofoli, 2009; Piore and Sabel, 1984; Pyke et al., 1990). They were once seen as the silver bullet in preventing de-industrialization in Europe. Then it became clear that global change also seized stable clusters, and they were taken over by external, transnational companies, often resulting in relocations, failures, and abandonment. A number of important industrial clusters still exist, such as the chair cluster in Friuli-Venezia-Giulia, the glasses cluster in Agordo/ Longarone, or the fittings and kitchenware cluster in Omegna, but often they have considerably transformed (e.g. the tile cluster in Sassuolo/Tuscany as a logistics platform). On the other hand, in a few cases, manufacturing activities were retrieved from Asia as quality and proximity matter more than low wage costs. Certain regions have reported that they have stabilized (e.g. the Lombardy region)[9] and that they mainly lack a good skilled workforce (e.g. Baden-Württemberg) (Prognos, 2009).

In some peripheral areas of the Alps, the population that had undergone several structural changes looks back bitterly on the manufacturing industry. Nuto Revelli (1977) describes the decline of rural life in the small villages of the West of the Piedmontese Alps by the pulling and absorbing forces of the Turin automotive works. This sentiment corresponds to interviews made in research in Domodossola (in the Eastern Piedmontese Alps), where once locally developed heavy industry outcompeted agriculture. As people reported, the companies attracted a workforce from all over Italy during the period of boom. They were located in new-built ('Alpine-styled') multistorey housing areas. In the consolidation period, the companies were directed from Milan, and in the declining period the sites were closed. As the companies vanished, so did the jobs. Industrialization had destroyed the old structures of the peasant society and when the manufacturing declined too, there was nothing left (Perlik, 2001: Chapter 10.2).

But these statements apply only to those regions where industrial production failed. In other Alpine regions, the development path from agricultural and artisanal skills to small and medium-sized manufacturing enterprises was successful. The specialized industrial districts of Italy had a longer standing and became a role model for the industrial persistence in the first period of post-Fordism. In other Alpine regions, the share of industrial production remains disproportionally high and outperforms tourism, even in famous tourist regions. In the Austrian Tyrol, the value added generated by the industrial sector is 17.9 per cent, compared to 13.8 per cent for the tourist sector; for jobs, the percentages are 16.1 per cent compared to 11.5 per cent, also in favour of industry. In the Swiss canton of Valais, with its strong tourist sector, industry has a higher value added than the tourist sector, and offers more jobs (13.8 per cent compared to 10.8 per cent).[10] The examples of the three countries show that tourism and industry can coexist quite well, a fact already stated by Ferlaino and Levi Sacerdotti (2000).

(c) Hydropower

With the new technologies of long-distance high voltage lines (since 1891), the locations at the source of energy lost their monopoly. The production of energy became a business in itself, not only for individual factories, but for the supply of the whole country and specific industrial clusters outside the Alps. It was not possible for local entrepreneurs or regional jurisdictions to bear these investments alone. The start of construction of large dams in the Alps between the wars became a symbol of national industrial performance and innovativeness. After the Second World War, it became part of the economic miracle of reconstruction. The capital needed for this large-scale national infrastructure was no longer available at the regional level. It came from nationwide private and public investors according their investment strategies and national development interests. This national interest was demonstrated in the Alpine countries with large dam projects (Switzerland: La Grande Dixence; Austria: Kaprun; Bavaria: Walchensee). For France, see Dalmasso (2008). Plate 4 shows the distribution of the most important hydropower installations over the whole Alpine arc.

The local jurisdictions benefited from these new large works differently depending on the national regulations, but not in the way that electricity generated new local manufacturing systems. The locals benefited especially during the construction periods by hosting a large number of workers, and by receiving infrastructure which connected them with the lowlands. In Switzerland,

Figure 4.4 Large dams have high impacts on the environment and the livelihood of the local population. Even those installations that were not contested have either winners or losers; it is a question of what scale and stakeholders are examined. This makes the search for fair social compromises even more ambitious.

Photo: The Albingia Dam in Val Bregaglia, Grisons/Switzerland. N 46°22.659′ E 9°39.636′, 8 January 2016.

the exploiting companies have to pay water rates for their energy production to the hosting municipality,[11] and these municipalities have privileges in the supply of electricity (which guarantees that energy consumption remains well accepted by their population). After 80 years, the use of the water, dam, and installations fall back to the hosting municipality. Certain municipalities are in quite a comfortable situation as a result of this high degree of autonomy and the high income they generate. Their problem is rather that they do not really know how to invest this money as they sometimes have a very low population. On the other hand, these rich municipalities have to pay into a compensation fund, to support poor municipalities in their canton.

The hydropower was intended to serve national rather than local needs, to enable construction of new industrial locations outside the Alps. This was already the start of a territorial cleavage between the supplying mountains and the deciding regions in the lowlands. It was this assigned calling to feed the new industrial hotspots of Venezia-Mestre that led to the construction of the Vajont dam near Belluno in the Italian Alps, to capture the headwaters of the Piave River. But a geological complacency audit led to disaster: A rockslide occurred, provoking flooding and causing the death of about 2,000 people in Longarone and two small neighbouring villages in October 1963 (Merlin, 1983). It was the second catastrophe caused by a large dam in the Alps. In 1959, about 400 people died when a dam for the irrigation of the Fréjus plain (Département Var/France) collapsed. Only two years after Vajont, in 1965, the Mattmark dam in the Swiss Valais was hit during the construction period by a glacier avalanche, killing 88 workers whose accommodation was directly in the flow line of the glacier (Ricciardi, 2015). It is not unusual for severe accidents to happen during the implementation of new technologies. The specificity of the Vajont case was the clear territorial asymmetry between the hosting location in the mountains and the lowlands (the industrial hub of Mestre), which reaped the main benefits of these installations. To make things worse, in the cases of Vajont and Mattmark, the companies involved refused to take responsibility for the disasters and the victims were treated badly.

There are cases in which the construction of dams was accepted by the local population. In the Swiss Bregaglia valley, the church bells rang when in 1954 the hydropower installations of the city of Zurich were inaugurated; it was a symbol of a fruitful cooperation between town and countryside. But often, such projects were heavily contested. There were severe protests against the immersion of entire valleys with Alpine pastures, causing displacements and the submersion of entire villages such as Graun for the Lago di Resia (Alto Adige/Italy) or Marmorera for the Lai da Marmorera (Grisons/Switzerland). Similar problems are reported from France (e.g. in the case of the dams of Isère and Ubaye in the Alps as well as in the Upper Dordogne, Massif Central) (Faure, 2008).

In some cases, a strong and furious people's movement achieved the abandonment of the project, such as in the Swiss Urserntal (Andermatt, canton Uri) and Rheinwald (Splügen, canton Grisons), both in 1946. People struggled against their displacement, arguing in terms of the destruction of inherited culture. In the 1980s and 1990s, the protests concerned mainly ecological questions, fighting the submersion of high Alpine valleys. The project of the Greina plain was impeded by national NGOs and prominent people nationwide who fought for the protection of the headwaters with an approach that, in 1978, was innovative: creating a foundation to pay the annual fees that the municipalities would have received through a hydropower dam. In the 1980s, some other projects were stopped (e.g.Val Bercla and Val Madris). In these cases, the argumentation was even more political, as it focused on the symbiosis between hydropower and nuclear energy. On the basis of pumped water, fuelled by cheap nuclear power, it is possible to fill reservoirs; the electricity thus produced may be sold at a higher price during peak demand. Several projects have not been realized. Over the years, it became apparent that, while providing some qualified jobs in the valleys, hydropower did not develop as a real job machine, due to its high automation. The benefits for the hosting municipalities differ depending on national legislation. But even if the municipalities are generously reimbursed by royalties (as is the case in Switzerland), they are not the decision-makers, and the price for hydropower is permanently contested.

The impact on the available quantity of water is severe, which means that not only the aesthetic aspects of landscapes are affected. Of much greater concern is the degraded biophysical quality and the reduced biodiversity caused by residual water discharge (Broggi and Reith, 1982). Nevertheless, hydropower is declared in mainstream definitions as 'green' and subsumed under the category of 'renewables'.

Hydropower developed from a local power plant for a single factory into an industrial sector of its own. This sector is now integrated into the continental energy markets and subject to volatile conditions. During the heyday of nuclear energy, hydropower in the Alps became precious as a just-in-time supplier for demand peaks; it became profitable to pump up the downstream water for reuse, even with the loss of pumping energy. The recent low prices of renewables have made the hydropower business difficult, as the high investment fixed in infrastructure cannot be refinanced.

In the southern countries, hydropower serves as a development tool, as can be seen from the Himalayas to Africa. In India, an investment campaign has been started to use the power of the headwaters of the big rivers such as the Ganges. It is intended to modernize the economy and transform the society from a predominantly agricultural to an industrial and service society, complete with international tourism, sports events, and resort towns. In Southern Africa, the water supply of the Johannesburg metropolitan area is provided by the Lesotho Highlands, under the Lesotho Highlands Water Project treaty (Nüsser, 2002; Rousselot, 2015; WCD, 2000). It promises prosperity for both parties, the Lesotho people and Johannesburg, but who will benefit and who will not is scale and actor dependent.

These few examples already show that mountain resources do not serve immediate or direct needs but are instead strategic assets. The question is who has the political power over this resource and who has the economic power to determine its use (Agnew, 2011). This relates to the issue of regimes of accumulation in terms of the long-term capital fixed in infrastructure, which fulfils the role of solving the problem inherent to capitalist societies: that of over-accumulation. This over-accumulation results in a permanent search for new investment opportunities and the invention of new commodifications. The investment in built infrastructure is one possibility (Harvey, 1982), and the commodification of landscape and its selected use is another.

(d) Tourism and outdoor leisure

Tourism is seen as one of the most important economic activities in the mountains. European tourism developed along the Côte d'Azur, in renowned spas in low mountain ranges, and in the Alps. In the 19th century, English upper-class sons came to the Alps to face new challenges in their workless life. Climbing high mountains was seen as a competitive sport, with spectacular first ascents on summits: One of the last achievements was the ascent of the 4,478-metre-high Matterhorn in 1865. The Alps were already then, in their most advanced parts, 'the playground of Europe' (Stephen, 1871). The social distinction of classes was expressed in specific cultural practices and different ways of life. It gave rise to professional local offers in personal services such as gastronomy, accommodation, rail- and ropeways, tour guides, and equipment manufacturers. Mountain tourism, over 150 years old, can now be seen as a regionally embedded, Alpine-specific sector that has created its own socio-economic milieu and trajectory.

In many parts of the Alps, mountain and spa tourism developed in an agricultural society in the decades before the First World War. This was often driven by local people who used accumulated wealth, risk-taking, and local power for investment in the new business of running hotels; in some cases, external people brought knowledge (e.g. in the case of Davos), but the development remained local, with all its positive and negative aspects. The first bloom of tourism came to an abrupt end with the start of the First World War, and there were many bankruptcies (e.g. the largest hotel, and one of the first Palace Hotels in Upper Engadine, the Maloja Palace, or the Wetterhorn ropeway at Grindelwald).[12] Many regions restarted between the wars, but in some cases, such as in the Chateau d'Oex region in the Swiss Alps, people did not risk a relaunch after the previous sudden end.

Early tourism developed into mass tourism in the 20th century, especially in the 1950s and 1960s after the invention of snow sports. Large-scale external investment entered quite late into this business, which was dominated by local families for a long time. Since the 1950s, mass tourism has encompassed the Alps, but with different models. While Switzerland pursued hotel tourism, Austria developed the model of small-scale pensions, often led by part-time farmers. France, however, following the post-war five-year planning of its economy, developed a model of large-scale winter tourism in the Northern Alps, financed by investment capital from Paris. This planned development, starting in 1964 and called 'Plan Neige', introduced the Fordist model of standardization, economies of scale, and mass consumption into tourism. This development took place only in France. It was based on the conviction of having the best terrain for skiing and that the expropriation procedures were in the public interest – and on the complete neglect of environmental issues (*Libération*, 1998).

Figure 4.5 Isn't it beautiful? The well-designed water reservoir for artificial snow in the ski-resort of Joshimath Auli tries to transmit the sentiment of the first electrical lights of 1879 in Badrutt's grand hotel Kulm at St Moritz/Switzerland. At 3,000 m altitude, the precipitation has to be defrosted by heating coils. It is understandable that emerging countries try to imitate global business models. But this makes it even more difficult to maintain balanced and cohesive livelihoods for the local people, as well as the original landscape aesthetics that new clients like to see.

Photo: Joshimath Auli, Uttarakhand/India, 7 November 2011.

In terms of external financing, Italy underwent a comparable development. In the Italian Alps, the development of ski resorts was promoted by the real estate business. A certain minimal standard of sports infrastructure was installed by real estate developers to sell apartments as second homes and as investments. However, tourist activities in the Northern Alps (such as the practice of hiking in summer or snow sports in winter) were not very successful; they mainly served as selling points. We find here a typical practice that affects peripheral regions: They are flooded by external capital (which seeks to be profitable), but this capital neither comes from the regional value added, nor from the same economic sector, which means that it does not follow the interests and the logic of the classical tourist sector with specific standards and rituals of hospitality, service, quality, and long-term interests – which corresponds to the common understanding of sustainability.

We were able to prove this with a case study comparing different provinces in the perimeter of the UNESCO World Heritage Site of the Dolomites. This geologically specific part of the Eastern Alps appears to be also homogenous in economic terms. In fact, the area consists of five districts (*province*) in three regions (*regione*) that each have quite a different socio-economic history. In particular, they include the trilingual (German/Italian/Ladin) Autonomous Province of Bolzano – Alto Adige (South Tyrol). The five districts collaborated in their candidacy for a common UNESCO World Heritage Italian Dolomites, which was accepted in 2009. Tourism was expected to benefit from this label, but this was not the case everywhere, as it developed differently depending on the area. Today, we see a completely different situation between the mainly German-speaking South Tyrol, where we have a small-scale pattern of prosperous hotels and guesthouses run by families, and the Italian-speaking provinces, which are now mainly developing second homes, but in the shadow of stagnation and decline. The differences result from different milieus of tourist entrepreneurs and – of at least the same significance – different provincial administrative regulations (Elmi and Perlik, 2014).

Tourism is, economically speaking, an export-based business: Local inhabitants offer services for an external clientele, with the specificity that the clients have to come to consume the product. Even if only 150 years old, Alpine tourism can be classified as an economic activity specific to the mountains, as it does for agriculture or certain industries. 'Specific to the Alps' means that it is linked to the territory by topographic and historic trajectories, and by its main actors, which means that it cannot be easily copied or relocated. On the one hand, the territorial capital of tourism constitutes regional stability. In 2007, the tourism sector in the Swiss canton of Grisons raised about 30 per cent of the cantonal gross value added (3,316 million Swiss francs) and of its jobs (25,530). Based on this, the direct core activities of tourism had a share of 25.7 per cent (Kronthaler, 2008). On the other hand it means that if important prerequisites are changing, the whole production system is at risk.

This is the case with Alpine tourism. For more than 20 years, this branch has been in a stagnant period: It is in a global competition between destinations, and it has high salary costs but restricted margins, as rising costs cannot be limitlessly passed on to the consumers. Tourism has high investment costs to adapt the offer according to rapidly changing demands by a clientele that is increasingly younger or more experienced. These days, the clients know what the alternative offers are and have more – worldwide – options than before. Therefore, the consolidation of the tourism sector has accelerated, beginning with the management of the infrastructure and other central services that are delivered by external transnational companies such as the French 'Compagnie des Alpes', an enterprise that had its roots in the Alps and has now diversified transnationally with investments in theme parks in Europe. Another tendency in tourism is observable: the growth of the outdoor business. The large providers are external, but, up to now, the market has also allowed local enterprises to participate, as the costs of market entrance for bungee jumping, rafting, and ski lessons are still rather low. But this also means that the locals are easily replaceable.

There is a large discussion on whether tourism can still be treated as a homogenous sector, as the differentiation of demands and offers and its amalgamation with temporary event management and multilocal residences has become evident. This debate is treated by the approach of post-tourism (Bourdeau, 2009) and cannot be deepened here. The other big transformation – besides this hybridization – concerns the transformation from tourism to dwelling and real estate management, which will be dealt with in Section 4.7.

(e) Second homes and multilocal dwelling

In economic terms, tourism is an export-based economy where the economic actors produce for external markets, whereby *export* or *external* is scale-dependent. It may mean international but also interregional or inter-municipal. In the case of tourism, the clients have to come from somewhere other than the place of production to consume the product: offers of leisure, gastronomy, sceneries, or 'otherness'. The enterprises that sell tourist offers may be owned by traditional local entrepreneurs or by international chains that operate a branch hotel in the given municipality. In both cases, the producers live and work more or less at the same place (daily commuting included).

Figure 4.6 Attractiveness is not driven by practical reasons. A dwelling with a lakeside view is rather a question of social status than an objective 'quality of life', a term that hides more than it explains. The old resort town of Nainital, Uttarakhand/India at 2,100 m altitude has developed into a highly prestigious location for the second homes of businesspeople from Mumbai, Delhi, and the Arabic countries. Habitable space is rare and expensive, further fuelling demand. Despite the danger of landslides, these new settlement areas of the multilocals have already spread to the hillsides, which were formerly inhabited only by the poor population and where landslides endanger the settlements.

Photo: The resort town Nainital, Uttarakhand/India, 2 November 2011.

The economy of second homes for multilocals or retirement migration follows another economic model: the residents, whether they are full-time or part-time, earn their money through external jobs or remittances (as freelancers, field managers, oil platform workers, or pensioners). They earn purchasing power to spend at their place of residence.

The construction of second homes in mountains began with the construction of small cabins on lots in rural areas in the 20th century, often inherited as family property. Examples are described from Norway in Flognfeldt Jr (2004). A similar development is described from the Czech Republic in Novotná et al. (2013). In the Fordist period, the growth of second homes ran in parallel with prosperity, with its most consistent expression the construction boom of the 1960s in the French Northern Alps. We see here already hybrid forms of tourism and residences, a hybridization that is still visible in new resort towns such as Andermatt in the Swiss Alps. Unlike the first cabins, the new private investment in second homes was also motivated by its role as investment object. Over the years, second homes became bigger and bigger due to higher wealth, new needs, and environmental regulations (e.g. sewage systems). With the abandonment of agriculture, farmhouses became available as second homes, either inherited or bought.

In the literature, there is a tendency to see a new repopulation of formerly depopulated areas in the Alps (among others, Corrado, 2014; Löffler et al., 2011). This might be true for selected areas, and also in the debate on the international migration of poor and refugee people. As a general tendency, permanent migrants to the mountains are rather rare, as shown by the difficulties mountain municipalities have in attracting qualified people for specific jobs. Trying to persuade people to 'come and work where others spend their holidays' is rarely successful, as the change from an urban milieu to a resort town in the mountains is often disappointing. Case studies that analyse movements to the mountains (either temporary or permanent) often ask for motivations: Answers include 'being near nature', 'landscape beauty', 'healthy environment', and 'quality of life', but they rarely consider questions of personal power such as the search for *altérité* (otherness) (Bourdeau et al., 2011) or symbolic capital and reputation (Perlik, 2011). Both – the difficulty of living permanently in a milieu imprinted by a strong local community and the increasing demands for changes and flexibility – cast doubt on the long-term sustainability of the residence model.

Nevertheless, there are many case studies showing that newcomers comprised of a mixture of loyal tourists, retired people, multilocals, and migrants have successfully stabilized weak mountain communities (see Table 4.3).

There is a lot of literature that runs under different labels: amenity migration, lifestyle migration, multilocality, second homes. The spectrum of cases covers all continents and involves all countries with new middle classes, and especially those with an explicit liberal land use (e.g. for Chile, see Marchant and Rojas, 2015). But multilocality is also a form of autochthonal people of the countries of the Global South who become integrated in market

Table 4.3 Seasonal variations in the population of a 'multinational' village in the south of France.

'All-year-round' Population	434
I 'Old' residents	ca. 30%
II New residents	ca. 70%

Alternative settlers
- Hippie generation
- Environmentalists

Repatriates
- Transgenerational migrants (3rd generation)
- Young, "town-refugees" rooted in the village (2nd generation)

Others
- Professionals (bakers, foresters, real estate agents, medical staff . . .)
- Commuters working in town while living in the country (lawyers, gardeners, teachers . . .)
- Former second-home owners

"Summertime population"	ca. 750
III Second-homeowners	ca. 40%

'Nameless' owners = 'tourists'
- Unknown or secluded persons

Well-known people = 'residents'
- Persons interested and involved in local life

IV Tourists	ca. 60%

Holidaymakers = guests
- Guests in holiday resorts
- Guests in health resorts
- Tourists in hotels, holiday flats, or holiday homes

Daytrippers

Total population	**ca. 1200**

Data and classification: Field research of Johanna Rolshoven. In: Rolshoven, 2001: 6 (I have slightly adapted the language).

Note: Until 1990, the French Southern Alps belonged (together with the Italian Piedmontese and Friulian Alps) to the most depopulated Alpine regions (in terms of permanent inhabitants). In the 1990s, the number of permanent inhabitants increased. This phenomenon was visible very early in southern France (cf. Kritzinger, 1989) and can be explained by the succeeding and overlaying processes of the 1970s neo-rural movement, followed by retirement migration from the north to the south of France (héliotropisme) and the most recent peri-urban development. Johanna Rolshoven's ethnological fieldwork in Provence (Rolshoven, 2001) also shows that the part-time presence of new population strata enabled local communities to stabilize.

economies and practise multilocality between work in distant cities and family support in the village of their birth (e.g. for Gojal/Pakistan, see Benz, 2014a, 2014b; for Ladakh/India, see Dame, 2015). The common thread is that multilocality describes practices that are different from tourism and the daily commute.

Figure 4.7 Construction in mountains is less standardizable than in the lowlands, whether in developed or developing countries. This always makes investment and construction in mountains more expensive than elsewhere. But this characteristic also creates a demand for well-qualified people who are skilled in manual work. This demand might be a sustainable option for the future of mountain economies if it is not linked with a speculative construction business, and if good school education is spread over the whole territory.

Photo: Street repair in the Indian part of the Himalayas near Shimla, Himachal Pradesh/India, 13 November 2011.

Box 4.1 Methodological problems of data interpretation

In practice, it is difficult to distinguish between an export-based and residential economy, as we can interpret the different service sectors as part of different value chains (an airport may belong to the tourist sector as well as to a local business cluster; the same goes for a restaurant). For operational purposes, we have to assign the different economic sectors to one of the two models. Then we can calculate the contributions of each sector and identify the economic structure of a certain municipality or region. In general, it is assumed that the restaurant belongs to the residential economy and the airport to the export-based economy. The main disadvantage of this aggregation for our topic is that the classification blurs the difference between tourism and second-home owners, which in our case is important, as the real estate sector and tourism each follow a different logic and have different implications for the regional development in mountains. But for a characterization that shows the economic change of mountain municipalities, we can work with these assumptions. We also have to admit that the current investments in resort towns operate with hybrid structures. They are comprised of luxury hotels and apartment buildings to be sold to an international clientele.

I do not name the practices of second homes 'migration', as I see multilocality as different to a definitive change in location (even if the people move again later). The difference concerns the impacts on the multilocal: They seek the advantages of moving as well as those of being sedentary, but they face higher costs of mobility. And the location is affected too: The multilocal is volatile; he or she cannot contribute to the community in the same way as monolocal newcomers.

(f) Construction

The construction sector is not specific to the mountains, but it plays a crucial role, as it was linked with all major infrastructure projects and all changes and enlargements of the housing stock. This concerned the construction of railway lines and motorways, large dams, and buildings for tourism, as well as the refurbishment of old farmhouses and new constructions for second homes. The maintenance of roads and protection against natural hazards (or repair of damage caused by these) can be seen as mountain-specific activities. These activities led in the past to an oversized construction sector with a considerable cluster risk. Today, of course, large-scale projects are carried out by large nationally or internationally consolidated construction companies or total contractors, and the workforce is recruited internationally (as it also was for the early tunnels), but regional enterprises are often included as subcontractors. Up to now the construction sector enjoyed a certain protection as access to mountains was restricted, and it is not very profitable to employ large firms for small-scale projects. On the other hand, the mountain topography restricted the perimeter and expansion of construction firms in the mountains. The construction business still has a strong regional component as calls for tender and supervision of the works also need locally anchored mediators for larger projects.[13] But larger structural changes have taken place. One reason is that now, several levels of subcontracting are practised, which transformed employed craftsmen to one-person enterprises who accept less favourable working conditions. The other reason is that one of the main characteristics of declining regions (such as East Germany) is the fall in construction orders. Building companies lose their home market and are forced to specialize and enlarge their market ranges. Consequently, there is an increase in multilocal living and working. In a more extreme form, we see this in the oil and gas industry (Saxinger, 2016).

(g) Water

Two other activities also have a problematic impact: water and raw material extraction. Mountains deliver 60–80 per cent of worldwide fresh water reserves.[14] Water resources, while plentiful, are restricted in amount and endangered by changes in climate. The distribution of water and the question to whom water is delivered constitutes a major problem, which will grow. At the moment, in most European countries, water is seen as a common good. It is not yet traded for the municipal water supply as an internationally distinctive brand.[15] There have always been attempts to open the water supply market to private companies, but mostly such attempts at deregulation have failed.[16] Big cities on the mountain fringes need water from the mountains, and irrigated large-scale agriculture (e.g. in the Italian Po Basin) needs millions of cubic metres of irrigation water, which is stored in large dams in the mountains. With the increasing concentration of population in these peri-Alpine metropolitan areas, the need for water will increase and the water catchments for their supply will be extended further into the mountains. This is similarly valid for the supply of Alpine resorts for hosting tourists and multilocal residents. The activities

Figure 4.8 Water in mountain regions affects two important social conflict fields: Who are the owners and who are the users of this precious resource, and what exchange conditions should be applied, especially when drinking water is transported over long distances to the lowlands? And, how long will this resource be available, given climate change and global warming?

Photo: The Rhône glacier, Valais/Switzerland. N 46°33.501′ E 8°17.753′, 24 September 2016.

in these resorts are concentrated on the peak seasons, causing particular problems in winter, when precipitation is stored as snow and water is lacking to dilute the increased load of waste water, overloading the sewage treatment system. Furthermore, artificial snow has become a widespread means of operating ski stations, requiring huge amounts of water (see Figure 4.5).

Up until now, neither selling nor importing water over long distances to supply other basins has been a big topic in European mountains. This may change, not only because of the enlargement of nearby metropolitan areas. As always, when gradients between economic activities open up, the lowland–mountain disparity feeds arguments to create new economic functions for the peripheries, which would mean that mountain municipalities begin to cooperate with private investors to invest in water catchments and a pipe system for long-distance supply. This would mean a new level of commodification of mountain resources with the question of a correct price and the risk of over-exploitation. It is clear that this question is strongly contested by the different societal stakeholders. The example of the Lesotho Highlands Water Project, the joint venture between Lesotho and the Republic of South Africa, shows that win–win solutions are often spoken about, but that it is a matter of scale in judging whether there are winners and losers – and in that example, the mountain population loses (Blanchon, 2009; Nüsser, 2002; Rousselot, 2015). There are other examples from the French (Serroi et al., 2015) and the Swiss Alps (Schneider, 2015). We also have to add that water is an important resource for the mining industry: During its production process, mining uses huge amounts of fresh water that then runs off as contaminated water.

(h) Logging, mining, and extraction of solid raw materials

Mining is no longer a relevant topic in the Alps and in other West European mountains, but it is very important for mountain ranges in other continents that have layers of coal, ore, or rare earths. Mountains offer many resources, but the sites are not large and easily exploitable. Therefore mountain topography plays a specific role under two aspects, socially and ecologically important. Many raw materials are accessible only now (but now with high performance), and many raw materials are needed only now (but now with much eagerness fuelled by its scarcity). The exploitation of these is potentially environmentally damaging, not only through chemical pollution, but also by their deep impact on landscape ecology (e.g. cutting the summits in the Appalachians to have open-sky mines instead of dangerous and expensive subsurface banks). Conflicts also arise through debates with local riparian organizations and concerned NGOs (Niederberger et al., 2016; Provo and Jones, 2011). Furthermore, mining requires a high quantity of water resources, which might be better used for public water supply, and finally, settlements for mining are often temporary, and abandoned after the exploitation. The remoteness of sites often makes mining take the form of an 'offshore' activity (i.e. the workers and technicians are flown in and out for a temporary time without the development of permanent

Figure 4.9 Extractive activities are always temporary, either because the resources are exhausted or the exploited good becomes technologically or culturally outdated. This question arises whether an exhausted site can be maintained or should be abandoned and become a ghost town. If we apply similar criteria to the recycling of waste – and view the establishment of a mining site in terms of invested efforts in human work and life and environmental impacts – then it seems worth planning early the reuse and transformation of mining locations after they are exhausted, to prevent working by the principle of 'after us, the deluge'. Idrija, at the edge of the Slovenian Alps, was the second most important mercury mine in the world. It has been a UNESCO World Heritage Site since 2012, together with the Spanish mine at Almadén.

Photo: The ancient mercury mine of Idrija/Slovenia.

settlement structures). This volatile use impedes efforts to make responsible use of the territory, as it means that no one is really interested in controlling environmental conditions for further use. It is a new form of shifting cultivation on a large scale. Changing this would require anticipating these reduced periods to avoid pollution, safeguard fair working conditions, and start a regional reinvestment of the taxes and fees obtained through the mining activity. Contrary to large-scale mining, the extraction of stones was – for a long time – a locally based small-scale activity. These small-scale activities have partly been abandoned due to the exhaustion of the sites, but are also under pressure from global supply. While in the 1990s, Sardinian rose granite began to invade Europe's capitals (including for the restoration of East Germany's historic monuments), stones now arrive from China in ships as additional cargo or ballast. The price differences are so high that even public enterprises that order stones to pave public streets have to buy globally instead of regionally. This constitutes a further loss for mountain-specific industries. Another aspect is that the globally traded extractive materials in general are a highly volatile business, where small changes in price decide whether the mine has to cease its activities, such as in the case of gold mining.

(i) Parks and biosphere preserves

The concept of national parks was first established in the Rocky Mountains at the end of the 19th century as a reaction to the colonization and transformation of the North American continent.[17] As a reaction to natural degradation, the concept claimed wilderness without humans as an ideal, although the indigenous native population had proved that they were able to develop stable economies in relation to the biophysical environment. Today, millions of international tourists visit the most famous of the national parks, which have undergone vigorous branding, leading to overuse and efforts by tourist organizations to disperse the influx of visitors to other regions.[18]

Historically, this concept has not applied to other continents. Mountain territories were cultivated by local populations; abandoning cultivated fields only occurred due to climatic aggravations or degraded soils, and was perceived as a defeat. Things only changed in the 20th century, when food production was secured. Rising productivity and global food distribution meant that mountain agriculture turned into a niche field of production. On the basis of different productivities, different population densities, and different value systems between stagnating mountain regions and growing urban agglomerations, conflicts of interest have increased: Local inhabitants claim their right to live and to produce, while the majority of the population, socialized in an urban environment, claims interests to preserve biodiversity and natural heritage in the name of humanity. The detailed argumentation in its logic and contradictions will be picked up again later.

At this point, it is necessary to describe the processes of a change in economic activities. In the past, under Fordist conditions, national governments tried to mitigate the differences in productivity by developing infrastructure. The decline of the Fordist paradigm brought up ecological arguments to 'take landscapes out of use', underpinned by monetary arguments calculating the economic value of biodiversity, water quality, and forests. Subsequently, landscapes as aesthetic values became labels and economic values. It is not a 'taking out'; it is another form of land use with other actors, which is often contested by local people.

In some places, local people have accepted changing their activity, at least partly, from food producing to offering site preservation services as rangers or local tour guides. This was the case in some regions in the Alps where establishing parks has become a new development goal. On the other hand, the local population largely opposes the policy of protecting large predator animals because the damage caused by such animals is increasing, making traditional pastoralism more expensive, a development that the locals perceive as a new form of colonization by external decision-makers. This development can be shown for the European mountains where the demographic decline of the peripheries gives way to the invasion of wolves and bears (especially in the Alps, Massif Central, Abruzzo, Pyrenees, Carpathians). With only a sparse population, these regions cannot play

Figure 4.10 The French Pyrenees National Park attracts hikers from France, Europe, and other continents. Bivouacking is allowed during the night. If the numbers of visitors are moderate and tourism is not the only activity, the interests of all stakeholders can be fulfilled, and the biosphere does not suffer.

Photo: The rest of the glacier of Vignemale near Cauterets, French Pyrenees. We can observe that soon the last heritage of the Pleistocene in the Pyrenees can be measured with a tape measure. GPS: N 42°47.571' W 0°8.487', 13 August 2016.

a relevant role, which means they are often left alone without much public support. They are of specific interest to certain groups of scientists (e.g. biologists) or to niche tourism (trekking and expeditions), possibly promising visitors the thrill of the reappearance of the big predators. This niche tourism produces added value as well as personal benefits, but mainly for urban stakeholders.

In emerging countries, national parks are seen as a strategy to modernize society and increase regional wealth, by developing from subsistence to market economies. These processes are conflictive and often displace the local population with their adapted practices of use. The Swiss social anthropologist Eva Keller shows in her work on the Masoala National Park, established in 1997 in hilly northeastern Madagascar, how European perceptions of nature are in contradiction with the interests of the local population. They see the national park as an affront to their traditional ways of life and their cultural values, compromising their livelihoods – for example when they need permits to pass certain areas (Keller, 2015). But it is not only the foreign postcolonial projection of landscape aesthetics or the political interests of a distant central power that wants to enforce such strategies with little regard for the interests of the local population – sometimes it is the mountain government itself that explicitly promotes this development. In the Nanda Devi region in India it is the mountain jurisdiction, the federal state of Uttarakhand, which owns the majority of the land. Uttarakhand wants to develop a modern tourist sector, valorizing landscape, spectacular views, and wild animals. They follow the American national park concept, where the human is strictly seen as the antithesis to 'nature'. In this concept, human pastoral activities have no place; in this case, the local communities quarrel with their regional government (Naitthani and Kainthola, 2015; Rao et al., 2000).

(j) Transformations of mountain economy

If we take the Alpine processes as a reference, then we can say: Mountain agriculture persists but it is transforming. On the one hand, it has a higher performance with fewer farms, fewer people, a higher input of pre-products, and an output of products with higher quality. On the other hand, we see an extensification, which delivers ecological services paid for by society. It is becoming less accepted to provide subsidies, as once widely practised in the countries of the Global North. De-industrialization is ongoing in Europe, and it also involves mountain regions. The extractive industries remain in the mountains on the whole, but the exploitation of the sites is temporary in a double sense: the duration depends on the thickness of the layers and the oscillation on the spot markets. We see as a very new tendency that the production of hydropower energy is also subject to these oscillations, due to an oversupply of renewables. Water as a liquid raw material is also a finite resource and a 'polluter', as the residual flows beneath a collector or dam necessary for the biocoenosis is not 'renewable' (a fact that is mostly neglected). Hydropower and solid raw materials generate a permanent debate about whom these resources should belong to and what the price for their use should be. The negative aspects of the solid raw materials make them less favourable in the larger public. They will certainly not disappear, but if the local or regional authorities see a possibility of changing into the tertiary sector, they probably will. This applies especially to landowners.

There do remain production systems that sell 'amenities', which in the literature means that they are based on commodities such as landscape aesthetics and well-being through environmental qualities. First, this means summer and winter tourism in the mountains. Second, it means owners of second homes. Often tourists who have known a certain destination for a long time decide to buy a house there later to be more independent, to feel more integrated in the local community, for retirement, or for all these reasons. In the Alps, tourism has been stagnating for a long time; it is seen as a 'mature' market and hardly profitable. There, tourism has been outperformed by second homes and hybrid tourist/real estate resort towns. I will expand on this in Section 4.7.

(k) The vulnerability of mountain production systems

Table 4.4 shows a typology of the six most relevant mountain production systems. It shows that the space given here to new inhabitants and the

Table 4.4 Typology of the six most relevant mountain production systems.

	Economic model	Product	Territorial function	Main actors	Local steering	Socio-economic function	Interest of main actors	Perspective of main actors	Development trend of production system
Tourism	Export	Intangible	Creator	Economy	+++	Economic site Habitat	• Liberty of action • Economic sustainability • Place to live	Permanent	Declining
Agriculture Manufacturing Artisanal	Export	Tangible	Creator	Economy	+++	Economic site Habitat	• Liberty of action • Economic sustainability • Place to live	Permanent	Declining
Multilocal dwelling	Residential	Intangible	Supplier	Civil society	– –	Habitat	• Place to live	Temporary	Increasing
Returned and retired	Residential	Intangible Tangible	Supplier	Civil society Economy	+++	Habitat Economic site	• Liberty of action • Economic sustainability • Place to live	Permanent	Increasing
Extraction Water Hydropower	Export	Tangible	Supplier	Economy Public sector	– – –	Economic site	• Liberty of action	Temporary	Increasing
Parks Nature Reserves	Export	Intangible	Supplier	Public sector Civil society	– – –	Economic site	• Liberty of action	Ephemeral	Increasing

Note: This table classifies the most important mountain production systems. They are differentiated between export-based (Export) and residential economies (Residential). They deliver tangible (e.g. food) and intangible (e.g. emotional values) products for their stakeholders. Furthermore, a distinction is made between creative activities due to the special regional development path (creator) and the function as a provider of rare resources (supplier). The main actors are divided into economic actors (entrepreneurs), public sector (state institutions), and actors of civil society (which can include both individuals and institutionalized cooperation). 'Local steering' assesses the degree of regional liberty of action. Depending on the regional specialization, the interests of the dominant players focus on the development of the region as a place of residence or as a production site. It is assumed that the regional connection increases with the length of stay (permanent stay vs. temporary stay). The last column indicates which economic sectors are in decline and which are growing. The colour subdivision distinguishes between dynamics, diversity, and creative multifunctionality on the one hand (dark grey), and stagnation, specialization, and dependence on the other (white). Under criteria of sustainable development, the expected paradox arises that the endogenous production systems have advantages but are losing importance, while functions that are in high demand (multilocal dwelling, extraction, etc.) are probably reinforcing the inferiority of mountain areas. An exception could be the winning (back) of the 'returned and retired': gaining back former emigrants and attracting and integrating new migrants (whether they come by choice, by need, or by force), provided that it is possible to make their life experience fruitful for mountain development, e.g. by setting up their own small businesses.

transformation into residential economies should not lead to euphoric and overhasty interpretations. First, such an economic model creates dependencies. A municipality is rid of its financial problems if it can host a philanthropic millionaire. But the millionaire can decide to leave at any time, if the municipality does not develop in their interest. Second, the model of ageing societies, in which the old people stay and the young go away for work, is certainly much more frequent. Here, the amenity migration literature certainly shows a social bias where the focus is too strongly oriented on the emerging middle classes and loses from view the peasants remaining in less accessible mountain villages. We can cite here the case of Japan, a society that is said to be very egalitarian. Japan is disproportionally strongly affected by demographic ageing. Here, we see the peripheral rural and mountain areas undergoing depopulation while the metropolitan areas are still growing (Feldhoff, 2011, 2013; Matanle and Rausch, 2011). In France, Giovanni Fusco and Floriane Scarella (2011) show the segregation processes occurring in the peri-urban expansion of Nice, where the workless and poor people, already on the outskirts, are further squeezed out to the adjacent Alps. Finally, we should mention the repopulation of certain Austrian Alpine valleys by migrants from Eastern Europe and, as described by Maurizio Dematteis (2010), the immigration of non-European foreigners to the Piemontese Alps in Italy.

It is generally recommended that sparsely populated regions develop a specialized economic cluster that gives them a unique selling proposition. Standing alone allows temporary monopolies and a better protection against the copying of knowledge. In fact, today, the only type of region able to compensate risks in case of a crisis is the metropolitan region with a multi-structured diverse economic pattern based on several clusters. The sparsely populated regions, by contrast, bear the cluster risk of monostructure, or the risk of a lock-in (losing innovation and competitivity), resulting in loss of loyalty by their main deciding actors, who may sell their enterprises to external competitors. When one key actor sells, others may follow. The buyers may appropriate the existing local knowledge and take it to their home base, causing the cluster to decline. In this sense, mountain clusters are fragile because of their small size and the lack of buffering alternatives.

With the integration of small-scale industrial sectors into larger groups, and following relocations, this embeddedness is weakened. It opens up opportunities for new production systems where the former activities showed signs of inertia and lock-in. However, it is not clear whether the new activities can reach the same stability as in the past. There are examples of new entrepreneurships in the Alps where people go back to their roots later in life or where they retry new activities (Meili and Mayer, 2015). They may be able to stabilize a local community but they cannot create many jobs. They cannot compensate for the loss of an economic cluster. Experience shows that the younger the production system, the more volatile it is. The old structures and knowledge become devalued, and for the new qualities there is no sufficient qualification, innovation, or competitivity. Such regions risk losing old qualities without regaining alternatives in the long run.

The findings can be interpreted as follows: the younger the production systems, the less endogenous they are – and the greater their dependence on external decision-making. This makes them very sensitive to relocation. This is a disillusioning result, as it gives an unfavourable perspective on new 'mountain-specific' value chains, which are seen as unique selling propositions and are expected to be sustainable. On the other hand, the embeddedness risks falling into the lock-in trap. In Alpine valleys, the main activities such as hotels are often in the hands of long-standing local families. They are fairly well protected against the comparative advantages of other tourist destinations, as long as the families have an intrinsic interest in keeping this trade, even if it is not very profitable. They might miss necessary adaptations to changed conditions and clients. They end up having to sell anyway, and the cluster dissolves when it is exposed to a benchmarked competition in which comparative advantages are important. One example is the history of the French 'Compagnie des Alpes'. This enterprise was already established through external capital, to operate ropeways and manage resort towns in the French Alps, after which it expanded to the Italian and Swiss Alps. The company accelerated the consolidation of an Alpine tourist industry before diversifying into business fields outside the mountains, while relocating its headquarters to Paris. The tourist sector in the Alps, estimated as a 'mature' market, lost importance. For the local people, this means that they have to precisely define new client target groups and new higher specialized offers on the global market in ever shorter intervals. In the same way, they have to reconfirm the loyalty of the main stakeholders (i.e. inhabitants, entrepreneurs, key clients, etc.).

4.5 The urbanization and metropolization of the mountains

First, we have to clear a question of definition. We have to distinguish between urbanization and urban development. Urbanization refers to the processes of sociation in its space-relevant expressions. This means the increase of a division of labour and of market economies, and the uses of space linked with these. Urbanization is independent of the morphology of a certain territory and of the built or non-built environment. It follows the already mentioned concept of the social construction of space. Urban development, on the other hand, means the increase in agglomerated forms of living and working. We will see that both forms are taking place in mountain areas. Metropolization means the emergence of a system of global cities which, by the socio-economic power of their citizens, can act as collective enterprises and enforce their interests nationally and internationally. In particular, they are able to integrate their rural and mountainous hinterlands to raise their own specific profile.[19]

(a) The global view

Mountains and urban development are often seen as a contradiction. Yet mountain regions such as the Andes, the Sierras, the Hindu Kush Himalayas, and the

Alps have always had a regular exchange with the lowlands for essential goods and services, and people have always moved between these two realms. Quite apart from such interaction, most mountain regions have been settled since pre-historic times, and the socialization in compact villages with common rules and institutions has displayed forms of social urbanization and led to the development of smaller or larger urban settlements in many mountain regions of the world. In 2000, about 27 per cent of the global mountain population, or 200 million of over 720 million people, lived in towns and cities (Huddleston et al., 2003). Some of these cities are capitals, including Kathmandu, with more than 2 million inhabitants; Quito, with 1.5 million; and La Paz, the highest capital in the world at 3,640 m, with 1.6 million inhabitants (La Paz and Alto) in the city proper and 2.7 million in the metropolitan area (see Table 4.6). Mexico City at 2,240 m is a megacity with about 8.9 million in the city and 21 million in the metropolitan area, making it the fifth largest metropolitan area in the world.

In global comparison, the rate of urban development is highest in South America and the Caribbean, where 47 per cent of the total mountain population of 53 million live in towns. In the mountains of industrialized countries, 36 per cent of the mountain population, or 20 million people, live in urban areas. The rate is lowest in Asia and the Pacific, with 14 per cent, which represents 46 million people (Perlik and Kohler, 2015, based on Huddleston et al., 2003). We have to take these data as minimum values, as statistics are always based on official administrative demarcations and mostly do not include sub- and peri-urban areas. If we also add resort towns, which appear (for reasons of marketing) as 'villages', it becomes clear that the functional urban area is much underestimated.[20]

The Alps are the most densely populated mountain range in Europe and were settled quite early (even earlier than some low mountain ranges). But the development of cities in the Alps, as well as in the Global North in general, was different from that in the mountains of the Global South, as it took place mainly outside the mountains. The towns in the Alps did not gain high interregional significance (Bairoch, 1985). The argument of a reduced food basis, mentioned by Jon Mathieu (1998), does not alone explain this trajectory: The characteristics of any city (valid already for the early towns) are that its founders had the organizational and ideological power to take the agricultural surplus from more and more distant places and to appropriate it, if necessary, by military means. In contrast to the weak growth of towns, the southern parts of the Alps developed a pattern of municipalities with codified municipal constitutions (Bätzing, 1984), which can be interpreted as an early urban development. But these villages remained small. The 17 bishoprics in the French Southern Alps also remained small; not one reached at least half the size of Grenoble.[21] So, we have here an early urbanization, but the balances of power impeded a larger centralization.

(b) Urbanization and urban development of the Alpine arc

Urbanization means much more than the process of city-building; it refers to all spatial aspects in the framework of the transformation of rural communities into global markets, including commuting patterns or the transformation to tourist destinations and part-time residences. It describes a process of spatial sociation and can hardly be quantified. By contrast, urban development is a more restrictive term that defines a measurable increase in urban enlargement. In the mountain context, we can subdivide urban development into city centre areas, as well as suburban and peri-urban settlements and resort towns.[22] The following calculation was made in 1999 as a quantitative analysis for the Alpine arc, based on the method of analyzing census data at the finest resolution, which is the municipal level. The analysis included all municipalities of the Alps, as well as all peri-Alpine cities and their potential commuter municipalities, even if they were outside the Alpine perimeter. It was a calculation with data from about 8,000 municipalities in eight countries, which had to be harmonized as definitions and time periods were never completely congruent. The parameters used were reduced to commuter relations, inhabitants, and job numbers, similar to the French agglomeration demarcations. The aim was to show – at the time, against the mainstream view of the rural Alps – that the mountains had undergone a similar development to the lowlands. As the prevailing opinion defended the rural Alps, the calculations had to be done rather conservatively and cautiously, so as not to overestimate urban development. The results showed that by 1990, a majority of nearly 60 per cent of the Alpine population lived in towns or agglomerations (Perlik, 1999, 2001). However, much more important was the result that nearly 20 per cent of the Alpine urban population lived in peri-urban areas belonging to peri-Alpine metropolitan areas. The significance of this result lies in the de facto integration of large parts of the Alpine arc into lowland (peri-Alpine) metropolitan areas. It is the expression of changed economic and socio-demographic linkages, merged fragmented labour markets, and accelerated transport systems. This functional shift generates a fragmentation of the Alpine arc into segments according to the spheres of influence generated by about ten peri-Alpine metropolitan areas: Munich, Salzburg, Linz, Vienna, Graz, Ljubljana, Milan, Turin, Geneva, and Zurich. In the case of Munich, the metropolitan area encompasses the whole German part of the Alps. There is only one metropolitan area within the Alps – Grenoble – that, up until now, has eluded integration into the larger Lyon metropolitan area. However, there was never one common Alpine interest, as there were always different points of view between the seven countries: The segmentation of the Alps according to the ten metropolitan regions (which became clearly visible in the 2000s) shows the end of the idea of a common Alpine space.

The thesis that an increased urbanization is taking place in the Alps is therefore evident (see Table 4.5). To show which parts of the Alps are affected, I measured urbanized Alpine areas that are oriented towards the lowlands (i.e. the peri-Alpine metropolitan areas such as Munich, Milan, Zurich, etc.). In the 1990s, this was nearly 20 per cent of 14 million people. Again, these numbers are counted rather conservatively. The peri-Alpine metropolitan areas attract this population as commuters. Meanwhile, this phenomenon has increased as a result of the process of European de-industrialization, which has contributed

Table 4.5 Population and jobs in the European Alps.

Population and jobs within the Alpine area

	In FUAs	Out of FUAs
Population 1990/91	59%	41%
Jobs 1990/91★	66%	34%

★ Slovenia not included; for Germany: 1987.

Municipalities and areas within the Alpine area

	In FUAs	Out of FUAs
Municipalities 1990/91	36%	64%
Areas 1990/91	26%	74%

Source: National census data at municipality level (LAU2). First published in Perlik (2001).

Note: Urbanization is comprised of more than the delimitable functional urban areas (FUAs) and is not restricted to agglomerations and metropolitan regions. But even according to this indicator, the majority of the population in the European Alps in 1990 lived and worked under agglomerated conditions.

to an increase in commuters and, in particular, the distance commuted. The peri-urbanization process at the Alpine border has increased in the same way, by hosting new migrants that have moved from the cities and become daily commuters.

A quick quantitative check with 2010 airline data showed, unsurprisingly, that most of the airports that are served by the two major low-cost carriers at that time were located on the Alpine fringes (Perlik, 2010). It is this location that attracts a higher critical mass of passengers for city tourism in the peri-Alpine downtown areas, as well as to the leisure resorts in the mountains. We see that the margins of the Alps do not constitute a distinct border between different economic spaces. With the orientation of the Alpine fringes towards the peri-Alpine metropolitan areas, we can consider a segmentation of the Alpine arc that no longer runs (if it ever did) according to similar 'Alpine interests', but according to the social practices and economic interests of the particular metropolitan area nearby. It is therefore not astonishing that practitioners, as well as researchers from Munich, Zurich, and Grenoble, have quite a different interpretation of Alpine development. This is important in terms of the administrative configuration or reconfiguration of regions; it shows the arbitrariness of any demarcation.

(c) The pattern of urbanization in the mountains of the Global North

For mountain ranges in the densely populated Global North, we can identify the following spatial patterns, taking the example of the Alps:

The urban areas at the peri-Alpine fringes: This system of large agglomerations or metropolitan areas is the location of mountain-specific high-end services and their headquarters. It also holds national and international economic functions that are fairly independent of the neighbouring mountains. The strength of these economic functions depends on the international integration and position of the national state in the global economy. With global tertiarization, the changed professional profiles and qualifications required in these metropolitan regions makes them attractive for highly qualified people from abroad, because of their leisure offer. The metropolitan enlargement also creates jobs for medium-high qualifications from the Alpine fringe.

The Alpine fringes: The piedmonts of the Alps came into early contact with lowland economies and thus started an early transformation to peri-urbanization. These fringes are highly dynamic. A considerable part of the Alpine urban population lives here (20 per cent already in 1990), and it is in close interaction with the peri-Alpine agglomerations and metropolitan areas. The links concern daily commuting from the peri-urban to the downtown areas, and the inverse processes where enterprises relocate from the city centres to the peri-urban areas because they need a larger and more affordable space. Furthermore, residential relocation processes take place for the same reason (affordable housing).

The interstices: The areas located at medium altitude have the most disadvantages – and nearly no advantages – to their location. In the early days of industrialization, these parts of the Alps were important as they were ideal during the period of early industrialization for the use of hydropower for local production. Now they are more difficult to reach than in the past due to their steep and narrow relief, which is less accessible by modern transport systems. Furthermore, they do not benefit from sun or snow. So, they now have neither the old nor the new qualities. Hopes were in vain that the automobile, as the ideal means of mountain transport through mass motorization and capillary roads, would solve the problem of inequality. Interstitial areas such as the canton of Uri or the Leventina valley in Italian-speaking Switzerland have lost much of their population, reinforcing the disadvantages of bad accessibility, as having fewer customers means that public transport will reduce their services to the area. Most parts of municipalities with 'poor potential' (a Swiss notion) now lie at these altitudes.

The resort towns: These places for leisure and high-end dwellings near the summits are the early tourist locations. They have the resources to adapt to changing client preferences, and the necessary means for disinvestment and reinvestment in new business sectors or to attract foreign investment. In the last decades, we have seen a transformation from tourism to the real estate business and second homes. The case example is Davos in Grisons.

The transit corridors: Municipalities along the mountain passes were favoured in the beginnings of mountain-crossing traffic. But they have lost out to the acceleration of transport. Higher productivity in the logistics sector means for these places that they are outperformed by the most efficient transport means, first by non-stop trains, then by base tunnels.

This model is more or less similar in the countries of the European Alps. It reflects the character of the mountains as a barrier between the metropolitan areas of Central Europe (Munich, Zurich, etc.) and Southern Europe (Milan, Turin), which give way to a use of space that is differentiated and also disparate. In the rural–urban dichotomy, only the interstices may still be called rural, and only with precaution. The processes of urbanization and the resulting patterns are similar in other European mountains such as the Pyrenees (del Mármol and Vaccaro, 2015; Solé et al., 2014; Vaccaro and Beltràn, 2009). The demographic processes show a shift from integrally dispersed settlements to a concentrated population with a change in socio-economic functions. This is a development that seems to correspond to secular and ongoing processes of population concentration, as described by Denise Pumain (1999) or François Moriconi-Ebrard (1993).

(d) Aspects of urbanization in the mountains of the Global South

In the mountain ranges of the Global South, the rapid growth of large agglomerations and metropolitan areas is much stronger, as shown by the examples of Kathmandu and La Paz (Table 4.6). In these cities several functions are overlaid: They are national capitals; they are the gateway to the international economy; and they provide the possibility of jobs for poor people seeking better living conditions, for example in the rise of mountain tourism as a new emerging economic sector. In the 1980s, the approach to Kathmandu Airport was considered

Table 4.6 Kathmandu and La Paz, two national capital cities in the high mountains.

Kathmandu, city [inhabitants in thousands]

	1971	1981	1991	2001	2011
	150	235	421	672	975

Kathmandu, metropolitan area [inhabitants in thousands]

	1991	2011
	915	1,500

La Paz, city [inhabitants in thousands]

1950	1976	1992	2001	2012
321	655	713	790	757

(*Continued*)

Table 4.6 (Continued)

La Paz, metropolitan area [inhabitants in thousands]

	1992	*2001*	*2010*
	2,050	2,350	2,840

Source: Kathmandu census data, General Bureau of Statistics, Kathmandu 2012. La Paz, city: INE census data (Instituto Nacional de Estadística Bolivia); metropolitan area (Departamento de La Paz): Hoffmann and Requena (2012), based on INE data.

Note: National capitals situated in mountain areas are rare; Kathmandu/Nepal and La Paz/Bolivia are the most important ones. The table shows their tremendous growth rates in the last decades. This development is not mountain-specific, as the tendency for extraordinary growth of a single national hub is common to many countries of the Global South. However, it marks a specific historic trajectory of people living in mountains to stay, and not to out-migrate to the lowlands. The tendency towards a concentration of resources to one national hub in the Global South is a result of poverty and is increased by global policies that favour agglomeration economies.

risky, and pilots were required to have special supplementary certification to be permitted to land there. Since then, air traffic to and from Kathmandu became transformed into a regular shuttle service. After the crash of an airplane some weeks before the great earthquake of April 2015, the runway was blocked, causing the cancellation of the 40 daily flights to and from Kathmandu, affecting about 5,000 tourists per day.

4.6   The Fordist period: a short honeymoon for the mountains

(a)   *The Swiss trajectory to Fordism and beyond*

The Swiss example represents a regime where social cohesion was experienced for a long time by balancing a strong regional heterogeneity within the national territory. The Swiss territory is comprised of cantons with topographic and socio-economic divergences: mountains versus lowland, cities versus countryside, four national languages and – still important in the 20th century – Catholic and Protestant sub-territories. These differences are also apparent within the cantons. Switzerland was perceived for a long time as an agricultural state which shared the myth of a common 'Alpine culture' of Swiss people. Nevertheless, Switzerland was, until the 1970s, one of the most densely industrialized countries in Europe.

The industrialization of Europe was based on the availability of liquid capital, accumulated in various ways, mostly through colonial trade. This process also involved the population of the mountain regions: In the 18th century, a proto-industry of cotton manufacturing developed in the Swiss canton of Glarus, based on the principle of primitive accumulation by family clans that made their fortune through the trade in mercenaries. In the lowlands, in Basel, the silk industry stood at the origins of industrialization; it was replaced by its suppliers, the up-and-coming chemical industry, which settled due to local salt deposits and by taking advantage of a border situation with different national regulations. And in Zurich, an industrial boom was induced by a constellation of political power and powerful entrepreneurs, who created new influential finance and research institutions.

By founding a nation state in 1948, the Swiss Confederation followed a policy of intensive interlocking and balancing of very heterogeneous regions in order to avoid polarization that could jeopardize territorial cohesion. At the same time, the agricultural-era heritage meant that daily social relations were characterized by an economically liberal entrepreneurial current. This meant, among others, that the syndicalist and political labour movement never reached the strength that it did in neighbouring countries. Entrepreneurial thinking is also the force behind the high degree of municipal autonomy (*Gemeindeautonomie*), which, in the crisis years of the 1920s, led to the municipalities being overstretched. This led to considerable impoverishment in rural areas, as the municipalities were no longer able to support poor families.

This constellation of values led to two characteristics: firstly, the question of territorial balance was always more important than thinking in terms of class antagonism. Secondly, Switzerland was 'neutral' during the Second World War; thus, it had no war damage and no ensuing 'economic miracle' by a Schumpeterian 'creative destruction'. But as a small country, Switzerland was home to important transnational companies and holding companies at an early stage. Both a protected internal market and early globalized companies enabled a Fordist social and territorial compromise, as in other European countries. With some delay, the economic returns also arrived in the mountain regions as classical trickle-down effects.

Already in the interwar period, mountain communities benefited from investments in large dams at high Alpine altitudes. Since the municipalities and even the mountain cantons could not finance these investments alone, private public consortia of the lowlands did so. They created the hydropower as a new economic sector which soon became an in-demand export product. The enormous investments in mountain infrastructure created a new, in part mythically exaggerated, solidarity between cities and rural areas and between lowlands and highlands.

This development path can serve as an explanation for the fact that the Swiss mountain regions were involved in the economic upswing in the 1960s and experienced a strong catch-up process, which however only became apparent in the 1970s. Meanwhile, federal policy had begun to elaborate legislation intended to favour the disadvantaged mountain regions and other regions affected by de-industrialization shocks (the crisis of the watch industry of the 1970s). In this framework, from 1974 to 2007, several programmes[23] provided large subsidies in the peripheral areas of the Alps and the Jura. The Investment Aid Act (28 June 1974, effective since 1 January 1975) saw the creation of 54 regions. Between 1975 and 2007, these regions received about 2,280 million Swiss francs in the form of loans with reduced interest, fuelling 8,500 projects worth about 19,300 million Swiss francs (Schuler et al., 2005).

(b) The two trend reversals in Swiss spatial development

The law on regional policy, decisions, and subsidies cannot alone explain the relative prosperous development that Swiss mountain areas saw in the 1970s, as these measures came too late to turn the spatial development. This development was characterized by a lagging behind of the rural and mountain areas in the key Fordist years of the 1950s and 1960s. But in 1974, the demographic development changed. Up until then, the urban agglomerations had gained population disproportionally. Since 1974, it was the population of the rural areas that showed a disproportional growth, while cities and agglomeration were below the Swiss average (Figures 4.11 and 4.12).[24]

Analysis of municipal level (European nomenclature: LAU2) data shows a disproportional population growth of all municipalities that are not part of an agglomeration: those municipalities that are generally called 'rural'. This astonishing disproportional growth continued until 1998, and only then turned in favour of the urban areas. The growth rate of employment corresponded to the rate of population growth (Schuler et al., 2004).

How should we interpret these two trend reversals? We mentioned already that during periods of growth, urban areas are the winners, while in declining periods rural areas had relative advantages. Looking at these years, we see that the Fordist crisis first announced itself in 1967 with a light depression; the oil crisis of 1973 made clear that the post-war growth period was ending. It was not a period of growth for the cities. Nevertheless, the intermittent recessions between 1974 and 1998 were too short to explain the long period of disproportional growth in the non-agglomeration areas. In other words, as the prosperous periods prevail over economic recessions, we would expect a more or less continuous decline of the non-agglomeration areas. This did not happen. In contrast, this period of more than 20 years saw an increase in public sympathy and support for mountain issues in Swiss society, despite a generally dynamic economy (which usually favours urban growth). We interpreted from this that there must be a second influence beyond the oscillations of the economic conjuncture, which we explained with the crisis of Fordism and the change in regime. We interpreted the relative growth of the so-called rural areas between 1974 and 1998 as the spatial expression of the Fordist regime of accumulation and regulation that dominated the 1950s and 1960s. But this spatial expression occurred only after Fordism had had its heyday. The equalizing development favouring rural areas took place at a time when the socio-economic driving forces had already changed to another paradigm of spatial development. The limits to growth start to become apparent in 1972 and the turning point comes in 1973, with the oil crisis marking the change in paradigm. This change only

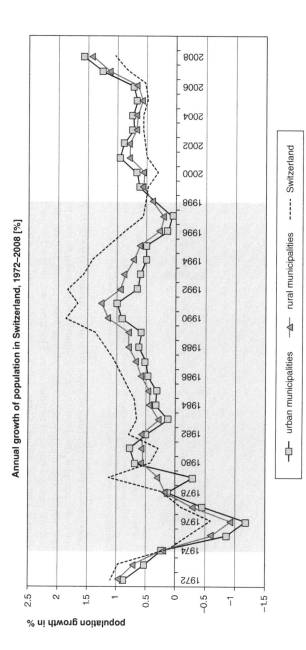

Figure 4.11 The two trend reversals of demographic growth in Switzerland. Since the end of the 1990s, an inverse process occurred, reinstalling the old territorial hierarchies. We have called this change the 'two trend reversals' (Schuler et al., 2004). The duration of this disproportional period of the rural areas is all the more surprising in that it does not follow the fluctuations in economic cycles. Therefore, we interpret the two trend reversals with overlaying larger mechanisms that are stronger than short-term market cycles: the prevailing social paradigm of Fordism that fuelled the decentral growth until the 1970s, and the post-Fordist change of the 1980s that introduced the renaissance of the concentration of power in the cities. The interesting aspect of the two trend reversals is that in both cases, the spatial expression of the social processes occurred with a considerable time lag as the peak of rural growth became visible when the Fordist period was already over. The second turn in the late 1990s towards a disproportional growth of the metropolitan areas also occurred late when the liberal–productivist regimes were already fully established. This disproportional metropolitan growth persists (Schuler and Perlik, 2011). In physics, these phenomena are called hysteresis.

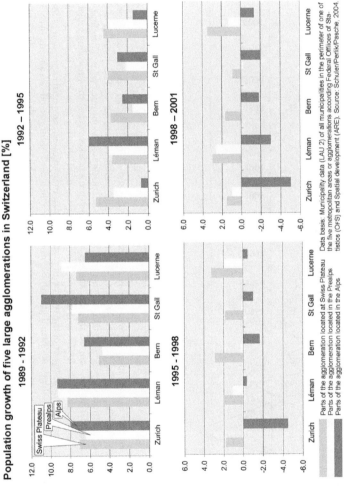

Figure 4.12 Demographic developments of five hinterlands of urban areas in Switzerland, 1989–2001. As part of our work on rural areas (Schuler et al., 2004), we analysed the demographic development of the hinterlands according to their geographical position (left column: Swiss Plateau, Schweizer Mittelland; middle column: pre-Alps; right column: Alpine parts). During the 1980s, the population of mountain areas (right column) rises high above average compared to other areas. This trend was reversed in the 1990s. In the context of metropolization, we can interpret these findings as a relative decline of areas with less accessibility and lost attractiveness in favour of urban and peri-urban areas. We interpret this as a paradigmatic change where the Alps lose their function as the centre of everyday life but remain attractive for leisure and part-time residence, which is not shown in demographic statistics.

became visible in society in the 1980s, and its spatial repercussions even later, at the end of the 1990s. The two trend reversals of 1974/1998 mark turning points in spatial terms. Socio-economically, the social convergence process culminated in the 1960s; spatially, this process (in Switzerland) took place in the 1970s and 1980s. Socio-economically, the post-Fordist turn began in the mid-1970s; spatially, it became visible only in the late 1990s. The spatial effects are thus 20 years behind – a phenomenon called 'hysteresis' in physics. We can compare these mechanisms with the functioning of a cardiac pacemaker, which triggers an impulse to which the response is never immediate: there is always a slight delay. The delay in this case is more than 20 years. This result is important, as it gives an idea of impression of the time periods that are necessary to implement new ideas, new paradigms, and social innovations in terms of their effects on territorial cleavages, disparities, and social and spatial justice. It shows that there are changes in paradigm. They are possible, but they take a long time. That again means that if we want to change anything, we have to start now if we want to have results 20 years or more later.

The process of disproportional growth of the peripheries lasted until the end of the 1990s and was linked with processes of peri-urbanization and a decentralization of public and commercial services. The Alps developed like the lowlands; they became functionally urbanized, despite maintaining a rural facade.

We remember the repartition and concentration of jobs in the Alps: In 1990, 66 per cent were located in towns and agglomerations, and the number of commuter municipalities has continued to increase (Table 4.5). The examples are intended to show that there was – for a limited period – a spatial development that did not follow the rules of an everlasting concentration process, but was in favour of promoting regions that lagged behind and developing them according to common national standards. This development mitigated existing large-scale disparities that were caused by gradients of productivity between lowland economies and mountain economies.

This tendency was driven by the political will under the prevailing Fordist paradigm (economic growth and redistribution by mass consumption for all), but always on the basis of an existing North–South gradient.[25] For the mountains, it had its repercussions in a massive investment in infrastructure. And at the same time, the mountain regions had the support of the alternative and left movement which saw in the preservation and development of the mountain areas a counter-model to the societal mainstream and growth paradigm (see the ethnographic work of Markus Schütz [2010]).

4.7 From tourism to metropolitan neighbourhoods

(a) Stagnating tourism

The majority of early resort towns in the Alps developed historically from mountain villages to tourist centres, such as the well-known resorts of Zermatt,

St Moritz, and Davos in Switzerland; St Anton in Austria; or Chamonix in France. Only the new French resorts of the 1960s were planned according to the central interests of a national central planning system and according to the placement strategies of Parisian investors. It was the first example of an industrial development of tourism. In Italy, the resort town of Sestriere was established on the initiative of the Agnelli family, the founders of the Fiat automobile company. While the Swiss, Austrian, Italian South Tyrol, and German regions generated a family-based model of accommodation in hotels, guesthouses, or on farms, the French and Italian models were based on real estate rentals and sales. In the first group of countries, local families mastered the transformation from agricultural to tourist services and kept the power over the local development in their own hands, with all consequent positive and negative implications.

Since the 1990s, tourism has stagnated in the Alps. National statistics show that while overnight stays in Alpine and rural regions are not increasing, urban destinations and business travel are increasing disproportionally (Table 4.7). Between 1992 and 2015, the number of hotels in the Swiss canton of Grisons fell from 920 to 780.[26] Furthermore it is a long-running general trend that the length of stays is declining. The profile of the clientele is changing. European tourists prefer destinations that are more exotic or cheaper; some cannot afford to go on holiday, and others practise other leisure activities. In France, this transformation and hybridization is discussed as 'post-tourism' (Bourdeau, 2009). Furthermore, tourism in general cannot generate high rates of profit as its product is sold to private consumers with a limited budget, and the conditions of production in a mountain context do not allow producers to benefit from economies of scale. The Alps are not alone in this development: A similar example of stagnating tourism is described in the Pyrenees (Vlès, 2012).

Tourist offices and associations are opening new market segments and attract tourists of the emerging countries from Eastern Europe, the Middle East, and East Asia. This target group appreciates Alpine tourism for its good reputation. But they do not seek the traditional offers that would call for a longer preparation or stay; instead, often the purpose of these trips is to shop for luxury goods. To this end, they might stay in only one place (e.g. a fairly large city with beautiful mountain scenery, such as Lucerne), and only for one night.

Those who go to higher altitudes stay in resort towns. Only there can they find an adequate offer and salespeople with the knowledge that is necessary for an ambitious international clientele. This means understanding, curiosity, and a liking for foreign cultures, and also advanced competencies in the language (e.g. already in 1990, the retail shops in Interlaken employed Japanese staff for their counter services to communicate with Japanese clients, and they made public signposts in Japanese).

Nevertheless, tourist destinations try to intensify summer tourism as it is said that only those destinations with offers for both summer and winter

Table 4.7 Overnight stays in the Swiss hotel sector in Swiss tourist regions

	1993	1995	1997	1999	2001	2003	2005	2007	2009	2011	2013	2014
Grisons	6,913	6,341	5,869	6,009	6,301	5,835	5,570	5,868	5,885	5,366	5,161	5,052
East Switzerland	2,118	1,881	1,809	1,839	1,945	1,803	1,875	1,989	1,973	1,972	1,933	1,979
Zurich region	3,738	3,629	3,738	4,055	4,400	3,892	4,208	4,879	4,717	5,234	5,478	5,607
Central Switzerland	3,239	2,999	3,050	3,163	3,169	2,788	2,961	3,448	3,271	3,371	3,414	3,533
Basel region	985	919	919	952	966	975	1,043	1,275	1,382	1,452	1,488	1,566
Bern region	1,153	1,138	1,121	1,186	1,216	1,128	1,282	1,423	1,399	1,434	1,484	1,479
Bernese Oberland	3,729	3,494	3,340	3,444	3,576	3,404	3,566	3,776	3,719	3,643	3,649	3,684
Jura	664	622	652	653	729	685	629	728	700	732	764	768
Lake Geneva region	2,556	2,472	2,357	2,430	2,503	2,386	2,340	2,535	2,490	2,564	2,603	2,656
Geneva	2,111	2,120	2,048	2,185	2,313	2,223	2,380	2,878	2,661	2,838	2,883	2,939
Valais	4,294	3,994	3,858	3,967	4,285	4,168	4,202	4,425	4,392	4,078	3,888	3,887
Ticino	2,948	2,711	2,918	3,002	2,963	2,518	2,539	2,756	2,608	2,372	2,405	2,313
Fribourg region	313	298	300	313	314	283	349	386	393	431	473	470
Switzerland	**34,760**	**32,617**	**31,980**	**33,197**	**34,678**	**32,086**	**32,944**	**36,365**	**35,589**	**35,486**	**35,624**	**35,934**

Source: BfS, n.d. The lines marked in grey indicate the Swiss metropolitan regions.

will survive. The winter season is under particular pressure, as climate change means that snow, needed for winter sport, is becoming increasingly scarce. Even artificial snow cannot change the current reality that destinations below 1,300 m altitude have to find a new position in – or give up on – tourism.

In this precarious situation, hotel owners have tried in recent years to regain competitiveness by means of political lobbying, on the one hand, and enlarging their capacity by building and renting out holiday homes, on the other. Additionally, to have the financial means for renovating their old stock, they invested in the construction of leisure residences to put them up for sale. Today, the important resort towns have a hybrid structure, consisting of tourist beds and residences, with a growing shift towards the latter.

(b) Peri-urban expansion

The growth of metropolitan areas provoked an urban sprawl towards the mountain fringes. Increased social and technical mobility allows people to live near the mountain slopes or at the bottom of the glacially deepened main valleys, while still working in the peri-Alpine city, which already has the advantages of the lowlands (i.e. hourly long-distance trains and an airport). A good example is Munich, which attracts for work highly qualified people who like spending their leisure time in the Alps. This sub- and peri-urban sprawl took hold of the foothills to the south of Munich very early. The people of Munich speak of 'Munich and our Alps'. The Lake Geneva region has similar amenities. Due to excellent air connections, Geneva is also an attractive hub for British people who work in the City of London and live with their families in Chamonix or Verbier (Geoffroy, 2007).[27] These constellations show that it has become even more difficult to distinguish between 'peri-urban' and 'resort towns': Chamonix at the foot of Mont Blanc has been a traditional tourist resort since the first days of alpinism. Bern, the Swiss capital, was early to extend its agglomeration municipalities in the direction of the Aare valley at the Alpine fringe. The completion of the Lötschberg base tunnel in 2007 (a strategic axis through the Alps, linking North and South Europe) made the inner Alpine Rhône valley (the canton of Valais with its small agglomeration Brig-Visp) accessible as a one-hour commute. Since 2000, the number of out-commuters from the Valais to the outer Alpine parts of the canton of Bern has tripled, reaching 1,500 people per day (in 2015). Commuting through the base tunnel (beneath the main watershed Rhine/Rhône) allows people to work in Bern and live in or around Visp or Brig, and this has been done since the opening of the tunnel. This inner Alpine valley can now be defined as part of the peri-urban perimeter of Bern. So, we have different processes that run in parallel. Since the end of the 1990s, the city has once again become attractive for dwelling. Prices are rising. People can afford to move to the suburban and near peri-urban fringes. The peri-urban perimeter is expanding. Those who can afford to live in the densely populated city can often afford (or have access to) second homes: in the mountains, at the coast, or in another city.

Between 1970 and 2010, floor space per occupant in Switzerland, according to the Federal Office for Spatial Development (ARE), increased from 27 m^2 to 47 m^2 per capita. The result is almost the same for city centres as for suburban communities because of the high number of one-person households in the city centres.[28] The eight small maps (Plate 5) show the development of urban sprawl in Switzerland. All eight maps show the proportion of the Swiss resident population living in multistorey buildings in 2000. Each map represents a different construction period. The darker red the dot, the higher the share of the population living in multistorey buildings (three floors or more) of that particular period. The dot sizes show the total number of people living in buildings of that period. The combination of the structure of the buildings (apartment blocks or detached houses), their position (inner-city, sub-, or peri-urban), and the total population allows us to interpret the spatial processes during one century where national census data were available at a municipal level. Here, peri-urbanization and metropolization are the processes that are the most interesting. The maps from 1981–1990 and 1991–2000 show that the buildings built in these periods are mostly individual houses (green = low degree of multistorey dwellings) and located in the peri-urban zones (the red dots in the inner cities are much smaller than in the periods before). This new approach to measure peri-urbanization clearly shows the enlargement of housing into the broad mountain valleys and beyond, a process that has become contested under the label of urban sprawl but has not yet halted. The enlargement of peri-urbanization also means that urban sprawl caused by peri-urbanization and urban sprawl caused by second homes are coalescing, as the maps in Plates 7a and 7b show.

At a larger level, we can detect similar processes of peri-urbanization in North America. The American mountain states (Arizona, Colorado, Washington, and Utah) have had a disproportional growth in recent decades. Since 2008, the 160 km between Albuquerque in the plain (nearly 600,000 inhabitants) and Santa Fe (at 2,200 m altitude) is linked by commuter train. As real estate prices in Santa Fe have risen tremendously (Glorioso and Moss, 2006), inverse commuting – from the metropolis to the mountain area – has become common. In their case study, Ray Rasker et al. (2009) show the linkages between residence cities and metropolitan areas in the American West by daily flight connections. Plate 6 shows that many counties have daily flight connections to the metropolitan areas on the West Coast, which constitutes a peri-urban constellation at an even larger scale.

(c) From tourism to residences

Recent development in the Alps sees tourism in crisis, and there is development similar to sectors such as the brewing industry: the big ones and the very small ones are surviving, and the medium-sized ones have to give up. Small-scale guesthouses, cooperatives, or agritourism have chances as niche players, and present ideas of near-natural uses and activities. The large ones may gain economies of scale by mergers or franchising and have the support of their banks. The medium-sized hotels tried to survive through hybridization, offering leisure homes for rent or trying to subsidize their hotels with money they raised through construction, rental, or sale of second homes for seasonal use by a multilocal clientele. But often these rescue efforts fail, and often after having had severe impacts on the landscape scenery (e.g. in the case of the Kulm Hotel at the Maloja pass/Upper Engadine). In most cases, then, hotels become transformed into condominiums. Table 4.8 shows the municipalities in the Italian Alps with the highest numbers of second homes. Plate 8 shows its distribution over the whole Alpine arc. The Alps are a role model for a development that meanwhile has also been described for other mountain ranges such as the Pyrenees (Clarimont and Vlès, 2009).

The new installations to host people for leisure and (multilocal) dwelling are mainly large building complexes with a hybrid concept consisting of condominiums, hotels, restaurants, and infrastructure for leisure (like golf driving ranges or spas). Examples are well known from North America, such as Canmore (Buxton, 2009; Nepal and Jamal, 2011). In Switzerland, the Andermatt Swiss Alps resort is currently under construction, initiated and financed by an Egyptian investor who made his money in the telecommunications sector. The project comprises construction of six luxury hotels, a golf course on former agricultural land, 490 apartments in 42 buildings, 25 villas on a former military area, and 15 new ski lifts. The existing winter sports infrastructure is being renewed and linked with the neighbouring ski region. Overall, 1–2 billion dollars are being invested in the construction of this resort for at least a decade. The local population was sceptical at first, but ended up being convinced by the personal engagement of the investor. In a vote on the project, 96 per cent were in favour. Directly after the decision, the real estate market of the municipality was 'dead'. People held on to their land in the hope of high rents later on, in the development of an internationally renowned resort.

The examples show that the tourist sector, as many other 'mature' sectors, depends on clear profiles of economies of scale or scope in the high-end or niche segment. This is becoming increasingly impossible to achieve at the local level. The tourist sector is transforming through disinvestment and reinvestment into a real estate business and attracting a different type of clientele. This clientele buys condominiums and houses and they are

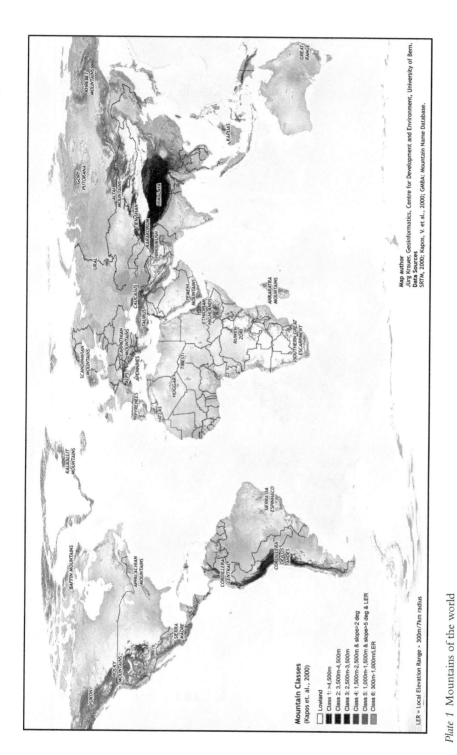

Mountain Classes
(Kapos et. al., 2000)

- Lowland
- Class 1: >4,500m
- Class 2: 3,500m–4,500m
- Class 3: 2,500m–3,500m
- Class 4: 1,500m–2,500m & slope>2 deg
- Class 5: 1,000m–1,500m & slope>5 deg & LER
- Class 6: 300m–1,000m/LER

LER = Local Elevation Range > 300m/7km radius

Map author
Jürg Krauer, Geoinformatics, Centre for Development and Environment, University of Bern.
Data Sources
SRTM, 2000; GMBA: Mountain Name Database.

Plate 1 Mountains of the world

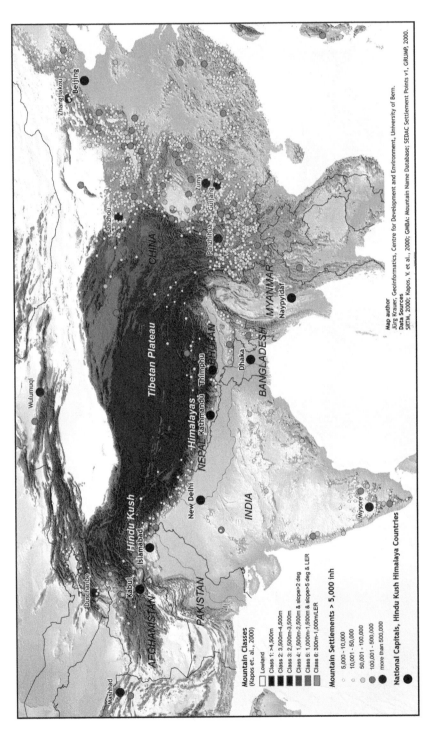

Plate 2 Urbanization in the Hindu Kush Himalayan region (HKH)

Mountain Classes
(Kapos et. al., 2000)

☐ Lowland
■ Class 1: >4,500m
■ Class 2: 3,500m–4,500m
■ Class 3: 2,500m–3,500m
■ Class 4: 1,500m–2,500m & slope>2 deg
■ Class 5: 1,000m–1,500m & slope>5 deg & LER
■ Class 6: 300m–1,000m/LER

Population in cities, 2000
(without Metropolitan Areas)

· 100,000 – 500,000
○ 500,001 – 1,000,000
◉ 1,000,001 – 5,000,000
● more than 5,000,000

Bogota
● Cities in mountain areas > 5,000,000

LER = Local Elevation Range > 300m/7km radius

Bogota

Map author
Jürg Krauer, Geoinformatics, Centre for Development and Environment, University of Bern.
Data Sources
SRTM, 2000; Kapos, V. et al., 2000; GMBA: Mountain Name Database; SEDAC Settlement Points v1, GRUMP, 2000.

Plate 3 The most important urban agglomerations in worldwide mountains

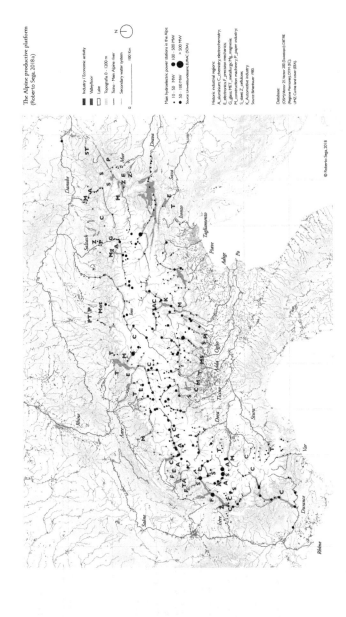

The Alpine productive platform
(Roberto Sega, 2018a)

Industry / Economic activity
Valleyfloor
Lake
Topografia 0 - 1200 m
Ticino - Main Alpine river
Secondary water system

0   100 Km

N

Main hydroelectric power stations in the Alps

• 10 - 50 MW
● 50 - 100 MW
● 100 - 500 MW
⬤ > 500 MW

Source: Umweltbundesamt, EURAC (ÖOA)

Historic industrial regions:
A_aluminium; C_chemistry-electrochemistry;
E_electronics; F_precision mechanics;
G_glass MET_metallurgy; Mg_magnesia;
M_construction machinery; P_paper industry;
S_steel; Z_cellulose;
K_Automotive-fiat industry.
Source: Bätzenhauer 1980.

Database:
OSM/Meteor 25 Vector 200 (Swisstopo) DIBTRE
(Regione Piemonte) DTM 75 (IC)
UHIC Corine land cover (EEA)

© Roberto Sega, 2018

Plate 4 The Alpine productive platform. Roberto Sega's map from his thesis (2018a) shows the hydropower installations in the headwaters of the alpine rivers. They enabled the industrialization in the Alps and their foothills and served to supply the urban agglomerations of the adjacent plains. In the meantime, large parts of the historic heavy industry sites of 1980 have been transformed, and even the small industrial districts at the foothills of the Eastern Alps, which since the 1970s have become famous as the "Third Italy", have partly disappeared. But we will still see the recent concentration of agglomerations at the adjacent plains (Italian Po plain in the south, Swiss Plateau in the north), whose population benefits from the Alpine resources. Although an enormous boost from renewable energies is currently hampering the economic performance of hydropower, the dams are very important for consumption peaks in the European interconnected energy supply network. Hydropower is not a renewable energy as the water lacks there where it has been taken away by canals and tubes. Therefore it is not an example for a "greening economy". However it mitigates the disparities between productive and consumptive areas.

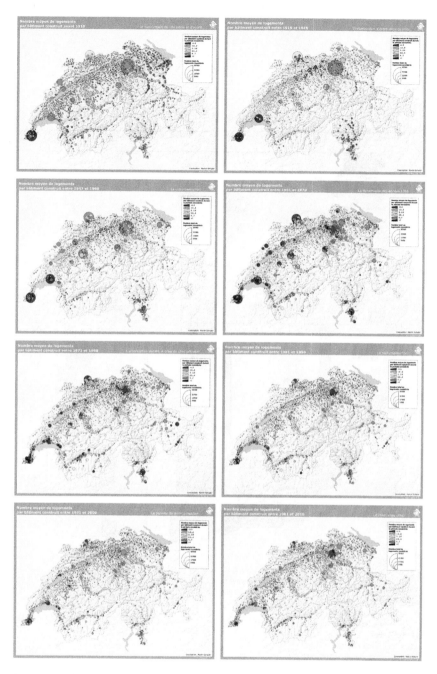

Plate 5 Spatial pattern of multiple dwelling units in Switzerland in long-term analysis (1900–2010). Each of the eight small maps shows the number of buildings new built within the indicated decade (discerned by the size of the dots). The different colours designate the average number of apartments in these buildings. We can see that each decade of construction had different impacts on spatial development, especially the peri-urban sprawl since the 1980s, where a lot of detached houses were built in formerly rural areas. The renaissance of the cities with its inner densification does not reduce the residences in the peripheries but may increase the consumption of space through an alternating multilocal use during different time of year.

Conception: M. Schuler; cartography: MicroGis Lausanne; source: Schuler et al., 2012, modified.

Three Wests

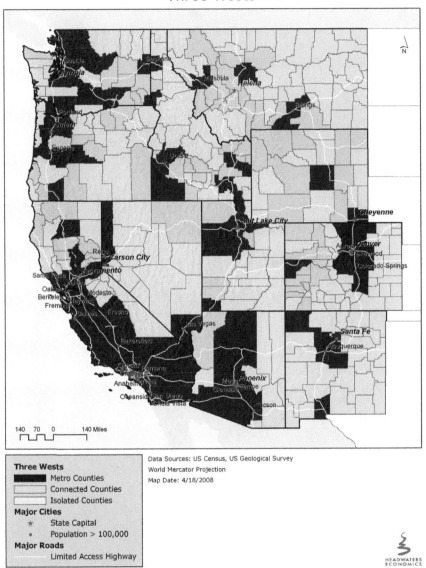

Plate 6 American peri–urbanization processes. The yellow areas indicate those counties that have regular daily flight connections to the metropolitan counties.

Source: Rasker et al., 2009.

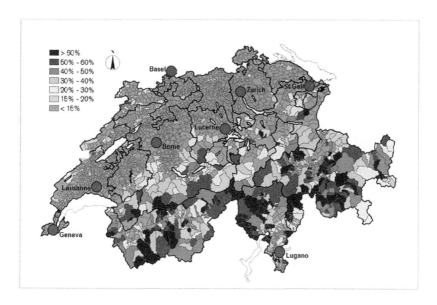

Plate 7a Shares of second homes in Swiss municipalities.

Sources: Credit Suisse Economic Research, BfS, Geostat; Schuler and Dessemontet, 2013.

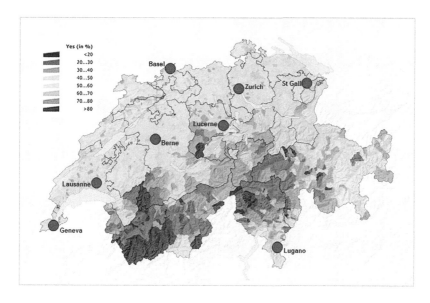

Plate 7b Approval of the initiative against second homes in Swiss municipalities. Providing second homes is one of the important business models in the mountain regions of developed countries. In both maps, the red areas are almost congruent with the Swiss mountain areas. The upper map shows all municipalities with a share of more than 20% of second homes compared to the total stock. The lower map shows the results of the 2012 vote in favour of a restriction on the construction of second homes in the interest of landscape protection. Here, too, the data are almost congruent: There is a widening gap between both regional types: an urban lowland majority is calling for greater environmental sensitivity while the mountain population feels overwhelmed and restricted in their freedom of action.

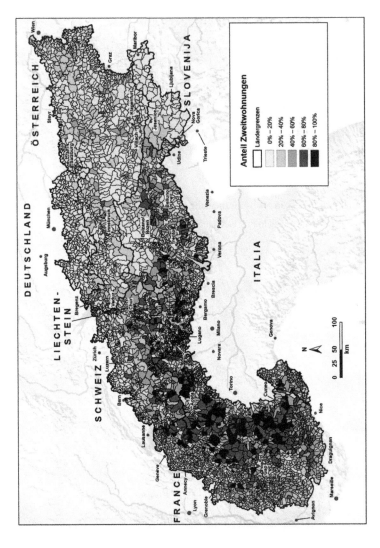

Plate 8 Distribution of second homes all over the Alpine arc. We see a gap between France and Italy on the one hand and the other countries on the other. This can be explained with a different historic trajectory of the tourist sector, a stronger position of the agricultural sector in the German speaking countries and different national regulations for these two sectors.

Source: Sonderegger, 2014.

Table 4.8 The 15 municipalities in the Italian Alps with the highest number of second homes in 2001

Municipality and provinces		Altitude [m NN]	Inhabitants 31.12.2006	Second homes 1981	Second homes 2001	Increase [%] 1981–2001	Number of beds [estimated] 2001	Hotel beds 2005	Rented houses [%] 1981
Bardonecchia	TO	1,312	3,063	5,785	7,404	28.0	34,498	1,777	11.3
Frabosa Sottana	CN	641	1,494	5,318	6,444	21.2	24,811	573	23.3
Aprica*	SO	1,172	1,733	3,735	6,189	65.7	28,129	1,244	44.2
Castione della Presolana	BG	870	3,413	4,802	6,057	26.1	31,593	744	36.9
Limone Piemonte	CN	1,009	1,575	5,583	5,956	6.7	22,809	700	13.3
Roana	VI	1,001	4,082	3,919	5,537	41.3	30,465	765	21.2
Pinzolo	TN	770	3,048	3,768	5,273	39.9	25,951	5,649	16.1
Sauze d'Oulx	TO	1,509	1,161	4,822	5,264	9.2	21,227	2,131	12.9
Valtournenche	AO	1,528	2,211	4,072	4,957	21.7	19,481	3,326	6.3
Ponte di Legno	BS	1,257	1,793	2,368	4,242	79.1	22,038	1,548	17.1
Gallio	VI	1,090	2,424	2,356	4,077	73.0	21,800	187	25.1
Sestriere	TO	2,035	907	3,390	3,880	14.5	14,549	2,635	14.7
Asiago	VI	1,001	6,550	2,347	3,854	64.2	22,561	1,838	25.9
Cortina d'Ampezzo	BL	1,211	6,150	3,331	3,680	10.5	23,918	4,391	9.0
Courmayeur	AO	1,224	2,969	2,948	3,520	19.4	20,651	2,833	18.4

*Data relating to the tourist conurbation of Aprica–San Pietro Aprica (Municipalities of Aprica, province of Sondrio, and Corteno Golgi, province of Brescia; 1621 inhabitants in the municipality of Aprica alone).

Source: Bartaletti, 2008.

not tourists (neither by economic definition nor in their self-perception). They have become part-time inhabitants who live in more than one location; they can be described as multilocal. In contrary to the hotel owners who often rent out second homes, multilocal owners do not rent out their property, which is often larger than their first flat in town. It is used multi-functionally to invite friends and members of their enlarged family, as well as for teleworking.

In Switzerland, this evolution predominantly affects the mountain cantons. In general, in Europe, where there are no strong gradients between agglomerations and their hinterlands in terms of security and physical health, one can assume that a reason for owning a second home lies in the 'otherness' – the possibility of having different experiences from everyday life. These expectations can be linked with key words such as high altitude, spectacular views, pleasant climate, leisure activities, calmness, rural milieu, authentic culture, wilderness, and better quality of life. Independently of the objective situation (the quality of life is not bad in European cities), there are advantages to alternating between locations, as one is able to benefit from both worlds, although the transaction costs are much higher, also compared to commuting (Weichhart, 2015). We can therefore assume that second homes and multilocality have become part of the symbolic capital of middle-class families, which belongs to their habitus and distinction. In an uncertain financial environment, the placement aspect is important, too. I thus named this form of living *Wohlstandsmigration* in 2007. Norman McIntyre (2009) used the notion of 'lifestyle migration'.

The phenomenon of multilocality is not restricted to the mountains. It also affects other types of landscapes such as coastal areas or the centres of renowned cities, such as Paris, London, or Zurich. It is estimated that 16 per cent of Paris apartments are occupied by multilocals (Chevalier et al., 2013), but this is difficult to measure. And it is not noticeable or visible, due to the size of such cities. In contrary, the impact of second homes is accentuated in regions with considerable depopulation.

In a large empirical analysis, Laurent Davezies and Magali Talandier (2014) outlined the relationship between the most important French agglomerations and the coastal and mountain regions. The former are defined as the productive systems; the latter as the residential systems. The analysis allowed them to discern which types of agglomeration are connected with which type of mountain or coastal region; which have relationships to nearby residential places; and which have relationships to residences far away. For example, they showed that the people of the Lille metropolitan area have close connections to the Alps, while people of the Nantes metropolitan area have secondary residences nearby at the coast. Based on these findings, Davezies and Talandier calculate the two types of economies together – productive (export-based) and residential – as productive-residential complexes, where they differentiate four main types and seven mixed types of territories according their characteristics of value adding (see Figure 4.13). This conclusion is quite interesting as it suggests a solidarity over the whole territory between the northern and southern parts of France, where the functional division of labour between production and consumption (reproduction) is not seen as a source of social cleavage but serves as an argument for compensation and sharing welfare benefits. But this interpretation runs counter to the larger tendencies where metropolitan regions act more and more autonomously and the political will for etatist subsidies wanes. Interpreting as a common unit the spatially divided productive and residential functions (separated over long distances) would only be justified if there is a common development goal between the regions, instead of competition. France as a large territorial state is therefore a special case in Europe, stuck together by national regulations. In view of the manifold cross-border relationships, the productive-residential system would – even in France – have to be thought of at a transnational or European level, a thinking which goes against the current trend in Europe. When the different territorial functions (the productive and the residential) fail to see their mutual interests and no longer cooperate, the social cleavage and the asymmetric relations will deepen. As will be discussed later, this is the direction the post-Fordist regulations took.

Returning to the spatial development in the Alps, we can say that tourism altered the trajectory of the ancient and already well-differentiated system of the agrarian society with artisanal products, local exchange, and some limited export-based activities. It replaced the old system by occupying ground and diminishing the status of peasant activities, but not completely. The old activities were well embedded and maintained a certain strength (which gave tourism unique features, for example by providing local food). Now tourism is losing significance, as it goes through a development similar to that of other 'mature sectors'. Tourism meanwhile has an over 150-year-long tradition in the Alps, but it did not become as stable as the ancient agricultural system had been. Now that tourism has become an activity specific to the Alps, it is increasingly being displaced by residences for multilocals. It will be interesting to track these developments, to see where and whether they can persist, and whether the new landscape amenities for dwelling will constitute strong value chains in the long run, or whether they are only a short-term phenomenon.

(d) Residential economies

With the relative and absolute loss of tourism in favour of residential living, the character of the local or regional economy changes. Why does it make a difference whether it is tourism or dwelling – or what is the difference between the export-based or the residential model? In the export-based economies, the stakeholders on site should have – in the ideal case – an interest in developing their territory by exploiting it as an economic space and using it for their own livelihood. In this sense, they should be interested in sustainable development, including economic growth, high environmental qualities, and social peace.

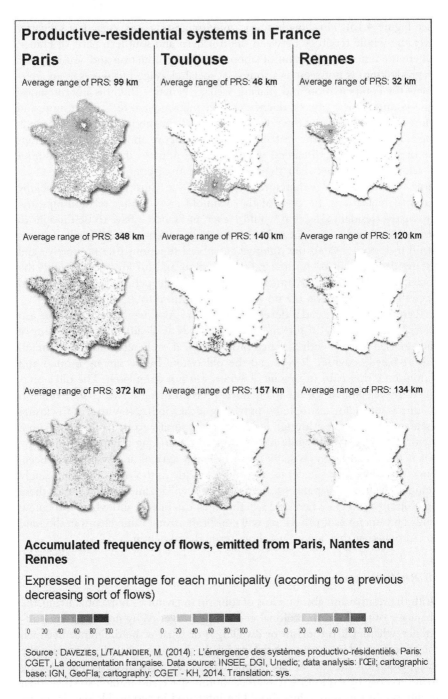

Productive-residential systems in France

Paris	Toulouse	Rennes
Average range of PRS: **99 km**	Average range of PRS: **46 km**	Average range of PRS: **32 km**
Average range of PRS: **348 km**	Average range of PRS: **140 km**	Average range of PRS: **120 km**
Average range of PRS: **372 km**	Average range of PRS: **157 km**	Average range of PRS: **134 km**

Accumulated frequency of flows, emitted from Paris, Nantes and Rennes

Expressed in percentage for each municipality (according to a previous decreasing sort of flows)

0 20 40 60 80 100   0 20 40 60 80 100   0 20 40 60 80 100

Source : DAVEZIES, L./TALANDIER, M. (2014) : L'émergence des systèmes productivo-résidentiels. Paris: CGET, La documentation française. Data source: INSEE, DGI, Unedic; data analysis: l'Œil; cartographic base: IGN, GeoFla; cartography: CGET - KH, 2014. Translation: sys.

Figure 4.13 The territorial interdependencies between export-based metropolitan areas and residential economies in France. The picture shows the approach of Laurent Davezies and Magali Talandier (2014) to cope with the territorial cleavage between the 'productive' and the 'residential', by analyzing the mutual dependencies of both

From this point of view, and in a first approach, it makes no difference whether the offered product is tangible or intangible. The main difference concerns the flux of goods and people and the character of the targeted markets. For tangibles, upstream products are imported and final products are exported. For intangibles, additional food, non-food, and equipment have to be imported, and the clients (tourists) have to come on site for its consumption. This is important for questions of road infrastructure and transport policies. To be competitive, the market has to be narrowly focused and highly specialized. To make such a specialization pay off, you need to host tourists from all over the world. The success of tangibles depends on the technical life cycles of the offered products; the success of the intangibles depends on a fashion-driven life cycle of the destination and on the mobility of the clients (in terms of financial and security aspects).

The residential economy attracts people who make or have made their money elsewhere. Depending on their activity status, they are multilocals or retired – or both. In the ideal case, these people should care for their territory as a place of living – and nothing else. This means that these places develop what is generally called 'quality of life'. It risks suppressing all the other facets of reality, such as the usual negative outcomes of production (like traffic) or socio-economic diversity in the hosting municipality. It produces a calm environment, but also segregation, gentrification, and perhaps isolation. The problematic aspects – such as pollution, over-exploitation of resources, stakeholder conflicts – happen elsewhere. Perhaps new 'problems' arise: it has become a running gag in the Alpine discourse that new inhabitants start legal action as soon as they feel disturbed by the bell of the last cow of the only peasant left in the village. Residential economies deal with intangible goods: They depend on perceptions, storytelling, symbolic capital, and marketing. They may fuel the local entrepreneurs of advanced artisanal skills for construction, retailing,

Figure 4.13 (Continued)
worlds on the basis of French employment zones in the years 2005 and 2006. In columns, they showed the three examples of Paris, Toulouse, and Nantes, which interact with their hinterlands as 'productive-residential systems' according to three main functions. These functions are commuting (first row), retirement (middle), and second homes (third row). An average distance was calculated according to the accumulated flows of residents between the residential location and the work location. The authors see a correlation between the large distances and the size of the metropolitan area, which is an indicator of their centrality and prosperity, especially in terms of commuting. They were also able to show that the second-tier metropolitan areas (Toulouse, Rennes) have a far smaller range of flows. It is not only that Rennes shows only about a third of the average kilometres calculated for Paris; it is also that the radius of flows is limited to the immediate hinterlands. This confirms the argument that the small metropolitan regions depend strongly on the attractivity of their adjacent areas, be it mountains in the case of Toulouse or seaside in the case of Nantes. These results become even more striking if the density of the flows is considered (in percentage, for each municipality); it then becomes apparent that people working in Paris have close links to the coasts (especially in the West) and the Alps (in the East). These analyses can be used as a striking argument against new territorial egoism (Davezies, 2015), which has emerged as a characteristic phenomenon of the current post-Fordist regimes.

healthcare, etc. These locations may become rich but they may also become boring and lose their adherents. They depend on external revenues from remuneration for freelance work, dividends, royalties, or – in the ordinary form of retirement – state pensions. Sometimes these municipalities develop the characteristics of a rent economy. These regions, which – in contrary to the regions of production – we can call regions of consumption, are very fragile and risk a lock-in situation, which prevents them from pursuing alternatives when the conditions change.[29]

There is another important point besides the economic model: the origin or the embeddedness of the main protagonists, which influences the interests in the development of the given location. For example, there might be a difference in the residential economy if the inhabitants are multilocal newcomers or if they are monolocal retired persons (independent of whether they were born here, moved here later, or are returning). Active and multilocal people will not have much time to care for their place of living, although they might develop a certain attachment. Retired people might have more time to be active as volunteers in associations or institutions; they are probably in it for the longer term than multilocals, who might leave more quickly. Nevertheless, in both cases, the young generation is missing. As a result, these municipalities lack the advantages of new knowledge and new dynamism. Ideally, new services will emerge that serve both long-term residents and those who have just moved in. However, there is a risk that the regional profile will erode.

4.8 The ugly question of financial flows: who pays for whom?

The spatial differentiation with the demographic shift from the peripheries to the agglomerations has raised increasing debates about who is financing whom: Do the cities pay for the Alps, or do the Alps provide all those resources that the cities no longer have, so that metropolitan support through transfer payments is more than justified? This was researched by the ALPAYS project in the framework of the National Research Programme 'Landscapes and Habitats of the Alps' (NRP 48) by the Swiss National Science Foundation (Simmen et al., 2005). ALPAYS was an analysis of financial flows according to the most recent regulations for vertical and horizontal compensation in Switzerland between mountain and non-mountain territories. The results were very differentiated and confirmed that the services delivered and consumed mutually are not really comparable: the beneficiaries and payers are changing, according to the understanding that taxes should be paid according to personal economic power. In the case of the Alps, this means that it is accepted that mountain people pay less taxes as they have an economy mainly based on tourism, which has a less specific value added. There were also astonishing results regarding the use of infrastructure. Alpine road and rail infrastructure is expensive because of the topography. But when looking at the use of infrastructure, we see that the highest costs are for the lowland infrastructure which is also used by mountain people. Mountain people who are not multilocal do not travel as often. But if mountain people drive to the lowlands (for business or leisure), they drive longer distances on expensive roads (motorways). These findings relativize the often-used argument of the costly Alpine infrastructure and the ecological impact of Alpine people. Some further results are shown in Box 4.2.

Box 4.2   Financial flows between the Alpine area and the rest of Switzerland

The National Research Programme 'Landscapes and Habitats of the Alps' of the Swiss National Science Foundation was conducted between 2002 and 2007. The results of the programme in general, and the ALPAYS project in particular, showed that the consensus on cohesive development goals in Swiss regional policy was still valid. This is despite the fact that during these years, the metropolitan regions again began to dominate Swiss policies. The ALPAYS results can be summarized as follows:

- The population of the Swiss Alps pays significantly less tax, as they earn less than people in the lowlands. Their per capita gains through financial compensation and subsidies are higher than in the rest of Switzerland. On the other hand, the Confederation saves money through lower expenditure on infrastructure in the Alpine region. All in all, the politically determined financial flows are clearly in favour of the Alpine area. This support can be seen as willingness of the lowland people to fund financial compensation.
- Tourism is an important source of income for the Alpine regions. Guests from the rest of Switzerland and abroad consume tourism services worth 5.6 billion Swiss francs per year (i.e. 3,800 Swiss francs per inhabitant of the Alpine region). The Confederation pays 6,600 Swiss francs per Alpine inhabitant for personnel and material expenditure in the Alpine area. But these costs are 500 Swiss francs per capita less than in the rest of Switzerland.
- 4.7 billion Swiss francs in the form of federal subsidies flow into the Alpine area. This is 19 per cent (or 500 Swiss francs) per capita above the rest of Switzerland (mainly for transport and agriculture); they reflect the difficult topographical conditions. The Alpine area delivers to the Confederation half of the taxes (per capita) compared to the population of the rest of Switzerland. This expresses the lower economic potential of the Alpine space.
- The Alpine area receives 710 Swiss francs per person per year in financial compensation. In the rest of Switzerland, the compensation is balanced. It was envisaged that the new law on compensation

(FiLaG, which was passed in 2003 and came into force in 2005) would benefit the Alps more than the rest of Switzerland.

- Switzerland benefits from an annual 940 Swiss francs per Alpine inhabitant due to Alpine ecosystem services (landscape and biodiversity).
- It is explicitly expressed that there is no overall balance possible because the different financial flows represent very different phenomena:

    - Market-driven flows favour one or the other area, according to the respective issue.
    - Politically driven flows run clearly in favour of the Alpine area. This support can be seen as conscious support of mountain areas.

An econometric model was used to measure the excess expenditure of cantons and their municipalities. One part of the expenditure can be attributed to socio-demographic factors, and another to specific geographic-topographical factors. Surprisingly to the authors, the excess expenditure by geographic-topographical factors and the reduced expenditure by socio-demographic factors are nearly balanced. The ALPAYS authors interpret this to mean that subsidies cannot be justified by specific mountain disadvantages alone.

The ALPAYS results can be taken to demonstrate two points. First, it shows how sensitive a society is when lines of social cleavage narrow to one single feature where basic material features become important (who pays for whom, who works more than others, who bears greater environmental burdens than others). Second, the results show that the general picture of regime change does not lead quickly or completely to an abandonment of the norms that formerly prevailed. As under Fordism, we can note also different forms of regimes in post-Fordism.

European municipalities have wide-ranging municipal autonomy. In some countries, this also includes substantial financial autonomy; in others, they depend considerably on federal grants. Switzerland has a broader autonomous status than its Alpine neighbours, giving it considerable freedom of action. This includes a high degree of fiscal and budgetary autonomy for major tasks such as the responsibility of school infrastructure. Unlike other Alpine countries, Swiss municipalities are largely financed by self-generated taxes, related to the taxation of residents. This system favours competition based on differing tax scales. In a context of high and increasing mobility, this system implies that people can 'optimize their taxes' by choosing their place of residence according to a municipal tax scale that is favourable to their particular income level. This is especially interesting for wealthy people. Living and working in different places has become the norm in most developed countries. Selecting one's place of residence according to a defined catalogue of amenities and low taxes fuels segregation and gentrification processes, which also leads to a reduction in diversity. In the past, many suburban municipalities of agglomerations grew by new inhabitants due to such gentrifying and segregating processes. With the enlargement of agglomerations, this tendency has also taken hold of peri-urban municipalities further from the city and resort towns in the mountains. It has implications on municipal strategies to specialize in attracting inhabitants rather than jobs. In many cases, municipal councils are happy when space-consuming enterprises abandon or relocate their activities. The municipalities of the Birs valley (Laufental) in the Swiss Jura region were recommended to give up any strategy to maintain the remaining industry in favour of attract-ing new commuters. The concept of innovativeness is partly interpreted to strengthen fiscal competition at the communal and cantonal levels. Obwald in Central Switzerland (with its famous resort town of Engelberg) tried to introduce a regressive tax system; its spatial planning had outlined a zoning for luxury residences at very attractive sites on large plots. Finally, after a negative decision by the federal tribunal, Obwald introduced a less aggressive system and the special zones for high-end residences were not realized. We can con-sider such strategies of tax competition by the municipalities in the framework of self-responsibility as an adaption according to the laws on 'new regional policy'.[30] These strategies depend on wealthy consumers with high purchasing power; in a larger sense, they depend on the wealth of the nearby metropolitan area that generates that added value. In the case of economic stagnation, the municipalities closer to the city and the municipalities with a high reputation will probably have fewer risks than others. In addition, bank decisions, credit providers, and marketing agencies generate a rating of which municipalities have the potential for investment and which do not. In this ranking, urban areas are advantaged by the structure of their more favourable population (age, education, unemployment rate, etc.), enabling them to enjoy better terms when assigning credit. These rankings are highly volatile in case of financial crisis, as Sanjay Nepal and Tazim Jamal (2011) mention in their conclusions on the British Columbia case studies.

Where municipalities are unable to finance themselves through their tax revenue (outside of Switzerland, this is the norm; in Switzerland, this concerns the poor municipalities), they are dependent on redistribution measures and subsidies. But as nations and regions have become indebted, they have reduced payments to the lower levels. Mountainous municipalities therefore have to accept the specialized functions assigned to them. In other words, they are losing federal support and reassurance; they do not have their own resources, except landscape amenities and their present reputation; and they have to agree to further develop according to a profile defined by the majority of the popula-tion outside the mountainous regions.

4.9 Summary: five main tendencies

On the basis of the approaches shown in the first part of this book, it is possible to weigh and to generalize the spatial processes described above. The aim is to show the commonalities between peripheral areas at a global level, in order to identify the current conditions that lead to an increase in spatial disparities. Although every territory has its specific trajectory and function at a national and international level, it is possible to identify the following commonalities: an increase in global mobility, the ongoing penetration of foreign capital, and a shift in territorial functions due to socio-demographic differentiation induced by the emergence of new upper and middle classes in the Global South. These factors devalue the productive aspects of mountain areas in favour of consumptive functions for an external clientele. In this sense, I subsume the transformation processes in mountains according to five main tendencies:

(a) Urbanization and metropolization

With the increase of the global division of labour, mountain areas become integrated in global circuits of commercial exchange and capital flows. This transforms mountain communities, even if the mountain morphology and landscapes remain 'rural' at first sight. This phenomenon is visible especially where we see pressure on cultivable and building land, on territories with high prestigious leisure and environmental qualities, and where considerable parts of the local population are absorbed by the non-agricultural economic sectors. We can find these transforming mountain areas all over the world: from the Pyrenees via St Moritz to Kathmandu, and from Alberta to the Chilean Andes. The increasing interdependencies in combination with the post-Fordist change shifts the relation between both areas towards market relations, which reinforces selective and efficient use of space and the commodification of landscapes.

(b) The decline of endogenous economies and the difficulty of substituting them

Endogenous economies and short circuits were seen as the silver bullet to revitalize economic life in declining mountain regions. But as the existing sectors belong mainly to agriculture, artisanal products, and private services, which are less skilled and less performing, they do not deliver attractive jobs and cannot attract an active population permanently. In contrast, endogenous economies are displaced (e.g. locally run ropeways) or fade away (e.g. small-scale agriculture). They can hardly be replaced with new types of production systems, and we see that the younger a production system is, the more volatile it is.

(c) A shift in value adding from export-based to residential economies

With the loss of old, mountain-specific production systems (agriculture, artisanal products, quarries, tourism), the local economy shifts from a productive, export-based activity to a consumptive, residential economy. This introduces other socio-demographic population strata, demands other skills, devalues the existing regional knowledge and identity, and may be part of new forms of socio-spatial segregation. It has not been clear how to deal with it to date, as isolation strategies will not help the current ancient population.

(d) An intensified search for mountain resources

In the framework of technological dynamics, the need for new raw materials such as rare earths has grown tremendously, and mining sites have again become important. Their geological location is mainly in the countries of the Global South. The significance of mountain water for drinking purposes has grown, due to increasing pollution of groundwater aquifers in the lowlands. Water is also the medium to store hydropower in large reservoirs. All these resources serve as most-wanted options demanded by the lowland economies, which makes mountain areas vulnerable to being overused. As distances become quicker and cheaper to bridge, this development not only concerns mountains in the core of a densely populated Europe (such as the Alps), but also the other mountain ranges as well.

(e) Mountains as border regions and hiding places

An aspect that is not depicted in this book concerns the new global migration and commodity flows. In the 19th century, mountains often came to mark 'natural' borders of the emergent national states. It was often said that this peripheral situation aggravated spatial disparities at the expense of mountains. In recent decades, one could hope that global cooperation would also allow transnational cooperation and development in mountain areas. But we saw a paradoxical effect: in peaceful regions, the reduced territorial functions in mountains (border guards or customs offices) reinforced depopulation, while mountains with strongly secured borders and military tensions (in the Himalayas) stabilized the territorial settlement but did not increase livelihoods. Furthermore, we can observe that territories where institutional functions are no longer present become part of the black economy. This topic has been relevant for the mountains of the Global South for a long time. It has also recently become important for Europe and is still an open field of research.

Notes

1 Developed countries: Europe, North America, Australia, New Zealand. Developing countries: Africa, Asia without Japan, Oceania (South Seas), South America.
2 Global trade at the end of the 20th century favoured, in general, the coastal metropolises, regardless of topography (for West Africa: Moriconi-Ebrard et al., 2016).
3 The scenario was made to demonstrate the strong dimension of international trade flows with its impacts on energy consumption, CO_2 emissions, etc. In his PhD thesis, Hug modelled the flows of tangible goods with the aim of finding strategies to reduce the energy consumption of Switzerland to 2,000 W per capita. His findings came to the conclusion that local economic circuits have nearly no influence on reduction compared to the high impact of global imports. In this light, the only – hypothetical – alternative

would be to re-agrarize Switzerland with agricultural land on the now densely popu-lated Plateau and to displace the 8.5 million inhabitants of Switzerland to the Alps.

4   The French Alps had 17 diocesan towns (Briquel et al., 1996).

5   The accessibility is still restricted today. The daily perimeter for construction work should not exceed 160 km, which determines a small-scale pattern of enterprises (from an interview with the owner of a pipelayer firm in Naters/VS, January 2000).

6   SR 901.1, Investitionshilfegesetz (IHG) decided 28 June 1974, into effect 1 March 1975, valid in revised form until 1 January 2008.

7   The ratio of deputies in the two chambers of the Swiss parliament showed 10.2 per cent (25) of the 246 deputies were farmers (legislative period until 2015). In the current legislative period 6.5 per cent are farmers (16 deputies).

8   See Crevoisier et al. (2001).

9   NZZ, 11 May 2015: *Lombardei als Konjunkturlokomotive* (author: Tobias Bayer).

10 The industry data refer to manufacturing, including the chemical industry; they do not include construction (which is also high). Sources for the Austrian data: NZZ, 15 December 2015: *Trotz 132 Millionen Nächtigungen ist und bleibt Österreich ein Indus-trieland*; NZZ, 16 November 2016: *Tirol in der Sackgasse des Massentourismus* (author: Matthias Kattinger). Sources for the Swiss data: Cantonal Office for Statistics and Pere-quation, 2011 census data; NZZ, 27 February 2017: *Das Wallis – innovativer als man denkt* (author: Dominik Feldges).

11 Between 2015 and 2019, the maximum fees are 110 Swiss francs/kW gross output of the hydro station (Loi fédérale sur l'utilisation des forces hydrauliques).

12 Thomas Mann described this situation in his novel *The Magic Mountain* with the exam-ple of the old high society in a sanatorium in Davos (written 1912–1924).

13 Information based on several interviews with representatives of the Basel architecture cluster in the framework of the European ESPON-Metroborder project.

14 See www.iscar-alpineresearch.org/documents/Factsheet_Mountains_english_000.pdf (accessed 26 November 2018).

15 A public good in the sense that it does not fuel the business model of a private company. The water is sold according to the efforts of public enterprises, which means paying salaries and taking a fee that covers the cost of administration.

16 In France, the privatization of water has progressed since the late 1980s: It was much contested by the population, who lost control over their local resources and the condi-tions of delivery (e.g. public fountains no longer serve a guaranteed quality of drinking water). The mayor of Grenoble was convicted of corruption, having been paid by the private company for the privatization. In 1994, he had to resign. Afterwards, the water supply was re-municipalized.

17 The first was Yellowstone National Park. The United States Congress decided in March 1872 to take out of productive use the area of the Yellowstone River: 'with-drawn from settlement . . . dedicated and set apart as a public park or pleasuring-ground for the benefit and enjoyment of the people'.

18 For the conflicts of use in the Californian Sierra Nevada, see Tim Duane (2000).

19 The transformation of territorial jurisdictions to collective entrepreneurs is not restricted to large cities. An example for this shift from the Fordist equal territorial development paradigm to ambitions of regional expansion is the case of the Carinthian city of Vil-lach in Austria in the 1990s. Its trajectory led from a company town (railroad) to an IT chip-producing site (Siemens/Infineon). The city became prosperous when the social democratic council decided to invest parts of their capital budget in venture capital, divesting shares from the national energy supplier (which was common for Austrian cities at that time) in favour of more profitable ones. This gave them far higher yields on the international stock market, but they consciously refrained from exerting influence over energy policies.

20 This is also mentioned by Brenner and Schmid (2014) in their critique on the United Nations' notion of 'urban age' (a notion that is based only on the inhabitants of cities

and the fact that these comprise – since 2011 – more than 50 per cent of the global population) (UN-DESA-PD, 2012); urbanization is not restricted to administrative city borders.

21 For example, Embrun in the Département Hautes Alpes, which was an archdiocese until the French Revolution. Today, it has little more than 6,000 inhabitants.

22 In the popular debate, this distinction is not made, and the notion of urbanization is rather restricted to the visible aspects of urban enlargement. I am aware that it is difficult to stay with this distinction, even in this book.

23 *Investitionshilfegesetz* (Investment Aid Act), decision in favour of economic regeneration areas ('Bonny-decision'), the 'Regio Plus' programme and the participation on Interreg (programmes of the European Union to stimulate cooperation between regions).

24 Up until now, I have implicitly assumed that population growth is an indicator for strength, but I should justify this explicitly. Under the current conditions of the growth paradigm, it is a bad sign when people leave: It means that the territories in question are given up and cannot defend their qualities anymore. So, we have to differentiate between current practices and other thinkable futures.

25 In the Swiss case, the particularity of an extraordinarily good cooperation with the Republic of South Africa played an additional role (SNSF, n.d.).

26 According to the Swiss newspaper, *Tages-Anzeiger*, from 27 August 2015.

27 For the multilocality practised by British residents in the hilly region of the Limousin in France, see Cognard (2011) and Richard et al. (2014).

28 For the year 2000: 42 m² per capita in city centre areas and 44 m² per capita outside (ARE, 2009a).

29 The choice of where to live may be influenced by incentives, but in the end it is arbitrary which places become attractive and which not. Without a sufficient 'export base', the municipalities make themselves dependent on revenue flows. In the extreme case, they become dependent on one single rich person who in turn becomes, through their taxes, the patron of the village. As long as this key person lives, the municipalities do not know what to do with the money; when the person dies, they have nothing.

30 The legal basis is the federal law from 6 October 2006 on regional policy (BRP, SR 901.0) and the act from 28 November 2007 about regional policy (VRP, SR 901.021).

5 The new role of mountains as global suppliers

The common characteristic of the five main tendencies identified in the previous chapter is the changed role that mountains are assigned in a globalized world under liberal-productivist conditions. In the past, they were relatively distinct regions with specific production systems, identities, and a spatial division of labour mainly on a national level. They were dependent on national state policies but had relative independence, as territorial solidarity at the national level was guaranteed. Now this solidarity is questioned and mountain regions have to manage their integration in global markets in a role as entrepreneurial-acting suppliers of specific resources.

As we have seen, mountains are developing not only residences. Other new resources of mountains have gained significance in the frame of metropolization, technological change, new consumption patterns, and abundance of liquid capital. First, this concerns in particular a new level of demand for raw materials (especially rare earths) and the rapid increase in global energy consumption (coal, fracking of oil and gas). Second, mountain headwaters are a reservoir of water for drinking, sewage, and now also for artificial snow. The demand for water has increased due to the concentration of the population in large agglomerations, the need for irrigation water for an intensified agriculture, and the growing pollution of aquifers and rivers. All three factors are interlinked, and all have resulted in a centralized water supply and rising demands that mountains were able to satisfy until now. Mountain water also plays a crucial role for hydropower purposes: in developed countries, it has the function of a costly product to substitute lacking energy for peak demands in a compound supply chain. For emerging countries, it is a still unused potential that they want to see rapidly exploited for the modernization of their national economy. The unrestrained expansion of hydropower benefits from its positive image – it is considered 'green' as it has no CO_2 emissions and no nuclear risks. In fact, the biophysical impacts are enormous and have been well known for a long time (Baghel and Nüsser, 2010; WCD, 2000). Third, global wealth enables and creates new options of consumption for prosperous citizens, and the paradigm of innovation-driven economic accumulation demands the commodification of new spheres with the development of new products. Both can be fulfilled with the valorization of aesthetic criteria by the concept of landscapes and the aesthetization of wilderness.

The awareness of ecological problems makes environmental public goods commodities too. Environmental commodities are calculated according to their value for the well-being of society (ecosystem services). Inversely, costs to restore polluted sites and to avoid biodegradation become internalized by assigning a price to the value of the ecosystem. Since the evaluation of these goods is always controversial between social actors, there can be no objective assignment of values. Under the conditions of asymmetric power relations between actors or between countries and a conventional growth paradigm, environmental goods tend to be undervalued.

This chapter will comment on the examples and processes of the previous chapter. I state that although mountain regions already had subaltern functions before, this position has been reinforced with a new role as suppliers of rare resources on a global level. I will treat five aspects which I see as the main impacts of transformation.

5.1 Asymmetric power relations

Mountain regions, even if they do not suffer depopulation, remain sparsely populated compared to outlying agglomerations or metropolitan regions. In the framework of global change, new knowledge, new technologies, and new economic sectors become concentrated in internationally linked agglomerations. They provide the necessary infrastructure, including large personal networks. The old mountain-specific economies are losing significance and competitiveness. Qualified local people have to out-commute to find a job that suits their (higher) qualifications. Social cleavages develop between an urban majority outside the mountains and a weakened mountain population. Decision-making about land use, the protection or consumption of mountain resources, and the overall consideration between conservation and development is caught in the dilemma between expert knowledge from the outside (which reflects the interests of the urban majority), and the interests of the local mountain population (which are quickly judged as being self-serving, as these communities represent the minority). These general conflicts are increasing, with policies that designate the mountains to a single use as supplier of raw materials or of aesthetic emotions. In Switzerland, the federal structure was in the past fuelled by differences between town and countryside, mountains and lowlands, religion, and four different languages. These manifold social cleavages had a moderating impact and an effect of checks and balances due to changing coalitions. Since the end of the 1990s, the conflicts of interest run along the urban vs. rural/mountain areas front, and both sides feel overstretched. The city folk express environmental arguments in favour of biodiversity. The mountain dwellers claim their right to be masters of their territory. A subject of blame-shifting is the reappearance of the wolf: the city people are happy; the mountain people shoot it whether this is legal or not. Mountain people want to produce, as do urban people; as in all productivist societies, production has a much higher prestige than reproduction. Urbanites want to designate the mountains as their own recreational space, or as a compensation area for disproportional damages to urban areas, or as a supplier, as mentioned above. The demography and the division of economic activities and political-administrative institutions create an asymmetric relation of power, as shown in the example of the Geneva metropolitan region (Bertrand et al., 2015).

The examples shown in Section 4.4 (especially of the Himalayan conservation policy and the Lesotho Highlands Water Project) contrast with the happiness about the increased interest in world mountains. This increased interest has put the public eye on preservation and environmental issues, which have increasingly become a common good on the political stage (Debarbieux and Price, 2008). On the economic stage, however, things have gone in the opposite direction, detracting goods from the public for commodification. It shows that the question is more complex and needs a more intensive discussion about disparities and liberties of action – a problem of which the authors are well aware (Debarbieux, 2013).

Asymmetry of power also guides the definition of demarcations. This concerns the scale for which the values and norms should be pertinent and at which level democratic rights and majority decisions should count (Agnew, 1994; Brenner, 2001; Swyngedouw, 2004). First of all, it concerns the question of whether mountains can or should form its own region with distinctive development goals. It also concerns the question of autonomy and solidarity, and the question at which level different framework conditions (peripherality, bad accessibility, economic weakness) should be taken into account for measures of compensation. Several of the examples we have already treated in the previous chapters are part of this discussion: Should mountain regions (which serve as leisure sites for lowland urban areas) be merged together with these productive regions, as in Davezies and Talandier (2014)? Is it a 'win-win' solution if Johannesburg and the state of Lesotho have solved their sectoral problems at the expense of the local population (Rousselot, 2015)? Is it, on a global balance, a sustainable solution to create distinct Alpine resorts (such as in Andermatt) and large protected areas, as in Slovakia (Meessen et al., 2015)? And of course, there is the question of which to prioritize: wolves or sheep, cattle herds or tourists?

5.2 Volatility combined with the renaissance of extractive industries

The global hunger for raw materials – rare earths and other metals, as well as coal – makes mountains attractive for the mining and wholesale business. The catch-up process of the emerging countries in their demand for energy in all forms, and the new technologies that use noble metals and rare earths, can be seen as the main drivers. Many of these extractive products come from the mountains. While most of the ore and coal layers in Europe's mountains have expired, the mountains in the emerging countries in the Andes and the Himalayas, but also North America, still offer tremendous reservoirs for all kinds of metals, coal, and also special stones for global markets. Beyond the global questions of the appropriateness of its exploitation – which involves, in general, the questions of recent technologies, global warming, transport flows, ecology and working conditions, and so on – these industries pose several problems. The locations have to be established in greenfield areas where settlements are pioneered and planned to be temporary. 'Sustainability' is excluded by definition, as these settlements are not foreseen to be developed as cities to live in with families, civil society, cultural institutions, and high education or research (Forget, 2015; Romero and Órdenes, 2004; see also, for West Africa, among others, Werthmann, 2000).

Mining has always been a temporary and volatile activity. Many towns became rich in the past by mining, only to decline once the mines were exhausted. It is not possible here to give a history of mining activities, but some examples. Laurence Moss (2006) shows in his book about amenity migration how regional consultants in the Rocky Mountains recommend the transformation to tourism and residences, because mining and logging has no future. John Provo and Mel Jones (2011) show the coal basin of the Appalachians in the United States for many years as an out-migration area due to poverty. Regions in the Alps such as Carinthia had the bad experience of the end of mining and resulting unemployment, subsequently deciding to abandon industrial activities in favour of non-mountain-specific tertiary industries. Today, large mines are part of a global supply chain that is defined by a few transnational companies (TNCs) and a high volatility of the financial system and currency exchange rates. The high volatility causes the problem that areas with traditional economies or even 'untouched nature' are transformed quickly with an uncertain future as there is no urban infrastructure, and often the workforce is imported for restricted periods, as on offshore platforms. The volatility generates uncertainty for the workforce, regional authorities, and the indigenous population.

Regional authorities bargain with TNCs about concessions in which the regional side has less power than the TNCs. The TNCs depend on the order of their shareholders and exert pressure to obtain favourable conditions by the granting regions. The regions, regardless of whether this is a 'mountain state' or not, have no choice but to accept (Forget, 2015) – if they do not, the TNCs threaten to move. The 'mountain government' would lose its global player for the 'modernization' of the state.

Meanwhile, a counter-public emerges. International NGOs try to ameliorate working and environmental conditions (such as in Switzerland with the 'Public Eye/Berne Declaration' or 'Solifonds' of Swiss syndicates, and also governmental institutions such as the Swiss Agency for Development and Cooperation, SDC).

With the example of water, we see that the exploitation of resources is always a problem of scale (Agnew, 2011). As mentioned, hydropower in the popular view is seen as a renewable energy, but the reach of residual water generates an ecological desert. The large-scale derivation of catchment areas with large dams for the delivery of water from Lesotho to Johannesburg is generally presented as a win–win situation for both partners, but the ecological problems are neglected and the communities of the Basotho people of the Lesotho highlands have lost considerable parts of their agricultural basis (Rousselot, 2015).

5.3 Biodegradation in global mountain areas

The remoteness of mountains to the centres of decision-making makes it difficult to control overuse and pillage. This is not caused by a lack of information, but results from the fact that the problem is far away and the number of people directly affected is small. Problems that occur in densely populated urban areas affect a population that is able to defend its interests: the direct impacts are more severe, so solutions are sought – these may be technical or a matter of shifting the problem to others (e.g. the relocation of the chemical industry away from Frankfurt in the 1990s). In mountain areas, a civil society that wants to influence national decisions is always less powerful due to a smaller demographic and educational basis. Even if problems are well known, there is less interest to solve them as the exploitation of mountain resources generates so many third-party advantages. Large parts of the stone industry have been relocated from Europe to Asia due to cheap labour costs, but also as this industry has high impacts on landscapes and is chased away from Europe for reasons of landscape protection. Relocating these industries makes the impacts invisible, as nearly no one looks at the new locations of quarrying, mining, or manufacturing.[1] The mining sites are not only volatile; they also have an enormous need for fresh water, which also means waste water that causes severe pollution. Also, agriculture is affected by these forms of global sourcing: it is a current and justified critique that the countries of the Global North have closed markets towards the countries of the Global South. But the incentives to produce cash crops in these countries point towards the installation of large monocultures. An example is coffee, with Vietnam now the second largest producer of coffee beans. Traditional coffee production used mixed cultivation, resulting in a cultural landscape of a rich biodiversity that becomes degraded by monocultural methods. Moreover, monocultural production also incorporates the extensive use of pollutant plant protection; dependency of farmers on the international seed market; and degradation of local knowledge, production, and living structures. In terms of agriculture, mountain areas are also implicated in processes of large-scale buyouts of land for food security of emerging countries and transnational companies, which has become known as 'land-grabbing' (Breu et al., 2016; Tejada, 2015).

5.4 Paradoxical effects of conservation

Mountains have become the subject of much interest in recreative qualities and linked to this, issues of nature protection, environmental action, and research – it has even raised spiritual approaches ('sacred mountains') (Birnbaum, 1998). As mentioned, mountains have become a public issue with the claim to be a public good, although their uses are becoming increasingly privatized. And this is not the only paradox. Mountain areas have often become the target of strict conservation measures by people who do not live there and are not aware of their way of life, influenced by the recent interdependency between the highlands and lowlands. Subsequently, they do not understand the motivations of local people and their interest in producing and productivity – an interest which dominates the globalized world, and which is expressed in its most extreme forms in the logic of production in the global metropolitan areas. So, the environmentalist movement, which has its merits against productivist thinking, has its blind spots too. It runs the risk of missing the target where it claims 'nature' in the understanding of a paradise without local people. An understanding that polarizes in terms of the use of intangible commodities in the mountains (without producing food) and tangible, highly productive goods in the lowlands, transfers own perceptions of an idyllic nature onto a territory that is topographically disadvantaged for human settlement, but where people nonetheless have tried to maintain their lives. As rare earths, energy inputs, and food specialities are no longer seen in everyday life products, an appreciation of the productive sphere is impeded. In this way, the bashing of mountain economies with aesthetic arguments of landscape protection is a certain form of 'Nimby': The population in the peripheries is expected to practise higher standards than its mainly urban critics themselves are willing to. Aesthetic arguments do not reflect the societal origins of these problems, and are therefore not suitable for treating them.

On the other hand, the local populations often do not see their role in an interdependent and interacting world. Although it is true that mountain populations have had a long experience of migration and the exchange of export goods over long distances, the willingness to attract foreigners is limited in the agricultural world, based on entrepreneurial practices in a stable milieu of restricted expansion. This helps to explain why, amid the recent worldwide migration to Europe, the communities most opposed to immigration are those that have had the least problems with it. A restricted personal and professional network impedes radical critique and innovation as there is no escape from the strong ties of local relationships. Both bear the risk of provoking lock-in phenomena. The lack of innovation in social issues has favoured the adoption of external models (i.e. the mainstream economic models of productivist thinking that, in the rural world, meant trying to increase production and minimizing reproductive work). The entry of the real estate business in the mountain economy, with the possibility of realizing high profits by zoning, rising land prices, and construction of tourist infrastructure, aggravated the problem.[2] Only this can explain that the environmental ideas in general (soil, water, and biodiversity, including big predators) did not obtain the necessary attention to develop a new relation between productive use and reproduction, and also between mountain people and the urban majority.

Box 5.1   Rebound effects due to a mechanistic definition of ecology

- The regional administrations of Uttarakhand with autonomy rights according to the highly ranked principles of subsidiarity practise the adoption of external concepts such as the idea of national parks in its American interpretation (see Section 6.1) to compete with other regions in modernization strategies, thus displacing the well-adapted pastoral practices of the local population. To fuel this strategy with the necessary energy, the main rivers are equipped with dams for hydropower. The orchestrated artificial wilderness at high altitudes corresponds with the intensification of use in the valleys to feed the increasing tourism industry, including the heating of water in the reservoir basin for artificial snow in new-built ski resorts. The government – which is not an external unit – practises a selective use of their own mountain resources, which are 'à la mode', thus sacrificing other potentials of the historic trajectory. A similar case is the example of the Lesotho Highlands Water Project (see Chapter 4).
- In the European Alps, the reappearance of big predators, such as the lynx, wolf, and bear, is highly contested by the local population as it complicates sheep husbandry. The urban population is happy about the new zoological biodiversity but does not want to pay for the increasing costs of maintenance in the mountains. The debate has become a question of sheep versus wolf, and the preferences are quite arbitrary; they depend on the power of the different social milieus to define the ecologically correct solution. Finally, the eco-balancing worsens when the local character of the food value chains is continuously degraded.
- The growth of metropolitan areas and its inner densification is the mainstream approach in European spatial planning. It is seen as the silver bullet to prevent urban sprawl, reduce transport flows, and offer attractive jobs. It is the answer to increasing per capita consumption of living space. The last calculations show that, indeed, the graph shows an attenuation in the last years. But it is not noticed that it has now become possible to use more than one residence due to the new possibilities of mobility (i.e. to 'divide one's time' between different places and to escape the densified dwelling situation by long-distance travel). The mountain airports of Kathmandu/Nepal and Cusco/Peru offer more than 40 flights per day. In Cuzco, a new international airport is planned at the Andean plateau at 3,700 m altitude. The speculation of landowners has already begun.

5.5 From the city into the wild and back

The recent debate about demographic and economic development in mountains shows that there are studies about depopulation on the one hand, and studies about remigration and repopulation on the other.[3] Both are true. Empirical data for the Alps and other mountain ranges shows that people who do their higher education outside these areas do not return, as there are neither adequate jobs nor the necessary creative environment that makes it attractive to return to their village of origin after their studies. There is a real brain drain of young, well-educated mountain people who are attracted to the large cities. These cities provide the whole range of higher education, services, culture, and also contemplative near-natural places. It is one purpose of higher education to impart a broader view, discourage self-serving thinking, and provide alternative approaches to solving a problem. It becomes understandable that people have to leave their narrow valleys for their studies and, in all likelihood, their ensuing careers.

As urban development in most cases has been late in reaching the mountains, there are only rarely national or regional capitals in mountains, which would offer attractive jobs in administration, healthcare, high-performing services, or universities. In a situation where university education has also become prestigious for emerging states and the hopes of young individuals, urban liberty, diversity, and culture offer the best options for a successful life. As the economic sectors of mountains are mainly specialized in low-level consumer services, large cities offer the highest diversity of personal preferences and the best opportunities for professional careers as they have work for both the highly qualified and low-skilled.

It has sometimes been said that the phenomenon of amenity migration constituted a counter-tendency, and that the change in personal preferences for the biophysical qualities and cultural assets of rural and mountain areas would make people accept lower wages, as in return they had the advantages of a healthy environment. Sheila Croucher (2012) underlines this argument. In contrast, Raquel Huete et al. (2013) show that this idealistic view is inadequate, arguing with the results of their comparative analysis in Alicante (Spain). They show that during the economic crisis, the 'lifestyle migrants' changed their mobility patterns in a similar way to other migrants. Furthermore, studies done in the 1990s showed that preferences for certain places depend on a person's stage of life. Young people go to the city after school and leave the city for a peri-urban area when they have families. At that time, the peri-urban fringes promised the highest benefits in terms of 'quality of life', especially for individual fulfilment and social prestige. Meanwhile, the centres of large cities have regained their attractiveness. They have also become attractive for families, as they offer better conditions for new constellations of all kinds of couples – those with strong or loose ties, or with their own or adopted children. And, of course, they offer more options for childcare. It becomes obvious that decisions about a resident's location is a material issue in their societal position and their stage of life.[4]

Mountain regions should not complain about the brain drain. It is the purpose of an academic education to train students to later take on leading functions in society, and in some countries, this education has been financed by the population through taxes. So, it is not justified to complain about the brain drain – it is probably the only appropriate logic for the concerned individuals. However, the decision-makers of mountain regions should look to encourage the young going abroad to remain loyal to their origins so that they may come back later. And probably the hope of mountain regions to attract people from urban regions in the lowlands is not in vain. As many left when they were young, some may come back during middle age, as often they have kept their family homes for emotional reasons.[5] And as there are empty houses outside the hotspots of tourism, there are opportunities to buy old farms, even for people without a mountain tradition.

But most important is the different situation. When people remigrate or are newcomers to the mountains, they do this with the knowledge of urban social practices and the option of being able to switch between two worlds. They may use the mountain residence as a multilocal home, and can choose between the best of both worlds: living in the mountains during the tourist season and living in the city when the weather is best there, or vice versa. And they can decide to stop the mountain experience and go back to the city (Camenisch and Debarbieux, 2011). In an article for the same journal, I named this in 2011 as Alpine gentrification, driven by the individual's search for reputation and social capital and deduced from theories of political economy. Meanwhile, Michaela Benson (2013) confirmed this argumentation empirically with ethnographic methods. With her findings, she explains the search of second-home owners to participate in and obtain 'authentic' experiences, a quality that obviously could not be reached with simple tourist arrangements. The search for authenticity serves as a specific means for social distinction.

We can explain these processes with Bourdieu's concept of habitus and the individual search for the accumulation of resources, perhaps in the form of social capital or symbolic capital. Today, these preferences are often summarized under the label of 'culture' (elaborated on in the 1990s with the 'cultural turn'), an approach that obscures more than it elucidates. However, with the analyses of mountain regions and the ongoing processes of out-, in-, and remigration, it is possible to be much more precise. The processes in mountains and in cities constitute a laboratory situation or an in-between comparison: they show the different opportunities that people have, and their individual trajectories. By showing this, it becomes clear that 'culture' is a specific resource that is a hybrid of power and economic strength. So, it is easy to explain that the most wanted way of life is to have one's cake and eat it: the flat in town and a second branch in the mountains, or vice versa. And it explains why it is easy for citizens to demand inner densification in cities – they have the alternative to migrate, to commute, or to use the mountains for a restricted period of time.

5.6 'Slowfoodization': quality products for urban elites

The general post-Fordist understanding of regional development is to raise productivity by entrepreneurial initiatives, as the national states have difficulties in financing equivalent living conditions in mountain areas. As production in mountain areas is more costly than in other territories (geography does matter), mountain economies cannot compete with lowland economies without offering specialities – products with a label informing about conditions of production and specific qualities.

The proposed concepts argue in favour of a consequent regional specialization and accelerated innovation according to the approaches of Schumpeter (creative destruction) and Krugman (avoiding competition on comparative costs). Such innovations give enterprises and regions an advantage in generating temporary increasing (disproportional) returns. These temporary monopolies allow them to avoid the competitive advantages of lower wages in the countries of the Global South. Michael Porter (1998) uses this argument too (demanding clients). In this way, the proponents of high quality/high prices argue that because the new markets are very fragmented, they have to be global to reach enough clients. This strategy is clearly export-based, allowing higher yields. It addresses the repeated argument that mountain products are too cheap. This may be true in general. But the conclusion that prices have to be high, and that the target market should be global, with a well-funded clientele of the emerging countries, has at least three shortcomings.

First, it implies that mountains, with their lower population and restrictive topography, could be as competitive as lowland areas by strategies of difference. This could only be possible if mountain areas enlarge their market range for highly specialized products on a global level, as they did with tourism offers for the new Asian middle and upper classes. It is doubtful whether the uniqueness factor will be strong enough to compensate for the lack of productivity compared to the lowlands. If it is possible, it raises the questions of over-exploitation and cluster risks. The quantities of organic Alpine-labelled food or exotic Himalayan drinking water will not be enough to sustain continuous mountain development, and the ecological costs of generating global brands on the basis of local production will be too high to maintain a credible sustainable development. Small, local economic circuits, however, do not deliver the push of productivity that is needed to meet the requirements of economic competitiveness.

Second, it is justified to demand higher prices for higher quality. But if a high-quality product is produced only to justify a higher price, then production might be justified by the self-serving interests of a company, but is not suitable as a strategy for a society trying to mitigate spatial disparities. It should also be noted that a large part of the surplus has to be paid to external consultants, as the mountain regions (with the exceptions of some resort towns such as St Moritz, Kitzbühel, Banff, Aspen) do not have the business services industries necessary to produce the communication strategies. The professional linkages between mountain region and lowland services are a clear indicator for an advanced urbanization process.

Third, the strategy of high-quality products implies that a 'willingness to pay' can be generated for ecological services and that the 'emotional surplus' for consumers will allow a higher level of prices. This argument reduces the market size to a niche market. It creates a niche of production that can be afforded only by a small rich segment of clients who are defined by social criteria, and not by the small local economic circuits often proclaimed (which again confirms the first argument, above). If we do not mind about the missed opportunities of small economic circuits, then the social selection of the consumers creates a problem. If mountain products are really so much better than lowland products, then they are essential for humans, and access to them should be affordable for all (the 'democratization' of consumption). If mountain products are not as essential as marketing would have us believe, then the higher price is not justified, and the wealthy clientele will notice this quite quickly when it has found a new product to consume.

It is clear that in reality, mountain regions have no other choice of how to act. But we should not be too happy with it and it will not solve the problems of the peripheries. The argument is not valid as a strategy to reduce the structural disparities of mountains. Used in this sense, the argument becomes affirmative and ideological; in the end, it turns against the mountain regions.

5.7 Metropolitan embrace and integration

Less than ever, mountains can be called independent economic spaces. The people inhabiting mountains have a long-standing knowledge in agricultural, manufacturing, and tourist activities. In the past, this was a comparative advantage – today it is a commerciable uniqueness. With the ongoing global market integration and mobility, this old tacit knowledge becomes codified – usable for all – or it vanishes to the same degree as the traditional activities become less attractive, are transformed, or disappear. This weakens mountain areas, and its population has to look for the renewal of its value chains by its own means and by arousing the interest of lowland people.

The character of investment in mountain areas is changing. In the Global North, where borders are stable and nation-building is finished, investment is no longer driven by territorial ambitions. Peripheries are discussed with a view to abandonment if they are believed to be declining and without future potential. Public investment requires the consensus of the whole population, which puts the topic of regional policies in a contradictory debate about normative development (or preservation) goals and stakeholder demands for low taxes. This turns public investment into economy-driven decision-making. Private investments in existing traditional value chains are exposed to the mechanisms of comparative advantages where lowland economies are favoured. Investment in mountains is seen as risky, and bank regulations do a ranking with special 'handicaps' for non-agglomeration and mountain areas (which means mortgages and interests are much more expensive). Mountain areas in emerging countries often receive specific national support for their development. Amid enthusiasm about this, it is often ignored that this interest, in many cases, is due to latent conflicts (e.g. at the Indian-Chinese border), as it was in former times in Europe.

The decreasing interest in mountain areas contrasts with the high interest to obtain access to selected mountain resources by appropriating property rights on land. In this sense, we see processes of large-scale land acquisitions also in mountain areas (e.g. Tejada, 2015; Nepali and Upreti, 2012). These tendencies allow transnational companies and state funds to invest capital according to their business strategies and their food security needs. The other main tendency comprises the practices of urban people to acquire real estate in adjacent mountain areas, to use the offered leisure services, and to use intensively the qualities of the mountains as a common good. These amenities make mountains a new and supplementary asset for mountain-near (peri-Alpine) metropolitan regions. These agglomerations are, on a global level, only second- or third-tier metropolises, but their mountain features give them a strong point of uniqueness. Although these mountain areas show only partly a densifying urban development, they are functionally integrating into the metropolitan areas and through this become completely urbanized. The intensified use of mountains as a common good prepares them for a new wave of commodification in the form of regulations against overuse or in developing new business opportunities. In paradox to the prevailing appraisal of diversity, this tendency signifies a pronounced separation of functions, which surpasses those of the days of the Athens Charta. Mountains become a neighbourhood of the metropolitan areas.

Notes

1 See the Indian documentary of Sudheer Gupta, *Black River Business* (India, 2009–2010).
2 An example of such mismanagement was the municipality of Leukerbad in the canton of Valais in Switzerland, which failed by a debt overload due to oversized investment in a new tourist infrastructure. Canton Valais is also heavily criticized because of its extensive zoning perimeter for settlements.
3 For example, Bätzing et al. (1996) show decline in parts of the Italian and French Alps. Corrado and di Gioa (2011), Löffler et al. (2011), and Solé et al. (2014) show repopulation in the Alps and the Catalan Pyrenees.
4 The gentrification processes in cities are explicitly a counterargument against the affirmative narrative of Florida's 'creative class'. One can also add that the neighbourhoods of large cities in the past have been transformed according to the interests of the powerful elites. The main difference to the Fordist period is that students, trainees, and sometimes even the workforce of the most powerful sectors have been added to those who are labelled as 'creative'. For another critical approach on the arbitrariness of the label 'creative', see Krätke (2010).
5 Agricultural economists often deplored that political strategies to sustain the existing settlement structures generated a bias in the balance between land offer and demand, impeding an efficient use of land, because market value, earning capacity value, and emotional value (by people that abandoned peasantry) are no longer congruent. This incongruency prevents a dynamic valorization of land use and slows down innovation and local entrepreneurship (Giuliani, 2002).

Part III

A new level of inequality

Figure 6.1 While mountains in former times were an obstacle, cities with a mountain environment now profit from it as this offers a unique selling proposition which their competitors do not have. The neighboured mountain regions have advantages, too but they have to face the transformation from producing locations to residential places. The consequences of these segregation processes in the long run are not yet clear.

Photo: Zurich and the Glarus Alps, 6 April 2010.

6 The shift from state-organized to liberal-productivist regimes

This chapter picks up the theoretical debate of Chapter 2. It explains the transformations of mountain areas according to the logic of accumulation regimes, and the corresponding modes of institutional regulation and its profound change in the 1970s and 1980s, according to the approach of regulation (Section 2.6). The application of the regulation approach to mountain territories may serve to add new facets to the use of this tool. But primarily, it serves to explain mountain development according to the relations between groups of social actors that act with different social resources and different degrees of shaping. The fact that different amounts of capital (in the enlarged sense of Pierre Bourdieu) influence territorial relations and development explains that it is not yet done that peripheral areas in general, and mountain areas in particular, find new market niches and new products in the Schumpeterian sense. In this way, this chapter is intended to show that spatial processes in mountains should be explained by political economy, while the solution later on has to be found mainly politically.

6.1 Characteristics of Fordist regimes

The 20th century saw a change in the characteristics of the capitalist societies of the 19th century. There was now a new relation between the private ownership of industrial and financial capital, and the society represented by the state: elements of planning, concerted action, and cooperation between the most important groups of social actors became constituent of the societal relation. This change characterized the shift to a new type of regime that was originally named 'organized capitalism' (Hilferding, 1927), and meant a joint action between employers' associations and the state trying to answer to one major critique of capitalism in the 19th century: its 'anarchist' character, where every entrepreneur is producing independently without knowing exactly the size of his markets and the needs of his clients. The notion of Fordism stands for a limited period of this 'organized capitalism': the post-war period with concerted action including now also the trade unions. It had its heyday between 1950 and 1973. Some of its main characteristics were valid in the interwar period before. Turning points were the publication of the Club of Rome's *Limits to Growth*

(Meadows et al., 1972) and the first oil crisis (1973). The fading out lasted to the late 1990s.

Fordism stands for its specific organization of production and social arrangements: economic growth and mass consumption. It includes all framework conditions and general rules of value adding (accumulation) and redistribution of added value (regulation) in a society that is organized on a productivist growth-oriented base and tries to avoid social cleavages and clashes through a welfare system and redistributed purchasing power for a broadening middle class. This model had different variants in the Western world, as well as in the countries of the Eastern bloc, but its mechanism was similar in both spheres. It was oriented to ensure the loyalty of its stakeholders with a powerful productivity (based on a centralized economy of scales) and the trickle down of benefits in the form of mass consumption of goods that were formerly restricted to the upper classes. The welfare state's services (especially state-guaranteed old age security and healthcare) made life more secure. The prerequisite for redistribution and mass consumption was high productivity based on standardized production. The economic model was demand oriented. A key economic figure was John Maynard Keynes, who proposed anti-cyclic state intervention to avoid economic crises by overproduction. The key political measure was the New Deal under President Franklin D. Roosevelt in the United States.

State residents not only earn benefits called 'wages' by their status as employees or entrepreneurs. They also obtain social benefits by their role as citizens of a certain society to which they pay taxes, carry out military service, or do voluntary work. This has advantages for economic growth. Societies with professionalized healthcare and guaranteed pensions have a higher productivity, as the adult children can follow a professional activity in the most productive stage of their life instead of having to support their parents, as is the case in societies with a large informal sector.[1] The conception of welfare states with a nationally different shape of social services was more or less the dominant model in Europe and the developed countries. In terms of concentration of work, the state combination of the former German Democratic Republic (a highly vertically integrated conglomerate of industrial production) was the most extreme and most optimized organizational form; in terms of redistribution by social services, Scandinavia was the reference model. Japan could be seen as a reference model for the redistribution of productivity gains within a cohesive society that makes great efforts to maintain its homogeneity. The French model was based on a strong national state with a high degree of central planning. The German model became known under the name of 'Rhenish capitalism'. It was characterized by the power of trade unions, which were able to work strategically together with their everyday antagonists, the employer's associations, and the state in concerted action; another characteristic was the financing of the large industrial companies by their banks, which hold important shares in these firms, so that the industrial pattern was protected against takeovers (the so-called 'Germany Plc'). Germany and Switzerland were exemplary in avoiding territorial disparities through federalist institutions. This territorial approach of the welfare state played an important role in mountainous regions in Swiss regional policies of the 1970s and 1980s.

In the controversial discourse on Fordism, it is often neglected that the new national states of the Global South were also part of the Fordist regimes, as the postcolonial access to those resources (from coffee to uranium) was also a prerequisite of the business model.[2] The reference to developing countries, therefore, is close and indispensable but characterized by its complementarity. In that way, Fordist regimes have largely depended on the colonial and neocolonial surplus (especially by using oil as the key resource of this period). The concept of Fordism is not Eurocentric. It is thus incorrect to say that Fordism can only be applied to a few advanced capitalist countries. However, the range of Fordist regimes is large, as also stated by the authors of the regulatory approach. The characteristics of the Fordist model are specific for each country or region, and should be analysed as such. For instance, a complete analysis of the regimes of social security by country would demonstrate this broad range, and explain why the homogenization of social security systems under the dominance of the Anglo-Saxon global model inevitably lead to a massive deterioration of the welfare state. The globalized model of a reduced welfare state provides security standards according to the lowest common denominator of all countries.

6.2 Spatial disparities of Fordism

Since the end of the 19th century, the rural and mountain areas were the suppliers of the workforce for industrialization and its concentration in fast-growing cities. At first glance, it confirms the picture of a continuously reproduced uneven development. Past empirical work (Berry, 1964; Cattan et al., 1994; Moriconi-Ebrard, 1993; Pumain, 1997; Pumain and Moriconi-Ebrard, 1997) showed secular trends of spatial concentration for decades. This concentration can be explained by two types of agglomeration economies. First, the typical economies of scale in its territorial expression, where the majority of enterprises of a certain economic sector are concentrated in one city or region, such as the former knife producers in Sheffield, Solingen, or Thiers, named localization economies or Marshallian districts. Alfred Marshall (1919) received his remake through Michel Porter's (1998) cluster approach. Second, the economies of scope. In its territorial expression, this means the high diversity of housing, manifold formal and informal activities, and a variety of service offers, which today can be found only in large metropolitan cities.[3]

Rural and mountain areas, however, saw a continued decline. Innovations were developed, especially in the cities, based on science and research at the newly founded polytechnical universities. The innovations were also first introduced in the cities, which further reinforced the differences and the spatial disparities between town and countryside. However, we saw the rise of specialized industrial districts due to local raw materials (e.g. the development of the industrial district of the Ruhr) or the generation of water power-related industries in the low mountains and the piedmonts. The development of those industries requiring many low-skilled workers allowed the affected areas to benefit from raised productivity in agriculture and led to a considerable rural industrialization.

The post-war period was characterized by an attempt by the national states to develop policies of regional equilibrium to avoid societal conflicts and to raise productivity, especially in the rural regions, with its changing agricultural sector. It was the concept of the welfare state to counter the existing disparities by social and regional measures with an approach of general modernization and the acceleration of economic structural change. If the scope and form of such compensation measures vary from one country to another, they have – in the developed countries at the time, in Europe and North America – one thing in common: they tried to anticipate and address the social cleavages and improve living conditions, even in the centralist states (or, in the case of France, explicitly through this centralism). It was exactly with the arguments of equilibrium that France developed a specific form of an industrialized seaside and mountain tourism. Many European countries experienced laws of financial compensation for mountain areas and other regional policy measures. The bloc of the 'countries of the real existing socialism' also followed the paradigm of regional balance by systematically ignoring cities and accepting their deterioration.

Box 6.1   Fordist planning practices in Europe – five examples

- *Equal industrial development in agriculture*: In the heyday of Fordism, the national/European planning paradigm was comprised of measures for the industrialization of European agriculture (Mansholt plan of the European Economic Community, EEC), which meant the shift from small-scale agriculture of manifold compounds to large-scale production. This was linked with a wave of protesting farmers.
- *Modernization of new infrastructure*: In Germany in 1967, the famous 'Leber-plan' provided a network of motorways to which each municipality was promised access closer than 20 km. In the 1990s, Switzerland planned and realized two base tunnels (instead of one) through the Alps in the interests of a regional equilibrium.
- *Spatial planning*: Large infrastructure was planned in the name of 'public interest' by the state and regional authorities. The technocratic paradigm included expropriations and violent conflicts (e.g. expansion of airports, nuclear power plants). Environmental issues did not play a role – they were not included in the model of permanent growth. The end-of-pipe technologies with very high chimneys provided a mitigated quality of air to all.

- *Urban development*: The ideal of a functionally separated city led to the transformation of city centre areas to central business districts, and the conversion of central neighbourhoods to locations for headquarters. But under the influence of the territorial compromise, cities could not exploit their areas to the full extent. Though the Frankfurt city government practised an intense exploitation of their central areas in the 1970s, it was unable to extend it to the residential neighbourhoods near the centre: the Westend was opened to land speculation but became occupied by a squatter movement; the other neighbourhoods were protected by zoning; the residing population held a strong position.
- *Mountain development*: The installation of large dams for the storage of water for hydropower was linked with the displacement of villages, sometimes against strong resistance from the local population. A better standard of living for all and new jobs were promised. In the Grison Val Bregaglia, the installation of hydropower was perceived as a new solidarity between the city of Zurich and the mountain population. Church bells rang when the hydro stations became operative.

The Fordist regimes combined an increase in productivity, the neocolonial relations to the countries of the Global South, and the welfare state paradigm in a nationally different and broad variety. This constellation allowed rich countries to reduce large regional disparities at a national level. Within the cities, however, the disparities increased. Economic structural change based on the international migration of low-skilled workers created a pattern of enlarging suburbanization with a transformation of the city centre areas and degradation of the centrally located neighbourhoods. The city centres became the 'vocation' for the service sector, according to the modernist principle of separation of functions. Land prices and spatial planning made the rising middle-class population move to the suburbs. This process was explained by the ground rent theory with the example of West Berlin and Frankfurt a.M. (Brede et al., 1976). Thus, the centres of cities decomposed, with temporary ghettoization and temporary uses until reinvestment and gentrification. These facilities housed the pioneers, the germ of the 'creative class'. At the time, this phenomenon was called the 'A-Cities' (Frey, 1981), where 'A' stood for all the disadvantaged members of the society: aged, aliens, asylum seekers, *arm* (poor), *arbeitslos* (unemployed), and *ausgegrenzt* (excluded). Fordism, in its Eastern bloc variant, tried to level the disparities between town and countryside. This was done by allowing systematic deterioration of the city centre areas for ideological reasons, as cities were seen as relics of the capitalist class structure.

The spatial disparities inherent to the Fordist regimes are complex and heterogeneous, and it is not possible to go into detail. Five key issues should suffice, which are of course not exhaustive, and moreover do not necessarily apply to all countries:

- *Skilled workforce*: The standardization of production and the increased product output made training of the workforce imperative for employers. This was in the interest of the enterprises as it enlarged the margin of decision-making for the workforce, and thus its productivity. Furthermore, it mitigated conflicts.
- *Spatial division of labour*: It developed as a functional divide between industrial structured agglomerations and vast agricultural areas of high productivity. Spatial planning as a specific form of social engineering claimed the division of functions. For example, in France, the spatial division of labour developed with the growth of large specialized areas: control function (Ile de France), manufacturing (Nord-Pas de Calais), and industrial and rural periphery (Lipietz, 1977). On the other hand, certain social standards should be accessible to all. Disadvantages between different territories, such as between mountains and lowlands, were mitigated by subsidizing policies.
- *Territorial relations*: According to the paradigm of equal development, national spatial planning also tried to induce economic growth in the peripheries, increasing the endowment with infrastructure and personal services. A polycentric urban system was consciously maintained and politically supported. The mountain and rural areas developed too; in many cases, this was because of investment in real estate due to suburbanization. The other reason was the state's financial compensation and measures of regional policy. In this period, rural areas caught up and grew faster than cities.
- *Higher education*: An important political project of European welfare states was to equalize educational opportunities, considered largely responsible for social and regional cleavages. In some countries, compensation measures have increased social permeability and helped underprivileged classes gain better access to education, but without jeopardizing the old elites. Paradoxically, in France, the country where Fordist concepts had and still have a high impact, the system of elite schools was never abolished, which went in parallel to the uncontested strong position of Paris. In contrast, in Germany, one result was the foundation of new university sites in third-tier cities (such as Bochum, Siegen, and Constance) and the upgrading of schools of engineering to universities of applied sciences.
- *North–South relations*: The high economic growth of the Fordist era was based, to some extent, on colonial and neocolonial relations where disparities were not questioned. The goal was to create social and territorial homogeneity in the mother countries. Everywhere in Europe, the welfare state model was based on neglecting the North–South issue, or, in other words, on profiting from the development gradient.[4]

Fordism created societal cohesion on a national level by a growth paradigm that favoured the socially disadvantaged classes at the expense of the countries of the Global South. Post-Fordism abandons this nationally restricted cohesion in favour of the globally emerging middle and upper classes, and at the expense of the disadvantaged, also in the wealthy countries. The problem of the uneven distribution of resources in the countries of the Global South has not yet been solved – on the contrary, and it is also increasing again in the Global North.

6.3 The mountains in the Fordist welfare state

During the Fordist period, mountains in the Global North long played the role of disadvantaged territories that had to be supported and subsidized in the interests of the nation state and the whole territory. Mountain areas were the target areas for trickle-down strategies to cope with depopulation. In particular, mitigation of difficult access to mountainous terrain and narrow valleys was at the top of the agenda, resulting in large programmes to construct new infrastructure. Some sectors profited from this – it led to a strong position of the construction industry and technical innovation and progress, such as geological prospection, tunnel engineering, ropeway building, or civil engineering to protect against natural hazards. The automobile was seen as the mountain-specific transport system, and investments in road systems therefore crucial, as already mentioned in Section 4.3.

The Fordist regimes of accumulation achieved enormous productivity gains in the post-war years. These increases favoured the old industrialized regions with their existing infrastructure, workforce, and skills. One of the first policy fields of the European Union was to develop a Common Agricultural Policy (CAP) to raise productivity through the industrialization of agriculture. It was linked with the EU's agricultural commissioner, Sicco Mansholt, a social democrat and farmer (a very unusual combination) from the Netherlands (i.e. from a country with large plain areas that had experienced a great hunger crisis in the 1940s). His policies became notorious: The Mansholt plan stipulated halving the agricultural workforce within ten years by radical modernization. It drew criticism from all sides – farmers, governments, and the early environmental movement – and had to be stopped. But the aim was clear and was finally fulfilled: to have fewer people directly involved in food production by considerably enlarging the surface area per workforce and abandoning less productive areas. This was particularly valid for mountain areas as they are especially costly in terms of labour. But at the same time, agriculture is the only economic activity that is possible for nearly all communities. Especially for the Alps, it was a classic trade-off between the interests of the local population and the interests of the central power. The European Union's agricultural policy at that time, which was aimed at increasing productivity, was tailored to the production conditions of the vast lowlands in the Netherlands, France, and northern Germany, and would have meant the end of mountain farming if it had been fully implemented. Given this situation, it was an advantage for mountain regions that only three of the seven Alpine countries were members of the European Union (Italy, France, and Germany). When Austria joined the European Union in 1995, it was able to influence European policy in the interests of mountain agriculture through alternative and more sustainable forms of agricultural development. Nevertheless, the thinking in quantitative growth and more output was part of all national agricultural policies. In Switzerland, a national marketing organization was established to valorize three kinds of cheese as international brands for mass consumption (Gruyère, Sbrinz, and Emmental) – the complete antithesis to the current trend of mainstreaming branded regional products with an artisan tradition.

The institutionalized spatial planning system in many European countries with a clear zoning in built and unbuilt areas protected the existence of the traditional family farming system for a long time. It can be assumed that this effect was not really noticed by the public. On the other hand, individual farming families profited from an upgraded zoning to building land during the period of increased agglomeration growth.

The workforce discharged as a result of higher agricultural productivity was proposed to find new work in the newly established branch plants nearby. As these branch plants were in consumer goods industries, and did not need skilled workers with much experience or apprenticeship, this was also a strategy to raise productivity in these new industries, which made consumer goods cheaper and more affordable, again raising the quantitative output of these products. Mountain family farmers were able to remain farmers by doing multi-professional work in the factory for the company and 'after hours' on their family farm (Lerjen, 1998). With this understanding of duty, they formed a counter-model to the classical industrial regions with a long-standing syndicalist tradition among the workforce,[5] which made it attractive to make new investments at these new places. An example of this shift is the family-owned enterprise Hoppe, a European specialist for door and window hardware, which had its origins in Velbert near Düsseldorf (the old German industrial cluster of door hardware) and established several sites in South Tyrolean Val Venosta.

The other economic development path went in the direction of tourism, where several business models were applied by local entrepreneurs or introduced by centralized planning strategies. These strategies are comprised of favourable regulations for the support of small-scale accommodation in farmhouses (in Austria), the targeted investment in industrial tourist structures (in France), or the dynamization of old existing tourism structures with popularization of new products, such as snow-sport-based winter tourism for mass consumption (in Switzerland). But topography, landscape, and spatial differences were still valorized only partly and, due to a lack of accessibility, less intensively. The French economic model of resort towns outside villages played a pioneering role by enlarging the industrial dimension onto a new economic sector, as well as vulgarizing it under the label of a 'democratization' of this new commodity. One can say that some large-scale tourist infrastructure to attract an international clientele, typical of the recent post-Fordist era, was already developed in the

1960s. While today private investors try to invest liquid capital profitably in large Alpine resorts, at the time the French state promoted regional development by investing in large tourist infrastructure. This political climate also saw the construction of the panorama road above the Ardèche canyon near the North–South Rhône transit axis, at the time one of the poorest French departments. A similar, although not realized, plan foresaw a similar road project over the Verdon canyon in the Alpes de Haute Provence, 100 km north of Nice.

In general, tourism as a regional strategy become possible through the emergence of new segments of lower middle classes that were able to consume new products. It also developed from the social compromise between employers and employees: in the form of social tourism, where cabins were run by enterprises, syndicates, or family associations, which became affordable only with paid holidays (in France, introduced by the Léon Blum government in 1936).

State investment policies tried to find new functions for mountain regions to mitigate their lagging behind and to use their specific advantages for the benefit of the lowlands. Development of the use of hydropower meant the construction of large dams financed by national private and public capital; existing enterprises of the mining and manufacturing industries were under state ownership or received national subsidies.

With growing social wealth in peripheral regions, retailers and banks opened local branches, ending the last signs of the subsistence economy and opening the door for similar consumption standards nationwide. However, this service offer in peripheral regions did not last. It ended with Fordism (Schuler et al., 2004). Branches were closed due to a combination of a new understanding of territorial services, devaluation of certain services, and changed demand. The closure of local post offices is accelerated by new forms of communication, schools closed due to fewer children and the demand for higher qualifications, and hospitals closed as new treatment techniques favour centralized units. During Fordism, certain characteristics of the old agrarian societies still persisted. This was due to delayed technological innovations in this sector in general (it was not the focus of industrialization in the first half of the 20th century), small-scale properties, and an absolute or relative poverty in the rural areas. Small-scale parcels of land in steep areas could only be cultivated by stone lynchets, requiring an abundant and cheap workforce. Modernization according to the productivity standards of other sectors was not possible. Federal subsidies were introduced to fill the income gap for farming families. Under the Fordist mode of regulation, specific mountain laws were passed to compensate for the disadvantages of living in remote areas under hard conditions of agricultural production. These laws provided direct subsidies to farmers to increase agricultural production for the realization of economies of scale. Grants were also given to industrial enterprises who saw the first signs of European de-industrialization. Municipalities received loans for the amelioration of infrastructure. These primary and secondary legislation acts were the expression of a consensus on trying to achieve equal livelihoods in the mountains as in the lowlands.[6]

Large parts of land were removed from the national commodity circuit because they were in the property of local families that did not sell, so there was a restricted exchange of real estate, and – as most was agricultural land – it was open space and (de facto) publicly accessible. The dynamics of real estate markets were reduced by national regulations. In the end, it was the combined effect of the European agricultural policy, the suburbanization of the 1960s and 1970s, and the heyday of mass tourism that made agricultural ground near agglomerations more and more valuable. It was integrated into the circulation of real estate capital by its transformation into building land (a 'symbiosis' between farmers and the construction business).

In developing countries, however, mountains mainly played a role on a global level for certain categories of food (especially tea and coffee) and for specific raw materials (at the time, mainly metals such as copper or chrome). Their exploitation and commercialization were organized according to colonial and neocolonial terms of trade. Mountain areas were also important as catchment areas for the construction of large dams (e.g. in Africa: Lake Volta, Ghana; Lake Kariba, Zambia/Zimbabwe; Cabora Bassa, Mozambique), mainly for hydropower to feed the extracting industries. Affirmatively it was justified as development aid in the framework of a modernization approach in North–South relations.

In the Fordist context, mountain territories had a stronger function insofar as they still profited from their 19th-century function of structuring the national states. In this nation-building process, they were part of national identities, and under this aspect, seen as a common good, although the usable ground was mainly private property and the territory was run by municipalities with certain autonomy rights. National and federal spatial planning institutions prescribed the rules for transformation, investment, and accessibility. They followed the social model of polycentric or central places development, with equal endowment of infrastructure in the name of mitigating disparities, with the promise of participating in economic prosperity. At the end of the 1970s, it can be said that the mountain areas of the Global North no longer showed any regional disparities in the form of large-scale pockets of poverty. Individual differences in income and wealth of course still exist, but they are not linked with mountains on the whole; they have become small scale and less visible.

6.4 The Fordist crisis

The model of growth and redistribution began to run out of steam at the beginning of the 1970s. Its economic performance declined and newly identified externalities undermined its reputation. The model came under attack from two sides. One was its low rate of accumulation: it could no longer maintain the desired rates of profit. The countries of the Non-Aligned Movement and of the Global South made raw materials more expensive and fought for a reformulation of the terms of trade in general. There was no sign of the start of a new cycle of growth with capital investment to induce new circuits of accumulation. But the model was also undermined as a result of changing preferences. New values and goods which had been blocked under the old regime were claimed by the new post-war generation: the protection of nature, the interests of the countries of Indochina and the Global South, and the personal rights of individuals. Subsequently, the regimes of accumulation were transformed, facilitating the creation of new resources and investment opportunities. This solution included the relocation of mass production to other countries, outsourcing of service activities, reinforcement of the financial business industries with new placement opportunities, and the shutdown of the Keynesian welfare state. It was also expressed by the shift in significance from tangible products to intangible products and the emergence of new services such as professionalized NGOs for landscape protection or other amenities. The change to new production models meant a change from the prevailing equality paradigms to strategies of distinction with more diversity – but also more inequality, which became an accepted part of societal relations.

The Fordist model, with its enormous growth rates, had been possible by the destruction of war. After the Second World War, the countries most destroyed, Germany and Japan, profited the most, as they were forced to rebuild their industries and could implement the highest-performing technologies at that time. They could generate increasing returns on the basis of temporal monopolies, as they were already facing the ruins in reality, before this approach to modernization became popular in the economic literature of the 1980s under the label 'creative destruction' (Schumpeter, 1942). At this time, during the 1950s and 1960s, the other developed countries were not under pressure to modernize. The old colonial powers still profited from their long time access to the basic resources of their colonies, before these became independent around 1960. The US faced disadvantages but could compensate this in part by their geopolitical position. Eastern Europe did not benefit from this situation due to its institutional system – there was never sufficient surplus to make similar redistributions as in the Western part of the world. These post-war shifts in significance already introduced the idea of permanent innovation into the sphere of production, but it was not yet visible as military technology was the driver of new technologies and fuelled the rebuilding of the destroyed countries. It was only in 1967 that the shadow of a small economic crisis began to creep over the dream of eternal non-cyclic growth.

It is generally undisputed that the phase of the mid-1970s marked a caesura that reflects the adaptability of capitalist societies. This adaptability mainly concerns two major points:

1   *Finding a response to the falling rate of profit in the former key sectors of the industrial societies of the Global North.* In the 1970s, the favourable conditions of the industrialized North began to decline and the markets of consumer goods became saturated. The response consisted of a flexibilization of the process of accumulation by an innovation-driven approach and by changing the modes of regulation from solidarity-driven regimes towards self-responsibility and subsidiarity.

2   *Reacting to the loss of legitimacy in society under sociocultural and ecological criteria.* The Fordist compromise was based on the model of eternal economic growth and its redistribution according to predefined welfare standards.

Ecological questions, the interests of ethnic and social minorities, and foreigners excluded from the mainly national welfare systems did not play a role, nor did the interests of the people of the Global South. The accumulation regime and the regulation mode were morally discredited by the academic youth of the upcoming new elites. This resulted in the emergence of an ecological movement, civil society, and professionalized non-governmental organizations (NGOs) as new, important types of stakeholders.

In fact, the consequences taken from the above points served to make the existing growth model more efficient through the optimized allocation of resources, the valorization of new commodities (including sociocultural and biophysical diversity), and redistribution of the produced surplus to the most dynamic social and economic actors. It was also the beginning of a new wave of internationalization and globalization. In the framework of this transformation, the different Fordist regimes – which were nationally diverse in terms of sociocultural and economic preferences, constellations of social practices (various relations between liberal and repressive elements in everyday life) or social systems (e.g. country-specific attitudes towards the organization of health care) – were reduced to a shrunk bundle of different liberal-productivist models where the Anglo-Saxon regime became the reference and the best known. It swept aside other societal models such as 'Rhenish capitalism'[7] in Germany.

In the literature, the change in regime from Fordism to the liberalist-productivist post-Fordism is described at length. The focus is on flexible production structures and individualized salary relations. As the new regimes incorporate new requirements for increased transparency, participation, and environmental issues, they are often provided with the attribute of 'sustainability', and are not a priori rejected, even under critical examination. It is often forgotten that in the majority of cases, the old 'Fordist' activities are subject to divestment and relocation: the success in reducing energy consumption and CO_2 emissions in one place is foiled by new consumption in the emerging countries. The societies and states of the Global North often present rent economies that were criticized at the beginning of the 20th century, from Veblen's 'leisure class' (1899) to Lenin (1917),[8] who both mentioned *avant la lettre* the amenity migration of the upper classes. The heavy, monotonous industrial work is delocalized, especially to other continents outside the triad of Europe, North America, and Japan. This new social and spatial cleavage must be taken into account in the interpretation of post-Fordism, particularly when regarding ecological sustainability and individual emancipation. The succession of liberal-productivist regimes to Fordism in many parts of the world does not imply a deterministic periodicity. In contrast, the two different categories of the regulation approach (accumulation and regulation) should serve as a tool and analytical framework to describe new, differing qualities, thus showing the possibility of social change. In any case, we have to avoid considering this course as linear or teleological.

If we accept this shift of regimes (Table 6.1) as a profound caesura – the fact that accumulation and regulation have been organized differently since the mid-1970s – it is important to concisely describe the differences in different

Table 6.1 Mountains in Fordist and liberal-productivist (post-Fordist) regimes

	Fordist regimes	*Liberal-productivist regimes*
Accumulation and regulation	Nationally restricted organized capitalism with distinct welfare systems	Transnationally organized capitalism with restricted homogenized welfare systems
Territorial function of mountains	Integral development and exploitation in the frame of national cohesion and security	Specialized development with selective exploitation of unique or rare assets
Urban system	Places for central services and public administration; dominating supply function (= use value oriented)	Cities as collective enterprises in global competition; dominating network function (= exchange value oriented)
Economic function of mountains	Export-based economies: commodification of tangible products (agriculture, manufacturing) and tourism	Residential economies: commodification of intangible perceptive goods (landscapes); enclose of public space
Mountain disparities	Measures to reduce pockets of poverty and of less specific value adding	Using disparities to highlight differences as potentials for new commerciable products

social fields and for different types of territories. In this book, this means the production of space in mountains and its relation to the lowlands.

6.5 The shifts between economic sectors as a response to the Fordist crisis

The privatization of the Greek state-owned ETVA bank in 2002 can be interpreted as an example of the changed power relations between manufacturing industries, the state, and business services industries which emerged as the result of changed models of value adding (from manufacturing to the real estate development services) and governance (from state to financial services).

While under state control, the bank was an instrument of the state for industrial and spatial development policies, financing spatial infrastructure such as industrial zones. It provided loans rather than investments. In its public character, it was similar to the German Kreditanstalt für Wiederaufbau (KfW Group). The interests of the bank were territorial development – as a Fordist institution, it acted in the interests of the national state. Greek industrial sites developed quite anarchically, often without the necessary infrastructure against pollution. In general, spatial planning was quite rudimentary. The institutions of spatial planning and industrial policy were interested in reorganizing the industrial zones as standardized locations that matched the demands of planning (e.g. access to motorways) and the environment (e.g. sewage systems).

Post privatization, ETVA's interests have changed. Private banks are rated and ranked according to successful interactions. The logic of industrial policies followed the logic of the financial business sector. Among the developments financed by the new ETVA were the Koropi industrial zone near the airport of Athens and an industrial cluster of maritime suppliers (pumps, maintenance activities, oil control emergency units, etc.), which was relocated from the port of Piraeus to Schisto (10 km inland, with no direct sea access).

The impacts can be summarized as follows (Perlik et al., 2013): In the case of Koropi, the land for the industrial zone at the airport was bought by the bank for inflated prices from the former agricultural owners. The infrastructure consists of electrical connectivity, road access, and sewage systems. As the land was expensive, the loans are expensive too. In 2013, the zone was not yet fully occupied by companies. Meanwhile, infrastructure demands have become much more differentiated. Electricity, road access, and sewage systems are no longer enough to match the needs of enterprises, which increasingly belong to the service sector.

In the case of Schisto, it was not the price of land that made the move expensive for the maritime suppliers. Instead, they complain of high fees imposed by Schisto municipality, which the suppliers say allow Schisto to profit from their difficult situation in general (fewer orders placed, bureaucratic hurdles, strikes). The suppliers say they are cheated by third-party advantages: Other stakeholders take disproportional shares from the value added that they, the suppliers, are generating. They also complain that they are still involved in collective action of the trade unions of the shipbuilding and harbour sector. They no longer see themselves as part of the harbour milieu, but the syndicates do. The former maritime cluster is being broken up: The suppliers are separated from the port and have partly lost their maritime profile, but the two antagonistic parties have not yet found the appropriate social practices for their labour dispute under these changed conditions.

The experiences with the planned industrial estates had the consequence that the unplanned estates remained attractive for the enterprises.

These mechanisms were typical for the change from Fordism to post-Fordism. The Fordist crisis is twofold: reduced rates of return on investment and the loss of confidence in state activities. The importance of the economic sectors shifted from the sectors of the real economy to the financial sector. According to the logic of the financial sector, liquid capital has to be placed in new investments to gain higher returns to resolve problems of over-accumulation of capital. The manufacturing sector serves as a means to justify investments in real estate development. A considerable part of the surplus is transferred from the manufacturing sector to the finance business industries. The sellers of land profited from rising land prices close to enlarging agglomerations. They were able to realize disproportional rents. The national state loses its influence to steer spatial planning and the focus of strategic economic investment.

6.6 Liberal-productivist mountains

(a) Mountains within the new regimes of accumulation

Continuous commodification of public goods

With the regime shift to post-Fordism, topography is systematically valorized under the label of specific and unique landscapes. This is partly due to the transformations within the tourist sector, but mainly to new preferences of consumption towards intangible goods. New offers and new demands fuel the real estate sector in mountain areas. When open land becomes building land, value is added; with construction on its surface, it becomes completely deprived of its character as a public good. In other words, it strengthens its character as a private commodity, accessible only to the holders of property titles. What began with the French industrialization of tourism is becoming the prevailing economic model in post-Fordism: investing in mountain areas for better returns in new emerging markets. Beginning with the hotspots, the mountain areas of the world become integrated into the circuits of commodities and large-scale strategies of accumulation of capital that have to deliver sufficient returns on investment.

These new markets open with the increasing mobility of individuals and the differentiation of new middle classes in the societal strata. As old, rare (tangible) goods of the Fordist era become widespread, and are therefore largely banalized (such as cars, no-brand potatoes, and other goods of mass consumption), new, rare goods emerge whose values are defined by their reputation or symbolic capital. The habitable property of new part-time inhabitants in second homes in the mountains has partly obtained the character of a positional good, due to its properties as a place for leisure, work, meeting family, and professional networking. Regions and landscapes receive the character of a commodity by being valorized with the instruments of branding in the framework of regional marketing. One can observe a shift in the relation between 'use value' and 'exchange value' in favour of the latter. While under Fordism, territorial development and land use were subordinated to the objectives of a cohesive state (which can be interpreted as *use value* in the interest of the society), regions should invent their own products to market for an international clientele (which can be regarded mainly as a form of *exchange value*). Regions become collective actors that should try to realize this commodification of attractive landscapes by attracting new inhabitants, as the number of inhabitants is important for tax income and payments of the federal state (in Germany: *Schlüsselzuweisungen*). This strategy changes the character of value adding from an export-based economy (via manufacturing or tourism) towards a residential economy (via new taxes, fees, retailing, and personal services).

Appropriation of public spaces

We can interpret the commodification of former public goods as processes of appropriation in the sense of Marxian primitive accumulation. Like the construction of buildings on common land in cities, the construction of rural buildings on open areas in the mountains, once used for pastoralism, deprives public users of the open space. One can argue that the exploitation of mountain landscapes with residences also corresponds to original (or primitive) accumulation. In the case of the small-scaled zoning for tourist infrastructure of the Swiss or Austrian type, one could still argue that the exploitation was done in a collective form according to a more or less consensus-based interest by those regional actors who once developed the territory and care for it. But if these communities want to survive they must accept newcomers and give them the same rights to participate. On the other hand, local communities have to pay attention not to be squeezed out by more powerful economic actors who act on international markets.

Nobody knows which options will open in the future. Real estate developers are a new type of investor on the scene: actors that are not linked to the territory. By creating a higher specific added value, they are competing with a sector that was traditionally closely linked to the territory: the tourism branch.

The exclusion from open space (by construction on open land) and the commodification of landscape (by new business models) is not new, but in its dimension has taken on a new quality. It corresponds to the fact that the state abandons certain responsibilities to a lower level (municipalities), and that these municipalities hand over several responsibilities to the private sector. This concept of the commodification of landscapes is based on the principle of subsidiarity. Subsidiarity allows administrations, institutions, and individual actors to develop social relations according to their specific needs, which are analysed, reflected, and negotiated on the local field. But this principle also requires self-responsibility and risk-taking where the protection of the weaker parts of society by solidarity systems becomes reduced. In the ideal case, the relation between subsidiarity and solidarity-based common rules is balanced to guarantee the interests of both the dynamic and the less dynamic parts of society. Our examples of processes in mountains show that the liberal-productivist change favours the dynamic parts. It offers more options, but increases the dependencies of mountain regions on lowland metropolitan areas and deepens the asymmetric relations to them.

From territorial cohesion to entrepreneurial uniqueness

The post-war prosperous Fordist period in Europe enabled national territorial policies to mitigate spatial disparities and to adjust mountain areas to lowland living standards, making them lose their character as integrally abandoned territories. Mountains were given financial support, in order to compensate structural disadvantages and establish equal standards and quality of living. At that time, during the 1950s and '60s, the Alps were a target of investment by light manufacturing industries, who saw setting up branch plants in the mountains as a way of engaging a workforce liberated by raised productivity in the agricultural sector. The local population had ambiguous views on the manufacturing industry in the Alps. In regions where later de-industrialization took place, it was perceived as a killer of the former, once-stable agricultural production systems, causing ongoing fragility. In some parts of the Alps, the manufacturing industry has been resisted until now. But even the manufacturing industries have hit difficulties. In the mountains, they are too far away from engineering competence and from financing (Crevoisier, 1998). When mergers take place, the companies may maintain the manufacturing units (at least for a while), but they economize on the up- and downstream services that are pooled and centralized in the metropolitan areas. They have to fight for the best 'heads' and recruit internationally. Foreign expats with high qualifications want to work in central urban areas, as this is there where they have their professional and private contacts.[9] An example is the watch and microtechnology industry in the Swiss Jura valleys, which is still producing there, but has moved parts or entire sites to the cities nearby (Biel/Bienne, Basel) to find skilled staff.[10] Such regions therefore face a double challenge: de-industrialization makes them lose parts of their production systems, and changed regional policies makes them lose the former guaranteed support of national institutions. They become 'business units' and have to reorient their own productive systems according to the intra-firm competition.

Searching and selling symbolic capital

Mountain regions have understood that the days of relying on subsidies are over: They are now subject to the logic of innovation and offer-oriented production. This has most affected the agricultural sector, which faces a number of challenges. As mountain agriculture cannot be as productive as lowland production, it always had to fight for its legitimation. Now, the aspects of production are called into question by new ecological demands and changed consumer preferences, such as the desire to consume less meat. Subsidies are no longer paid mainly for a high output, but rather for greenkeeping and as an 'insurance function', e.g. for food security. This leads to a completely changed self-perception in a world where production counts much more than reproduction, and it means abandoning the illusion that agricultural production is an independent entrepreneurial activity. This is the paradox: The cutting of subsidies should enable family farmers to be entrepreneurs as in former times, while at the same time the subordinated position towards wholesalers and retailers has increased. Family farmers have to consider the prescriptions and suggestions of external experts on modifications as well as market opportunities. This means, on the one hand, its transformation towards agro-tourist services, artisan activities, or production of luxury food for an elite clientele (slow food movement). This also means divestment and reinvestment by profiting from a transformation of agricultural land to building land.

The tourist sector is in competition with global destinations that are cheaper and more attractive. Tourism takes on a more hybrid character (Bourdeau et al., 2004) as it merges with other events. The stakeholders of small villages invent new forms of tourism such as agro-tourism or – in Italy – the *albergo diffusa*, which offers tourist beds in several houses of a small village, run as a single hotel. The dilemma they face is that such small-scale solutions do not really resolve the problem of a lack of jobs, while larger tourist installations would have a high impact on the environment, destination profile, and targeted clients (Vaccaro and Beltràn, 2009).

We are currently in the heyday of offer-oriented entrepreneurial strategies. Mountain regions are invited to search for new niches of production. This means valorizing intangible values such as nice landscapes, by transforming them into symbolic capital. Urban people demand experiences of 'otherness' in mountainous areas, such as scenic landscapes. They argue in terms of aesthetic beauty in 'wilderness', biodiversity, rare species, and ecosystem services. These demands are not necessarily valid in the long-term, but they have the characteristics of commodities that benefit from a temporary monopoly, and therefore generate high returns (in the sense of Krugman) in positioning 'nature' and 'landscape' as prestigious and emotional commodities for urban people. Constructible areas may be offered as new residences for commuters, multilocal, or retired people, or, in the best scenarios, for new active permanent dwellers (see Section 4.7). Commuters and multilocal people have a strong attachment to the city where they work and spend money, reflecting an urban way of life. But this new clientele also creates a new relationship between the urban agglomeration and their so-called rural hinterlands. They are willing to bring more purchasing power and the demand for new social and personal services into these hinterlands, if there is an offer and if they are welcomed by the permanent population. This clientele is believed to be – under certain conditions – very loyal to the hosting regions: If they can be persuaded to stay for longer, their hosting region will gain supporters.

Changed model of value adding from export-based to residential economies

With the change from agricultural, manufacturing, or tourist production clusters to specialized dwelling, the regime of accumulation in mountain areas turns from an export-based model to a residential economy (Davezies and Talandier, 2014; Segessemann, 2016; Segessemann and Crevoisier, 2015). This change is more than a simple change in economic definition. It entails the abandoning of production systems and the shift to a rent economy, where regional wealth depends on the prosperity of individuals who earn their money elsewhere. This can create problems of cohabitation between the locals and the newcomers, especially as the local norms and values depend strongly on manual work and a clear idea of the direction of one's life ('life plan'). The change in the economic model may create an increased dependence on external revenues, which may also be the source of mutual misunderstandings.

Selective use of territorial capital

As most mountain territories did not develop their own, strong, export-based metropolitan economies, they are dependent on external support. However, the regime shift meant a reduction in aid allocated by national governments to mountain areas. New policies are combined with demands on mountain areas to develop their own regional entrepreneurship. Mountain regions respond to this by restructuring their offers of leisure and dwelling and addressing it to an international clientele, focusing on selling emotions, a good reputation, and landscapes. This means they are forced to abandon traditional forms of activities even if they would have liked to pursue them, and they probably have to commercialize their cultural practices. The transformation concerns mainly the resort towns at high altitudes and the commuter villages at the borders to the lowlands. These municipalities risk an overuse of their territorial capital, and they also risk missing out on developing alternatives that could mitigate the cluster risks. The medium altitudes in between have partly maintained the structures of the old economy. These parts are not attractive from the point of view of amenities, as they do not have spectacular views, enough sun, or enough snow in winter. They are too far away to be integrated into the peri-urban fringe. Their economy remains fragile.

Lowland–mountain linkages

The urban majority expects services from the mountain regions and their population. These services differ from those of the past. With the emergence of global markets, the economic functions have been narrowed to complementary products that are unavailable elsewhere (e.g. calmness, spectacular views, non-polluted water, raw materials). On the one hand, this is a restriction. But on the other, it offers new potentials that are sometimes seen as an inexhaustible source of innovation strategies (such as in the past, Fourastié's optimism on the potential of the services industries, 1949). It is useful to maintain a certain scepticism in this respect. This model is more than ever based on the hope of a productivist growth model elsewhere; it applies the production of emotions for better selling and uses old folkloristic clichés as marketing strategies. This is part of the business services industry that is metropolitan based and cannot be controlled by mountain people. In a sociological understanding, this can no longer be named rural. The rural aspects remain (more or less) in the morphology of the village and the persisting perception of former ways of life. But the socio-economic functions transform, as the municipalities become integrated into an extended agglomeration. Under aspects of increasing wealth and new services, this development is mainly positive. This new relationship causes new dependencies and defines a new functional hierarchy that has to be renegotiated.

(b) Mountains within the new modes of regulation

New practices of inclusion and exclusion

The loss of traditional value chains and the turn to residential economies makes it necessary to change strategies away from creating jobs to attracting inhabitants, to be able to maintain and enlarge a sufficient local service offer. But this raises the questions of who will come and how to deal with new people who practise other ways of life, have other preferences (in the case of the urban middle classes), or do not really come by choice (in the case of a temporary workforce for tourism). Many of the case studies cited in this book on amenity migration and multilocality stress the point that many villages still exist only because they were repopulated by new inhabitants, even if these are only part-time residents. One problem is that local people fear being overwhelmed by people who do not share their habits. As mountain villages do not offer the anonymity of a city, there are fewer possibilities or alternatives for individual 'life plans' and social interaction, and a greater risk of misunderstandings or conflicts. The topic of inclusion and exclusion becomes a crucial question for both sides, the autochthonal people as well as the newcomers, and a combination of mutual ignorance, the number of new people, and the pace of change may inhibit a common understanding. Experience shows that foreigners are well accepted when local people have got to know them better.[11] But efforts by newcomers in being accepted or locals in accepting them may end up failing.

Considering these aspects, the new modes of regulation make it more complicated for mountain regions: In the past, they had to adapt to the needs of external clients for specific products. Now, the autochthonal population in mountain villages is challenged to find a way between adapting (according the new liberal-productivist offer orientation) and maintaining parts of their endogenous value system. They have to work hard to attract new inhabitants to renew their communities, and they have to adjust to a new balance of inclusion and exclusion. This mainly concerns appreciation in everyday life, but also includes aspects of political citizenship and ownership of the large land properties of mountain communities, which is, in many countries, a privilege only of the old families of the founders of the village. The question of inclusion or exclusion is therefore a question of the mode of regulation: Who may participate in the territorial capital that reaches from simple mutual acceptance to property rights on traditional club goods (artificially scarce goods) such as the wood from the public forest?

A new repartition of national resources

The Fordist crisis began to affect the peripheries when it became clear that an equal growth strategy such as in large cities would have negative ecological impacts, and that there is no such thing as a free lunch in the use of resources (which corresponds to Bourdieu's concept of agonism, or the metaphor of the zero-sum game). In this sense, mountain regions have been affected from two sides: The liberal-productivist shift provoked an intense debate about the allocation of classic investments such as infrastructure, social services, public transport, and subsidies to less densely populated parts of the territory, according to a simple investment per capita calculation. And, on the other hand, the delayed methods of production in mountains, the specificities of the cultural landscapes, and the awareness of the value of spatial differences became a new resource in itself, and provoked a trade-off against the objectives of equal living standards.

The ensuing transformation had two negative consequences for the mountains. First, it gave a push in the direction of centralization and concentration of economic functions, culture, and demography in weakening the territorial capital of the mountain regions. Second, it turned the public opinion of the urban majority from its former position of support for mountain people towards a position of alienation. There are certainly many reasons for this alienation. A bit shortened, we can attribute it to a combination of elitist habitus, economic efficiency thinking, and a purist ecological view.

From 'Alpinophilia' to 'Alpinophobia': a new form of the spatial cleavage between highlands and lowlands

With the new liberal-productivist regimes, the mountain regions lost their influence and shaping power. In this relationship between centre and periphery the metropolis is the more powerful, with larger interests at the global level and the power to impose its interests on its hinterlands. But the hinterlands have the power to irritate, and also to betray the city – as in cases involving bilateral treaties, zoning plans, the research profile of a publicly financed university, or public transport policies. It is like in ancient Roman times: the central power in Rome levied taxes, tolls, and tributes on the suppressed tribes, who committed petty crimes when trying to betray the occupying power. In Switzerland, the practice by sub- and peri-urban municipalities to attract wealthy inhabitants by keeping their taxes low – harshly criticized by the mayor of Lausanne in the 1990s – started a national debate on the 'exploited city'. What began as an intra-agglomeration conflict was extended to the whole territory, and had impacts especially on the mountain peripheries. It was the turning point where many decision-makers abandoned their former self-perception of Switzerland as an Alpine country. At the end, the former, at times euphoric, solidarity with the rural areas turned into a bashing of the whole periphery, with a debate about the best allocation of financial resources and the best use of space (Diener et al., 2006; Eisinger and Schneider, 2003). This is a debate in which the urban majority has the shaping power: the power over names, wording, and the definition of sustainability.

With the regime shift, the differing interests form a new territorial cleavage or reinforce the existing one. The struggle to obtain a share in the distribution of resources and to influence the shaping of power takes on a new quality. Both sides – metropolitan areas and mountain regions – develop and reinforce regional egoisms and compete over questions of identity. The conservative turn in the mountain regions, combined with the increased significance of the dynamic urban habitus, eroded the solidarity between the urban centres and the rural-looking peripheries. Urban people argue with a demand for better environmental protection. Mountain people claim their right to decide on their own – with the argument of long existing tacit knowledge in the mountains. In Switzerland and France, this cultural conflict is fought over the right to shoot remigrating wolves. The right to construct houses for second homes in oversized dwelling zones is another topic contested by the urban majority. Vice versa, the Alpine Convention is often rejected by the locals, as they see only restrictions and external domination by 'Brussels'.

Urban people claim the public interest in mountains with the argument that they are better informed about the ecological risks. They argue in the interest of world heritage for humankind, involving NGOs and political institutions. At the same time, a commodification and valorization took hold of the very last mountain peak.[12] There we see an opposing trend. On the basis of higher productivity due to the privatization of public goods, new urban middle classes have the necessary resources to be occupied in environmental issues as a hobby or philanthropic activity (or to donate the NGOs as modern sale of indulgences). Mostly, it is forgotten that this prosperity is generated by productive activities all over the world, while steering activities are concentrated in the metropolitan headquarters outside the mountains. The mechanisms follow the principle of large transnational companies in generating a high rate of value added, which can then be given – by the creation of a foundation – to the public as a gift. The idea of political responsibility and democratic institutions is therefore elegantly sidestepped and abandoned.

External people are not familiar with local practices and the locals may not be aware of the latest scientific research on biodiversity. The mountain dwellers do not accept that they alone should have to implement stringent environmental protection measures while the global node economies do not follow these principles – but at the same time the two sides fail to see that they are both also profiting from these global interdependencies. The main problem with the new modes of regulation, insofar as they concern mountains, therefore seems to be the emergence of a new cleavage between the metropolitan lowlands and the rural-looking mountains, which is deliberately fuelled by identity-driven isolationism or nationalism. It foils the efforts of transnational social integration, as well as transnational regional economic cooperation, which would be necessary to cope with a globalized world. But it also foils the future options of the young generation remaining in the mountains.

Notes

1 For this, I refer to the comprehensive ethnologic fieldworks of Claudia Roth in Bobo-Dioulasso, Burkina Faso on intergenerational relations (Roth, 2010, 2014, 2018).

2 At least two prominent members of the Swiss government of the 2000s made their fortune as entrepreneurs, with close business activities with apartheid South Africa, which was prohibited according to several United Nations resolutions from the 1960s.

3 These are also referred to as urbanization economies of a Jacobsian type. The epigone of Jane Jacobs (1969) is Richard Florida (2002), with his redefinition of Jacobs' citizenship to a valorizable 'creative class'.

4 For example, in the 1960s, the Swedish ASEA company (today the Zurich-based transnational ABB) participated in the construction of the large dam of Cabora-Bassa in the Portuguese colony of Mozambique. Furthermore, nearly all Western countries maintained good economic relations with South Africa during the period of apartheid – despite decisions by the UN stipulating the contrary – to maintain access to noble metals and as an important export market.

5 This picture has to be differentiated according to different countries and different periods of industrialization. For example, some French Alpine valleys had an early and strong

manufacturing industry, and there was also a strong syndicalist movement among agricultural workers in less densely populated rural areas like the Dordogne and the Limousin.

6 We mention here as examples the Swiss LIM Law and the Italian Legge Regionali. An overview of worldwide mountain legislation is given in a report based on the Mountain Forum's Electronic Conference on Mountain Policy and Law in 1997 (Lynch and Maggio, 2001).

7 Denomination for the social market economy, the German version among the Fordist regimes (Albert, 1991).

8 In *Imperialism, the Highest Stage of Capitalism*, Chapter 8. Lenin bases his analysis in large parts on the critique of rentier capitalism expressed by the British economist John Atkinson Hobson:

> The greater part of Western Europe might then assume the appearance and character already exhibited by tracts of country in the South of England, in the Riviera and in the tourist-ridden or residential parts of Italy and Switzerland, little clusters of wealthy aristocrats drawing dividends and pensions from the Far East, with a somewhat larger group of professional retainers and tradesmen and a larger body of personal servants and workers in the transport trade and in the final stages of production of the more perishable goods; all the main arterial industries would have disappeared, the staple foods and manufactures flowing in as tribute from Asia and Africa.
> (Hobson, 2011/1902: 335)

9 See Diener et al. (2006). 'English in professional life' was one of the indicators to demarcate urban Switzerland from the remaining few rural areas.

10 The Swiss Jura has preserved up until now, and after several crises, its watch and microtechnical industry. But during the consolidation process, merged enterprises have withdrawn the specialized services and given the orders to companies outside the Jura region, which reduced the diversity of the cluster (interview, Olivier Crevoisier, Université de Neuchâtel). In contrast, the neighbouring Basel metropolitan region not only hosts the headquarters of several transnational pharmaceutical and biotechnology companies, but also provides all the specialized services for them.

11 In Switzerland, examples of immigration over a long period, from 1956 (Hungarian refugees), 1968 (Czechoslovakian), 1973 (Chilean) to 1991 (shelter for Kurds at a place of pilgrimage in Central Switzerland) and later (Tamils), show that a better (positive) knowledge and a minimum of shared values can raise large and even unexpected movements of civic engagement. For a detailed history of Swiss migration (in- and out-migration) see Holenstein et al. (2018).

12 For many environmental NGOs, the Virgental in East Tyrol/Austria was for many years the spearhead of sustainable development because the local population rejected modern tourist infrastructure and insisted on traditional ways of life. In the end, they sold the name of their local mountain, the nearly 2,800-metre-high 'Mullwitzkogel', to their main sponsor, an industrial meat company in Vienna, which now calls it 'Peak of Wiesbauer' (according to the name of the brand). One can see this as an example that an overload of regionalist identity turns identity into its opposite, abandoning all regional dignity in one go.

7 The new spatial disparities

After having developed the new picture of mountain areas according to the logic of different regimes of accumulation and modes of regulation, I will now try to show the pattern of regions under the liberal-productivist paradigm. I take the functional division of labour between metropolitan regions and mountain regions as a starting point, and construct two types of regions that appear as collective entrepreneurial actors on the global market of commodity exchange and placement of capital. At the end this chapter, I try to give an answer to the hypotheses established at the beginning of the book in Section 3.7.

7.1 A new pattern of disparities

(a) New homogeneities

The Fordist model claimed homogeneity in a national context. In post-Fordism, heterogeneity has become the new paradigm. At first sight, this contradicts the frequent critique that the globalized world would become homogeneous, rootless, and atopical. Neither one nor the other is true. It depends on the scale we look at. And there we have the paradox that the big picture gives us the impression of a world of high diversity, while on the small scale we see homogeneous segments.

In the business sphere, common interests are now based on a cooperation that is more flexible than before ('weak ties') and is limited in duration ('projects'). In territorial issues, regions cooperate with counterparts of a similar economic structure, similar prosperity, and similar demographic structure – and at the same time they compete with them. Metropolitan regions together define their strategic interests, which they defend against other regions at a European or global level (such as the cooperation between the four wealthiest regions, Baden-Württemberg, Rhône-Alpes, Catalonia, and Lombardy). Of course, we must keep in mind that it is the organizational and financial power of the most influential companies of the (export-based) economy that gives the necessary background for the entrepreneurial appearance of metropolitan regions.

Nevertheless, each private entity and each public jurisdiction tries to develop unique selling propositions according to the Krugman argumentation (avoiding direct competition by measurable comparative disadvantages).[1] We observe the emergence of homogeneous regions according to productive functions such as steering (in headquarters) and manufacturing (in specialized peripheries) – and of reproduction (in other specialized peripheries) with high export-based value adding, on the one hand, and consumptive residential economies, on the other. But unlike the past, these functional differences do not reveal large-scale differences that would become visible in GDP, as incomes from freelancing, pensions, and remittances also fuel those regions with few jobs. At the European level, this crystallizes into the following types of space with a certain homogeneity. These types are not developed empirically and may be discussed. The national and regional capitals of these territories develop certain common strengths that define their negotiating power in a new system of hierarchies. They have some similarities to the large regions of the Fordist period, but they differ in scale and in their transnational character:[2]

- The 'Pentagon' of Europe's most performing metropolitan areas.[3]
- Spain and Southern Europe as Europe's orchard.
- Central and Eastern Europe as a large manufacturing cluster.
- Eastern European countries as bulk suppliers for energy.
- The historic metropolitan city centres as amenity destinations for tourism based on low-cost air traffic.
- Rural-looking recreation territories based on the commodification of landscapes.
- The mountains as a menagerie for an impression of the 'wild', with rare species and animals.

These new functional entities (i.e. their actors and institutions) develop their own logic, norms, value systems, and strategies to pursue their interests. Those parts of society that are not part of such core competencies lose economic and societal influence. From the global point of view, these new entities offer better visibility and attract foreign capital as direct investment. Under the aspect of increasing intra-national hierarchies and social cleavages, we can also interpret this as a weakening of territorial cohesion.

(b) Equal, equivalent, unequal

In the conflict of goals between productivity growth and regional cohesion, the old Fordist virtues of territorial equality have had their day. They have been replaced by the principle of equivalence, with greater diversity, functional specialization, and complementarity between the different territories. It is a promise that the disadvantages of less centrality will be offset by a higher quality of life in sparsely populated areas without sacrificing acquired standards of living such as life expectancy, health, and education. In reality, the promises are difficult to keep because these standards are knowledge dependent, and when parts of a territory become peripheral, it is mainly because of a lack of knowledge, which in turn is tied to inhabitants. Functional specialization is based on a change in the accumulation regime that now gives absolute priority to continuous innovation; in the case of mountain regions, this is the development of new products linked to landscape and regional food. If successful, these regions can renew their economies. If not, it is discussed whether even the equivalence goal can be safeguarded, e.g. in Eastern Germany. The regions are thus free in a dual sense: They are free to innovate according to the creativity and interests of their local actors, and they are free of reinsurance by the nation state. This change in the mode of regulation (combined with the primacy of innovation in the accumulation regime) urges the peripheral regions to gear their development strategies to the needs of global markets, although they often do not have the necessary knowledge to do so. The associated territorial restructuring means an increase in the hierarchies between mountain areas and lowlands, comparable to the restructuring of large companies.

(c) The double freedom: subsidiarity and self-responsibility

Regional struggles against the interests of national states' decision-making and planning, on the one hand, and the recommendations of economic experts in favour of increased innovation, on the other, have led to a shift in the territorial responsibility from the national to the regional level, following the arguments of subsidiarity.

We now see that this was advantageous for those that were already strong. A state that opposes such developments finds itself under pressure by regional nationalist movements or strong regional governments. Italy was the first example, with the separatists of Lega Nord (the demand for an independent 'Padania' state), but also other economically powerful jurisdictions such as Catalonia, is trying to rid itself of the poorer parts of a nation. In general, the metropolitan regions use more subtle practices through the use of financial power, as in Bavaria, Baden-Württemberg, or Zurich. Such regions can take advantage of the whole range of functional landscapes to provide the benefits of a metropolis. This includes primarily the areas of recreation and rest, segregated luxury residential areas for a new clientele, accommodation for highly qualified migrants, cultural venues, or ecological compensation areas as a green belt around the city (e.g. Frankfurt, Geneva, Toronto). However, they also contain industrial areas relocated from the city centre to the urban periphery, specialized agriculture (often organic, including urban gardening) for urban needs, and residential peri-urban sprawl due to a lack of affordable living space. Thus, the metropolitan areas are not restricted to the dense classic 'urban' area, but they also include – and this is a new trend – functionally the whole range of spatial and economic structures.

In this way, very few areas can withstand the thrust of metropolization. Those that do often have a mountain topography and are poorly accessible. Often, they are target regions for national or European support (e.g. through structural funds). But to be eligible, they also have to prove a certain capacity for innovation and adaption to metropolitan needs. If this is not the case, they are labelled 'of poor potential' and abandoned in national strategies.

(d) Diverse metropolises: the functional integration of the rural

The described processes generate a new pattern of disparities. At the beginning of the post-war period, we saw 'France and the French desert' (Gravier, 1947; Lipietz, 1977). At the end of Fordism, the peripheries had caught up, making interregional disparities less visible by generating small-scale intra-regional disparities (for Switzerland: Schuler et al., 2004; for the Alps: Bätzing et al., 1996). Today, under the liberal-productivist regimes, the metropolitan regions have grown, often overlapping in the lowlands. In the mountains, the interstices between the peri-Alpine metropolitan areas and the resort towns at high altitudes – the narrow lateral valleys at medium altitudes – develop weakly. Their former advantage (small-scale hydropower for modest industrialization) has gone, and there is not enough sun to attract people. Often, they are skipped over by public transport.[4] The urban position often justifies the abandonment to make a new use of such 'Alpine fallows' by enabling other activities (Diener et al., 2006). The reasoning oscillates between economic efficiency, ecological efficiency, and cultural superiority thinking. Of course, the concerned regions protest loudly and qualify these statements as paternalistic.

The power of the cities is a new development. In the 1980s, the cities, and especially their central areas, were in decline as they accumulated the unintended effects and unsolved problems of the Fordist growth regimes. It was the time when Alexander Mitscherlich (1965) spoke about 'the inhospitality of our cities' and René Frey (1981) developed the concept of the impoverished A-cities. An exodus to the suburbs and the peri-urban areas was the main tendency. This tendency was largely reversed in the 1990s: now, nearly everyone wants to live in the central neighbourhoods, which have undergone or are undergoing gentrification, a process that began in global cities such as London or Paris and which is reinforced by individual or institutional placement strategies, the rise of a new type of tertiary business sector, and the demand for second homes. Meanwhile, these processes are also taking place in second-tier cities. The gentrification process has reached the suburban municipalities, and the poor part of the city population is squeezed out to the outer fringes. The former poor A-cities are now the Triple-A cities, and the real winners of the liberal-productivist turn.

We see the following territorial cleavages arising. At the global level, we have the international competition between large metropolitan areas for dominance in the most centralized economic and steering functions. At the national levels, we see conflicts of interest between the metropolitan city centre areas and their suburban fringes regarding tax regimes, public transport, and financing of metropolitan public services and cultural offers. Finally, we have conflicts between the metropolitan areas and their peripheral hinterlands in terms of political and economic priorities and investments and compensation, which are steeped in sociocultural differences, misunderstandings, and controversies (e.g. in ecological questions). While the differences of interest between city and the suburbs have a long tradition, the global competition between metropolitan regions and the deepened gap between them and the hinterlands are a new phenomenon, and linked with the liberal-productivist turn.

7.2 Triple-A as key qualities for the metropolises

Below, I discuss the thesis of the new inequalities in terms of the regional characteristics that were considered key for cities and regions in the regional competition of the liberal-productivist era. These characteristics are traditional tangible assets (e.g. excellent infrastructure or high tax incomes by a performing economy), as well as intangible assets (e.g. knowledge or global networks and alliances). Tangible and intangible assets enable a jurisdiction to influence the processes of value adding and the administration of wealth, and to create an environment of elevated living conditions. They are comprised of three essential factors:

1   The ability of a global or second-tier city to manage its metropolitan area and to respond proactively to changes or uncertainties (economic, social, and political) with its strategic capacity, to avoid loss of regional prosperity or significance ('adaptability').
2   The ability of a global or second-tier city to continuously renew the link with its population and stakeholders under conditions of increased mobility (socially and spatially), attracting new inhabitants (especially highly qualified ones) and integrating them such that they develop loyalty towards the territory in a long-term perspective ('attractivity').
3   The ability of a global or second-tier city to mobilize existing shaping power to continuously enhance its reputation and external visibility under the conditions of an increased territorial competition and concentration of economic functions ('authority').

These three factors include an economic component, which highlights the resource feature and denotes a regional accumulation regime (e.g. how regional knowledge is generated), and a political component, which addresses a mode of regulation (e.g. the ability to integrate migrants from different cultures and in mixed social constellations).

These three key points are outlined below. I try to provide examples of trajectories, both positive and negative.

(a) Adaptability

With the development of automotive technologies, the centre of gravity shifted towards the lowlands and the urban pattern became more centralized. Industrialization caused new cities to spring up near manufacturing sites, which attracted migrants. Already during this period, the historic cities were able to adapt to and participate in the economic prosperity of industrialization. The knowledge accumulated in medieval towns and the latent innovative power of their populations were so strong that they were able to continuously adapt to fundamental changes during phases of upheaval. The power of the guilds was broken and the city walls were demolished. During the course of industrialization, the cities expanded into their hinterland and the patricians began to invest in the then new economies.

But industrialization had also its roots in rural and mountain areas, and during the 20th century these grew to industrial clusters. In some small towns, the enterprises promoted the foundation of vocational training centres and universities of applied sciences, and sometimes such cities were even able to finance a theatre, as in La-Chaux-de-Fonds in the Swiss Jura. In the post-war period of social compromise – during the years of the economic miracle – they were politically supported and grew. They seemed to become equal with the large historic cities. Then, the Fordist crisis brought a change in paradigm and a decade of industrial divestment. The small and medium-sized cities lost not only their source of revenue (taxes and jobs), but also – and this was much worse for them – many of their active stakeholders. It became clear that they did not have sufficient knowledge to adapt to the new situation of having to act entrepreneurially.

On the other hand, the large historical city centre areas – which had suffered from degraded housing and the bad image of polluting industries during the Fordist period – were able to strengthen their tertiary sector, as a range of examples show.

- One example is the development of Frankfurt. Being the loser in the decision about Germany's post-war capital, it nevertheless gained central institutions of the finance industry. At the same time, it remained home to a large segment of modest inhabitants and manufacturing sector jobs, and traditionally had a social democratic municipal government. The strategies turned, when in 1977 the government changed and relaunched the city as a hotspot of urban life – with high culture, museums, and the tacky reconstruction of historic buildings lost during the war. Afterwards, a green government introduced the paradigmatic concept of a green belt around the city (Keil and Lieser, 1992), and, nearly in parallel, the chemical cluster imploded by accepting a merger, making way for some small-scale industries. We can see this constellation as emblematic of post-Fordist change. With metropolitan de-industrialization and the invention of green spaces, the city turned the last disadvantage it had compared to rural areas (environmental degradation) to a new strategic advantage: regaining open space and environmental qualities, and creating a new social dynamism that became attractive for socially mobile people.
- Other cities followed, such as Glasgow and Bilbao. They did this in the same way, with huge investments into culture to become a global player. Bilbao, an industrial town in full transformation, took reputed architecture

for a branch of the Guggenheim Museum. It became successful, although the architecture of Frank Gehry at that time was already a remake of his established style. For a mass public, the architecture was spectacular. It put the city into the headlines of lifestyle magazines and launched it to become a destination of urban tourism served by low-cost carriers. It was the precursor to copying 'best practices' from other regions by creating 'landmarks' and symbolic 'lighthouses', a process which became known as 'Bilbaoization'.

- The French city of Metz tried to replicate that success with a branch of the Centre Pompidou. The financial commitment of the long-established Wendel family (who had dominated the mining region of Lorraine for decades) was expected to be a very important sign for the renaissance of the Lorraine region.[5]
- Barcelona (1992) and Turin (2006) were able to land the Olympic Games and transform their economies from industrial or company towns into second-tier metropolitan areas.
- Historically, Basel gained attention first. In 1431, its powerful citizens were able to attract an 18-year-long international event, the Catholic Council, which became the cradle of a first economic cluster: the artisans of paper, writing, and printing. With industrialization, it became a company town in the late 19th century. On the basis of accumulated wealth, the urban elites transformed the industrial pattern from an early textile industry to chemistry, evolving from bulk production to chemical specialities, and then on to pharmaceuticals and biotechnological products, with a shift from production to research and development. This caused spillovers, with the emergence of a cultural cluster in fine arts, electronic music, design, and architecture.

The examples provide three lessons. First, the trajectory of the past influences the capacity to adapt. Future development can be derived from the past or the trajectory (i.e. the territorial capital). Second, the prevailing paradigm of governance (i.e. the mode of regulation) has an overlapping range of possible options, which means that other trajectories are always thinkable. Third, in strong cities, divestments of certain production lines and products do not result in de-territorialization, but in a reinforcement, a re-territorialization (Zeller, 2001; Zeller and Messerli, 2010).

The large cities were able to reappear at the top of centrality, after the equalizing period of Fordism when their old economic activities were relocated. They have developed a diversity of production systems where each is stable enough to buffer against shocks and to have enough adaptability to make partial divestments and reinvestments into other economic sectors. This process is not guaranteed forever, and each city or metropolitan region has its own specific constellations. It always depends on the capacity to keep loyalty and confidence at the location. The constellation of the stakeholders with their formal and informal rules and their social and economic interactions (the *untradeable interdependencies* of Michael Storper) play a fundamental role in creating this loyalty. In the ideal case, the intra-regional diffusion of knowledge is facilitated, while, on the other hand, foreign competitors cannot draw too much knowledge out of the region to their home base.

The liberal-productivist regimes favour competition between territories and justify it with arguments of subsidiarity and municipal autonomy. Rural areas are encouraged to follow this strategy and sometimes take it too literally, making them lose the solidarity of the urban majority, as the above-mentioned example of the Swiss canton of Obwald shows (Section 4.8). By attracting rich migrants to settle there, the canton was able to clean up its treasury, but it will not necessarily gain active citizens. Moreover, the canton confirmed with this aggressive attempt the existing complaints against regional egoism expressed by many urban people.[6] One can suppose that such regions often suffer from lock-in phenomena as they have a reduced base of stakeholders, and therefore a limited pool of knowledge. These constellations and restrictions make it difficult for them to adapt at a national as well as an international stage.

Major cities do not have these problems. Here, the potential of active stakeholders and profitable enterprises is broader and more diverse – and local conflicts can play a constructive role, which is a paradox only at first sight. They may speak with different voices, but they find ways to settle internal disputes, and find compromises and consensus. This allows them to become visible at a larger scale, and heard at a national and international level.

(b) Attractiveness

If a city has established and safeguarded a good reputation, demographic and economic development is met with positive feedback by ever more people.[7] Metropolitan city centre areas absorb the dynamic people. 'Attractiveness' describes the ability of a city or region to convince new people to come and settle there, and to retain them as loyal stakeholders. Attractiveness can be expressed in many ways, and generally this variety of opportunities plays a major role in the decisions of individuals and business sectors. Firstly, it is a large permeable labour market that facilitates the transactions of seeking and finding jobs and skills to cope with the uncertainties of daily life. However, this does not mean that the decision process in favour of the metropolis is made through a rational choice evaluation. On the contrary, it is rather the expectation about the future potential of a certain location, based on perception and reputation (i.e. symbolic capital that is not objectifiable). Closely linked with these perceptions are the expectations about the density of existing and potential social face-to-face networks for individuals and families, and the opportunities for the integration of newcomers, especially foreigners and minorities. Secondly, there is the full range of cultural and recreational benefits. This does not only mean well-known commercial offers of 'high culture', but also the ability of newcomers to insert their own culture and create new forms of it. It includes all the offers with no direct or immediate profit, even if parts of it become valorized later.

Attractiveness, therefore, is of particular importance. This is because of the changed position of cities under liberal-productivist conditions. As mentioned above, under Fordist conditions cities and regions were part of an integrated national and regional urban system, and as such, focused on territorial governance in the national framework. But global competition means that these restrictions are dropped. Cities receive a 'double' liberty (Perlik, 2001): They can develop a dynamic economy (with advanced economic sectors), but they also run the risk of failing, without the national solidarity and financial backing of the past. The only regions generally excluded from these risks are national capitals, which host the political clusters of national states.

- In France, the new capability to attract investments and inhabitants after the regime shift had a decentralizing effect. The old centralist system was one of the cornerstones of the equalizing Fordist system – under the untouched superiority of Paris. In recent years, the old French regional capitals such as Lyon, Marseille, Lille, and Nantes gained in significance by taking on new political and economic functions (partly in the framework of an explicit national decentralization policy where national institutions had to move), which also made them attractive for new inhabitants.
- In Germany, the same process had a centralizing effect, reflected in the new global strategies for the metropolitan areas, which include a new form of competition between them. The large cities are no longer the central places for their hinterlands. Frankfurt and Munich struggle to be the top German locations for the business services industries. The city of Hamburg tried (unsuccessfully) to poach the headquarters of the national German railways from Berlin, by promising to sell them their commuter railway system.
- In Switzerland, the city and canton of Zurich were equipped with strategic transport infrastructure first, as they were able to pre-finance it. They were refunded but had to pay the mortgage themselves: The Swiss Confederation thus saved money by not having to pay interest. This practice followed the principles of public–private partnership. Realizing an investment earlier means reaping its benefits earlier. In this case, the infrastructural advantage led to an intensification of intra-Swiss metropolitan competition and to Zurich becoming the undisputed leader of the city hierarchy.

It becomes crucial for the development of a region to safeguard and enlarge the critical mass of economic clusters, and of a wealthy population (with demands for sophisticated products), which helps to maintain the loyal support of the majority of active stakeholders. Active stakeholders – which also include the most severe critics – claim to want to participate in developing the territorial capital of a region.

Attractiveness also means the capacity of the local economy to receive credits and mortgages with good conditions. Peripheral regions are concerned with two aspects. First, they are too far away from the financial centres and their professional networks (Crevoisier, 1998); furthermore, the number of local bank representatives have been reduced and the remaining bank offices have less authority to decide than before. Second, credits cost more in the periphery, as the risk is evaluated as being higher. As seen above, the major banks have established a credit rating system that differentiates between regional potentials according to defined indicators, i.e. criteria such as classification as an urban area, positive demographic development, or a high level of tertiary education of the population. Peripheral regions receive a 'handicap' as in golf, in the form of a multiplier on the rates of interest.

This search for the best spot is nothing new. It applies not only to the location of businesses but also to homes. In the past, limited mobility meant that this search was limited to a narrow radius and was only valid for the power elite. Today, new technologies and lower transaction costs make it easy to change residence over long distances. The most important change, however, is that the residential area today is generally decisive for success: not just for a few but for a growing social class in the service sector. The central residential area becomes important for all those who need communication and face-to-face contacts for their career, even in their 'free time'. Thus, the centrality of the city is increasing and this search for centrality is no longer restricted to the companies but now also applies to the choice of residence of individuals. Management and staff of new small enterprises in the business services industry have their work and life in city centre areas. On the one hand, this is a reappropriation of the old patrician places, and on the other, a new appropriation of poor neighbourhoods by the so-called creative class. The only novelty of the concept of 'creative class' is that now, not only its established executive members count as 'creatives', but also the young blood: students, trainees, and certain specialists, as well as job-seeking people of a sector that is seen as innovative. It is now rather the sector that counts, and not only the leading staff (as was exemplified in European Rotary club hierarchies).

In this position, urban and metropolitan areas generally have an advantage because they already have, by definition, a higher density of interaction and offer many arguments to motivate highly and low-qualified 'creative' people, and – above all – to make them stay. The critical mass of agglomeration advantages generates economies of scale and scope that are perceived externally as having an excellent reputation and that induce a self-amplifying mechanism. In this process of individual accumulation of symbolic capital of having a job and a flat in the metropolis, it does not matter anymore that the most important locations (e.g. Los Angeles and Tokyo) are the places most exposed to earthquakes and tsunamis. This clearly disproves geo-deterministic arguments, without, however, completely eliminating biophysical dependencies.

We have already shown that in the context of European de-industrialization, personnel qualification structures are changing, and therefore so are those of urban populations. This is not a problem for cities with old urban traditions, which have transformed into metropolitan areas. They can maintain their position by taking over a new role, the role of a decision-making centre with an enlarged liberty of action. At the peri-Alpine fringe it was, as already mentioned, Turin which underwent this transformation from its industrial focus to a business services industry. Other examples are Cologne and Dortmund as leading cities in the Rhine and Ruhr metropolitan regions.

Nevertheless, during the Fordist period, other towns with no historic urban functions were able to acquire important regional positions. The strong position of the secondary sector has enabled unions and social democratic and socialist parties to defend social and political affairs offensively, and to anchor common urban interests into the collective consciousness. These plans reflect a range of ideas, from philanthropic paternalism to, at the time, new models of the welfare state; some of them were innovative at the time of their first application and their significance extended beyond national borders. Examples of those company towns in the Alps were Ivrea and Domodossola in Piedmont or the industrial towns in Styria. But we find towns like this all over Europe where a decentralized industrialization took place during the 19th and 20th century.

The case of Ivrea is revealing. In contrast to neighbouring Turin, it lost its territorial capital after the takeover of the Olivetti company in the 1990s. The takeover was experienced as a double loss, as the former family-owned company was known as a social model during a time of cultural, educational, and architectural prosperity in this town of 23,000 inhabitants at the Piedmont of the Alps.

One can assume that small and medium-sized cities in the mountains have better prospects than cities of a similar size in the lowlands. Even under the conditions of a reduced presence of the regional administration in the peripheral areas, there will still be a need in the future for a minimal infrastructural endowment. In the mountains the topography constitutes 'protection by distance' favouring a small-scale settlement pattern. But this pattern of small and medium-sized cities will become more differentiated. Some cities will try to invent new functions, amenities, or events to be present on the global tourism markets, whether these functions are really needed or not. Others will pursue a specialization in places of retirement or commuting, and still others will continue to decline. Hierarchies will increase. Although there is still a possibility for new market niches, one should be aware that under the process of ongoing metropolization, there is less 'need' for medium-sized cities: They are not part of a metropolitan region and the problem of attractiveness will persist.

More important than the question of *whether* it is possible for a city to become attractive is *how long* this attractiveness will last, and to determine whether it is possible to integrate new residents as active participants and to retain them. The continuously growing significance of professional and personal interaction – and the fact that at least in Europe, up to now, only a few signs of real agglomeration disadvantages exist – leads to the conclusion that in the near future, migration will take place selectively in favour of metropolitan areas, including their peri-urban and leisure fringes.

In post-Fordism, the city becomes a new commodity for a new type of stakeholder: inhabitants who can use the urban fabric as an instrument to simplify their everyday life, and as a resource to ameliorate their symbolic capital and thus promote their careers. The new stakeholders are more successful than in the past in defending their interests. They are at the same time more selective in choosing their location, and mobile in their decision to leave (cf. exit and voice, Hirschman, 1970). Only cities that are able to host such new stakeholders remain attractive for investment and maintain their prosperity.

(c) Authority

Who has the power to define and influence strategic decisions? There is a social cleavage between town and countryside, even if rural and suburban regions sometimes dominate over urban areas in questions of traditional culture and identity. In terms of investment in infrastructure or strategic decisions of where to locate a headquarters, the interests of metropolitan areas are relevant. Large metropolitan areas, as well as second-tier metropolises, have an advantage over less densely populated areas, due to their demographic composition, economic weight, and political networks.

The decline of the Fordist paradigm of equal development is accompanied by a loss of significance of the effective shaping power of national states. This is due to the increasing shaping power of cities involved in global networks. They need to react more quickly and are more flexible in terms of the demands of their stakeholders (i.e. companies and inhabitants). Metropolitan areas contribute disproportionally to the GDP of their countries, with their high concentration of a large portion of the national population. It is obvious that they want to and can exert an influence on national policies (e.g. in infrastructure investment or tax policies).[8]

What has changed? The ability to impose demands and political claims on the state depends on the differential of power between the metropolitan cities and the peripheral regions. In Fordism, this gap was primarily determined by a mode of regulation that gave a strong position to collective arrangements, especially in the form of rate support grants and subsidies – with all the consequences that this entails, from democratic legitimacy to possible nepotism. It led to a balancing between economic and political power by redistribution, but it also led to forms of concentration of both. In post-Fordism, the difference in power is determined by market rules. The economic logic of economies of size and scope deploys self-reinforcing effects. This results in polarization according to the theory of development poles (Perroux, 1964), technical lock-in (Qwerty phenomenon), or 'too big to fail'. Decisions of the public sector always had to be justified. In times of financial scarcity of the public sector, the criteria for space-relevant decisions of investment follow additionally the criteria of economic efficiency. It results in investments being made where they display the highest sectoral profit: Decisions on the location of advanced medicine, national institutes of research, airports, and commuter train systems are subject to this logic and metropolitan regions, as collective actors, have the capacity to direct the trajectory through targeted funding.

In the case where the state has lost part of its financial power due to increased debts, some wealthy cities and regions can step in to enable immediate construction of the infrastructure they need. They pre-finance the most performing infrastructure, or by developing investment models of public–private partnership. They thus benefit from the tremendous advantage of being the first with higher accessibility and higher productivity. They will be reimbursed later but have to pay the capital costs themselves rather than the federal state doing so. Examples are the already mentioned canton of Zurich, which partially financed the further expansion of the commuter railway system, or the *Land* Baden-Württemberg in Germany, which funds the protection against noise along the routes of the ICE high-speed train. These practices produce long-lasting spatial structures and generate long-term strategic benefits. Metropolitan areas with a highly qualified tax-paying population and strong economic sectors dominated by a large city have the financial power to unite more easily in political decision-making and in making themselves better heard outside the most important economic and political decision centres. With accumulated knowledge and wealthy regional stakeholders, they know the general tendencies of international territorial development and can react more quickly than others to current trends, which also gives them shaping power. The cities that do not have such a constellation do not have a sufficient budget, and often follow outdated trends.

Metropolitan regions have the capacities to elaborate concepts of unique selling propositions that they present on international markets with professional marketing offices. They are able to recruit a staff of experts, volunteers, and sponsors that serve as a think tank, multipliers, and facilitators of the city's interest. They make the region visible at an international level. With this advantage, they have the power to play a role in the network of globally acting cities, which is important in the case of negotiations about national and transnational regulations and the decision-making about headquarters, but also in the definition of new tendencies of ways of life for their target groups.

In relation to their hinterlands, the urban and rural peripheries, the cities should at least theoretically be able to steer a dialogue about common interests, best use of available territorial capital, and the potentials to valorize it without over- or under-exploitation of the resources. The competencies of defining assets, developing concepts, and planning should improve shaping power to define key societal and economic questions and put them on the political agenda. In reality, the relation is not as harmonious. In many cases, the relations with the hinterlands are not good. The potential losers in this situation are sub- and peri-urban municipalities of large metropolitan areas that are sites of heavy infrastructure and serve as residential areas for a poorer clientele: municipalities under a flight path or near motorways and railway lines. With an increasingly dissatisfied population, these municipalities can make life difficult for the dominating city, if the city does not take into account their interests. Such conflicts can arise from egoistic positions on both sides. The onus is on the cities, as the stronger partner, to seek to resolve the problems if they want to make exhaustive use of their potential. These quarrels between centre and periphery also exist between the lowlands and mountains: in the Alpine states, urban interest groups sought regulations on higher environmental standards, resulting in the Alpine Convention, a multinational agreement within the law of nations. Although the Alpine Convention has as its mission the overall protection and the sustainable development, certain mountain regions still oppose it, as they see their long-term interests restricted. Here again, while the peripheries can disturb the urban dominance, they remain in their inferior position.

Nevertheless, despite the short duration of the Fordist period, there are remnants of the social and territorial compromise of the time. Today there is a certain consensus in European policies that polycentric development is favourable to pursuing the goal of a cohesive societal development in Europe. In this sense, the stabilization of smaller (second-tier) metropolitan areas has become an objective in the European discourse (Parkinson et al., 2012). The urban hierarchy in Europe has resharpened, but the urban fabric has been densified by the second-tier cities. However, the mountain areas have not yet profited from this.

7.3 The 'R-regions': the new clusters and their risks

The vast majority of mountain regions do not have the characteristics of the 'Triple-A regions'. Today, it would be theoretically possible to hold a powerful position as a global city in the high mountains, based on high technology and sophisticated mobility systems – like the new-built 'smart cities' on the Arabian Peninsula. But the historic trajectory took a different direction, with national and regional capitals in the lowlands developing historically and defending their positions. Even if such a scenario would make sense, it will not happen: it is a typical lock-in situation, changeable only after catastrophic impacts that nobody wants. The evolution of transport technology since the industrial era of the 19th century brought systems that can bridge long distances on flat land with high speed. A technological push to surmount the vertical dimension, and with the same efficiency as the flat areas, might be possible, but the existing infrastructure and political acceptance will be the obstacle. Therefore, we have strong indicators that the options of the A-regions will not be the options for mountains. And the mountains have already been assigned other functions. I call them the R-regions, which stands here for 'resource'. Of course, everything can be a resource, every tangible commodity and untraded tacit knowledge. The resources we are referring to are those that are closely linked with the new demands of the emerging middle classes in a globalized world. These demands are concentrated in large conurbations: energy, water, rare earth. Its citizens also ask for spaces of recreation, rehabilitation, and temporary living. Conversely, mountain regions make offers with affordable space and low taxes to generate such demands. But mountain areas are also the destination of venture capital in the real estate business, for which its owners seek a secure haven. In this logic, it should be invested to create value added to find a quick answer to the problem of over-accumulation. In this case, the quality of the resource is its generation of rents through investment in construction on formerly open land.

(a) Raw materials: mountains for feeding the world

As mentioned above (Section 4.3), geographer Strabo has already documented how, in Liguria, the Romans took advantage of the abundance of forests for their tremendous timber needs. This dependency of the lowlands on mountain resources did not change until recently, as shown in the large-scale exploitations of ore and water to feed the hunger of the global markets. It is a characteristic of mining that the layers expire and that the significance of certain materials changes according to new technologies and other global demands. The conditions in which these resources are exchanged have always been highly contested and are at the origin of many violent conflicts.[9] The global processes of metropolization are aggravating these problems, as certain resources become degraded and have to be substituted (e.g. water, which has to be transported over long distances into large conurbations), or which change rapidly in value because of oscillating prices, reputation, or technical needs, so that the whole business becomes very volatile.

New mining sites are located independently of urban settlements. It is random whether they lie in a populated area or not. It is probable that the new-found sites lie in vast, sparsely populated areas, and the fields are exploited by surface mining like the tar sands near Edmonton or the coalfields in the Appalachians (Provo and Jones, 2011). For exploitation, the workforce may be flown in or there will be shanty towns during the exploration period. Often the former inhabitants are chased away: They will not have the chance to decide independently according to their own experiences and interests, as the relations between the exploiting stakeholders and the local communities, even if they are transparent, are asymmetric. Mining sites may generate a sudden boom in existing centres with existing infrastructure, which are chosen for all the services around the exploiting sector, forming a real production system. We know this from the oil-producing countries in Europe, where Aberdeen in the UK and Stavanger in Norway became hotspots. We can assume that in many cases, environmental issues are not at the top of the agenda, and that the conditions are always dependent on the character and transparency of the negotiated contract. Again, it depends on the size of the affected population, and their knowledge and experience of whether they can resist a displacement or see environmental arguments taken seriously by the companies.[10] It is not automatically an advantage if the administrative decision-makers are based in the mountain region or not. There are regional examples from Argentina (Forget, 2015) or Lesotho (Rousselot, 2015) that show that also the governments of 'mountain states' have such a strong interest in valorizing the resources that they override all protests. On the other hand, we also have a few examples where protests were successful.[11]

In each case where mountain regions receive a new function for export-based activities, it is a huge challenge (and an open question) whether the local decision-makers are able to transform the dynamic in the fast-growing locations to a continuous urban development that goes on after the boom.

(b) Resort towns: the mountains as symbolic capital

Under the conditions of agrarian society and the industrial era in the first half of the 20th century, amenities linked with biophysical and aesthetic features ('nature', 'beauty of landscape') were restricted to the upper classes of the aristocracy (hunting, contemplation) or the upcoming bourgeoisie (sports). The first statement giving a contemplative view on mountains and landscapes was found in a correspondence of the Italian poet Francesco Petrarca (1304–1374), who wrote a letter dated 26 April 1336 to his confessor, an Augustinian monk, that he had ascended the 1,912-metre-high Mont Ventoux in the French pre-Alps just for pleasure. It is contested whether Petrarca really climbed the mountain, but he gave details that he could only have from his own experience, even if the date is incorrect. Nevertheless, the report marks a new perception of nature. In a society where most people have to look out for their daily survival, social practices are focused on activities to feed and ensure the safety of the family, which Pierre Bourdieu named as 'economy of the necessity'. No peasant would ever have had the idea to go on a summit if not necessary (i.e. for reasons other than hunting or pastoralism). Bourdieu named the practices of the bourgeoisie as 'economy of the possibility': Each activity and investment mean an option for those who do not need to struggle for daily life. Activities that are done mainly for enjoyment deliver new intellectual knowledge and new ideas for practical life, especially in terms of creating new contacts with other people that may serve as social networks, that again deliver new knowledge for daily decision-making. Going on holiday at the Côte d'Azur or in the mountains at the fin de siècle, being among the first who do sports in winter, Japanese or Chinese people travelling to Interlaken, Switzerland on holiday – such exclusive practices are very prestigious and are part of personally incorporated resources in the form of symbolic capital.

With an increased standard of living and increased and cheaper mobility, holidays in far-off countries are affordable for broader parts of the population. Practices of visiting mountains and enjoying their natural (biophysical) and cultural amenities have trickled down in recent decades. While tourism in European mountains has seen a stagnation and decline over several decades, developers and tour operators see chances in new destinations such as the Himalayas or the Andes. In Cuzco, Peru, an international airport is in the planning phase (and fires the imagination of landowners). In Europe, declining Alpine tourism has been partly replaced by multilocal residents (Elmi and Perlik, 2014). For Europeans, tourism in the Alps is no longer prestigious, but to have a secondary residence has several advantages. Due to the concentration of the business world in agglomerations, many people have been attracted to the large cities, where space is restricted and renting has become expensive. Those people often consciously practise an urban way as a distinctive habitus; they prefer living in the centre and reject dwelling in detached houses in the sub- or peri-urban fringes. In recent years, living in the city has seen a strong renaissance. Public opinion has turned against space-consuming dwelling in peri-urban areas and is in favour of 'inner densification'. Those who possess a secondary home enjoy the best of both worlds in switching from one place to another, perhaps with the argument of better health in the mountains or simply as a distraction. The new types of families and personal relationships (living apart together, patchwork families, etc.) increase multilocal arrangements. New secondary homes are equipped with the Internet and all the other features that are necessary to be connected and to invite larger families or friends. These tendencies have also been fuelled by the growing wealth of the last decades, which made it possible to abandon farmhouses and to inherit (Sonderegger and Bätzing, 2013). This facilitates access and gives an additional emotional value. Furthermore, and depending on the situation on the financial market, the acquisition of real estate has become a strategy to save private capital, a situation that fuelled real estate developers (Heeg, 2012).

The loss of economically less productive production systems such as agriculture or artisanal production follows the same mechanisms as in the lowlands. At first sight, the crisis in tourism follows the same principles of abandoning a less performing sector. But the decline of tourism is more than a mere economic structural change. As mountain villages transform into resort towns, the local population is losing its former power to define the productive character of local economies. The tourist sector was a mountain-specific, export-based production system with local specificities and local liberty of action. The economy in resort towns is a mixture of large-scale hotel and sports infrastructure and real estate business. The consequence is that the character of the entrepreneurial work changes, and the region goes from being export based to a residential economy, leading to a change in the economic hierarchy and an intensification in the societal debate over who is working and who profits. For France, Laurent Davezies and Magali Talandier (2014) solve the problem by counting productive and residential economies together as productive-residential systems (*systèmes productivo-résidentiels*), which suggests a certain symbiosis between the productive and the residential parts. It is doubtful if public opinion accepts this symbiosis. In any case, it will probably not work for other countries and for the future. One reason is the increasing internationalization of the real estate business, making such a symbiosis more and more difficult to discern. The other reason is the high degree of local autonomy in many countries. While the urban majority expects the mountain regions to develop according to their perceptions, the mountain municipalities claim their autonomy. Finally, mountains do not want to see themselves as a residential part of the symbiosis, while urban regions do not want to subsidize the mountains.

In short: the transformation of mountain municipalities into resort towns makes the mountains depend on external business models, which they cannot control as tourism in the past, although the main protagonists are often local people. The economic type of value adding changes, which may solidify the territorial cleavage between highly productive lowlands and rent-seeking, residential, consumption-oriented mountains.

Box 7.1 Possible development paths of the residential economy

In mountain areas, the economic trajectory can be described as: mountain agriculture → manufacturing/tourism → residential economy. Currently three different paths of residential economies seem probable:

1 **Retirement:** The purchasing power of second-homeowners and newcomers offers a higher standard of living, with social services nearby, a cultural offer beyond the basic services, and above-average accessibility. This trajectory is bound to a prosperous environment that ensures a continuous influx of new residents who earned their money elsewhere. The place needs to have a good reputation if the newcomers are to stay loyal for a longer time. Reputation can, to a certain degree, be purchased from the outside by marketing specialists, if the municipality has enough funding. Federal support is necessary for financing infrastructure. On the whole, this most probable 'medium' scenario creates a fragile situation as it always depends on external loyalty.

2 **Non-tourist services in the old Alpine village:** The valorization of mountain regions as recreational and residential areas is accompanied by personal services, such as concierge or cleaning services, or real estate agencies. This specialization in personal services related to age, health, or well-being could possibly be diversified and developed into high-end services such as financial intermediaries, legal consultants, etc. Such upgrading also offers a distribution channel for locally produced food products. It helps to maintain the tourist industry, and neighbouring villages transform by accommodating temporary or permanent migrants to supply locally offered services such as nurseries, schools, and culture. This economically strong development creates jobs. It is the wishful scenario of most regional managers. Sometimes such a process is induced by chance, as in the case of Andermatt, Switzerland. But in this 'strong' scenario, too, the achievement is linked to a good performance and dependency on global markets.

3 **Dormitories:** In this case, the residents are only weakly integrated into municipal life as they are often absent. These may be people who inherited homes but have left to work elsewhere. Or they are newcomers who have come from the outside in search of affordable space. These inhabitants, at least initially, do not participate much in local life. During this time, they cannot contribute to creating a demand that would create local jobs. However, this 'weak' scenario may turn in the medium term, with greater integration of the newcomers through social relations, by establishing their own trades, and by the change in generation if these people are there for the long term.

(c) Reserves: mountains as an urban menagerie

It is an old experience that frequent flyers are not the ones who suffer from the noise pollution of their flights. Take-offs and landings affect less populated areas and those with a poorer population.[12] Affected areas will not change their social structure because of the noise. Less populated areas will accept problematic infrastructure because they have less information for an early mobilization and less bargaining power to prevent its installation. And if the plans are well known, the argument of creating jobs is so strong that sometimes the jurisdictions bid to get it (e.g. the French municipality of Bure in Lorraine with its 82 inhabitants; in the early 1990s they engaged themselves to be selected as the site for the laboratory on nuclear waste storage).

We see in this example from a rural depopulated French region that places that are abandoned by human activity do not have better protection against man-made risks – on the contrary. While in the agrarian period the population was adapted to the local capability of food production, an increase in population could put the community in danger. With a secure food supply by global logistics chains, a higher population becomes an advantage, and a decline through migration can put the community in danger. The mountain population knows these mechanisms. Therefore, the transformation of agricultural land into national or regional parks is not popular among the local population. It restricts the options for economic activities and for future population growth, and – most importantly – it puts into question the accepted productivist growth model in general, without offering a trusted alternative. The remaining population is encouraged to change the nature of their work, from a productive (value adding) to a reproductive (caring) character – to become a supervisor or ranger for landscapes, for example. One could fully agree with this position if general opinion and societal consensus would go in the same direction. But as we saw with the post-Fordist turn, the productivist model has been reinforced so that the recommendations to begin with sustainable development in the mountains are reminiscent of the principle of 'recommending water for the public while drinking the wine alone'. The scepticism among the mountain population who refuses to see the future potential in a regional development that imposes on the mountains only the reproductive activities while claiming all the attractive and highly productive activities for the urban headquarters, is understandable and justified. Furthermore, it is not plausible to reduce the small-scale lots of mountain farming with the argument of biodiversity (especially in favour of the flagship animals), while the competitivity of small-scale agriculture is permanently undermined by large-scale exploitations in the flat areas that have reduced the biodiversity to a minimum.

The reserve approach follows the logic of a separation of functions where pure, selective use offers the most efficient outcomes. In this way, this approach corresponds very well to the new liberal-productivist regimes. In the end, the environment does not benefit from this, as some protected areas serve as a free pass for a high invasive investment in the built and open environment with rather few protective regulations on cultural and environmental heritage. In short: With their specific trajectory, sparsely populated regions missed the opportunity to develop leading capacity and are confronted with a brain drain and the risk of being decoupled from future opportunities and well-being. Instead, they are invited to develop features that are seen as important by the majority of the population in the lowlands, but not practised by them. The problem is not whether these objectives would be right or wrong, but that they are unilaterally enforced by this majority, a majority which itself does not reject the liberal-productivist growth model. As these demands are not developed in an endogenous reflection process, we see much defiance from the people of mountain regions against external environmental propositions and against tendencies that change the traditional organization of work and life in these areas.

(c) Rents: valleys as a vessel for financial placements

In the thematic issue of the *Journal of Alpine Research* from 2015, 'Mountains as Global Suppliers', there was one resource missing: landscape as a vehicle for capital investment. The commodification of mountain areas has not only been reinforced to develop regional production systems. We have to add another resource: the quality of regions as a label for investors to solve the problem of reinvesting their accumulated financial capital. This is valid especially under liberal-productivist conditions, where the financial sector has gained a prominent position in the hierarchy of business. This importance gives it a strong negotiating power in pursuing its interests and needs. This is not the place to treat the aspect of shifts of influence between the business services industries in the framework of post-Fordist change. But we have to focus on the role of investments in the 'hardware' of long-lasting infrastructure as a circuit in the valorization of capital (Harvey, 1982).

The problem of over-accumulation is inherent in capitalist societies. We see this in fluctuations on the stock markets where liquid capital is handled in relation to the expected return on investment. The search for new investment products is therefore nothing new. What is new, however, is that the new accumulation regimes systematically play on the emotions that can be stirred by the issues of environment and nature, with the design of investment products that cater to achieving social prestige (classic yearning for ownership) as well as the sensitivity to environmental issues of a new type of habitus.

This has not been the case to date, at least not to this degree of consistency. Tourism in the Alps came into being in response to a new demand, in this case by bored English bourgeois boys looking for a sporting challenge (Hobsbawm, 1975; Stephen, 1871), and in response to the decline in agriculture. After the war, planned capital spending as an investment strategy in the tourism and real estate sector in the mountain region was first implemented, initially exclusively, in France in the frame of its planification strategy between 1964 and 1977 ('Plan Neige'), and then later also in Italy. In France and Italy, investment in winter tourism has been linked to real estate right from the start. In France, however, these investments were also part of a national project in the context of centralized regional planning (*aménagement du territoire*). For a long time, investment in the mountains was mainly linked to investments in regional production systems of the real economy (above all tourist infrastructure such as mountain railways and sports facilities). The placement of financial capital, primarily for investment purposes in the real estate industry – i.e. detached from regional production systems of the real economy – only became widely established in the 2000s. It goes hand in hand with a continuous loss of importance of ski tourism and the takeover of the tourism infrastructure (especially local mountain railways) by transnational companies.

In the real estate business, new prestigious resort towns are planned as hybrid high-end developments (hotels and sale of condominiums) to minimize the risk of this business model. Due to the high price of the condominiums, it can be assumed that the investment strategy is in the foreground, in contrast to investments in tourism or even in regularly used holiday homes. Unlike during the heyday of tourism, the aim is no longer to satisfy the need for leisure accommodation, but to create new investment products through new needs. In this specific case, it is a category that encourages people to spend time in the mountains as well as invest capital in real estate there.

This new generation of investment targets is in line with current recommendations on regional development to offer new differentiable products for global markets. In terms of its size (see Table 7.1) and purpose of use, however, it is above all a reaction to the returns achievable on the capital market. Capital placement in new major developments is thus the attempt to overcome the latent crisis of over-accumulation, by making the most distant lateral valley conform to the market laws of financial capitalism. In this logic, for the investor it is an advantage of mountain areas to have different and sometimes 'extreme' features.

Mountain areas can be considered as laboratories, because extreme places show much more clearly and earlier the intended and unintended effects of offer-oriented strategies: Every offer will find its market, regardless of whether it is useful or necessary. If the investment of venture capital was in vain and the investment fails because there is not enough demand, it was economically successful, at least in the short-term, to reduce the level of liquid financial capital and temporarily solve the problem of over-accumulation. As long as that is only the problem of the investors concerned, it is not a major problem. For mountain areas affected by financial collapse, however, the problem will persist, as it excludes other, more solid opportunities for the local population. The conditions of a small population, combined with the specific conditions of a steep and endangered topography, represent a financial risk that makes any mortgage more expensive and reduces the willingness to invest. This also makes mountain areas more vulnerable to external investors (both in terms of an uncritical acceptance and a hasty rejection).

In its function as a place for investments, the territory no longer plays a role as a site to promote the real economy. It is only the vehicle in which to

Table 7.1 Important investment in Swiss Alpine resort towns in the last 15 years

Investment projects in Alpine resorts	Key figures	Remarks
2004: Schatzalp Davos/ GR	Investment sum: 160 mio CHF Investor: local plus external investors (still missing) Architects: Herzog & de Meuron (CH)	105-m-high tower with condominiums (the highest building in Switzerland at that time). Cross-subsidization to preserve the old historic hotel Schatzalp. Not abandoned but uncertain (lacking investors).
2007: 'Andermatt Swiss Alps', Andermatt/ UR	Investment sum: 2 milliard USD Investor: Egyptian businessman with the Orascom company Architects: several	Hotels, condominiums, golf driving range on an old military site. Partly realized, partly under construction.
2008: 'Crystal', Celerina/GR	Investment sum: 200 mio CHF Investor: Regional ropeway company Architect: M. Botta (CH)	Hotel with 300 beds in a 17-storey, 77-metre-high tower plus four 4-storey buildings for second homes. Rejected 2008 by the elector's assembly with 72%.
2010: 'Royal d'Aminona', Crans-Montana/VS	Investment sum: 650– 700 mio CHF Investor: Russian investors Architects: regional	Based on a zoning legislation from the early years 2000 the municipality of Mollens/VS decided a large construction zone for a new resort close to the already existing Crans-Montana. Construction has already begun. An environmental NGO fought at the Federal Court. In January 2016 it decided that the five towers aspect of the project had to be cancelled.
2015: 'Femme de Vals', Vals/GR	Investment sum: 300 mio CHF Investor: two locals Architect: Thom Mayne, USA	Extra slim hotel tower with only 107 rooms in the high-end sector. Access by regular helicopter service (up to now highly contested in Europe). History: The municipality sold the spa to the investor who promised the most to invest. Then, the new owner presented the plan for the highest tower of Switzerland, 381 m (as the Empire State Building). No chance to be realized due to lacking permission for helicopters and hydrology (mineral water sources). Interpretation: bargaining chip for a smaller unit.

Sources: Accessed 4 January 2016

www.24heures.ch/suisse/suisse-romande/Ampute-de-ses-tours-le-village-d-Aminona-sortiratil-de-terre/story/26615234
www.nzz.ch/celerina-will-kein-neues-wahrzeichen-1.698823
www.tagesanzeiger.ch/leben/gesellschaft/Grandios-gescheitert/story/26596273.

place surplus capital that has been taken out elsewhere. As such, mountain valleys have a similar function to some suburban parts of urban agglomerations which become a container for unwanted urban infrastructure as a spatial garbage dump. This comparison is not meant as a comment on its aesthetic impact on the environment. Built infrastructure such as blocks of flats might be of high architectural quality and even constructed according to ecological standards. The criticism refers to the purpose: the fact that such buildings are not constructed to solve any regional problems or individual needs – but just to satisfy the purpose of the investors. That is what Neil Smith (2007) calls 'nature as accumulation strategy'.

7.4 What is the novelty of this message?

Changes in territorial significance are common throughout history, and also characterized the Fordist period (Storper and Walker, 1989). This is not astonishing. What is surprising in retrospect is a long convergent development in the countries of the Global North, during a post-war period of about 30 years. This process has ended, and also led to a transformation of sparsely populated areas, which can no longer be called rural nor deserted. The transformations these areas undergo are dependent on their stronger neighbours. Those areas offering emotional amenities become functionally integrated in urban agglomerations as the recreational part of a sharp spatial division of labour. Those offering raw materials and water become integrated in the global wholesale circuit.

This chapter argues in favour of the thesis that the paradigmatic changes of the 1980s did not express a gradual change, but a fundamental reorganization of the spatial distribution of resources and power. This implies that the new regimes manifest new spatial inequalities that are greater than the inequalities of the previous period and are specific to the new liberal-productivist regimes. I argue that mountain areas are becoming functionally integrated into the metropolitan areas at the piedmonts of the mountains ('peri-Alpine') and fulfil a role as specific suppliers. The strategies of metropolitan areas follow the logic of private enterprise (i.e. they elaborate distinctive profiles, aspire to high positions in international rankings, and seek permanent visibility in the competition of international cities). They promise growth under the label of 'quality of life'. Mountain regions are invited to participate in fulfilling this promise.

Poverty is still an issue, even in wealthy societies, but it is no longer linked to mountain areas as a whole. Regional disparities are hidden, not expressible by GDP, but by reduced access to commercial and public services and higher education. The regions rich in territorial capital host competitive firms with attractive jobs, which have a dynamic, highly educated, and skilled population that is part of important political networks. In this competition, mountain regions are structurally disadvantaged. This affects the aspects of creation of value adding (regimes of accumulation), as well as the shaping power for its division (mode of regulation).

(a) Regime of accumulation

The large-scale spatial and functional division of labour

Defining diversity or homogeneity, social equality, or winners and losers are questions of scale. Questions of scale are political questions that depend on the power of definition (Agnew, 1994). In which territory should social standards be the same, regional infrastructure share the same standards, and regions have similar levels of prosperity? And of course: What administrative delimitation should be made for this? Should we take the poor parts together or should we mix poor and rich parts into one region? In the first case we very quickly see disparities but also increases in growth; in the second case, the disparities are hidden and the need for action is less obvious.

Capitalist societies show their capacity to adapt. They develop – after the Fordist crisis of accumulation of the late 1960s and then the 1970s – new forms of accumulation and regulation. The new liberal-productivist regimes are based on the unleashing of mobility that began in the late 1980s. This made it possible to break up the large, vertically integrated industrial groups that had grown at their original location. They were dismantled into separate business units, sold, and merged at new locations worldwide. At this point, global free trade is flourishing, and the idea of economic growth is developing to its extreme, while the Meadows report, 'Limits to Growth', had just shocked the world.[13]

With the political will to raise productivity and the technological means to achieve higher mobility, the extension of the accumulation processes at a global level became possible and allowed for the capitalization on differences in salary relations and ecological standards between countries. It allowed distances to shrink and made it less expensive to organize the production all over the world instead of in one integrated factory. On the other hand, it made suppliers follow their clients close to their new production sites. The new regimes of accumulation apply a combination of economies of agglomeration (on the basis of a global economy) and the diversification of products (by modification or innovation), which generates uniqueness or new marketing methods such as certified regional products. This combination is quite promising for delivering increasing returns with a disproportionally higher margin for a limited time. It accelerates the hierarchization of production and orders, and at the same time the demand for uniqueness. This also concerns the differentiation in low-skilled services and high-quality services (Häussermann and Siebel, 1995). It also relates to manufacturing (high-tech or low-tech) and agriculture ('organic' or 'budget').

Concerning the exploitation and development of space, the mentioned aspects of the new regimes generate a vast new functional division of labour between territories, which still follows the principles of comparative advantage but at a global scale:

- We see continental specializations: China as the world's factory, India as a data warehouse, Brazil as a global petrol station, Europe as an engineering base for high-end goods, the US as a global headquarters as well as consumer of products manufactured in Asia.
- At a global scale we observe diversity but at a regional level we find a monostructured pattern. Only the most important nodes in this hierarchy (the metropolitan areas) maintain diversified functions. They generate higher margins of added value, and their inhabitants are wealthier and pay higher taxes. This constellation has a self-reinforcing effect, creating spillovers and the emergence of additional economic clusters. Metropolitan regions develop as 'Jacobs'-type diversification (e.g. university plus banking sector plus high-end culture plus informal culture); mountain regions develop as 'Marshallian'-type with specialized clusters (such as tourism). The former attracts so-called 'creative' functions; the latter hold disproportionally repetitive activities.
- This observation is valid if interpreted from an abstract economic point of view, as well as from the local level of the city. Indeed, at this local level, gentrification processes reduce diversity, and displace small industries and craftsmanship from the city in favour of high-end dwellings and the 'creative industries' (Klaus, 2004; Läpple et al., 2010; Smith, 1996). In the 1970s, it was estimated that city centre housing in the European city would soon no longer be affordable due to the mechanisms of rising ground rent for offices and large department stores. Under changed liberal-productivist conditions, this perspective has to be modified. Department stores have become an endangered species, retailing has been reduced to a selling point for international brands, and dwellings have survived in the form of gentrified neighbourhoods. Today, the demand for flats in the city by the 'creative class' is insatiable; it eliminates other trades and feeds the real estate economy. In addition, major new investment projects within the metropolitan competition contribute further to displacing the previous population (Moulaert et al., 2001).
- For the mountains, this means that regions are transforming their demographic and economic structure to fit a narrowed profile. Tourist regions are more or less squeezing out a young generation that does not want to work in agriculture, tourism, or real estate, while at the same time they have to recruit an unqualified workforce from far away. Wilderness areas squeeze out peasants and pastoralists as there are too many (at least perceived) contradictions between both sectors. Real estate investments in emergent countries squeeze out subsistence economies as well as biosphere activists. And so on. An example is the Lesotho Highlands Water Project between the highlands of Lesotho and the metropolitan area of Johannesburg (Baghel and Nüsser, 2010; Rousselot, 2015): As the mountain state

of Lesotho can generate rents by selling its water reservoirs to the metropolitan region of Johannesburg, both partners seem to be winners. It is the population in between that has lost access to its pastures and is the loser in this deal. It is the basis of a new type of rent economy.

- The functional division in diversified metropolitan hubs and specialized subordinate peripheries reproduces the old paradigm of functional separation. As the cities remain multifunctional, this lack of diversity in the peripheries carries less weight, as the dominant segment of the population (in number and deciding power) lives in the urban areas. The 'right to the city' movement sees this problem but is interested mainly in their own clientele – those who already live in the city and are in danger of being displaced. In this respect, they run the risk of addressing social problems primarily from the interests of the urban subculture milieus (and thus risk remaining attached to a culturalistic perspective – culture seen as 'end' and not as 'means'). In doing so, they overlook the relations of economic and political power on a larger scale. Meanwhile, the people in the peripheries hope to be protected by traditional, non-urban, nationally based versions of the welfare state (i.e. by exclusion and isolation).
- Large-scale depopulation and out-migration occurred regularly in war contexts and following industrialization in the 19th century. In addition, economic sectors transform continuously and industries relocate. This is not new.[14] Unlike Fordism, the liberal-productivist regimes present a qualitative leap: Territorial integrity, guaranteed by the national state, with the result of a more or less balanced regional development, is called into question. Regional development becomes subject to market dynamics with the argument of subsidiarity, bureaucratic slimming, and more flexible options. The goal of 'equality' turns to 'equivalence'. Difficult to maintain even this, it is also put into question. Uneven spatial development is not only accepted by these practices – it is even considered positive. The range of justifications is comprised of quite a heterogenous and in some way unholy alliance: It stretches from conventional arguments of economic efficiency and resource allocation by economic stakeholders, through regional development approaches as new economic geography (distinction as a competitive advantage) (Krugman, 1991), to the traditional environmental movement (the idea of 'wilderness'), and new approaches of the 'creative classes' (the concept of 'Alpine fallow'). Inequality also becomes a resource – a resource that may create a higher value added due to greater diversity.
- Two of the dimensions of sustainable development – economy and environment – become compatible with each other through a productivist efficiency thinking which becomes inherent to both. The contradiction of both towards the third dimension, the social question, remains and deepens.
- Finally, territorial integrality is called into question in those parts of the Global North that have faced no violent conflicts for a long time. In a world where borders have become permeable for the flows of goods, toll stations in the mountains have become obsolete.[15] The restriction and

regulations are applied to specific goods in the logistics centres in the low-lands to become transported via the main corridors from one country to another – even crime, contraband, and fraud, and their suppression, are no longer a business specific to mountain border regions. Even for border protection there is less and less need to fortify the higher altitudes with garrison towns or other hard symbols of territorialization.

The new division of functions between the city and the (former) countryside describes a new quality in their relation, compared to the previous regimes. Not only is this change new in its dimension (a scale jump) – it is very significant in its changed logic: functional disparity is released from its perception as being socially unjust; instead, it is reinterpreted positively as a new resource and an option even for disadvantaged peripheries.

The new role of the landscape in the process of value adding

With the decline of agriculture and reduction in strategic territorial functions – and in the framework of the regime shift – mountain regions have been rec-ommended to do more than before for their economic survival. This involves inventing new value chains and qualifying their population for this entrepre-neurial task, for example by the LEADER programmes of the European Union.

The mountains in Europe are – in large part – no longer entirely depressed areas (Bätzing et al., 1996; Gloersen et al., 2004; Stucki et al., 2004). The catch-up processes of the peripheries between the 1970s and 1990s made it easier to reduce or to reorganize subsidies that were given in the name of national regional policies to mountain areas. The Fordist crisis put mountain agriculture and industries under pressure. Recommended strategies are now to produce traceable unique products that follow the highest environmental and animal protection standards, and include the valorization of landscapes. Uniqueness strategies are not demand-oriented strategies, but offer-oriented, which means that the focus lies on the innovation of new products, which could perhaps find customers and new uses, even if the product is not useful under functional or ecological criteria. The invention of an emotional story of a certain landscape added to an anonymous piece of meat makes it a competitive commodity in the interest of the economy of that region.

Mountain regions still have constructible space and they lack inhabitants. Land use is defined by local, regional, or federal consensus (zoning); attracting new inhabitants is subject to competition with lowland cities. Valorizing land-scapes for construction zones has become a way of attracting new inhabitants and generating new value chains around construction, refurbishment, retail, personal services, etc. The landscape serves as the ensemble of selling argu-ments, promising calmness and 'otherness'. Owning a second home there, as a place for leisure, an alternative location for desktop work and family get-togethers, etc. makes life better and – especially in prestigious places – enhances individual reputation in the interaction with one's social networks. These are arguments for people who have chosen a life in a densely populated city centre. One could add the function of the placement of savings, especially in times of financial insecurity. In this sense, mountain landscapes serve as a location for 'Alpine gentrification' (Perlik, 2011), similar to the processes in reputable city centres across the globe. This is what is happening in mountains and coasts all over the world, especially in emerging countries, as documented by an increasing amount of literature: Among the most recent are Marchant and Rojas (2015) for Chile; Glorioso (2006) for the Philippines; Otero et al. (2006) for Argentina; Janoschka (2009) for Costa Rica. For the individual, the economic role of the landscape is twofold: one can distinguish between the use value of living multilocally in an environment rich in nature, near amenities that satisfy the needs of recreation and health on the one hand – and, on the other, an increase in personal reputation by the possession of positional goods (symbolic capital), which functions as exchange value. Mountain regions with many assets such as spectacular views, famous summits, many sun hours, and snow in winter, may be encouraged to specialize on these amenities.

'Landscape' has received an additional role defined by the urban majority who pin their perceptions about nature, projections, and hopes on a more sustainable way of life in the mountains. This results in a broad range of use from open (unbuilt) space with public access, to reserves protecting wild animals. Its promoters follow the interests of new forms of individualized tourism but also the interests of scientific research. These propositions may create economic activities for stakeholders in mountain regions, as there are national parks, UNESCO Biosphere Reserves, and UNESCO World Heritage Sites (Liechti et al., 2010; Schaaf, 2006; Scheurer and Küpfer, 1997). World Heritage Sites may create new local jobs and make the concerned regions known to a worldwide clientele. Such landscapes, although seen as near-natural, 'wild', or even idealistically as 'pure nature', become, as new intangible commodities, completely integrated into global markets and displace older forms of subsistence economies where these still existed. With the deterioration of environmental quality in the sub- and peri-urban areas, the demand and value of these near-natural landscapes are increasing. At the same time, this demand is becoming concentrated on ever fewer and more distant destinations. With the globally growing number of wealthy people who can afford leisure in such areas, the mere increase in traffic already creates an ecological problem.

The described transformations turn mountain regions into suppliers of newly created commodities based on landscape assets. These commodities may be creations of the mountain regions or they may be explicit demands from the urban milieu. In both cases, success will depend on whether the mountain regions are able to meet the demands of their clientele, which is becoming more and more international. As in the case of the cities and towns of the Alps (Perlik, 2001), we again have this double liberty. The mountain regions are free from the former paternalism of the subsidies of the federal state, but they are now also free from security; they are part of a market where the clients hold strong positions.

'Landscape' has become a new product which, on the surface, follows the market rules of innovation-driven offers and reputation-driven demand. The main actors of these mechanisms cannot be reduced to a single group.

In this situation, it is not clear which side offers the more sustainable options: The regional decision-makers are incentivized by the hope of regional wealth and follow their individual interests of shaping power, which may be short-sighted and self-serving. The global community of mountain users represent the new collective knowledge and sees itself as the ideal stakeholder but has a restricted interest in mountain areas for the selective use of landscape aesthetics and certain cultural brands.

(b) Mode of regulation

Increased asymmetric shaping power

The topographic conditions and the technological trajectory have favoured a development of the lowlands rather than the mountains. This double impact seems irreversible. As mountain people also have access to high education, they become attracted to the places that offer activities according to their competencies. And the metropolitan areas are interested in attracting them. Consequently, under spontaneous, unregulated conditions, demographic and economic power will still shift towards the lowland metropolitan areas. Furthermore, in the last 20 years, the need for a strong, secured territorialization of the peripheries has declined. The abandonment of intra-European frontiers with the shift of administrative functions from border towns to more central locations has led to certain territories being cut off from regional development. Although unpopulated territories remain part of the state territory, up to now there was no need to implant a new Brasilia or Chandigarh into the mountains.[16] Mountain areas therefore face the situation of being suppliers of rare goods, which will increase with the degradation of resources elsewhere, especially in terms of water and food.

Power asymmetries are likely to remain. These were aggravated during the shift from Fordism to post-Fordism with the reinforced functional division of labour and the concentration of new high-end services at fewer locations than before. During this transformation, metropolitan problems gained in significance to the detriment of mountain issues and mountain areas. Metropolitan areas generate and attract new problems in a larger dimension. Examples include traffic congestion, new migration flows, or new poverty due to a lack of affordable housing or jobs – as well as their increased attractiveness to people in situations of precarity. But as the number and diversity of citizens increases, so does the potential of self-healing capacities as well. Furthermore, this diversity enables cities to communicate these problems, to put them on the national agenda, and to gain greater support by the state. The large metropolitan areas become visible on the political agenda. The problems reach 'economies of scale' to attract knowledge and financial support to resolve them. Liberal-productivist regulation means, in this situation, that the resources help deliver the optimal returns.

Less attention is paid to the less populated regions. They are expected to find solutions in discovering niches to justify their continued existence. The visible impacts of the shift from a balanced mode of regulation to a difference-focused mode of regulation are as follows. Planning strategies emphasize the differences between landscapes, land uses, and economic profile. Subsidiarity-based approaches give more entrepreneurial freedom to local jurisdictions but abandon their reinsurance. Private and public investors place their capital according to the highest return on investment. In this constellation, mountains rarely have the necessary Triple-A rating. Young people leave small munici-palities for higher education, and if they come back, then only later in life. Recommended 'best-practice' strategies are to find niches for high-quality/high-price products, ignoring that this is a zero-sum game as it generates a cannibalizing effect between the peripheral regions. The proclaimed strate-gies of producing high-quality food seem reasonable, but the jobs created and the specific value adding of its agriculture cannot maintain mountain econo-mies, neither by the quantities produced nor by the strategy of keeping prices high by producing exclusively for the upper classes. Independently of this, urban agriculture has caught up in inventing new forms of production, such as producer–consumer cooperatives. Also, other assets of the mountains are transferable, even snow sports (with the extreme example of halls of artificial snow, far from mountain areas).

There are certainly exceptions. In Europe, the mountain regions have gained purchasing power by becoming the locations of second homes of multilocal dwellers. In Switzerland, the political system still systematically favours the peripheries, as for historical reasons their weight in parliament is disproper-tional. This is the source of great dispute, as it enables mountain regions to intervene against the interests of the majority of the population, even on issues affecting only urban areas.[17] This means the actors in the mountain regions may undertake little pinpricks against the dominating lowland centres to defend their interests. Nonetheless, in the greater strategic goals, they lose.

The separation of spatial functions, although an outdated planning paradigm, has re-entered into practice, especially in the search for economies of scale and through social segregation processes. This spatial separation facilitates an asym-metric relation between territories. Both parties do not negotiate regularly. They risk losing their mutual understanding and each side feels outsmarted by the other. In reality, both depend on each other. Amid global competition, met-ropolitan regions need their hinterlands. For their part, mountain areas need the metropolitan regions as clients and funders. But mountain regions are more dependent: Their landscape asset is very vulnerable to change such as new construction projects (buildings, infrastructure). Damage to the landscape asset increases the danger of losing the loyalty of the urban sphere. The relationship has become very volatile and the urban party has the upper hand, more able to withdraw its solidarity than the other way around.

The oscillation of power, with strengthening or weakening of the political weight of certain regions or states, is not new in itself. The qualitative leap from Fordism to post-Fordism is the fact that the territorial approach (which was the foundation of the old conception of the nation state) lost its importance, and at the same time regimes are established that rely completely on the market solution in spatial development. The national institutions lose much of their power. The regulation of social questions is transferred to lower institutional levels or even to the individual. The ecological question has been redefined as symbolic capital: It has been transferred to a question of reputation, and by this mechanism a selected part has been internalized into the price system and serves as proof of the performance of ecological assets (especially flagship species such as panda and whale) as market solutions in the environmental economy.

It results in an asymmetric division of strength and weaknesses that reduces the power of negotiation of mountain and peripheral areas. Balancing instruments according to market rules cannot rectify these asymmetries. Political instruments are discredited and have been weakened in the past.

Appropriation of open space

The new regimes of accumulation claim a culture of interaction where the consumption of goods and services seems to be free. But of course, this is not true as the hardware is produced in low-wage countries and the software is given away in exchange for personal data. The search for new niches in the mountain economy is linked with the commodification of space for new business options. This practice has existed for a long time and was always contested by groups for environmental preservation or the heritage of the built environment, or simply by those in favour of preserving the existing landscape. The individual loss is not up for debate here. The fundamental change is that the public is deprived of open space by the construction of dams, second homes, or mining operations. The former open spaces were used multifunctionally. This is an important quality, especially in an area where there is a lack of usable terrain, and especially in a debate always critical of the negative aspects of urban sprawl. It shows the ambiguity of the demand for inner densification, which also deprives the public of access to open space.

Open space does not automatically mean public good. Often, it is private property that gives freedom of use in the framework of local and national regulations. But it makes a difference whether a plot is used for agriculture, where the public has minimal access as a visitor, or whether it is blocked by a building. It is an old problem: New constructions use the existing built and near-natural environment as an asset to valorize a project, which changes the setting of this environment. The difference to former times is that the new investments have a higher impact and are less reversible, while at the same time they are more volatile. Furthermore, the ideas are rarely locally born: Due to the increased market size, local communities have to adapt and to copy external models; they are overstretched by external knowledge and external market power. The regime shift has reinforced this dynamic. There is no difference concerning the form of property. The state as landowner, even if it is a mountain state, often acts in the same way as a private company. If the owners see a means to valorize the territory, they squeeze out the other stakeholders, as the example of the Himalayas (Section 4.4) has shown.

Here, we can state that the regime shift from the Fordist to the liberal-productivist regimes reinforces the problem of appropriation of new resources without considering the public interest or paying the correct price to the mountain producers.[18] This is not an argument to restrict investments only for locals (they practise the same, or, due to a lack of knowledge, even worse methods as external investors), but to more carefully balance the different logic and interests of public and private stakeholders.

7.5 Summary

We come back to giving an answer to the four hypotheses from Section 3.7.

(a) 'Diversity' is an opportunity for the urbanized areas

Self-responsibility: Abandoning the former paradigm of equal territorial development seems to open new opportunities for more regional diversity. Paradoxically, often the contrary happens. It is argued that an equal endowment with the same infrastructure is not financially viable, and also counterproductive, as every region has different needs. With the liberal-productivist paradigm, the individual regions become more responsible for the performance of their economy. They need different infrastructure to distinguish themselves from their neighbours. In this sense, the regional economic activities become reduced to their core competencies in a manner analogous to the economic model of private enterprises. In the positive case, the regional trajectory may go on in differentiating and growing by providing jobs and knowledge not only in the dominating sector, but also as spillovers to other sectors. A certain manufacturing sector may spread in developing specialized schools, commercial services, contract logistics, etc. In the negative case, a regional monostructure generates a cluster risk. In the case of an erosion of this cluster, the specific knowledge of those involved becomes abruptly devalued.

Diversity becomes a resource: Diversity becomes an asset and a commodified resource. Metropolitan regions have several industrial clusters. The diversity increases the attractiveness for job seekers, residents, and new immigrants. It also serves as reinsurance against the cluster risk of one-sided specialization. Over the last 20 years, regional competition has intensified and innovation cycles have accelerated, and many regions have lost their production systems. Mountain regions as sparsely populated regions do not have the protection of several production systems as metropolitan regions do. The higher their specialization, the more specialized and limited their clientele. The supraregional companies must constantly renew their product range and open their markets globally.

This increases the risk of over-exploitation of regional resources (e.g. environment) as well as the risk of decline in the case of failure.

Limited potential: Due to their sparse population, mountain regions are traditionally the site of production systems linked to their topographic specificities, i.e. agriculture, mountain-specific industries, and tourism. In the Fordist era, administrative, social, and retail services completed the spectrum. With the economic and demographic transformation, the limited options of mountain areas have narrowed again. Reduced access and a lacking agglomeration impede economic activities that are not dependent on the existing territorial capital. Activities and jobs linked with calmness are rare, and the possibilities of working independently from the main office in town makes part-time or freelance work in the mountains attractive but creates no new production systems. It remains tourism (in decline) and specialized leisure and dwelling.

Selective use of landscapes: The transformation of mountain economies creates new economic clusters, but they rely mainly on the selective use of landscape-related amenities. This is a reduction of diversity rather than an enlargement. The diversity argument plays only at the global scale as a form of diversity between large but internally rather homogeneous regions. It can be appreciated and used only by those people who often move between such different geographical macrostructures. This new spatial configuration means – and up to now, this was not discussed – a depletion for the less mobile people and a personal enrichment for those who are mobile and can afford to enjoy spatial diversity at large scale.

We can conclude that 'diversity' is not a neutral term, but that it follows divergent interests. It depends on the dominant stakeholder who defines what she or he sees, consumes, and believes to be a worthwhile part of the spectrum of diversity. Second, the considered scale determines what we see as diverse, whether we look at the local level or whether we take the big intercontinental picture.

(b) The commodification of 'landscape'

The transparent agro-manufacture: In the mountains of the Global North, agricultural production has been partly abandoned. It has been substituted by public remunerations for greenkeeping, hazard protection, and assurance for the future.[19] The remaining areas for agricultural use serve in the production of new types of luxury goods: mountain cheese labelled as such, rare wines, craft beers, organic food, and lard – all emotionally boosted by geographical designation of origin. These new uses by the invention of new – tangible and intangible – products deliver in sum a higher return on investment for the involved stakeholders (the farmers, landowners, entrepreneurs, and planning experts) than the output-oriented mass production of the Fordist era.

The invention of emotions and the valorization of symbolic capital: While the densely used urban areas have become intensively valorized and the public spaces have become concentrated and generally reduced, there is a potential to open up new markets for the valorization of new commodities. These include spectacular views, through the construction of new infrastructure; invention of new outdoor sports; corporate assessment courses in five-star hotels; and family events at exotic places (e.g. Japanese weddings in the Swiss mountains).[20] And the new urban middle classes develop these dynamically changing demands as their consumption promises access to new forms of symbolic capital: quickly accessible second home condominiums for weekly trips, old farmhouses for hosting family and friends, new and traditional gastronomic trends, the whole range of outdoor leisure activities including new sports fads, cheap air fares, etc. No matter whether the client has to pay direct entrance fees or whether this is included in the costs of transport or accommodation, we see a differentiation of offers as a consequence of the Fordist crisis.

Requirements of space: The business model of post-Fordism – supply of industrial products by transcontinental trade, redevelopment of the environment, increase of the functional division of labour by growth of the service sector, increased mobility – opens up new opportunities for 'dividing one's time' between big cities and places with landscape amenities. In the big cities, the brownfield areas of old industry become attractive for new inhabitants. In the mountains, the same can be said of former sites of early industrialization, old farms, abandoned military sites, and unprofitable old hotels. The public discourse on the impacts of urban sprawl with the demand for inner densification has generated the astonishing paradox that the most opposing interest groups suddenly share the same opinion: planners, architects, unaffected citizens and environmentalists. In this harmony, it is overlooked that likely impacts will favour those who hold the property rights. The shortage of space makes the offer more expensive, new building land delivers value added, and citizens learn the new practices of multilocal dwelling and can afford to double their space in square metres (when the space of their second home is added to their first). The losers are the people in the less favoured parts of the suburban fringes who find themselves facing rising rents, and the environmentalists who will pay the price for favouring the flagship species wolf instead of the ordinary sparrow.

The commodification of public space in the form of labelled landscapes and residential zones (as consumptive regions) is a specific application of Krugman's new trade theory. It enables an escape from the dilemma of competitive advantages with the repeated creation of new products.

(c) The revival of cities – with integrated mountains

The urban narrative: With the post-Fordist turn, the discourse of regional policy has changed: It is now determined by the urban stakeholders. They argue that the metropolises are the engines of growth, which is why it is necessary to improve their condition in general, and to solve problems such as traffic congestion in particular. It is too costly to provide advanced infrastructure for all.

It is easier to resolve environmental problems in large conurbations than in the periphery: Open land should remain open, also because the densely used urban areas need the open spaces for recreation.

The mountains as metropolitan neighbourhood: The new practice of multilocal living gives mountains a supplementary population, which, in the case of the Swiss Engadine, swells from a permanent 10,000 to more than 100,000 in the winter. But these temporary inhabitants neither pay taxes nor vote there. Nonetheless, the affected mountainous areas can still benefit from this functional integration. They profit, in particular, from wealthy clients, and can provide a better retail offer and better social and cultural services. The increase in population has a positive effect in that it enables the permanent inhabitants to recoup their investments in costly infrastructure such as swimming pools, public transport, and art museums. If the new part-time inhabitants establish a long-term relation to their hosting municipality, the municipality may benefit from their specialized knowledge. However, their rural profile decreases. Also, metropolitan regions can reap benefits from their mountain neighbours. Especially for the smaller second-tier metropolitan areas, the extended offer of land, more leisure options, and cultural events at mountain locations represent supplementary assets in the competition with other world cities.

The functional integration: The post-Fordist turn is linked with the renaissance of the city, which became an attractive place in which to work and live. But it was also linked with a new hierarchization, in which metropolitan regions were the main winners, and small and medium-sized towns the losers. Large second-tier agglomerations (regional capital cities) had the opportunity to become part of the system of metropolitan areas in a second-tier position. Small and medium-sized cities lose their function as decision-making centres and are functionally integrated into metropolitan areas. Second-tier metropolitan regions are rather small to safeguard their long-term position. But they can defend themselves against decline by using their specific assets and unique benefits for specific target groups. Their performance depends on their ability to generate new resources. One of these resources is having the capacity to functionally integrate the neighbouring regions with their mountainous characteristics into their own sphere of influence as a valorizable resource. This means that the peri-urban fringes of the city have enough dwelling or building space and an extraordinary offer of leisure activities, and the city is able to coordinate a close cooperation among the different jurisdictions.

We can thus conclude the hypothesis as follows. The interest in the peripheries and mountainous regions has changed, as has the situation of these regions: Today, there are no large pockets of poverty in the Alps. These achievements are still based on the spatio-social compromise of the Fordist welfare state, but it is overlaid with liberal-productivist practices. The new use of the Alps and similar mountains brings increased purchasing power to these regions, reducing existing economic disparities to a small scale. Furthermore, it masks the fact that recent disparities now rely to a stronger degree on hierarchies that have been shifted in favour of the metropolitan regions.

(d) The territorial capital of mountain regions is made more fragile

The liberal–productivist regimes influence the future trajectories and potentials of the mountains. New options open up while the doors of important alternatives close. In the final evaluation, the weakening factors dominate:

External interests: On a national level, in most cases mountains host the minority of the population. With population growth and migration flows in favour of lowland conurbations, this bias is increasing. Liberal–productivist regimes only sharpen the different profiles between highlands and lowlands. This has consequences on the interests of the principal stakeholders in the different territories. In the case of diverging interests and values, the urban interests will dominate, as they host the majority and the more powerful population. With this backing, the urban majority may succeed in defining the standards of decision-making. Nevertheless, the peripheries may disturb this dominance through anti-elitist arguments. But this is not the expression of societal influence and strength; rather, it is the sign of decline.

Logic of the real estate business: Mountain regions enlarge their building zones to profit from the real estate boom in hosting rich clients. A demanding clientele raises the reputation and the added value of services (Porter, 1998), and also the quality of services for the locals. Under Fordist conditions, spatial planning depended on a combination of non-transparent expert decision-making and democratic legitimation. In the framework of post-Fordist regime change, both experts and democratic legitimization lose their influence. The Alps transform from productive regions to residential places according to credit conditions and the decisions of private investment in real estate. With the proliferation of building zones and the valorization of land, mountain regions turn from productive economies to rent economies.

Gentrification: Local actors can benefit when they sell land to new in-migrants, but they lose influence when they are dominated by different interests of the newcomers, who may squeeze them out because of rising land prices, high rents, and costs of services and fees. This effect of relative or absolute displacement is shown in the examples of Santa Fe, New Mexico (Glorioso and Moss, 2006), or the new resort of Andermatt in Switzerland. I call these processes Alpine gentrification (Perlik, 2011). The change in demographic structure and the transformation of the regional production system towards specialized dwelling devalues the previous tacit knowledge more quickly than in cases in which the regional trajectory is only modified. The new flat owners will have a certain influence on the development of the resort, but they may be less engaged as their focus of everyday life is outside.

Knowledge: Every structural change devalues existing knowledge and brings new ideas that add new knowledge. Long-existing knowledge is often tacit knowledge that is regionally spread and hard to copy. In contrast, new, externally born knowledge is codified and has to be regionally adapted. So, the outdated knowledge lacks application and has no further use, while the new knowledge is still in a phase of trial and error and not yet competitive. In this development, the territorial capital is thinned out.

Landscape: This is a resource that is consumed only by tourists and multilocal dwellers. Both groups are searching for 'otherness' compared to the lowlands. This means that the resource can only be exploited in an extensive form, which does not question its qualities of uniqueness, authenticity, and image. In contrast, the locals have an interest in maintaining a similar standard of living to the lowlands. The requirements therefore are contradictory: When the landscape is extensively used, it does not contribute to raising the number of jobs and the standard of life; if the landscape is intensively used, it becomes devalued. In this tendency, both alternatives degrade the territorial capital – either by weakening local stakeholders or weakening their main resources.

Mountain-specific economic activities: Tourism undergoes a period of consolidation, which is a sign of general decline. The number of actors and number of sites become reduced. Even Alpine hydropower cannot produce profitably and has an uncertain future. Most of the mountain-specific activities are under pressure due to their small-scale and domestic orientation, which means small markets and less attractivity for young academic graduates. With the downturn of many of these enterprises, the mountains lose most of their specific production systems. Of course, this opens up new opportunities, and it is understandable that the parts of the population that were a minority in the old company towns are happy to now have new options. But the new activities are less linked with the historic trajectory, and are therefore more volatile and mobile.

Local food products: Extensive production in mountains favours the creation of specialities that can be sold with higher margins. Producing specialities could contribute to the attitude of people towards food change (less waste, environmentally friendly, shorter transport distances, better working conditions), and the quality of food may rise. But what was once a subsistence crop of small-scale farmers, new pioneers, or indigenous people in the mountains is now becoming a lifestyle product for global markets (e.g. quinoa). Furthermore, we see a certain banalization to the detriment of mountain regions. We now find organic products in supermarkets (which provide guaranteed supply chains), urban gardening and contract agriculture are growing (by urban neighbourhood networks and cooperatives), and with the decline in tourism, mountain agriculture is losing its outlets. Large parts of the value chain are based outside the mountains – those that generate the largest shares of value adding (research and development, marketing and retail). Current food production follows the logic of a division in luxury products and cheap mass products. This relativizes the hopes that have been pinned on mountain food products. High-quality food from the mountains has not yet mastered the larger parts of the value chain, and suffers from the elitist development that results from an increasing social cleavage in the Global North and the emerging countries. Organic and mountain food both depend on the clients' purchasing power and fashion cycles. These value chains are important, but in their present shape they do not safeguard a distinct and sustainable mountain economy. They may not be part of a mass market, and have to struggle not to be squeezed out.

New in-migrants: New migrants may have an enormous potential to create many new opportunities in the mountains. New stakeholders can bring new knowledge, even if they are present only temporarily. Whether in-migrants are perceived as an enrichment or not strongly depends on the local actors. The mobility of people has given rise to new forms of attachment to a region that results in joint projects designed by a multitude of external people who work together with local people and realize joint activities in alternative tourism, landscape, technical preservation, or social work.[21] The possibilities and the specific capacities of active retirees can be a definite asset to repopulating an area.[22] But currently, the main migration flows favour the large cities, even for people not actively seeking to climb the career ladder. Even the current migration flows into and within Europe are not yet seen as an opportunity for sparsely populated areas, and as future options for foreigners are always better in an agglomeration, nobody wants to go to the peripheries voluntarily. Migrants coming to mountains by choice (like retirees), by need (labour migration), or by force (refugees) will certainly influence the direction of development (the trajectory) (Perlik and Membretti, 2018). If this process is successful, they may increase the existing territorial capital in the long run.

Of course, the question arises: Isn't a gradual change that affects mountain areas just a change that can be explained by new communication technologies and reduced distances? Why are the changes not simply explained by the phenomenon of 'globalization'? We can answer that 'globalization' is not specific enough, and that even in the context of global integration, states and regions have different options for regulations. However, this global integration has led the different national states to abandon their own long-grown traditional welfare state regulations in favour of a minimal common denominator, which means that not only goals of 'equal' development have been abandoned, but also the goals of 'equivalent' conditions of living. It was a conscious decision to strengthen those economic structures that reinforce territorial dynamics and increase the effects of agglomeration economies. New technologies (mobility), new production and business models (vertical disintegration and subcontracting), and continental relocations attack the regional production systems and integrate the mountain areas into larger urban markets. Unlike the Fordist model of regulation, this integration is not part of an agreement between the important stakeholders (federal institution, associations of economy, chambers of commerce, unions, spatial planning, etc.), legitimized by political decisions. The integration of the mountain hinterlands into adjacent metropolitan areas takes place in the framework of global economic change and competition. Mountain regions may take new chances and their own development strategies, but they lose the unconditional territorial 'insurance' by their national states. With the functional integration of mountainous regions in their expanding agglomeration, the metropolitan areas increase their own territorial capital and connect the hinterlands into their network of commuting perimeter, leisure offers, and labour markets. The mountain regions may maintain the parts of their territorial capital that are useful in the framework of this integration, shedding the parts considered to be inefficient. The disparities are no longer expressed in differences in GDP and purchasing power between mountain areas and lowlands. Rather, new and deepened functional hierarchies with an asymmetrical steering power have emerged.

Notes

1 Every metropolitan region and many of the medium-sized towns are well equipped with professional marketing organizations. Most of them, especially those with an active citizenship, also have their own institutions founded by a cooperation of civil society and the principal economic actors or institutions (e.g. 'Metrobasel' at Basel, 'Bern neu gründen' [Founding Bern Anew] at Bern, Association Europäische Metropolregion München e.V., Torino Strategica, etc.).

2 One could already find monofunctional macro-regions before, but only at a national level. See Lipietz (1977: Chapter IV) for France, or the example of the Ruhr area in Germany.

3 London, Paris, Milan, Munich, and Hamburg (BBSR, 2011).

4 This is the argument used to give them up, with economic and environmental considerations and the supremacy of urban culture. But by sacrificing the 'peripheries of the periphery', new structurally weak parts are created among the formerly less peripheric areas.

5 *Le Monde*, 12 May 2010.

6 After this decision to introduce a degressive tax system, the municipal parliament of Zurich had to decide whether to grant urgent aid to Swiss mountain cantons that were affected by flooding. In general, such aid is voted on quickly and with generosity. Here, the aid was given only after a long and controversial debate.

7 For example, the high attractivity of Berlin, Barcelona, and Copenhagen for students.

8 The London metropolitan area contributes 20 per cent of the UK's GDP. Its financial district is located in the city of London ('the City'), which has a parliament that is constituted of representatives of the companies located here, proportional to the number of their employees. A representative of this parliament is always present in the House of Commons as a lobbyist (oral information from the British film-maker Lee Salter, see the documentary *Secret City*).

9 An empirical study made at the University of Lausanne showed that intra-national conflicts are threefold, numerous and much more violent in those regions with petrol resources (Morelli and Rohner, 2013).

10 Finally, new economic sectors and technological innovation are always a process of trial and error. This concerns the settling practices in mountains as well as in modern

industries. In the Alps, the peasants had to find rules for the clearing of woods to maintain protection against natural hazards. Working conditions on offshore oil platforms ameliorated only after the Piper Alpha accident in the North Sea in 1988, which caused 167 deaths.

11 This was the case for several dams for hydropower in the 20th century in Switzerland. Recently the Association against a larger dam at the Grimsel (canton of Bern) could delay the planned project until the times changed and hydropower lost its profitability – they prevented the company from producing a huge loss in its operations.

12 This phenomenon is particularly striking in the case of Zurich: the approaches to landing are mainly 'outsourced' over German territory and the relatively poor north of Zurich, while the rich lakeside shores in the south of Zurich are explicitly kept free as premium dwelling sites.

13 This is particularly interesting as it occurs just after the signs of an oil peak. This episode clearly shows the impacts of rebound effects. After scarcities or pollution emission, technological innovations are undertaken with the result that people make so much use of it that the technological gains are soon overcompensated (Sorrell and Dimitropoulos, 2008).

14 Among many others: Storper and Walker (1989).

15 Currently, during this book is written, this process has come to an end in the context of the nationalist vogue of isolationism against supraregional rules and human rights obligations towards refugees. The Austrian government began in 2016 with strict border controls at the Italian–Austrian border. It has announced – if it estimates as necessary – to close this intra-Alpine border by military means.

16 One could argue that several states in Africa newly constructed or shifted their capital city, such as Nigeria, for political reasons. Of course, this is thinkable also for other parts of the world, but such a decision would have to be prefaced with an enormous deterioration in the relations between the lowlands and mountains, to justify such a high politically driven investment. It is unthinkable without a scenario of appeasement of previous violent conflicts.

17 One example is that in the debate on migration, those regions with the lowest proportion of migrants are those most vehemently opposed to migration. Another example from Bern: in a cantonal vote, the rural majority blocked the expansion of the tramway in the city of Bern as they found the costs too high.

18 We have to consider that logic varies between parties. In fact, external investors do pay the correct price as, according to their logic, they take the risk of doing business in peripheral regions. The long-term risks of the mountain producers, however, are not considered.

19 One may subsume here the reserve areas for a possible later use, as well as the areas for ecological compensation with instruments such as the set-aside incentive scheme for arable land of the European Union (EEC no. 1272/88).

20 The city of Lucerne, which invented this tourist offer in the 1990s, had to work hard in the following years to reject the image as a mere tourist resort and to regain, at least partly, its historic role and position as an important constituent city in the Swiss urban system.

21 There are many groups active in peripheral areas of the Alps engaged in the reintegration of young people who are disabled, delinquent, or in drug abuse rehabilitation or treatment.

22 We refer to the example of external volunteers for the reconstruction of the narrow-gauge tourist railway between Realp, Uri and Oberwald, Upper-Valais, or the even smaller ropeway 'Älplibahn' operated by volunteers at Malans, Grisons. Another example is the long-distance trail 'Grande traversata dei Alpi', which had been supported by Germany and other European countries (Vogt, 2008).

Part IV

The new disparities and possible alternatives

Figure 8.1 In sparsely populated areas, the continuity of a permanent population is especially important to avoid socio-demographic decline, and in consequence also environmental degradation. As mobility is rising in every country, and it is a legitimate interest of people to search for a better life elsewhere, governments have a high responsibility to strengthen the territorial loyalty of inhabitants. It is a challenge and could be a chance to integrate and embed new segments to a population.

Photo: An unknown convention of women on a Sunday afternoon in Gairsan, Uttarakhand/India, 6 November 2011.

8 Liberal-productivist mountains

Three main aspects

This chapter first recapitulates the question of mountain specificity. I then focus on three topics that seem to be most relevant in characterizing liberal-productivist regimes in their social and spatial effects on mountain regions. This is done with the aim of finding practical action to cope with the negative aspects of these regimes, and to benefit from the new options that have opened up. These practical actions are described as counter-tendencies. Counter-tendencies cannot solve the problems of the underlying paradigm, but they can help new paradigms to emerge, and eventually alternative regimes to replace liberal-productivism. I do not see the future of the mountains in developing some best practices or distinction through unique selling propositions, which is the current state in regional development. Instead, we should go further. If mountain habitats and mountain economies are to survive in the long run, more profound social innovations must be developed that go beyond the liberal-productivist logic.

8.1 Recapitulation: the specificity of mountains

We have tried to discuss the specificity of mountains in this book. The usual arguments are as follows:

1   The physical disadvantages of a steep relief that does not allow standardized mass production, and which is particularly exposed and fragile towards biophysical uncertainties such as climate change.
2   Specific cultural practices of mountain agriculture and a pastoralist tradition that shows commonalities and differences over different mountain ranges.
3   A resource-rich territory that serves as a genetic pool and a reservoir of rare species.

In the light of recent knowledge, we have to relativize this common understanding. Under the conditions of an abundance of liquid capital all over the world and the availability of sophisticated and advanced technologies, former tacit and non-standardized practices become codified and standardized, which – in theory – could mitigate the development gap between lowlands and mountains and can – in general – cope with the mountain fragility. At the same time, the physical particularities are levelled (but are highlighted by marketing poetry). The global uncertainties of climate change can cause large irritations, probably not directly because of the mountain topography, but because of its global impacts on the economy, ecology, migrant flows, and politics.

The argument of common mountain cultures and identities, as well their diversity, also have to be relativized. Of course, the pre-modern agricultural practices to adapt to mountain conditions have persisted in modern societies for a long time; they still influence recent development. But they do not determine it. The national decision-makers live outside the mountains, and the mountain people send their children to the lowlands for a better education.

Finally, the resource pool and the reservoir matter for future generations. But they matter in a double sense. It is not only the survival of the biogenetic pool that interests the involved stakeholders, but also the valorization of it: mountain species for bio-pharmaceutical research, Alpine fallows as reserve areas to be built, mineral deposits for electronic devices, and the traditional reserve of a cheap workforce on a global labour market. This means that mountain specificity today is characterized by a superior potential for market development and strategic investment. In the emerging countries, the specificity lies rather in the geology of old basement complexes for mineral deposits; in the countries of the Global North, it is more the creation of new intangible amenities.

The mountain specificity therefore will not give us a clear order to act. We have to take our decision-making from normative criteria such as the presumed interests of the next generations, the Mountain Agenda from 1992, the UN Sustainable Development Goals (Table 8.1) – or risk-avoidance strategies such as the Climate Protocol (the 2015 Paris Agreement) to prevent the destruction of the planet. On the other hand, we can learn from the specific trajectories of mountain areas, from the good as well as the bad. The choice of possible trajectories is vast, and it is up to society to decide in which direction to go.

The question of mountain-specific problems remains. It was progress that transnational initiatives created transnational cooperation and treaties such as the Alpine or Carpathian Convention. But we have to distinguish between basic scientific questions and technical questions such as biophysical transformations, development of large protected areas, natural hazards, water quality, and noise pollution, on the one hand – and their interdependencies with external influences, on the other, such as an increase in traffic or demographic change. To study the interdependencies between highlands and lowlands, the perimeter of topographically demarcated mountain ranges is too narrow, and a national or transnational/European cooperation will be needed. To analyse mountain-specific questions, even the cooperation of all countries of the mountain range might not be enough, as this level is too restricted. For these questions a global exchange of current knowledge is necessary, as we see in the scientific debate on climate change. Questions such as forestry, plant migration, natural hazards,

Table 8.1 The United Nations Sustainable Development Goals.

United Nations Sustainable Development Goals	
Goal 1	End poverty in all its forms everywhere
Goal 2	End hunger, achieve food security and improved nutrition and promote sustainable agriculture
Goal 3	Ensure healthy lives and promote well-being for all at all ages
Goal 4	Ensure inclusive and quality education for all and promote lifelong learning
Goal 5	Achieve gender equality and empower all women and girls
Goal 6	Ensure access to water and sanitation for all
Goal 7	Ensure access to affordable, reliable, sustainable and modern energy for all
Goal 8	Promote inclusive and sustainable economic growth, employment and decent work for all
Goal 9	Build resilient infrastructure, promote sustainable industrialization and foster innovation
Goal 10	Reduce inequality within and among countries
Goal 11	Make cities inclusive, safe, resilient and sustainable
Goal 12	Ensure sustainable consumption and production patterns
Goal 13	Take urgent action to combat climate change and its impacts
Goal 14	Conserve and sustainably use the oceans, seas and marine resources
Goal 15	Sustainably manage forests, combat desertification, halt and reverse land degradation, halt biodiversity loss
Goal 16	Promote just, peaceful and inclusive societies
Goal 17	Revitalize the global partnership for sustainable development

Note: In 2015, the member countries of the United Nations adopted the programme 'Transforming Our World: the 2030 Agenda for Sustainable Development', a set of 17 Sustainable Development Goals (SDGs) to end poverty, protect the planet, and ensure prosperity. Each goal has specific targets to be achieved over the next 15 years.

or watershed management are treated at a global level, and new global mountain knowledge enters the Alps or Carpathians or Rocky Mountains via this exchange. Mountain stakeholders need access to this expert knowledge and an exchange on a global scale; in return, they can contribute their long-standing experience to be engaged as consulting experts for mountains in other continents. This is valid especially for the Alps, the most populated high mountains with the longest research tradition. At this point, mountains should be supported by the lowlands to enable universities and high-level research units to be located in the mountains, as there they can demonstrate their specific mountain competence (e.g. University of Central Asia). This also necessarily means that mountain regions have to develop more medium-sized towns to international-oriented cities with highly diverse urban qualities to attract students and lecturers. This is only possible in this 'cohesive trajectory': For the mainstream trajectory, there are already enough and better performing universities outside the mountains. And in the regionalist scenario, regions trying to go it alone probably lack the resources to be competitive.

8.2 The myth of cultural and environmental diversity in post-Fordism

(a) The increased role of culture as a means of distinction

Culture is seen in this book as an umbrella term for social and economic practices. From a spatial point of view, the transition from Fordist to liberal–productivist regulations means the abandonment of the logic of developing the identical pattern of infrastructure, industrial production systems, and quality of life everywhere. This development favours a spatial concentration of the most profitable activities in the metropolitan areas, and the conversion of less profitable areas into consuming regions for housing and recreation. It is a strategy to raise the specific productivity of territories and organizes territorial development selectively and according to the criteria of economic efficiency. The high spatial diversity attributed to post-Fordism is visible only on a global, intercontinental scale: Asia as the world's factory, South America as energy supplier and strongbox for the diversity of food, and Africa as mining extractor.

Looking at mountain areas on a small scale (i.e. the local and regional level), the opposite is the case. In the mountains, we often see the installation of high-quality homes in exceptional locations for affluent clients. In its extreme form, these strategies lead to secured neighbourhoods ('gated communities'), a development that has progressed in certain emerging countries and megacities. This is stimulated by strategies to attract a rich clientele as the real estate business receives higher margins and jurisdictions raise more taxes and have fewer problems. Meanwhile, diversity exists mainly in the urban areas, and only where neighbourhoods are not yet completely gentrified.

Under current conditions, mountains have to specialize to create a sharp profile. In the ideal case, the specialized sector might be quite diverse, but they rarely have the headquarters of their economic clusters: the financing, the commercial services such as advertising, etc. Furthermore, this specialization covers the sectors with specifically low value added (retail, personal services, and also tourism). It means that mountain regions do not have the endogenous growth to become rich and diversified according to the needs of a globalized world.

The local population can profit from enlarged retail and services if they share the offer with additional clients (tourists or multilocal inhabitants). They have to address their services according to the demands of their major commercial target group, and can receive new knowledge through this. This changes the complexity and diversity of their offer in favour of international brands, which means a reduction in diversity. As mountain regions do not have the high degree of diversity that has now been accumulated in large cities, the functional disparities between mountains and metropolises are sustained and increase.

What do these statements on diversity mean under the new regulations of post-Fordism? First, they disagree with the commonly used argument that highlights the enormous cultural diversity of mountain regions. In a globalized economy, this diversity is eroding in places which have become disconnected from current trends: in general, it is difficult to preserve it in its former authenticity. If mountain regions and communities profile themselves as international resort towns, this diversity will erode even more quickly. However, diversity in its broad range has become a high-ranked value. It implies that individuals have more choices of action. The advantage can be seen in analogy to Mark Granovetter (1973): a multitude of weak ties multiplies the range of information, provides broad knowledge, and allows a bundle of practices appropriate for many situations of everyday life and for strategic individual goals. A high diversity allows a greater choice for the personal consumption pattern and includes a great emphasis on personal liberty for work, residence, and leisure. These values have become important in societies that have eradicated direct poverty. And they are also characteristic of post-Fordist regimes because they serve as personal resources, i.e. symbolic capital, for a social ascent. Of course, the erosion of cultural diversity also applies to the large cities – diversity there is becoming a myth, too. But the bundle of possibilities to evade the fully commercialized and gentrified zones is much broader (which, again, is an indicator for the advantage of agglomeration economies).

Diversity allows individuals to emancipate themselves from societal restrictions – and means that the options for a change of social practices increase. Not having enough of this quality limits a mountain region's options for transformation and innovation.

What is new is that, due to higher mobility, it is possible to move more easily from one homogeneous space to another. With the specialization of mountains, we observe a broadening of homogeneous spaces. It can be concluded that cultural diversity that is attributed to liberal-productivist regimes is a myth. As in the past, it is affordable only for a part of the society that has the means to travel or to live multilocally: between metropolises, mountain resorts, the coastline, or across the globe (in its caricatural form: Paris, New York, Marrakech). Those who are immobile – trapped in repetitive and poorly paid jobs – are found in areas suffering social collapse where the cultural offer and the 'quality of life' are on a downward slide. It is obvious that the main criteria formulated by Edward Soja in search of 'spatial justice' are not met. For the advantaged parts of society, the 'uneven spatial development' invoked by Neil Smith (1984) becomes an engine for their empowerment and creativity; for the others, cultural diversity has the warmth of a film by Jean-Pierre and Luc Dardenne in the rubbish heaps of the Wallonian city of Liège. Finally, 'cultural diversity' is a matter of scale and perspective; it unfolds when considering the global aspect but restricts when examining the local or regional level.

(b) The increased ambiguity of environment as a basis of life and new commodities

The crisis of Fordism was also a crisis of faith in unleashed growth and accumulation with limitless natural resources, and a growing awareness of the fragility of ecological systems. It is the merit of this discussion about the usefulness of the environment for humankind for making obvious and tangible the destruction of the biophysical environment by pollution and the sealing of vast swathes of soil with concrete. This sensitivity to the environmental question emerged by citizenship in the form of the ecological movement, but also by scientific empirical research showing the advantages of biophysical processes (in terms of economic savings through ecosystem services) for humankind, which was a new approach. But the monetarization of pollution also makes the ambivalent double character of this debate appear. In this process of quantification, ecological values show that they do not represent a proper intrinsic value independent of any social relations. In this process, environmental qualities not only have a use value to society or to individuals (clean air for breathing, other health benefits). Ecological values are also defined by their exchange value (i.e. specific access to amenity-rich resources that have now become rare and are therefore exchanged by market mechanisms and subject to societal regulations).

The exchange value of near-natural environments is not only expressed in their absolute and relative scarcity. If it were, one could make efforts to improve environmental standards. In the case of housing, scarcity is repeatedly reproduced, since a flat not only meets the basic requirements of being a dwelling, but also reflects social hierarchies in terms of reputation (symbolic capital). Living in a quiet residential area with a view of a lake becomes a constituent element of social distinction as much as other social groups do not have easy access to this type of housing. Furthermore, in the liberal-productivist era, conscient zoning in luxury housing areas becomes an important factor for municipalities to attract wealthy people and to exclude less affluent residents that cost money. This aspect is new: in the Fordist era, the preferred places were the suburban areas and the city centre areas were abandoned. Now the symbolic capital of living in the periphery has become devalued. The significance of symbolic capital in general has increased but it is concentrated in emblematic places in large cities and temporarily in famous resort towns.

Another aspect is the common critique of urban sprawl and the demand for inner densification. People who are able to afford a flat (however small) in a central area can easily make this demand, as they may have access to a second residence in the mountains. What seems ecologically prudent becomes the opposite if it generates a rebound effect of consuming twice the number of square metres of living space. And there is another point that can be qualified as a 'Nimby' practice: If one already owns a secondary home in the mountains, then it is an advantage if the number of houses is restricted, to maintain the comfortable and quiet situation and profit from rising land prices.

This shows that the commitment 'to the environment' has two aspects. Enjoying pleasant scenery does not imply automatically an ecological awareness or a real intrinsic desire for it.

The new preferences for a concentration of jobs and the densification of residential areas – and against urban sprawl – touch the environment only superficially. These preferences are often linked with a generalization of high mobility and the pursuit of multisite working and living. Here, again, we can draw the conclusion that the environmental issue only becomes a problem for groups or individuals who are financially unable, cannot move due to family obligations, or who do not want to leave because they are emotionally strongly attached to the region of origin. At the global level, biophysical changes only become a problem when people are not able to leave the hazardous environmental conditions. From this point of view, and from the perspective of 'sustainability', the driving force is rather the foresight to escape the big world disorder, than an ecological argument or a preference for a particular landscape. The fact that there are so many people who cannot escape is a strong argument to avoid environmental damage. It is in its last consequence a social argument and not a biophysical one.

8.3 The non-innovative destruction of territorial capital

(a) Restricted options in post-Fordist trajectories

The concept of the persistent impacts of the different forms of capital, as well as the approach of evolutionary economics, shows that historically accumulated goods, values, and practices – although not determining – influence recent and future action. So, the historic path brings both an expansion and a limitation of the degrees of freedom for the future. Enlargement refers to new options, the further accumulation of wealth, and the blossoming of creativity on the basis of the existing development. Limitation means that by choosing a certain development path, some other alternatives become obsolete. Where a town has been founded, there is no more space for primary vegetation. Conversely, it is improbable that an additional metropolis will grow in European mountains above 1,000 m altitude.

Advantaged by agglomeration economies, metropolitan areas are meanwhile the only jurisdictions that do not have the problem of being dependent on one single economic cluster. They have several production systems that give them the necessary diversity to show a sufficient robustness against crisis or misman- agement in a single sector. In times of a generalized crisis, however, peripheries and mountains regained attractiveness, as we already knew from Switzerland (Schuler et al., 2004), and which was confirmed in recent years by in-migrants during the Yugoslav Wars (Dematteis and Membretti, 2016) and in Greece after the beginning of the financial crisis (Kasimis and Papadopoulos, 2013). Worldwide risks, migration, and needs for all kinds of mountain resources again justify keeping every part of a territory settled and in a similar shape.

It is thus all the more important to preserve and develop territorial capital in the peripheries, and to prevent it from being sacrificed. But the logic of agglomeration economies push mountain economies in the opposite direc- tion, into a selective exploitation of mountain-specific assets such as landscape- related activities, construction, tourism, and real estate business, etc. If land prices around urban agglomerations rise, there might be a change in zoning.

Agriculture is abandoned if farmers can sell their land to real estate inves-tors or if they themselves invest in new blocks of flats. The same goes for traditional extractive or manufacturing industries left in the suburban fringe: They are losing the support of their specific entrepreneurial milieu, which decreases with each company closure or relocation. They come under pressure, as the economic structure changes from manufacturing to business services industries, while at the same time land prices rise in the whole region due to the attractiveness of the city. The resulting changes in labour markets, busi-ness environment, and industrial know-how force the remaining manufactur-ing industries to relocate, as their industrial milieu has broken up. The usual recommendations favour apartment buildings at these sites. In the case of the mountains, regions are losing their cultural heritage and their tacit knowledge in this transformation process, while the success of gaining comparable skills for new productive activities is not guaranteed. So, what is once lost will not come back; destruction of territorial capital will diminish the options for the future, and this is especially valid for sparsely populated regions (i.e. for mountain areas). In this way, we have a true specificity of mountains, albeit a negative one.

While the growth regimes of the Fordist area had negative impacts on moun-tains through highly invasive infrastructure and severe pollution in the core countries of industrialization, the liberal-productivist regimes are more subtle and less visible. Severe pollution of rivers and air has been eradicated from the former strongly industrialized countries by relocating heavy industry to the emerging countries. The problematic impacts of the post-Fordist regimes are different: Mountain areas have little choice but to globalize their production systems – often against their will, as they cannot manage this or do not want to share the consequences in terms of the impacts on sustainable development. In this process the territorial capital of the mountain population risks becom-ing lastingly devalued, followed by out-migration or the replacement of the population by people lacking the tacit knowledge which once constituted the territorial capital.

8.4 The reproduction of territorial cleavages

(a) Productive and consumptive regions

The existing liberal-productivist regime has increased the problem of over-accumulation in capitalist societies, and the necessity to reinvest the accumu-lated surplus at higher returns on investment than in the past. This makes it necessary to find new places for investment, maybe by creating 'smart cities' for the development of technical devices, or a new resort town for the marketing of an intangible emotion. Both cases concern mountain areas in specialized but inferior functions: The devices require noble metals and the resort towns require the construction business and a workforce for hosting services. The spe-cialization divides territories into two different types. On the one hand, highly productive metropolitan areas as the location of the majority of jobs in general, and nearly all executive jobs. These are the areas with export-based economies and high value adding. On the other hand, peripheral areas that are used as residences for long-distance commuters or as second homes. In the literature and in the historic-political development of states, we find evidence that societies with a multitude of social cleavages are more stable than societies with one sharp gap between two antagonistic classes or ethnic groups. In the 1970s, the Norwegian sociologist Stein Rokkan, who also worked for the United Nations, worked on violent conflicts and how to prevent them by regional cohesion. He developed the concept of 'cross-cutting cleavages', according to which states, regions, and ethnic groups with a bundle of less important conflict lines in their society are better off than societies with one deep cleavage (Rokkan and Urwin, 1983). A high number of smaller disruptions in a society is not as severe as one single conflict line. A bundle of social cleavages may overlap incongruently, making them unable to disaggregate the system as a whole (cross-cutting cleavages). Every individual of a distinct group of stakeholders is part of another group of stakeholders and makes alliances with other groups, which limits the intensity of each possible conflict.

We find examples of this approach in West Africa, where different ethnicities that have been strongly linked by history have institutionalized their relations by exchanging targeted altercations, known as 'joking relations' (Radcliffe-Brown, 1940; Roth, 1996). In Switzerland, Rokkan's approach was used to explain the long-time territorial and social cohesion in Switzerland as 'nation by will' (Joye et al., 1992; Schuler and Perlik, 2011).[1] The plurality of small divisions (denomination, language, town versus country, lowland versus mountains) that have formed in Switzerland (and which are not congruent) explains that these conflicts are of low impact; they prevent the disintegration of the state as there are, ideally, changing coalitions. At the same time, the principle of a planned imbroglio of institutions (which was further strengthened with the foundation of the Swiss federal state in 1848) confirmed the principle of multiple cleavages that divide the blocks of homogeneous stakeholders, split between members of the same social class but also bringing together heterogeneous groups of stakeholders.

Considering these reflections, the polarization into two types of territories – the productive value adding and the consumptive residential ones – seems very problematic. According to the proverb, 'He who pays the piper calls the tune', and the question of 'who contributes how much to the community and how much they benefit from it' is quickly raised. All societies know the implicit obligation that each individual and each collective have to contribute to the wealth of a given society. Although this imperative differs in its rigidity between countries and changes in time, there is a certain universalism. In a world where paid work to have access to tangible and intangible resources is so important, it is hardly imaginable that at the very end, there is no conflict when one part of the country mainly produces and the other part mainly consumes. We can already observe the territorial conflicts between southern and northern Italy, where accusations fly as to who is productive and who has been abandoned in terms of investments in infrastructure. According to Rokkan and Urwin, a multitude of small societal cleavages prevents larger conflicts because there is rarely a situation in which one completely homogeneous group stands against another. In everyday life, there are changing constellations of cooperation that make real conflicts rather unlikely, while a situation in which the same dividing lines always occur will generate a deep gap. If in a globalized world some ancient cleavage lines lose significance (e.g. the language), the deepening between producing cities and unproductive hinterlands may be dangerous and should be avoided.

8.5 Regional strategies to cope and to counteract

(a) Common regional strategies: adaptation or isolation

If a significant reversal of spatial power relations in favour of mountain regions seems unlikely, the question arises of how to cope with the latent loss of territorial capital. The most commonly applied strategy is to incorporate the new leisure and residence functions in the regional trajectory of transforming the old production systems into new ones (e.g. becoming a greenkeeper or landlord of holiday accommodation instead of farming). Or, more promisingly, to invent new business ideas that link former knowledge with new demands. This is how all outdoor leisure activities were created, from bungee jumping to educational trekking tours. It may work, but it will reduce the diversity of territorial capital, as explained in Section 8.3. These activities are less place-dependent due to increased mobility, and they will also have a shorter life cycle than the former production systems, as they are part of dynamic lifestyle practices. So we cannot really see much progress in these strategies, although there hardly seems to be a pragmatic alternative.

A completely different coping strategy is to reject all transformations and maintain one's identity as a mountain community, asking for financial support in the form of subsidies or higher (politically defined) prices for the use of mountain resources. This is contradictory, as peripheral regions demand through this strategy to be financed by a national or European community, using the argument of their inferiority compared to the metropolitan regions, while, on the other hand, they have to welcome the disproportionally high value adding of these dynamic nodes. Furthermore, the verification of strong traditional identity leads, as we have recently observed, to the deepening of social and ethnic cleavages and the tendency of exclusion. We see the mighty lock-in effect: the local stakeholders lose their former openness and innovativeness; they fail to adapt permanently to external influences. In this case, the institutions, the relations between actors, and existing infrastructure again work as capital in the sense of Bourdieu, but this time they are a hindrance to overcoming the crisis. A change might be possible only after the pressure of suffering has become too strong.

(b) New neo-ruralism

The neo-rural movement of the 1970s in the Western countries was a first attempt to counteract the paradigm of growth and environmental destruction. Such movements have also taken place recently. All over the Alps, neo-rural movements can be found, with people who have migrated from the cities to abandoned villages in the mountains. The effects of the new immigration of urban people to rural or mountain areas are discussed controversially. In any case, we assume that the new inhabitants have some interest in the mountains. This interest can create an untapped potential for the active development of the hosting municipalities. This applies to permanent residents (e.g. the specific knowledge of the retired), as well as for part-time, multilocal residents (who make the mountain region known outside). Multilocality brings patchwork families together and combines work, dwelling, and leisure for temporary and specific situations. In the form of repeated individual practice, this might generate a specific attachment. There are examples of associations whose members live outside the Alps but meet in the mountainous region to pursue joint activities such as the operation of a cable car or a railway line, or for pastoralism in summer at high altitudes, or to repair ancient dry walls of stone lynchets. These are examples where newcomers become well integrated because they make efforts, and thus meet a culture of openness. If these practices become more widespread, mountain regions could generate a new demand for service, which could make it possible to close the gap between productive and residential economies. Although the numbers involved do not alter the general picture, in any case we do not have profound reasons to abandon sparsely populated regions and to proclaim a new 'empty', 'natural' space.

The effect of all these activities is very small and currently insufficient to alter the main tendency. But they help to maintain existing settlement structures. In a negative view, this could be seen as a delayed effect in a continuous process of decline. In a positive view, one can see here a movement that helps to maintain settlements and infrastructure, supports the local administration with external knowledge, and works as a lobby against abandonment. It is a huge potential for a future development in a double sense. First, the new inhabitants and volunteers can bridge the current period in which the sparsely populated regions continue to lose massively in importance, in the hope that the qualities of sparsely populated areas will become important and popular again: Mountain areas as a place of diversity preserved for the future. Second, these new initiatives could develop a creative force that may release new experiments and forms of governance in the sense of social innovations. Social innovations in rural and mountain areas are new forms of local cooperation that go beyond established economic models and state intervention.

(c) Social innovations in peripheries

With the liberal-productivist turn, the welfare state did not disappear completely. In Europe, support for the peripheries is still observable, which means that there is a societal consensus that these areas are disadvantaged and cannot be profitable. But this support varies according to the financial means of the public institutions. The financial crisis of 2007 has reduced the scope of policies, but regional policies were not all abandoned. The national state still provides infrastructure, and a system of financial compensation persists. It is one result of a national research programme in Switzerland that mountain development is based on two pillars: value adding and value appreciation. If there is no appreciation and support throughout society for the peripheral areas, then valorization strategies will also fail (Lehmann and Messerli, 2007).

Untradeable interdependencies play a role in civic engagement and network-building. Sometimes this happens on the basis of expected returns in the future, in the sense of 'paying it forward'. Sometimes it is in testing new ways of life and new forms of institutions (e.g. forms of associations). Such initiatives open up possibilities for social innovations. Social innovations, seen in a transformative view, are distinct from the offer-oriented approach as they go beyond technical and social engineering: instead, they try to find new relations between local actors in peripheral areas to overcome structural inferiority (EC, 2017, Klein et al., 2014, Moulaert et al., 2013, Perlik, 2018). If mountain areas succeed in developing new forms of socio-economic relations, they can maintain the loyalty of their own inhabitants and attract the support of the inhabitants of the metropolitan areas, as well as that of visitors, part-time residents, and buyers of specific products at a fair price. By doing this, they can stabilize their production system and their population and might have the potential – in the sense of a grass-roots initiative – to also influence social relations at a higher level.

Finally, the highlighting of 'landscapes' as the new buzzword, which I criticized for its aesthetic approach, has at least its merits of opening up a view of things other than traditional productivist growth. In other words, it allows other forms of growth and other trajectories than the usual infrastructure-dominated ones, and it may ameliorate the conditions in preserving public space and public accessibility.

(d) Persistence, resistance, and hysteresis

The concept of the regulation approach offers a logic to interpret a certain constellation of societal stakeholders and practices that differ over time and are found in a multitude of regional variations. This was named a regime. Each regional or national regime treats different social fields with a different focus, particularly the question of risk-taking, expected growth rates, land use, and checks and balances. Therefore, the liberal-productivist turn has been applied differently, depending on space and time. In this regard, for example, the Fordist regime of Rhenish Capitalism in Germany was abandoned later than in other countries, only seemingly paradoxically during the social democratic government in the 1990s (especially with cuts in the social system), while the French Fordist system remained more or less inert until now, even (or precisely because of this) under right-wing governments.

Concerning the mountains, Switzerland made this paradigm change as a 'metropolitan turn' in the mid-1990s. In contrast, comparable Austria still sees itself as an Alpine country. It did not takeover the self-perception of an Alpine metropolitan region. We see that the outlined generalized picture of liberal-productivist economies did not take hold completely. It penetrated in different forms and with a time lag and makes it impossible to speak about one single regime.

The export-based value chains still exist (such as agriculture, artisanal production, and tourism). Furthermore, the new investment projects in resort towns are often combinations between residences and tourism, meaning that tourism and jobs related to the new real estate owners remain. The mutual solidarity at the national level between lowlands and mountains is not yet really abandoned. On the contrary, we observe the merger of mountain communities as a strategy to give them more influence on national policies; they also increase their openness towards the lowlands to renew relations of solidarity. Concerning the relations between urban city centre areas and their sub- and peri-urban hinterlands, common interests and contradictions differ from case to case. Also, in the other countries of the Alps, the local population is still present and defends its interests. If we take the examples of the regaining of population in the peripheries, especially the Greek example mentioned in Section 8.3, then we see that there is a need for populated peripheries, but also the opportunity for enlarging their potentials.

Note

1 The Swiss journalist Roger de Weck argues the same way when he invokes the multitude of interlaced institutions for the social and territorial cohesion of Switzerland. Each institution, each region, has its own interests but has to work together with others in changing constellations – a strategy that he now also observes with the European Union (de Weck, 2009). Similarly, Christian Schmid (2006) argues with 'borders, networks, and differences'.

9   Three possible trajectories for mountain regions

This penultimate chapter will try to draw three broad options for mountain regions under the current conditions of liberal-productivism. We call these options trajectories. They differ in the general coping strategies of mountain regions towards internal (regional or national) transformations and external (global) impacts.

In the publication *Alpenstädte* (*Towns in the Alps*) published in 2001, for the first time metropolization was addressed and empirically proven for a large mountain range – which was the merit of this work – but with much caution, having rather conservative results. So, metropolization processes were clearly seen but consciously under- rather than overestimated, to have a 'right-side failure'. Meanwhile, 15 years later, metropolization has become, in spatial terms, *the* expression of the liberal-productivist change of the 1980s. Now we can pose the questions again, and we should pose them more radically:

- Should we – for research and policies – include the peri-Alpine fringes in the mountain perimeter? This would take into account the new realities. If not, what would be the consequences?
- Should we maintain the mountain-specific approach? What will be the economic, social, and political weight of mountain areas if we give it up? How can we avoid regional egoism if we keep it?
- What are the possible alternatives between the current mainstream tendencies and their rejection?

Scientific discourse and public debate on future Alpine development are dominated by two opposing positions. On the one hand, we see the demand by urban people to integrate the Alps into the value system of landscape protection, referring to biodiversity and aesthetics, and – at the same time – into global economic circuits, referring to the need for greater productivity, economic wealth, and market options. These positions accept the abandoning of weak areas according to their own logic of efficiency. On the other hand, we have the proponents of the preservation of traditional structures and the demand for local freedom of action against urban paternalism, claimed by mountain people and local and regional jurisdictions. So, we see two strategies:

- Continuing metropolization, justifying it through the arguments of economic efficiency, ecological efficiency, and social superiority ('high culture') of the city. This position relies on the urban majority demographic in the lowlands with its economic weight, claiming, on the one hand, the economies of agglomeration as an argument for concentrating jobs and services in the city and, on the other, profiting from the distinctive qualities of the countryside. The result is a territorial cleavage between highly productive areas and residential areas. The additional argument to this mainstream position is a vulgarized critique on urban sprawl and the demand for a general densification within cities. This argument can be called the 'new productivist mainstream' of the liberal-productivist period. The trendsetters are already well advanced, as already mentioned above: the concept of an 'urban Switzerland' can be seen as established, and meanwhile, ideas of the Asian-type city state (Singapore) have been evoked, with a responsibility only for the dynamic parts of a territory and an economically ultra-liberal mode of regulation. This development path can be named as the mainstream trajectory.
- Trying to generate a common Alpine identity based on a presumed common history of mountain farmers, artisans, and small-scale tourism. To reduce the pressure on the Alpine territory from 'outside' the Alps, it proposes a very narrow definition of the Alpine arc, restricted to its 'rural' parts. This is done by proposing a delimitation according to geomorphological (relief) criteria and the exclusion of the dynamic peri-Alpine urban fringes. By excluding urban dynamics, one hopes to strengthen the political position to maintain and prolong traditional cultivation with a moderate development. This rural paradigm, the so-called *ländliche Makroregion* (rural macro-region) (Bätzing, 2011), starts with an assumed common identity of the Alpine regions and the expectation that Alpine economic clusters can be competitive towards the economy outside as niche players for high-end food and tourism. At the same time, this position implies that with existing settlement structures (decentralized population, small towns as local markets), the urban dimension remains restricted to small and medium-sized towns with functions as pre-industrial marketplaces.[1]

In Section 9.3, I will sketch an alternative trajectory that tries to draw the consequences of the weak points of the current discussions: the increasing inferiority of the peripheries in the existing mainstream trajectory and the latent regional egoism that underlies the mountain-specific discourse.

9.1 The trajectory of liberal-productivist mainstream: city states, private cities, and the alliance of the wealthiest

It is the trajectory described in the book as the current process: Metropolitan areas are the nodes of decision-making and specialized services; peripheries and mountain areas are locations for resource extraction, residences, and leisure. It is the logic of agglomeration advantages, increased spatial division of labour, and the continuous creation of product innovations to gain disproportional returns on investment. As lucrative investment strategies become harder and harder to find, investment in the green economy and in mountain resources is a current option.

(a) The normative assumption

The trajectory follows the assumption that continuous surplus allows reinvestment to satisfy society's demand for technological progress, and that parts of the value added may be used to increase individual wealth, purchasing power, and consumption. The mechanisms of market laws are predominant.

(b) The characteristics

This trajectory generates highly diversified productive metropolitan cores in the lowlands and highly specialized mountain areas. In between, we find peri-urban areas that are more or less segregated according to the socio-economic status of their population. Land use has reached a new quality in efficiency by the commodification of new assets – aesthetic aspects which have become a new symbolic capital, under labels such as *landscapes, urbanscapes,* or *cityscapes.* Regions have to guarantee their own economic earning power. The non-metropolitan regions have to develop distinctive features and niche strategies to remain competitive. Such strategies may be tax reductions to attract specific economic activities or wealthy residents. The territorial model is coherent with the main tendencies in a globalized economy to avoid direct competition by the innovation of new commodities and to find new fields for investment. According to this logic, it is consistent to abandon a territorial jurisdiction if it seems no longer profitable. Key political actors propose strategies similar to those applied in economic life: splitting companies into a profitable and a less profitable unit to create higher market capitalization. In Europe, this can be observed with separatist movements in Lombardy and Veneto (northern Italy) or in Catalonia (Spain). The argumentation is always the same: the complaint that the other parts of the country are not productive enough or waste resources, and that a 'freelance' strategy would be more propitious.[2] Consciously or by naivety, its proponents do not consider the repercussions on other stakeholders: Mobility costs (especially labour mobility) and transaction costs in general would rise, especially at the expense of poor individuals and even many enterprises. The argument that the weaker regions may take unjustified profit from subsidies is so strong that even the 'insurance effects' of redundant and diversified but less productive structures are disesteemed. This attitude differs from the regionalist and separatist movements that occurred in the 1970s, when regions claimed more autonomy due to cultural assertiveness as minorities against the central state and social decline (Northern Ireland, Basque region, etc.).

What is new (i.e. specifically liberal-productivist) about these arguments? In the past, differences between different regions were seen as 'collateral damage' of economic competition, to be resolved with the intervention of the state through planning and compensation. Today, the argumentation has changed, and larger differences are seen as an incentive to be more diverse, efficient, and profitable. In practice, this generates a polarization between declining regions and new investments in upcoming gentrifying neighbourhoods, smart cities, and even private cities that are developed by commercial investors.[3] This indifference towards the purpose of producing only to raise value added, is already disturbing in the sphere of economics. It is even more disturbing in territorial issues. Cities and regions not only have the function of an economic use of space, which may run according to market rules; they also represent the platform for social life and the relationships between different individuals and collectives. Private cities and also 'city states' with willingly intended segregation are attempts to produce 'clean' solutions by excluding all parts of society that might not be as productive as the dominating elites. This means a reinforcement of the dominant economic and hierarchical position of the current leaders by abandoning all the elements that can cause additional frictions, elevate transaction costs, and endanger a position of strength.[4]

In this trajectory, mountains no longer play the role of a specific precondition of distinct forms of production or living that should be sustained because of their cultural quality. Cultural specificities of its people serve as commercializable folklore; the topography has become the 'landscape' brand. Agriculture may hold an organic or a nostalgic brand according to the targeted groups: 'organic' to achieve higher prices for the milk paid by the citizen; 'nostalgic' to transport isolationist ideas towards the electorate.

(c) Why has this trajectory become attractive?

This trajectory seems to solve the problems of regions with low value added or with declining industries: If one activity breaks down, there are dynamic local or external actors with the capacity of innovation to develop new business models so that the destination may regain a new life. It corresponds to the idea that market signals are the best sensors for transformation and that disparities are mitigated through self-regulation. It corresponds to the dominant liberal-productivist model.

(d) Shortcomings and weaknesses

Fluctuations in investment returns always affect individuals who were not aware or had no choice but to be part of the uncertainties of market movements. So there are always winners and losers, and in general there is no compensation of risk. Mountain areas harbour an additional risk, as they are often in fragile territory and present unique situations due to their topography. So, we often have the situation that the pioneers of a resort sacrifice open space for living and working, which may fall into decline during a crisis. Then the land and the landscape are devalued – economically and ecologically – and the failure affects not only individuals, but possibly the whole local society and territory. These mechanisms are not reflected by price signals. An extraordinary weakness is, of course, that this approach does not take into account individual and societal preferences beyond tradable and calculable indicators.

(e) The counterproductive and dangerous impact

The dangerous impact lies in the fact that in the end, this approach is not really innovative, as it shows no transformative *social* innovation. It accepts changed preferences only if the shift has already taken place, and it cannot anticipate new tendencies such as the preservation of ecological and cultural heritage. In this way, this approach is always on the side of the possessing classes, and never on the side of the non-possessing, displaced, and deprived – and so it lacks innovative potential, too.

(f) Three short scenarios

Scenario 1: Mountain regions that can pursue their tourism sector by maintaining both winter and summer seasons, focused on high-end clientele, have good chances of survival as long as the number of middle-class people in the emerging countries is still on the rise. Real estate business and residences become more significant compared to tourist activities. By enlarging residential zones the ground is sealed and the open land is withdrawn from the public. The piedmont fringes become densely populated, as migrants from the lowlands ascend and people from the lateral valleys descend. The new transport infrastructure bridges larger distances, traversing mountain ranges through tunnels. On the whole, the mountains gain people and new investment. The medium altitudes and lateral valleys have less potential and pursue depopulation. They have three options: They may serve as reserve locations for poor people who cannot afford to live in large cities or in the resort towns in which they often work. They may also serve as reserve places in times of economic crisis. Those sites which contain raw materials and water reservoirs may develop according to market oscillations. In most cases, they do not employ many people.

Scenario 2: During the construction boom, the available surfaces were sealed with condominiums. But now the tourist sector is declining due to climate change or intensified competition. The attractiveness for residents vanishes. Many of the apartments are empty. As the attractiveness to tourists and residents has diminished, agriculture, retail, and other services are in decline too. Certain projects for residence towers are cancelled. This provokes an enormous setback as many ideas, financial means, and especially time invested are burnt. There are not many alternatives. The workforce in tourism has already sought other destinations. People who came from abroad to work in the few positions requiring higher education qualifications in tourism and other services have already left. There will be no financial aid from the public sector as public institutions have been made 'lean'. There is no political will by the population in the lowlands to support the exaggerated plans of mountain entrepreneurs, as these projects completely contradict urban preferences and values.

Scenario 3: As in scenario 2, the considered region falls into decline. But contrary to scenario 2, the important local families are able to abandon the old business model of real estate speculation. A new generation of local owners tries with some success to find new ways to attract people from the lowlands and give them the opportunity to pursue artistic and other creative activities. Often, they are descendants of the owners of the old hotels and second homes and have large working experiences outside the mountains and in other sectors. They have fresh ideas and are willing to abandon their former expectations of basing their life on economic rent. They also accept the risk of losing money. In this way, they are able to relaunch the location with new activities and other business models.

9.2 The trajectories of exaggerated identities: a topographically demarcated Alpine region

In this trajectory, the regional stakeholders try to defend the traditional position of their region with the argument of specific framework conditions, specific culture, and regional identity. It is an attempt to fight against reduced autonomy and increasing inferiority and decline.

(a) The normative assumption

The normative assumption for this trajectory consists in the interpretation of the common historical development path, which is still seen as strong enough to legitimate common regional interests and to fuel a common social movement. Another normative assumption lies in a specific interpretation of the sustainability concept, where the quality of traditional mountain production systems is seen per se as superior to recent production systems. In the justified critique on the liberal-productivist mainstream, the ambiguous character of the past mountain economies is mainly neglected. Both these assumptions – general common mountain or Alpine interests and the specific understanding of sustainability – are strongly questionable, as I have tried to show in this book.

(b) The characteristics

Mountain regions have the specific disadvantage of higher costs of production and organization due to a sparse population. They have the advantages of a huge potential of rare tangible and intangible resources. Often their populations are part of ethnic minorities. In this respect they claim specific support, regulations, or even autonomy. In the past, this argumentation resulted in creation of several new Himalayan Federal states of India, the Canadian Nunavut Territory for the specific interests of the Inuit, or the autonomous regions in Italy for linguistic minorities.

The debate about the appropriate strategies for mountains is not new. Should we pursue a strategy of a common mountain development in the Alps to bring together regions by arguments of common history, problems, and strategic interests? Or should we – according to the Alpine arc segmented into different metropolitan regions – merge the lowlands and the mountain parts to mitigate risks and potentials by increasing the exchange between lowlands and mountains, and thus accept a certain hybridization? The European Alps are the most advanced mountain range in this debate. In the Alps, this discussion began in the late 1980s with the demand for an international agreement on environmental protection. It had its first proponents in environmental NGOs, regional institutions, and also academic positions. In the scientific debate, there was a huge discussion whether the peri-Alpine metropolitan areas should be part of Alpine policies to create economically stable regions and allow a compensation of wealth within a broader demarcated region (Martinengo, 1991), or whether they should be excluded to apply regional policies only to the 'real Alps' (i.e. to promote the disadvantaged traditional rural economies) (Bätzing, 1991).

If we look at the map of the Alpine Convention from 1991, we see that this demarcation was already quite arbitrary. There are states such as Switzerland that took a very rigid demarcation, leaving out Geneva, Bern, and Zurich, although the Alpine summits are clearly visible from there, and daytrippers use the weekends to invade the mountain destinations with daily tourism. There is Germany, which has the smallest share of the Alps; it claimed a large demarcation, interested in having more influence, but nevertheless, Munich remained on the outside. There is Austria, which tried to benefit from both sides: bringing in a tertiary structured city such as Salzburg but leaving out the strongly industrialized Graz. Both are in a similar geographic position, but Graz is the location of a manufacturing automotive cluster, and Salzburg is famous for music. Leaving out Graz, one hoped to benefit from a higher degree of freedom in developing Styrian industry.

It seemed plausible to apply this understanding of a common Alpine space – similar historic development paths and current problems – to a common political strategy that aimed at uniting the regions of the Alpine arc to protect the environment and rare resources against degradation and squandering. In this logic, it makes sense to delimit the Alpine arc strictly along topographic lines in order to maintain homogeneous areas with many commonalities and to strengthen 'Alpine awareness' and identity in this area. Consistent implementation of this approach would lead to an institutional relaxation of the existing links between the highlands and the lowlands with its metropolitan regions and strengthen the development of a transnational intra-Alpine economic area.

(c) Why does this trajectory seem an attractive counter-model?

The idea is that the institutionalized cooperation between regional societies with a common socio-economic background may serve as a counterpart to the external forces of global change, and that it may create a more solidary society based on rather homogeneous mountain communities. It is seen to be a propitious strategy to maintain the specific qualities of mountain-specific production systems by reinforcing regional identities and rejecting the prevailing interests of enlarging metropolitan areas. One of the strategies to maintain regional specificities against the global impacts tries to intensify the endogenous potentials and short regional economic circuits. It is meant as an answer to the post-Fordist global growth regimes. Its proponents refer to regional movements struggling against water and hydropower reservoirs in the Alps constructed 'for the thirst of the plain', expressed through public action and watch-fires against transit road traffic through the Alps. Such movements are important to show the price of the productivist growth regimes, the ecological impact, and the regional asymmetries. If they are successful, they contribute to concrete alternatives of development. But we have to discern between regionally embedded social movements and political regionalism. Political regionalism is not the precondition for successful regional and social movements. Its promoters, however, see Alpine regionalism often as the legitimate antithesis to the liberal-productivist mainstream, as this approach is stated as a regionally homogeneous alternative against the impacts of external dominance in general, which they hold responsible for socio-economic change.

(d) Shortcomings and weaknesses

This trajectory has many shortcomings and weaknesses, although it seems to offer a good option for joint action against the liberal-productive model. First, the promoters are not free of narrow-minded self-interest to protect their own little garden while the world burns outside. In this sense, alpine activists and their NGOs show the same weaknesses as their colleagues who defend the superiority of urban culture. The professionalization of NGOs has produced loyal and efficient experts who do not respect the legitimate interests of other stakeholders, even though they also benefit from these stakeholders' global practices. Secondly, the assumptions of common alpine interest are highly questionable. The argument of the Alpine arc as a common economic area had its legitimacy as a criticism of the inferior function of the Alpine regions, with the aim of awakening more self-confidence and creative power. But if the starting hypothesis of the assumed common interest is wrong, the stakeholders involved will not find a way to cooperate. The idea of creating a macro-region without the peri-Alpine fringes with their metropolises thus denies the realities and tries to realize commonalities for which we cannot find a material basis. The mountain regions themselves disagree on this issue.

Even the Alpine Convention, although it also includes development goals, is contested. Many Alpine regions are sceptical about this European treaty, as they see too many restrictions for their development. This has not really changed, especially in Switzerland, where the mountain cantons are largely opposed to the convention's obligations. When the Swiss Statistical Office conceived the statistical units of NUTS2, the mountain cantons were against a common mountain unit 'Alps'. Instead, they preferred a territorial structure with seven NUTS2 units, where five of them hold parts of the Alps as well as peri-Alpine parts. The argumentation was that this demarcation would better reflect the regional cooperation and communalities than a model containing an all-Alpine unit, which would have merged parts that normally do not work together as much. Third, interpreting the Alps today as a topographically demarcated territorial unit means denying the spatial and socio-economic transformation of recent decades (i.e. the segmentation of the Alpine arc into subregions). The development of the last 20 years runs counter to this and cements the current picture of the demographically grown but segmented Alps.

While the Alpine regions did develop a common political rhetoric, they follow different economic development paths, with each Alpine segment oriented to its peri-Alpine regional metropolis – Milan, Turin, Geneva, Zurich, Munich, Vienna, etc. (Perlik, 2001). Since then, the significance of the peri-Alpine metropolitan areas has continued to increase. So, we have a situation where identity-building and marketing language converge, while socio-economic practices diverge towards the different metropolitan catchment areas. We can also see this characteristic in the results of a small-scale case study of the Dolomites, where five Italian provinces have received the UNESCO World Heritage label. The provinces work together in a common promotion campaign but the stakeholders practise completely different economic development strategies. As mentioned above, this differs fundamentally between the two German-speaking provinces and the three Italian-speaking provinces.

Fourth, the arguments for a socio-economic Alpine space seemed to be justified under the assumption that there is a common Alpine interest of the Alpine population that makes it useful to work together against the strong and densely populated peri-Alpine neighbours on the practical level. And it was a counter-model on the societal level expecting that the Alpine experience could deliver an emancipative alternative to the productivist optimism of eternal growth. Concerning the emancipative approach, the small circuits of an Alpine economy – where it still exists – no longer have the shaping power to show a real alternative to the mainstream scenario. Furthermore, the examples already mentioned above from India and Argentina and show that regional governments and administrations do not do a better job when they hold the responsibility for a homogeneous mountain state. On the contrary, they are encouraged to use their comparative advantages or monopolies to over-exploit regional resources and sell them on global markets, which they cannot fully master. The increased importance of land-grabbing and the role of local authorities and global investors are further proof of that.

(e) The counterproductive and dangerous impact

The counterproductive effect lies in the exclusive character of an exaggerated thinking in terms of identity. Strategies to strengthen regional identities are generally not harmless. The attempt to force areas that are differentiating themselves and developing into the corset of a supposedly common identity must fail, because a stabilization of the mountain areas is only possible through the acquisition of new knowledge that is generated by the exchange with schools and universities and by migrants from the outside. Decoupling from the peri-Alpine metropolitan regions is therefore counterproductive. One could stop here, as the European strategies already go in the other direction: The future European Alpine Macro Region (EUSALP) has a very large demarcation. But the idea to create a topographically restricted perimeter persists, and it plays an important role in the discussion about development strategies for the Alpine arc, Scotland, and other regions in the world. Paradoxically, mountain areas had in the past – in the equalizing Fordist period – the power to point out the differences between mountains and lowlands, thus stimulating sustainable developments: be it by obviation of high impact projects (e.g. the large dams in the Greina high plateau and other valleys of Switzerland) or through legal action (by the inhabitants of Longarone, as the victims of the industrialization of Mestre, Venice). In both cases, the people of the mountain areas had the power to persuade the rest of the country to reconcile the contradictions of interest. This mechanism also worked in transport policies: mountain people found allies who understood that there is an asymmetric pattern of charges and benefits by transit routes through the Alps, although mountain people also eat oranges that cannot be cultivated at the Gotthard Pass. Through these actions, mountain people showed that they were able to develop innovative ideas and influence societal processes; in this case, by changing European transport policies.

But here we see the ambiguous impacts of isolated success, the effect of progress restricted to the island of the happy few. Post-Fordist governance and accumulation have weakened territorially based solidarity towards a market-driven solution where specific disadvantages and asymmetric power relations are not properly considered. It is easy to denounce engagement against noise and fine dust pollution as a 'Nimby' attitude. As the mountain population does not understand the metropolitan population, and vice versa, the lowland majority does not support the mountain population. The mountain regions' power to persuade as an alternative model of society has been eroded. In principle, being an island of difference may be progressive, as a way of persuading other territories and parts of society to take the same path. But such an island may also be a community garden only of one's own to gain rents – and this model will fail as it comes under pressure from the outside. But the problem remains to be solved: how to create a comparable – similar – development between different regions while maintaining sufficient sociocultural differences to minimize social and environmental risks. These are normative objectives in the interest of personal and societal benefits, regardless of whether these objectives are called human curiosity, quality of life, or contemplation.

The question of the identity-based trajectory goes beyond the question of specific mountain disadvantages, as it constitutes the background of regionalist and nationalist identity-based self-assurance, which excludes those parts of societies that are ascribed other identities. In this sense, regionalist identity thinking (with a unilateral way of defending acquired living standards) has developed as a prototype of nationalist movements in Europe. Mountain and rural regions find themselves not in the first line. However, being distinctive from others is always ambiguous. In its positive form, it can show an alternative model for a better way of living for all; in its negative form, it remains restricted and represents only regional egoism. It is not clear at the beginning how it will turn out. Raising regional identity and distinctiveness of mountain areas was once linked with the hope that mountain regions would emanate a positive impulse also for the lowlands. In recent decades, the externally driven impacts have become so strong that distinctiveness has become a means to save one's own skin. Mountain value chains and regimes alone are not strong enough to serve as a counter-model to the liberal-productivist trajectory. This approach is either not heard, or else it is quickly integrated into the range of marketing strategies of the global mainstream.

The disturbing message of the topographically demarcated identity-based scenario is its isolationist regionalistic approach. It reinforces a cleavage between highlands and lowlands that confirms the difference between highly productive metropolitan economies, and leisure and dwelling landscapes with less value adding. There are no indicators that mountains can establish economies of similar strength in an interdependent global world. There are also no indicators that would show that the lowland inhabitants would subsidize a weak mountain territory without seeing an advantage (in the form of a consumptive use) for themselves. The regionalistic approach, therefore, will reinforce existing cleavages that are based on specific identities. Inflating the sentiments of identity confirms self-consciousness and diversity, but it is also a strong lever to produce exclusion of otherness and strengthen existing prejudices and disparities. In its most extreme form, it becomes a nationalist discourse that runs against the objectives of European integration, while nevertheless profiting from this integration through social and physical security and economic wealth. The experience of the failed Yugoslavian case shows that it is not always possible to create cross-cutting and institutional interdependencies, but we can also see that the failure to create stable interdependencies tears down the value and welfare system for the large majority.

What is the future of mountain areas in the identity-based trajectory? A functional Alpine macro-region based on mountain culture (whatever this would still be) would need to create a common socio-economic space, and it would be imperative for the different parts of the Alps to cooperate closely. This would require construction of new infrastructure, especially efficient longitudinal rail and road systems with an hourly service between the main first- and second-tier Alpine cities. We would need some cyclopean work on the 'hardware' of infrastructure: trans-European networks with base tunnels for high-speed trains from Geneva to Vienna and from Genoa to Munich. Furthermore, airports in every medium-sized town with daily flights not only to the major European hubs but especially to each other: e.g. Chambéry – Bolzano,

Linz – Cuneo and Sion – Leoben. And we would need a plan to interlace the different Alpine institutions by creating common administrations for specific topics, etc. All this in the interest of creating a new common economic space.

Nevertheless, it would result in an artificial economic space, which would host mainly the weak economic sectors. It would create an entity similar to Greece, with much tourism. It is therefore obvious that both in Europe and in the mountain regions themselves there is a lack of understanding or support for such a mountain segregation strategy. The argument for the 'real mountain' demarcation, denying existing functional linkages, was the idea to reinforce the interests of the disadvantaged agriculture and decentralized small-scale tourism, and to reinforce the population of the Alpine territory in the face of the peri-Alpine metropolitan regions. This attitude creates a paradox, because it requires the Alpine regions to unite within the Alpine arc across national borders (which is hardly possible in sparsely populated or uninhabited high mountains) and to develop a position of defence towards the densely populated lowlands (which is only likely to cause short-term harm to the metropolitan regions). In order to work together efficiently, it would be necessary to intensify intra-Alpine traffic with new high-performance roads and flight connections; social services would have to be homogenized – in the absence of financial resources it would probably mean at the lowest common denominator – finally, it would require considerable efforts to construct artificially a common Alpine identity. One could imagine a transnational league of Alpine wrestling or a mountain football league with seven instead of eleven players – typical constructions from the early days of nation-building. It would be necessary to regain the full spectrum of production systems and the full diversity (which is the crucial advantage of metropolitan areas), and this would mean an overestimation of one's own capabilities. It would result in building metropolitan structures, which, in the end, would mean a separatist scenario. On the other hand, existing linkages would have to be torn down, especially in economic aspects that would mean the end of many traditional producer–user relations and the end of small-scale mountain trade.

A narrowly restricted Alpine macro-region would pose the problem of the lack of its own value adding, a problem that cannot be eliminated, even if the terms of the current exchange are improved in favour of the mountains, and even if the liberal-productivist economic model were replaced by less aggressive regimes of accumulation. As long as human labour remains an important indicator for social life, productivity gradients that are too steep will not be tolerated by any society, as this will automatically call into question issues of social justice. And these questions will not be answered by emancipative action or social innovation but by the opposite: resentment and exaggerated identity. This is why spatial disparities, struggles for a better distribution of value added, and migration movements will persist. At the same time, it is questionable whether the Alpine population would support such an isolationist strategy. It may be conservative in adopting societal changes, but the majority have a rural history and largely share an entrepreneurial culture and a migration experience

(Holenstein et al., 2018). It is doubtful that it would start such an isolationist experiment. Such an attitude is rather to be expected in a paralyzed and shrinking region, such as in certain parts of eastern Germany, or in successful regions, such as the separatist movements already mentioned in northern Italy and other parts of Europe.

(f) Three short scenarios

None of the three scenarios of the identity-based trajectory are very pleasant. As they are all quite improbable, I do not deepen them here: I only sketch out the consequences of the identity-based trajectory.

Scenario 1: The autonomous mountain region has the monopoly on rare resources and is in a strong position towards the federal state to retain considerable parts of the value added. This region will profit from the revenues and develop as a rentier state for the sake of its long-standing population. It is likely that manual labour and traditional trades will vanish – or at least no longer be practised by the locals. Locals try to protect themselves against unwanted immigrants, but at the same time, they also try to attract their lacking workforce from abroad – a dilemma in which old practices and traditional values become relativized and polished. In its extreme form, it is comparable with the Gulf states. In mountain regions, the Kathmandu region in Nepal is a good example; in its modest form, it has similarities with South Tyrol. A new and deeper gap is generated between those who have old rights of citizenship and the newcomers. It may become the origin of deeper conflicts on the division of wealth and on different cultural practices.

Scenario 2: The alliance of the disfavoured mountain regions unites areas across different states: 'MountExit', demanding greater autonomy. Wanting to maintain traditional culture and rejecting urbanization, they become cut off from urban lowland agglomerations and will observe that they lack specialized services and urban functions. It is not possible to replace the lost networks with the external economy. Mountain infrastructure is costly to maintain, and material wealth degrades. Young people leave the mountain areas in search of a better education, and they do not return. Even the most loyal but mobile people leave the region, as they will not tolerate a whole society living under sub-par productivity standards. We will see 'shrinking mountains'.

Scenario 3: The ties to the lowlands are loosened, and the transnational ties within the mountain areas are strengthened, as in scenario 2. The supranational institution, in our case the European Union, is asked for funding in the name of cohesion and willingly accepts, but it makes the obligation to create competitive economic and institutional structures – which have to be taken from the European best practices list. This results in a much quicker and more radical modernization than elsewhere. The traditional socio-economic relations become discredited much more quickly, as the demands for mountain competitiveness incite 'creative destruction'. I showed this through the examples of the Indian Himalayas. In the Alps, at least the 14 million people are pleased finally to have a real Alpine capital with good intercontinental flight connections.

9.3 The cohesive trajectory: leaving regionalism behind

This trajectory seeks to avoid the shortcomings of the mainstream as well as the regionalist trajectory. It tries to preserve mountain economies and habitats by overcoming regionalist thinking and trying to ameliorate the relationship to the lowlands. Up to now, this trajectory existed only at a national level. Instead of a national scale or a mere trans-mountain scale, this trajectory aims for a supranational (i.e. European) approach.

(a) The normative assumption

The cohesive 'European' trajectory is based on two points. There is the search for reduced regional disparities and equalized or equivalent living conditions between metropolitan areas and peripheries, regardless of whether they have a mountain topography or not. Cohesive societies are not necessarily homogeneous. Cohesive societies are seen as more stable towards external impacts, more tolerant towards newcomers, and less aggressive in intra-societal relations. In this way, they are supposed to generate more wealth in quality and in quantity, and they seem to be perfectly adapted to follow the Sustainable Development Goals of the United Nations. In addition, larger territorial units are expected to be in the long-term in a better position than small autonomous regions, as the individual members of a larger area are less subjected to direct evaluation of their productivity. While these mixed entities (a constellation of high and low productivity) will probably have lower growth rates, this constellation might be – if it is the accepted consensus – more sustainable.

(b) The characteristics

A distinctive, alternative path would have to fulfil the prerequisites that it does not reinforce the processes of metropolization or fuel regional egoisms and xenophobic isolation. If we understand Stein Rokkan's approach in the right way and add all the experiences of the past – such as the positive example of Switzerland and the negative example of the break up of Yugoslavia – then we should create a mountain strategy that accepts being interlaced in a global world and is open to it. If we take the European example, 'Brussels' has become the enemy image for all nationalist and regionalist movements, as it has become synonymous with centralist decision power and dissipation of money. But among all complaints (which are hypocritical, as subsidies for their own interest group are rarely rejected), it is forgotten that integration of a multitude of cultures and practices is always costly. However, trying to maintain homogeneity through violence costs more. In this way, all the programmes of European cooperation for research, subsidies, and education – independently of their direct content value – have the merit of bringing together people who have to work together and get to know each other better, enabling them to gain respect for one another. Maintaining heterogeneity and diversity means that it is necessary to maintain and also to regain at the same territory a certain coexistence of production and reproduction, as well as between export-based and residential economies.

Abandoning the concept of the entrepreneurial region

Mountain areas will also henceforth be disadvantaged by their topography and a lack of people. They will decline without compensation. Compensation does not mean mainly financial support, but rather the extraordinary appreciation by autochthonal as well as external people. Mountainous regions cannot hold their positions if they do not have the solidarity of the urban majority outside, even if they produce the best organic food or offer the most luxurious wellness spas. But they also have to produce, which means activities within and beyond traditional agriculture, tourism, manufacturing, and leisure. Consequently, mountain regions cannot maintain an unchanged mountain tradition; they have to develop new activities that ideally have a close link to traditional professions and fulfil a real societal need. Their products have to be sold on international markets. Of course, this requires the extension of value chains, a postulation that is as boring as it is old. But this postulation would receive more credibility if it could be uncoupled from the demand for direct and immediate competitiveness. The recent turn to territories as 'subsidiary' business units would have to be reconsidered and not abused to increase spatial polarization. This should be done with the aim of being sustained again by national and supranational solidarity, which is linked with persuasion and not by performance. The exchange and cooperation between lowlands and mountains should not be restricted to the peri-Alpine adjacent metropolitan areas, as this would reinforce the asymmetric complementarity between highly productive urban areas and less productive mountains. This would clearly be a task for national and – in the case of Europe – European compensation. National states would regain the capability to define higher welfare standards.

Lowland–mountain linkages, renewed

The political implementation of new knowledge cannot be treated at the level of the mountain ranges alone, and again requires the exchange with the lowlands. The most important question common to the Alpine arc is transport across the Alps, where different countries have different interests, and the reduction of transit traffic in one country means an increase of traffic on the transit route in the neighbouring country, just like the water in communicating pipes. Although the European Union is part of the Alpine Convention, there is not much progress on this issue, as there is no general support within Europe to limit the overall transport volume through Alpine regions. In contrast, the logic of the mainstream trajectory reinforces the building of new capacities, although they were and are highly contested by the local population (as the second pipe of the Gotthard road tunnel and the TAV high-speed railway line between Turin and Lyon). The example of the TAV shows that the inhabitants of mountain regions have to face the reality of increased mobility and their integration as neighbourhoods of metropolitan areas. This makes it necessary to work together with the near metropolitan regions to negotiate and to maintain their own interests. In the conflict about the TAV, abandonment would only be possible if the dissident population of the piedmonts and the concerned mountain population worked together. But this also means that those mountain regions are open to discuss and to respond to the demands of the metropolises. Such a strategy might be more propitious than the current strategy, which positions a mountain destination on a global market to visit one unique feature under the laws of marketing poetry. This might take away some of the glamour of certain high-end resort towns but bringing in more ordinary features would be a more feasible solution for all. This strategy would include a reduction in the high specialization and a shift in the dependency on tourist or real estate activities towards a more mixed economy. In the end, this strategy is a step towards reducing the power of the metropolitan areas in favour of a more territorially anchored responsibility. Mountains would be one more economic cluster in the diversity of metropolitan clusters. In fact, they already fulfil this task, as they host Asian tourists who visit Zurich for shopping and museums, and to take trips to the Alps. The relations of these phenomena have to be better negotiated and ameliorated in favour of the mountains. If such a strategy is taken, then many of the discussions about new types of regions to raise subsidies for regionalist interests could be abandoned.

Indeed, the Alpine arc could also become a space to host new migrants from the international migratory flows who come to work rather than for the consumption of amenities. This could save the demographic basis of marginalized regions and serve as a new model to withstand a polarized regional development dominated by the metropolitan regions. In the past, mountains were often territories that served as spaces of transit and exchange. The exchange with the metropolitan regions has become necessary under the tendencies of recent years. It would be a strategy to try to integrate the international flows with the intention of profiting from the global changes that have begun to affect the European peripheries.

Accepting but renegotiating lowland–mountain relations

It is a common argumentation expressed by local people in the Alps that they do not want to become a museum without modern infrastructure and detached from the lowland agglomerations. This argumentation is based on long experience, and the observation certainly is not wrong. Often traditional heritage of built and unbuilt environment is sacrificed in the name of accessibility, competitivity, and assumed expectations of tourist clients. However, external visitors would expect to find even more 'otherness' and a greater distinction from the urban sphere in the form of authentic heritage. On the other hand, in questions of cultural liberalism and social solidarity, the urban population would often expect an adaptation of the rural population and more 'similarities' than in the past.

(c) Why does this trajectory seem an attractive counter-model?

We can assess the liberal-productivist path and the mountain-specific identity-based trajectory as having failed: the former, market-based approach produces high territorial and social disparities; the latter, identity-based approach produces exclusion and rent-seeking. An alternative trajectory should avoid both, as high disparities and exclusion contradict the normative values of social and spatial justice as well as international conventions that seek to promote sustainable development, such as the 2030 Agenda for Sustainable Development of the United Nations. An alternative trajectory should also question the model of permanent high economic growth rates, and the principles of territorial competition.

This trajectory would be a counter-trajectory to the post-Fordist model, which encourages regions to appear as enterprises on global markets. But it is also an alternative to an Alpine region that limits its identity to topography and refuses to look beyond that. No one wants a return to the technocratic administrative approach of Fordist subsidy policies, but a limitation of regional competition, consciously accepted by both the mountain and the lowland populations, would be a kind of social innovation.

(d) Shortcomings and weaknesses

The weaknesses of this trajectory lie in the uncertainty over whether the mountain areas remain strong enough to maintain advocates in the lowlands, i.e. people who are interested in mountain and environmental topics and the well-being of the mountain population. It is also an open question whether possible changes are quick enough to avoid severe global disturbances: This is the uncertainty contained within every social movement, whose success or failure can only be stated if it has been tried. Another possible weakness lies in the open question of whether a value adding that veers from the productivist model is able to maintain the existing standard of living or whether it has to be diminished, and to what degree, and how this might contradict the objectives of equality and reduction of disparities.

(e) The counterproductive and dangerous impact

It is worth discussing whether the sacrifice of a 'region-specific' approach in mountain strategies is justified. However, supporting mountain areas no longer works in the old Fordist sense with regional policies providing financial aid according to political, region-specific aims. Under post-Fordist conditions, mountain regions act on global markets as entrepreneurs and they do not have much choice. They cannot always do this according to region-specific and sustainability values. In this sense, while risky, it seems appropriate to treat mountains and their inhabitants the same as other parts of the territory. This means, of course, that participative methods of decision-making are accepted best practices and that the fragile ecosystems are treated according to the state of the art.

(f) Three short scenarios

Scenario 1: Mountain regions and adjacent lowland metropolitan regions begin to work more closely together than before and are able to avoid stronger asymmetries of power between highland and lowland areas, by taking better account of their mutual expectations and needs. In this sense, lessons have been learned from the errors of the Fordist and post-Fordist regimes. Cooperation is now based on a certain spatial division of economic functions, but the hierarchies are less pronounced than they were in the past. In particular, the clear separation between productive and consumptive functions has been abolished, as it was possible to maintain and stabilize job opportunities in the peripheries. Mountain areas have regained a new variety of different activities. Commuting flows have been reduced. The real peripheries were reduced to small unpopulated interstices between two metropolitan catchments. This scenario became possible through intensified supranational cohesion and integration policies. By contrast, in contested questions such as urban sprawl and landscape preservation and heritage, rural areas have adopted urban expectations and developed their own competencies in this field. The main impulse for reinforcing cooperation and cohesion came from the highly productive metropolitan lowland areas.

Scenario 2: High urban–rural linkages and lean spatial hierarchies as in scenario 1. However, the initiative did not have its origins in the metropolitan lowlands, but came as grass-roots action from the mountain peripheries, which were able to reinforce their position in national and supranational states and institutions. These initiatives started with a large number of re-migrants who were born in the mountains and came back after years of education and professional activity internationally. In the beginning, it was uncertain whether this scenario could be successful, but it spread, eventually succeeded, and later became dominant.

Scenario 3: With an initiative starting like in scenario 2 (from the bottom up), the egalitarian model is spread, but it does not become very popular, remained fragile, and in some cases had to be given up.

Notes

1 A dominating 'Alpine capital city' is not the aim of this position, as the structural changes necessary to achieve this would destroy the majority of the intended objectives of this model. This means, at the same time, that highly specialized and rare, expensive goods (such as high-end medicine) would not be available in the Alps in the long run.

2 After having written this, the majority of England and Wales opted on 23 June 2016 to leave the European Union. It is the same mechanism: 'If we can decide according to subsidiarity in our own interest we have enough for us'. And in this constellation, it serves as an anchor for the losers of a globalized economy threatened by social decline. Ex-post analyses showed that it was the population of the abandoned Midlands who voted in majority for Brexit, independently of their class situation – while in London even the poor voted to remain in the EU (Los et al., 2017).

3 The first examples are the so-called Charter Cities or Zonas Especiales de Desarrollo Económico in emerging countries of Asia and South America. The original was Celebration, a planned city at the Disney World area in Florida, built in the 1990s based on the plans of Walt Disney in the 1960s.

4 We also see that logic among the poor population. What is superficially named as populistic – the xenophobic exclusion of minorities by the autochthone people – should be described better in economic terms as rigorous individual entrepreneurship of safeguarding one's own older investments in individual life. In the concrete case, it means the attempt to gain back the status of lost middle-class belonging, promised and partly realized in the heyday of Fordism. In the past, the popular left parties controlled and channeled xenophobia, which also occurred latently during Fordism. For a sociological explanation of the changed social world in northern France, where working-class neighbourhoods turned to supporting the racism of the extreme right-wing Front National, see the auto-ethnographic reflections on the family by Didier Eribon (2009) about the 1960s milieu of the housing estates of Reims, France.

10 Beyond liberal-productivism

10.1 Which way should we go?

As mentioned repeatedly, the main spatial impacts of the post-Fordist turn can be seen in the vast de-industrialization of the countries of the Global North, the renaissance of the city as a powerful collective actor, and the transformation of rural areas for specialized urban functions. This changed the role and profile of all types of regions, and the cultures and identities of their people. I also stated above that culture is a derived category. Culture denotes a setting of practices based on rules to explain and organize everyday life (from language to greeting rituals), which have to be learned and accepted to be part of a community of shared values and social standards. It is a resource that can be named as symbolic capital, which costs the investment of time to master it. No one can be blamed for defending their own practices, identities, and living standards against devalorization. This is especially valid for the modest classes, which did not develop social and spatial mobility in the last decades as a personal asset. It has become popular to name as populists those who defend their interests against mainstream practices. This description blurs more than it elucidates. In particular, it brushes the responsibility for the newly produced social cleavages from the deciding elites to the deracinated people with devalued skills who run behind the Pied Piper.[1]

Those who are now deracinated and devalorized profited for decades from their collaboration with the elites by consumption of products of cheap labour, which dequalified them at the same time. They had forgotten the knowledge acquired in the first half of the 20th century, that the play-off between regions and their population does not help the poor. Identity-based egoism, which argues from a globally comfortable position to preserve privileges without questioning social disparities, shows the ugly face of post-Fordism – regardless of whether it promises a separatist state, a nostalgic return to the 1950s, or a nationally demarcated socialism. This also counts for the stakeholders in mountains, and it points out a specific danger of the 'mountain-specific' approach. Yes, they have specific conditions that must be considered in specific policies, but they are also not so degraded to justify better treatment than others: The mountain population in the Global North is still much better off than those in an Indian shanty town. And the mountain population of the Global South is not as subjected to social benchmarking as its lowland cities. So, the problem is not a mountain-specific one, but again a social one: who defines the rules and who defines who gets what in the division of the commonly produced wealth.

A trajectory that wants to go beyond the post-Fordist regimes has to balance between these two contradictory positions, saying clearly that neither the liberal-productivist mainstream nor the isolated identity-based mountain approach can be alternatives. The former does not escape the growth logic at the expense of the typical Fordist middle classes. The latter is not open to the problems of others, especially those of the poorest on the globe. Making mountain regions strong and relatively independent from the lowlands was intended as a counter-position to the global mainstream. But this strategy uses either the same logic of value adding (which means establishing similar structures as in the lowlands: competitive value chains and efficient transport infrastructure) – or it has to beg for money from the richer regions (and which will not be given without conditions). Both trajectories have never really taken into account either the legitimate interests of the countries of the Global South or the interests of poor people living on the fringes of the metropolitan areas. Both the mainstream and the regionalist trajectories do not seem appropriate for the mountains, nor sustainable for the individual regions or emancipative in terms of societal issues in general.

10.2 An alternative to liberal-productivist and to identity-based trajectories

We have therefore sketched a third path, which has all the disadvantages of not having been experienced, researched, or elaborated. It is the path of intertwining different territories and different interest groups, encouraging them to work together in a coherent way, to avoid accentuating identities or promoting unreflected strategies of uniqueness, exaggerated subsidiarity, self-responsibility, and the suppression of competition.

It seems crucial to restrict the polarization that is induced by increasing metropolization, as well as to avoid a unique and deepened social cleavage that inhibits territorial cohesion. The long-standing practice of the Swiss Confederation of maintaining cross-cutting institutions as well as low-grade cross-cutting cleavages was seen in this sense as successful. It was a strategy that Yugoslavia tried after the Second World War, but which tragically failed. If we want to learn from this sad experience, we should abandon the identity- and specificity-focused model, even though it has many adherents in the rural and mountain world. The principle of producing many small cleavages corresponds to the principle of the 'strength of weak ties' of Marc Granovetter, and also to the recommendation to regularly change partners as in 'square dancing', as expressed by Masahisa Fujita at a conference in Palermo in 2013:[2] Be open-minded and try to create multiple networks. This argument in favour of 'weak ties' certainly has some shortcomings and has to be balanced with the region-specific path.

The territorially embedded regional network of local communities has its merits, as it produces regional differences and stable societies in the periphery. It should not be given up nor played off against. It is argued that new experiences such as alternating cooperations (included the hosting of new inhabitants) and the collaboration with other regions can deliver new knowledge for peripheries and can give them new options. It has to be pursued with the aim that, in the end, the relations between centres and peripheries lose their asymmetric character. This is not a plea to deny mountain-specific problems and the necessity for specific solutions. But the undisputed need to resolve mountain-specific problems must not overlook universal questions of societal well-being nor end up fuelling regionalist self-serving interests.

10.3 A use-value-dominated view on economic diversity

It is well known that it is costly to maintain suboptimal production sites, as well as to produce in mountain regions. But production costs may change, and the question of whether there is an interest or not to invest resources is one of political will. This is a lesson we have learned recently in the debate on energy production and societal costs – before Fukushima, no one believed that renewables could compete with nuclear power. Interestingly, it is also costly to maintain several small cleavages, as well as to cooperate in different constellations and in different languages. The 28 member states of the European Union, in 2016, used 24 official languages, which they wish to preserve. Switzerland, with its 8.3 million people, has four national languages, three of which are designated official languages and used in every political transaction and documentation. Having higher costs in strategic questions can never be an argument, as costs always reflect current structures, offers, and preferences that may already be outdated when the calculation is made, as preferences change quickly in a dynamic world. In this sense, it is not false to undertake 'active' industrial or agricultural policies, but these policies should be explicitly transnational or supranational. To conclude, a high diversity of a multitude of production systems, as well as a diversity of low-grade social cleavages, is in the interest of a cohesive and sustainable spatial development. Under both aspects we should sometimes accept disproportional costs compared to other locations (the situation of mountains, with their reduced accessibility and topographic gradients, makes this more clearly visible than elsewhere). If a certain activity or profession is appreciated, then it should find its support in society. This can be resolved only by political solutions: through consensus-oriented policies that give a stronger weight to stakeholders other than owners of financial capital.

10.4 The myth of the quality food approach

The now common 'best practice' strategy is – as comprehensively explained in this book – to produce specialities, which makes the products on offer more expensive and allows a higher return on investment. This is the offer-oriented, market-based strategy that is shared by a broad alliance spanning regional poli-cymakers and Alpine experts to environmental NGOs. It is true that in the past, the prices for mountain specialities were (too) low and the asymmetry of power still comprised negative terms of trade. But here again, we find the problem that attempting to correct the disadvantages by setting higher prices quickly turns to over-exploitation, as higher prices signal higher margins. This was the case with the transformation of cultural land to construction zones for second homes, and it may happen with all other resources too. In the Alps, these pro-cesses of over-exploitation may lead to increased gentrification or, in the case of certain trends in food production, to a 'slowfoodization': high-end products for a restricted clientele that consumes it for its symbolic capital rather than for its taste. We have there a microeconomic entrepreneurial strategy that is feasible for some specialized producers, but not for all. Furthermore, this strategy rein-forces the functional division of labour between a rich urban clientele working in the metropolitan areas with access to amenities of the mountain regions. The peripheries turn into territories of consumption. It is foreseeable that this strategy will not be sustainable. Furthermore, it may fail as the enlargement of production at a global market level will not attract sufficient demand and the innovations will be degraded with increased production. This is a normal pro-cess in the life cycle of consumer goods. The old clientele, up to now loyal to mountain issues, as domestic tourists or supporters of mountain demands, will turn away.

Which offer should mountain regions provide? In our argumentation, this is not the central question. Mountain regions should offer what they are able to produce in a diversified range, and the customers should pay the correct price for it. Of course, a quality-based production can command better prices and should be supported under the aspects of being environmentally friendly and socially fair. But we all have reasons to doubt that this offer-oriented approach will save the mountains from their inferior position in the national and global context.

10.5 New and better-reflected relations between metropolitan and mountain areas

If we take one of the first arguments about the disadvantages of mountain regions – the sparse population compared to the metropolitan regions – then it seems an illusion that mountain regions should open up markets at a global level on an entrepreneurial basis. Such relations would always be asymmetric. A seemingly easy way would be to accept the formula 'Munich and its Alps', where we replace Munich with any near metropolitan area: 'Toulouse and its Pyrenees', 'Denver and its Rockies', etc. However, the terms of the relationship would certainly have to be clarified.

Both sides, the lowlands with their metropolitan core, and the mountains with their rural-looking urbanized structures, have to make compromises and negotiate their positions. The mountain regions will have to accept that the urban population has different demands on the mountain territory than in the past, and that it is the lowland majority that defines the new trends in leisure, social practices, and consumption patterns. On the other hand, the metropolitan population has to accept that the mountain population is the only responsible body taking daily care of this territory, and that a mainstreamed mountain population will be so boring that no one will visit these places anymore. 'Urban–rural linkages' is the buzzword for these negotiations but is probably not taken seriously in practice. Nonetheless, there is certainly much potential to develop these aspects further (e.g. see the thematic edition of *JAR-RGA*, 103(3), 2015, especially the contributions of Meessen et al., Serroi and Rousselot).

To avoid a sharp functional division of labour between export-based and residential economy, on the one hand, and between metropolitan areas and peripheries, on the other, we have to break up the strategy of being offer oriented alone. Mountain regions have to take notice of the new rules of global capitalism, but they have the right to question these rules. If the rules remain unchanged, the mountains will lose both their old qualities of a topographically and culturally adapted way of production, as well as their population.

Beyond the negotiations with the neighbouring metropolitan regions about the complementarities of the regional profile, the European mountain regions must engage themselves in the debate on European regional policies and territorial solidarity. This means temporary and changing cooperations, as well as a mitigation of regional competition. In the interest of a cohesive and sustainable mountain development the aim should be to reinstall the solidarity between rich and poor regions and political support for the whole territory at national and transnational levels. This also means reducing the regional rhetoric on exaggerated hopes of regional self-responsibility.

10.6 A new understanding of embeddedness

The trajectories should show that it is possible to think in the direction of a more general change in paradigms. The change from Fordism to post-Fordism makes it possible to think that other stakeholders, other preferences, and other spatial patterns may or should gain significance, to lead to a more cohesive and sustainable development. This also concerns the questions of mountain regions and peripheries. Under the liberal-productivist system, it became an advantage to break up the territorially based systems of production and to dynamize the renegotiation of contracts at the global level. The effects are well known: relocation, de-industrialization, and a spatial division of labour across the continents. It will not be possible to re-establish territorially anchored production systems as in the past. They were often too narrow for the local people themselves, and often not open for other people. This makes it difficult today to defend the identity-based trajectory. Under current global policies it is in fact dangerous, as it is directly oriented against social and territorial cohesion. However, regional embeddedness remains important and should also be supported by the lowland populations. Regional embeddedness should be understood as responsibility for the territory, but integrated into the framework of a suprar-egional/supranational citizenship that would encourage people to care about what happens beyond their own valley.

10.7 Questioning the innovation–driven growth model to preserve cultural and biophysical diversity

The problem that humans make large impacts on the biophysical sphere exists independently of institutional regimes and the number of people living on earth. However, there are differences between regimes that take higher risks and others that are more risk-averse. The liberal-productivist model has inte-grated environmental and cultural questions according to the logic of efficiency (i.e. technology and market rules). This means that people's needs and interests do not have first priority, and impact prevention plays an inferior role to the rise in productivity as promised by innovation. The fact that the most important char-acteristic of post-Fordist regimes is that they are offer-oriented and innovation-driven makes them highly dynamic. This is not a general criticism, as the right relation between persistence and dynamic is always time- and place-dependent. But a higher dynamic makes societies more vulnerable to failure, and this general latent vulnerability is reinforced as the global relations of power have increasingly uncoupled and become more resistant to public control. It is no longer the single pollutant that is the problem, but the reinforced dominance of the paradigm of growth. People are more aware of risks than they were in the past and they are willing to engage. Success in environmental action or for cul-tural issues is good, as it reinforces the members of civil society in their power to act. But it would need a transformation of the liberal-productivist model to reduce the dependency on growth, accumulation, and resource consumption, which is characteristic for this model.

10.8 Changing paradigms towards use-value-oriented regimes of accumulation

Up to now, it was never discussed in the Alpine debate that the conditions for Fordist growth, as well as the global exchange of post-Fordism, included a strong North–South component. It is only on the basis of the high productiv-ity of production sites in emerging countries that Alpine farmers can afford to work with cheap computers and that the price of organic food has fallen enough to allow it to penetrate the urban middle-class milieu. Increasing this division of labour (based on global exchange or economies of scale) is a prom-ise to further increase profitability to maintain mountain farming. However, using this strategy of cheap imported fodder and auxiliaries at the same time undermines credibility of mountain farming. The concentration of produc-tion at optimized but temporary locations increases the destruction of cultural and biophysical resources. It also increases the territorial cleavage by differ-ent land use and productivity. Both mountain strategies – exposing mountain uniqueness for global high-end tourism or subsidizing policies for mitigating productivity gaps – are based on differences, and on disparities too. But if disparities become too large, they contradict all concepts of sustainability and also the Sustainable Development Goals of the United Nations.

Territorial capital is expressed by the loyalty of its stakeholders to their region. If this loyalty is no longer given, it is impossible to maintain the existing production systems. If the productivity gap between metropolitan regions and its peripheries becomes too deep, it is difficult to remain confident. This means that peripheral regions must have the chance to transform, and metropolitan regions would have to lower the expected returns of their economies.

Maintaining weak economic sectors would be possible if the prevailing regimes of accumulation would compromise on the average rate of profit. This would mean having increased patience with sectors that do not generate high returns on investment, as well as accepting 'mature' production systems in the processes of value adding. A general levelling of realizable returns in the different economic sectors would be necessary, which would have to run at the expense of the financial services sector. While agriculture has the goodwill of large parts of the population due to its territorial attachment and the combination of old and new practices (especially organic cultivation, wine, rare species), this is not the case with the manufacturing industry. In contrast, there are many examples of third-party profiting due to the activities of private equity companies or to real estate transactions.[3] This leads to reflections about the sense and purpose of production in general. It results in the use value aspect (producing for which purpose) having to be strengthened compared to the exchange value. This certainly would wipe out some manufacturing value chains of the real economy. But overall, it would give an enormous boost to the real economy compared to the financial production system. It would facilitate access to investment capital, and, even more importantly, access to the most creative and best-qualified people. And of course, the costs of global mobility have to be internalized in such new regimes.

Both the rise in productivity to avoid excessive disparities between mountains and lowlands, and a social climate to accept spatial differences in productivity, are necessary for cohesive development. Such development requires integration of two principles: the qualities of territorial capital, and the qualities of urbanization. Accepting the qualities of territorial capital means that the historic trajectory and the experiences of the regional stakeholders are respected and seen as an enrichment on the large scale. This value will persist, at least in its minimal form, as a spatial reserve for future generations as insurance, as long as a region is populated. In this sense, there have to be clear signals by national policies that every part of a territory has to be appreciated in its regional differences and different potentials, and that there is a common understanding to guarantee equivalent living conditions for the whole territory. This aspect focuses on the qualities of difference to be honoured by citizens, and on political support.

On the other hand, mountain regions have to be aware that they are an integrated part of global processes that accelerate the division of labour, market exchange, and the codification of knowledge, which means that this knowledge is ubiquitously available. These global processes are condensed into an increasing urbanization, which not only means a certain morphological concentration in cities, but also the change of economic activities towards an increasing differentiation and new specializations. New regimes of accumulation would have to consider both – the interest to maintain and stabilize the specific territorial capital, as well as the interest to participate in the diversity of recent urbanization. This is only possible if future regimes of accumulation change the relations between exchange value and use value in favour of the latter or, expressed in the terms of Lefebvre, in the direction of the spaces of representation of the lived space (the 'vécu').[4]

10.9 Changing paradigms towards a solidarity-oriented mode of regulation

The liberal-productivist model of distribution of produced surplus enabled the deconstruction and reconstruction of the big companies and generated the start-up firms that outperformed the traditional integrated companies. The returns on investment were unleashed, as was the principle of earning astronomic sums, avoiding taxes, and being able to make donations and create foundations. It is more prestigious to finance a private university than to pay taxes, as it generates visible symbolic capital by showing the name of the sponsor on a plaque, and of course it allows donations for every egomaniac whim (such as the irrigation of golf courses in the Californian desert). With the liberal-productivist model was linked also the predominance of the Anglo-Saxon business model of accumulation and the corresponding mode of regulation. As these revenues (or the symbolic capital) cannot be consumed during one human life, we see here the renaissance of the pre-democratic aristocratic model – an allocation that runs completely against universal values of the European model of the Enlightenment. Again, we can say if there was a paradigm shift in this direction of extreme individualization, there should exist also an alternative counter-tendency. Mountain societies – where they still exist, and where they have not been transformed by real estate managers – might provide the idea of a counter-model of a territorially based equilibrated society. But to have an influential voice at the national level, they have to accept the realities of urbanization. Moreover, mountain societies cannot create a counter-model as they are too weak: They have to regain the solidarity of the urban population that they have lost. Practising openness only by profiting from the business model of global tourist markets will not help and is counterproductive, as it counteracts this cooperation between mountain and lowland areas.

10.10 Economic analysis but normative participatory decision-making

Mountain-specific production, culture, and identity are, in the end, economic categories that refer to the acquisition of resources and social power: Who is at a specific place, and since when? Who has invested in a certain activity to sustain his or her livelihood? Who has, as a result of this, the authority to define the relevant values? Who has to adapt to whom? Who will be integrated, and who will be excluded? It is the paradox that in the current discourse, this argument of power relations is explicitly refuted (especially from the adherents of the 'cultural turn'), and yet the logic of market rules is applied in the cultural debate as never before. Therefore, identity-based reasoning must be taken seriously (and probably more so than recently) for local issues and practices of individuals in everyday life. And the 'economic' character of the identity question – the long investment of individuals in their own social and symbolic capital in a certain place – should not be denied.

Here we see a paradox that could not be resolved up to now: The tensions about accumulated culture and identity are caused by market mechanisms, but they cannot be resolved by market-driven instruments. They have to be negotiated politically. This is a result of the reinforced agglomeration economies and the new hierarchy gaps between mountains and lowlands that were shown in the preceding chapters. The consequence is not to develop new commodities, but to reduce the influence of market-driven instruments in favour of democratically based political decision-making. It also means a readjustment of the shares of value adding that the individual production clusters receive. It would be a readjustment in favour of tangible goods at the expense of the intermediary services industries. This is not a question of a redistributive social policy, but a question of decision-making power and of negotiating how much of what is to be produced and which production systems have what weight in society. It means a shift in the relation between the exchange value and the use value, in favour of the latter. It means a strengthening of those parts that Henri Lefebvre (1974) probably meant when he spoke in his threefold dialectic of *spaces of representation*: a greater emphasis on concrete needs and less emphasis on abstract accumulation. These considerations imply – for all actors – that generally lower productivity increases are accepted, but also reduced expectations in terms of returns.

Notes

1 In this context, it is striking that the voting results on migration in European countries show the highest xenophobia where the lowest rates of foreigners live. This is independent of a mountain topography but correlates strongly with a 'peripheral situation' in everyday life, in which the accustomed security (physical as well as cultural) is attacked by new competitors. To call in this situation for a 'left populism', as can be heard in the European intellectual debate, now seems rather hazardous.

2 See www.rieti.go.jp/users/fujita-masahisa/53rd_ERSA_Congress_ppt.pdf (accessed 26 November 2018).

3 See the example from Greece (Perlik et al., 2013) in Section 6.5.

4 I tend to interpret Lefebvre's *veçu* and the Marxian *use value* as being quite similar. While having some sympathies for the *veçu* as it contains an implicit critique on the prevailing model of growth and accumulation, I prefer the term *use value*. Those two terms are indeed not synonymous. *Espace veçu/lived space* constructs a difference between production and reproduction, a difference that is certainly justified today under the aspect of destructive

production (affecting human lives and environment) and under the ideal towards a more free, self-determined use of time. *Gebrauchswert/use value*, however, sees both – production and reproduction – as an essential part of human nature, independent of time; the problem is the repartition of work, the existence of class structures, asymmetric decision-making power, and finally, the crucial question of *what* should be produced. In this way, *use value* seems to me more categorical. This is a problem that is also inherent to new approaches such as *post-growth theories* or the notion of *post-material societies*.

Bibliography

Aerni, K. and Egli, H-R. (1991) 'Zusammenhänge zwischen Verkehrs- und Siedlungsentwicklung in der Schweiz seit dem Mittelalter'. *GH*, 46(2), pp. 71–78.

Agnew, J. (1994) 'The territorial trap: the geographical assumptions of international relations theory'. *Review of International Political Economy*, 1(1): 53–80.

Agnew, J. (2011) 'Waterpower: politics and the geography of water provision'. *Annals of the Association of American Geographers*, 101(3): 463–76.

Albert, M. (1991) *Capitalisme contre Capitalisme*. Paris: Le Seuil, coll. Histoire immédiate.

Amrein, T. (2014) 'Migratory trajectory and recomposing of Alpine societies: palimpsest of collective identities in the lower Valais'. *JAR-RGA*, 102(3). Available at: https://rga.revues.org/2570 (accessed 1 August 2017).

André-Poyaud, I., Duvillard, S. and Lorioux, A. (2010) 'Land and property transfers in the Mont-Blanc region between 2001 and 2008'. *JAR-RGA*, 98(2). Available at: https://rga.revues.org/1236 (accessed 1 August 2017).

ARE. (1996) *Grandes lignes de l'organisation du territoire suisse*. Bern: ARE.

ARE. (2005) *Rapport développement territorial*. Bern: ARE.

ARE. (2009a) *Monitoring de l'espace urbain suisse*. Bern: ARE.

ARE. (2009b) *Faktenblatt Zweitwohnungen der Schweizer Bevölkerung. Zusatzauswertung des Mikrozensus zum Verkehrsverhalten 2005*. Bern: ARE.

ARE. (2011) *Projet de territoire Suisse*. Bern: ARE.

ARL. (2006) *Gleichwertige Lebensverhältnisse: eine wichtige gesellschaftliche Aufgabe neu interpretieren! Academy for Spatial Research and Planning Positioning Paper*. Hannover: ARL.

ARL. (2019) *Multilokale Lebenspraktiken. Kompendium*. Hannover: ARL (forthcoming).

Arnesen, T. (2009) 'Recreational home agglomerations in rural areas in Norway as emerging economic and political space'. In L.A.G. Moss, R. Glorioso and A. Krause (eds), *Proc. of the Conference 'Understanding and Managing Amenity-Led Migration in Mountain Regions', May 2008*. Banff: The Banff Centre, pp. 93–102.

Arnesen, T., Overvåg, K., Ericsson, B. and Skjeggedal, T. (2011) *Recreation and the Making of the Multi-House Home: Emergence of New Relations between the Urban and the Rural*. Lillehammer: Eastern Norway Research Institute (ENRI). Available at: http://distriktssenteret.no/wp-content/uploads/2013/09/notat_second-homes_ostlandsforskning.pdf (accessed 1 August 2017).

Arthur, W.B. (1989) 'Competing technologies, increasing returns and lock-in by historical events'. *The Economic Journal*, 99: 116–31.

Auken, P. van (2010) 'Seeing, not participating: viewscape fetishism in American and Norwegian rural amenity areas'. *Human Ecology*, 38: 521–37.

Auzeby, F. and Le Gouhinec, T. (2001) 'Migrations de retraités en Languedoc-Roussillon'. *INSEE Repères*, 15: 1–8.

Aydalot, P. (1984) 'À la recherche de nouveaux dynamismes spatiaux'. In P. Aydalot (ed.), *Crise et espace*. Paris: Economica, pp. 38–59.

Aydalot, P. (1985) *Économie régionale et urbaine*. Paris: Economica.

Aydalot, P. (ed.) (1986) *Milieux innovateurs en Europe*. Paris: Groupe de Recherche Européen sur les Milieux Innovateurs (GREMI).

Baghel, R. and Nüsser, M. (2010) 'Discussing large dams in Asia after the world commission on Dams: is a political ecology approach the way forward?' *Water Alternatives*, 3(2): 231–48.

Bagnasco, A. (1977) *Tre Italie: la problematica territoriale dello sviluppo italiano*. Bologna: Il mulino.

Bagnasco, A. and Trigilia, C. (1993) *La construction sociale du marché: le défi de la troisième Italie*. Paris: Ed. de l'ENS.

Baiping, Z., Shenguo, M., Ya, T., Fei, X. and Hongzhi, W. (2004) 'Urbanisation and de-urbanisation in mountain regions of China'. *MRD*, 24(3): 206–9.

Bairoch, P. (1985) *De Jéricho à Mexico. Villes et économie dans l'histoire*. Paris: Gallimard. English version. *Cities and Economic Development: From the Dawn of History to the Present*. Chicago, IL: University of Chicago Press.

Balsiger, J. (2015) 'The European Union strategy for the Alpine region'. In S. Gänzle and K. Kern (eds), *A 'Macro-Regional' Europe in the Making? Theoretical Approaches and Empirical Evidence*. Basingstoke: Palgrave Macmillan, pp. 189–213.

Balsiger, J. and Debarbieux, B. (2015) 'Should mountains (really) matter in science and policy?' *Environmental Science & Policy*, 49: 1–7.

Banskota, M. 2004. 'The Hindu Kush Himalayas: searching for viable socioeconomic and environmental options'. In Banskota et al. (eds), *Growth, Poverty Alleviation and Sustainable Resource Management in the Mountain Areas of South Asia*. Kathmandu: ICIMOD.

Baran, P. (1957) *The Political Economy of Growth*. New York: Monthly Review.

Baran, P. and Sweezy, P. (1966) *Monopoly Capital: An Essay on the American Economic and Social Order*. New York: Monthly Review.

Bartaletti, F. (2008) 'Résidences secondaires en Italie en chiffres et en mots'. *CIPRA-Info*, 87: 13–16.

Bartoš, M., Kušová, D. and Těšitel, J. (2007) 'Amenity migration: driving force for rural development?' *Agricultural Economics & Rural Development*, 4(3–4): 57–69.

Bartoš, M., Kušová, D. and Těšitel, J. (2009) 'Motivation and life style of the Czech amenity migrants'. *European Countryside*, 1(3): 164–79.

Bätzing, W. (1984) *Die Alpen. Naturbearbeitung und Umweltzerstörung. Eine ökologisch-geographische Untersuchung*. Frankfurt: Sendler. [4th edn (2015) completely reworked: *Geschichte und Zukunft einer europäischen Kulturlandschaft*. Munich: CH. Beck].

Bätzing, W. (1991) 'Die Alpen im Europa der neunziger Jahre'. In W. Bätzing and P. Messerli (eds), *Die Alpen im Europa der neunziger Jahre*. Bern: GB, pp. 247–91.

Bätzing, W. (2011) 'Makroregion Alpen und Alpenkonvention – Gegensatz oder ideale Ergänzung? Die europäischen Makroregionen zwischen Aufwertung von Peripherien und Stärkung von Metropolregionen'. *Vortrag auf der Fachtagung: Perspektiven für die Alpen – was können Alpenkonvention und eine makroregionale Alpenraumstrategie dazu beitragen?* Wien. 19 September. Available at: http://www.alpconv.org/en/organization/groups/WGMacro regionalstrategy/Documents/20111223cipra_a_tagung_20110919_alpenkonvention_mak roregion_baetzing.pdf?AspxAutoDetectCookieSupport=1 (accessed 5 November 2018).

Bätzing, W., Perlik, M. and Dekleva, M. (1996) 'Urbanisation and depopulation in the Alps: an analysis of current social-economic structural changes'. *MRD*, 16(4): 335–50.

BBSR. (2011) *Metropolitan Areas in Europe.* BBSR-Online-Publikation January. Bonn: BBSR. Available at: www.inta-aivn.org/images/cc/Metropolisation/background%20documents/ Metropolitan_Europe_BBSR_Study.pdf (accessed 1 August 2017).

Bebbington, A. and Bury, J. (2009) 'Confronting the institutional challenge for mining and sustainability: the case of Peru', *Proceedings of the National Academy of Sciences*, 106(41): 17296–301.

Becattini G. (1979) 'Dal "settore" industriale al "distretto" industriale: alcune considerazioni sull'unità di indagine dell'economia industriale'. *Rivista di Economia e Politica Industriale*, 5(1): 7–21.

Béhar, D., Estèbe, P. and Vanier, M. (2012) 'Pôles métropolitains: du "faire territoire" au "faire politique," ou la nouvelle bataille de l'interterritorialité'. *Métropolitiques*, 18 May. Available at: www.metropolitiques.eu/Poles-metropolitains-du-faire.html (accessed 1 August 2017).

Benko, G. and Lipietz, A. (eds) (1992) *Les régions qui gagnent.* Paris: PUF.

Benko, G. and Lipietz, A. (eds) (2000) *La richesse des régions. La nouvelle géographie socioéconomique.* Paris: PUF.

Benson, M. (2013) 'Living the "real" dream in La France Profonde: lifestyle migrants and the ongoing quest for the authentic'. *Anthropological Quarterly*, 86(2): 501–25.

Benson, M. (2015) 'Class, race, privilege: structuring the lifestyle migrant experience in Boquete, Panama'. *Journal of Latin American Geography*, 14(1): 19–37.

Benson, M. and O'Reilly, K. (eds) (2009) *Lifestyle Migration: Expectations, Aspirations and Experiences.* Farnham: Ashgate.

Benson, M. and Osbaldiston, N. (2014) *Understanding Lifestyle Migration: Theoretical Approaches to Migration and the Quest of a Better Way of Life.* Basingstoke and New York: Palgrave Macmillan.

Benz, A. (2013) *How Migrants Made Their Way: The Role of Pioneering Migrants and Solidarity Networks of the Wakhi of Gojal (Northern Pakistan) in Shaping the Dynamics of Rural – Urban Migration.* Crossroads Asia Working Paper Series 11. Bonn: Crossroads Asia.

Benz, A. (2014a) 'Multilocality as an asset: translocal development and change among the Wakhi of Gojal'. In H. Alff and A. Benz (eds), *Tracing Connections: Explorations of Spaces and Places in Asian Contexts.* Berlin: Wissenschaftlicher Verlag, pp. 111–38.

Benz, A. (2014b) 'Mobility, multi-locality and translocal development: changing livelihoods in the Karakoram'. *Geographica Helvetica*, 69(4): 259–70.

Berry, B.J.L. (1964) 'Cities as systems within systems of cities'. *Papers of the Regional Science Association*, 13: 147–63.

Bertrand, N., Cremer-Schulte, D. and Perrin, M. (2015) 'Strategic spatial planning and territorial asymmetries. Grenoble and greater Geneva: two Alpine city regions put to the challenge of coherence'. *JAR-RGA*, 103(3). Available at: http://rga.revues.org/3126 (accessed 1 August 2017).

Bertrand, N., Souchard, N., Rousier, N., Martin, S. and Micheels, C. (2006) 'Quelle contribution de l'agriculture périurbaine à la construction de nouveaux territoires: consensus ou tensions?' *Revue d'économie régionale et urbaine*, 3: 329–53.

BfS. (n.d.) *Quarterly Data of Tourist Overnight Stays.* Bern: BfS.

Birnbaum, E. (1998) *Sacred Mountains of the World.* Berkeley, CA: University of California Press.

Blanchon, D. (2009) *L'espace hydraulique sud-africain: le partage des eaux.* Paris: Karthala.

Bobek, H. (1928) *Innsbruck – Eine Gebirgsstadt, ihr Lebensraum und ihre Erscheinung.* Stuttgart: Engelhorn.

Boltanski, L. and Chiapello, E. (1999) *Le nouvel esprit du capitalisme.* Paris: Gallimard.

Borsdorf, A. (2013) 'Second homes in Tyrol: growth despite regulation'. *JAR-RGA*. Hors-Série. Available at: https://rga.revues.org/2262 (accessed 1 August 2017).

Borsdorf, A. and Hidalgo, R. (2010) 'From polarization to fragmentation: recent changes in Latin American urbanization'. In P. van Lindert and O. Verkoren (eds), *Decentralized Development in Latin America: Experiences in Local Governance and Local Development.* Milton Keynes: Springer, pp. 23–34.

Bösch, M., Renner, E. and Siegrist, D. (2008) '"Brandscaping": from traditional cultural landscapes to "label regions"'. *MRD*, 28(2): 100–4.

Boscoboinik, A. (2018) Becoming cities, losing paradise? Gentrification in the Swiss Alps. In I. Pardo and G.B. Prato (eds), *The Palgrave Handbook of Urban Ethnography.* Berlin: Springer, pp. 519–36.

Boumaza, N. (1997) 'Grenoble, un mythe urbain moderne'. *RGA*, 85(4): 175–85.

Bourdeau, P. (2009) 'Amenity migration as an indicator of post-tourism'. In L.A.G. Moss, R. Glorioso and A. Krause (eds), *Proc. of the Conference 'Understanding and Managing Amenity-Led Migration in Mountain Regions', May 2008.* Banff: The Banff Centre, pp. 25–32.

Bourdeau, P., Corneloup, J. and Mao, P. (2004) 'Outdoor sports and tourism in French mountains: towards a sustainable development?' In B.W. Ritchie and D. Adair (eds), *Sport Tourism: Interrelationships, Impacts and Issues.* Clevedon: Channel View, pp. 101–16.

Bourdeau, P., Mao, P. and Corneloup, J. (2011) 'Les sports de nature comme médiateurs du "pas de deux" ville – montagne. Une habitabilité en devenir?' *Annales de géographie*, 680: 449–60.

Bourdieu, P. (1979) *La Distinction.* Paris: Les Éditions de Minuit.

Bourdieu, P. (1986) 'The forms of capital'. In J.G. Richardson (ed.), *Handbook of theory and Research for the Sociology of Education.* New York: Greenwood Press, pp. 241–58.

Bourdieu, P. (1994) *Raisons pratiques. Sur la théorie d'action.* Paris: Seuil (édition allemande, 1998).

Bourdieu, P. (2012) *Sur l'Etat. Cours au Collège de France 1989–1992.* Paris: Raisons d'agir/ Le Seuil.

Boyer, R. (1986) *La théorie de la régulation.* Paris: La Découverte.

Boyer, R. (2004) *Une théorie du capitalisme est-elle possible?* Paris: Odile Jacob.

Boyer, R. (ed.) (2018) *La Théorie de la Régulation au fil du temps.* La Plaine-Saint-Denis: Éditions des maisons des sciences de l'homme associées.

Boyer, R. and Saillard, Y. (2002) *Théorie de la régulation, l'état des savoirs.* Paris: La Découverte Recherches.

Braudel, F. (1966) *The Mediterranean and the Mediterranean World in the Age of Philip II.* 2 vols., 2nd rev. ed., transl., 1995. Berkeley, CA, Los Angeles: University of California Press.

Brede, H., Dietrich, B. and Kohaupt, B. (1976) *Politische Ökonomie des Bodens und Wohnungs-frage.* Frankfurt: Suhrkamp.

Brenner, N. (2000) 'The urban question as a scale question: reflections on Henri Lefebvre, urban theory and the theory of scale'. *International Journal of Urban and Regional Research*, 24(2): 361–78.

Brenner, N. (2001) 'The limits to scale? Methodological reflections on scalar structuration'. *Progress in Human Geography*, 25(4): 591–614.

Brenner, N. (2010) 'Critical sociospatial theory and the geographies of uneven spatial development'. In A. Leyshon, R. Lee, L. McDowell and P. Sunley (eds), *The Sage Handbook of Economic Geography.* London: Sage, pp. 135–48.

Brenner, N. and Schmid, C. (2014) 'The "urban age" in question'. *International Journal of Urban and Regional Research*, 38(3): 731–55.

Breu, T., Bader, C., Messerli, P., Heinimann, A., Rist, S. and Eckert, S. (2016) 'Large-scale land acquisition and its effects on the water balance in investor and host countries'. *PLoS ONE*, 11(3) Public Library of Science 10.1371/journal.pone.0150901.

Briquel, V. (2001) 'L'avancée de la périurbanisation dans les Alpes du Nord françaises et ses liens avec la croissance récente de la population'. *RGA*, 1(1): 21–40.

Briquel, V., Chéry, J.P. and Ravix, B. (1996) *Premier panorama de l'état de l'environnement dans les Alpes françaises*. Grenoble: CEMAGREF.

Broggi, M.F. and Reith, W.J. (1982) 'Beurteilung der Restwasserfrage nach landschaftsökologischen und ästhetischen Gesichtspunkten'. In *Schlussbericht der interdepartementalen Arbeitsgruppe Restwasser*. Bern: EDMZ, pp. 82–192.

Brugger, E., Furrer, G., Messerli, B. and Messerli, P. (eds) (1984) *The Transformation of Swiss Mountain Regions: Problems of Development between Self-Reliance and Dependency in an Economic and Ecological Perspective*. Bern: Haupt.

Brundtland Report. (1987) *Our Common Future: Report of the World Commission on Environment and Development*. Oxford: Oxford University Press.

Brunet, R. (1989) *Les villes europeénnes: Rapport pour la DATAR*. Montpellier: RECLUS.

Bucher, D., Bürgi Bonanomi, E., Dey, P., Elsig, M., Espa, I. and Franzi, S. et al. (2015) *The Commodity Sector and Related Governance Challenges from a Sustainable Development Perspective: The Example of Switzerland – Current Research Gaps*. CDE WTI IWE Joint Working Paper No. 1. Bern and St. Gallen, Switzerland: CDE, World Trade Institute (WTI) and the Institute for Business Ethics (IWE). Available at: www.kfpe.ch/WorkingPaper-com modity (accessed 1 August 2017).

Bullough, O. (2018): *Moneyland: Why Thieves And Crooks Now Rule The World And How To Take It Back*. Sydney, Melbourne, Auckland, London: Allen & Unwin.

Burkhalter, R., Ramseier, U. and Messerli, P. (1992) 'Verschärfter Standortwettbewerb im europäischen Städtesystem'. *DISP*, 28(110): 11–24.

Bury, J., Mark, B.G., Carey, M., Young, K.R., McKenzie, J., Baraer, M. et al. (2013) 'New geographies of water and climate change in Peru: coupled natural and social transformations in the Santa River Watershed'. *Annals of the Association of American Geographers*, 103(2): 363–74.

Buxton, G. (2009) 'Planning for amenity migration: can amenity migration pay for itself?' In L.A.G. Moss, R.S. Glorioso and A. Krause (eds), *Understanding and Managing Amenity-Led Migration in Mountain Regions*. Banff: The Banff Centre, pp. 103–6.

Cabodi, C., de Luca, A., Di Gioia, A. and Toldo, A. (2014) *TOWN: Small and Medium Sized Towns in Their Functional Territorial Context*. Case Study Report Italy. Luxembourg: ESPON.

Cadieux, K.V. (2009) 'Competing discourses of nature in exurbia'. *GeoJournal*. Available at: www.springerlink.com/content/011l270045011v73/fulltext.pdf (accessed 26 November 2018).

Cadieux, K.V. (2013) *Landscape and the Ideology of Nature in Exurbia: Green Sprawl*. London: Routledge.

Cadieux, K.V. and Hurley, P.T. (2011) 'Amenity migration, exurbia, and emerging rural landscapes: global natural amenity as place and as process'. *GeoJournal*, 76(4): 297–302.

Cahiers d'études africaines. (2006) *Parentés, plaisanteries et politique*. 184, plusieurs articles.

Camagni, R. (1998) 'The city as a milieu: applying the GREMI approach to urban evolution'. Presentation GREMI Workshop, 29–30 June, Paris.

Camagni, R. and Capello, R. (2010) 'Macroeconomic and territorial policies for regional competitiveness: an EU perspective'. *Regional Science Policy & Practice*, 2(1): 1–19. Available at: http://onlinelibrary.wiley.com/doi/10.1111/j.1757-7802.2010.01016.x/full (accessed 29 June 2017).

Camenisch, M. and Debarbieux, B. (2011) 'Inter-communal migrations in Switzerland: a "mountain factor"?' *JAR-RGA*, 99(1). Available at: http://rga.revues.org/1368 (accessed 1 August 2017).

Capello, R. (1998) 'Économies d'échelle et taille urbaine: Théorie et études empiriques revisitées'. *RERU*, 1: 43–62.

Castells, M. (1972) *La question urbaine*. Paris: Maspero. [(1977) *The Urban Question*. London: Edward Arnold].

Castells, M. (1996) *The Rise of the Network Society, The Information Age: Economy, Society and Culture Vol. I*. Malden, MA and Oxford: Blackwell.

Cattan, N., Pumain, D., Rozenblat, C. and Saint-Julien, T. (1994) *Le système des villes européennes*. Paris: Anthropos, coll. Villes.

CDE. (2009) *Mountains and Climate Change: From Understanding to Action*. Bern: Institute of Geography, University of Bern.

Charlery de la Masselière, B., Bart, F., Racaud S., Bonnassieux A. and Baron, C. (2017) 'Mountains and urbanization in East Africa'. In B. Nakileza, S. Racaud and F. Bart (eds), *Dynamics in the East African Mountains*. Dar es Salaam: Mkuki Na Nyota Publishers, pp. 35–54.

Chevalier, S., Lallement, E. and Corbillé, S. (2013) *Paris résidence secondaire. Enquête chez ces habitants d'un nouveau genre*. Paris: Collection Anthropolis, Belin.

Chipeniuk, R. (2006) 'Planning for amenity migration in communities of the British Columbia hinterland'. In L.A.G. Moss (ed.), *The Amenity Migrants: Seeking and Sustaining Mountains and Their Cultures*. Wallingford and Cambridge, MA: CABI, pp. 163–74.

CIPRA. (2011) *Alpenscène no. 95 – Qui réveillera la belle endormie? Un bilan après 20 ans de Convention alpine*. Available at: http://www.cipra.org/fr/publications/4586/956_fr/at_down load/file (accessed 26 November 2018).

CIPRA Austria. (2011) *Die Alpenkonvention*, 65. Innsbruck: CIPRA Austria.

Clarimont, S. and Vlès, V. (2009) 'Pyrenean tourism confronted with sustainable development: partial and hesitant integration'. *JAR-RGA*, 97(3). Available at: https://rga.revues.org/978 (accessed 1 August 2017).

Clivaz, C. and Nahrath, S. (2010) 'The return of the property question in the development of Alpine tourist resorts in Switzerland'. *JAR-RGA*, 98(2). Available at: http://rga.revues.org/1198 (accessed 1 August 2017).

Cognard, F. (2010) *'Migration d'agrément' et noveaux habitants dans les moyennes montagnes françaises: de la recomposition sociale au développement territorial. L'exemple du Diois, du Morvan et du Séronais*. Clermont-Ferrand: Université Blaise Pascal.

Cognard, F. (2011) 'Les migrations résidentielles des Britanniques et des Néerlandais: une figure originale de la nouvelle attractivité des moyennes montagnes françaises'. *Espace populations sociétés*, 3. Available at: http://eps.revues.org/4672 (accessed 1 August 2017).

Cole, J.W. and Wolf, E.R. (1999/1974) *The Hidden Frontier: Ecology and Ethnicity in an Alpine Valley*, reprint with a new introduction. Oakland, CA: University of California Press.

Coleman, J. (1988) 'Social capital in the creation of human capital'. *The American Journal of Sociology*, 94(Suppl.): 95–120.

Convertino, A. (ed.) (2006) *AlpCity Project Final Report*. Turin: Interreg IIIB Programme Alpine Space.

Corrado, F. (2010) 'Fragile areas in the Alpine region: a reading between innovation and marginality'. *JAR-RGA*, 98(3). Available at: https://rga.revues.org/1169 (accessed 1 August 2017).

Corrado, F. (2014) 'New inhabitants: processes of re-settlement in mountain areas'. *JAR-RGA*, 102(3). Available at: https://rga.revues.org/2545 (accessed 1 August 2017).

Corrado, F. and di Gioia, A. (2011) 'La provincia piè-montana torinese tra neoruralismo spontaneo e nuovi processi territoriali'. In Proceedings 'Il ruolo delle città nell'economia della conoscenza', Torino, 15–17 September, pp. 1–19.

Coté, S., Klein, J.L. and Proux, M.U. (eds) (1995) *Et les régions qui perdent ...?* Actes du colloque de la section développement régional de l'ACFAS 1994 tenu à l'UQAM les

17 et 18 mai 1994. Québec: GRIDEQ. Available at: http://semaphore.uqar.ca/458/1/ LES_REGIONS_QUI_PERDENT.pdf (accessed 26 November 2018).

Courlet, C. (1997) 'Globalisation et recompositions territoriales dans le Sillon alpin'. *RGA*, 85(3): 48–60.

Cretton, V. (2018) 'In search of a better world in the Swiss Alps: lifestyle migration, quality of life, and gentrification'. In A. Boscoboinik, H. Horáková and R. Smith (eds), *Ethnography of Rural Spaces: Between Utopia and Neoliberalism*. Münster: Lit Verlag.

Crevoisier, O. (1998) 'Structures spatiales différenciées de financement des grandes entreprises et des PME régionales'. *RERU*, 4: 625–40.

Crevoisier, O. and Camagni, R. (eds) (2000) *Villes et milieux: innovation, systèmes de production et ancrage urbain*. Neuchâtel: EDES.

Crevoisier, O., Corpataux, J. and Thierstein, A. (2001) *Intégration monétaire et régions: des gagnants et des perdants*. Paris: Harmattan.

Crivelli, R. (2007) 'Il paradosso della città alpina'. In C. Ferrata (ed.), *Il senso dell'ospitalità*. Bellinzona: Casagrande Editore, pp. 129–42.

Croucher, S. (2012) 'Privileged mobility in an age of globality'. *Societies*, 2: 1–13.

Dalmasso, A. (2008) 'Dams and development in the French Alps in the inter-war period'. *JAR-RGA*, 96(1). Available at: https://rga.revues.org/405 (accessed 1 August 2017).

Dame, J. (2015) 'Multilokalität im Himalaya: Diversifizierung der Lebenssicherung und neue Mobilität in Ladakh, Nordindien'. In J. Poerting and M. Keck (eds), *Aktuelle Forschungsbeiträge zu Südasien. 5. Jahrestagung des AK Südasien, 23./24. Januar 2015*. Göttingen: Geographien Südasiens 3, pp. 37–40.

Dansero, E. and Mela, A. (2007) 'Olympic territorialization: the case of Torino 2006'. *JAR-RGA*, 95(3). Available at: https://rga.revues.org/281 (accessed 1 August 2017).

Davezies, L. (2015) *Le nouvel egoïsme territorial*. Paris: Seuil.

Davezies, L. and Talandier, M. (2014) *L'émergence de systèmes territoriaux productivo-résidentiels*. Paris: La Documentation française.

Debarbieux, B. (2013) 'Le paysage alpin, impossible bien commun de la Suisse et des Suisses?' *JAR-RGA*, Hors-Série. Available at: https://rga.revues.org/2285 (accessed 1 August 2017).

Debarbieux, B. and Price, M. (2008) 'Representing mountains: from local and national to global common good'. *Geopolitics*, 13(1): 148–68.

Debarbieux, B. and Rudaz, G. (2015) *The Mountain: A Political History from the Enlightenment to the Present*. Chicago, IL: University of Chicago Press.

Debroux, J. (2006) 'Migration d'actifs vers l'espace "rural isolé." Éléments d'analyse sur les liens à l'espace d'arrivée'. *Norois*, 200(3): 80–9. Available at: https://norois.revues. org/1817 (accessed 1 August 2017).

Debroux, J. (2011) 'Stratégies résidentielles et position sociale: l'exemple des localisations périurbaines'. *Espaces et sociétés*, 144–5(1): 121–39.

del Mármol, C. and Vaccaro, I. (2015) 'Changing ruralities: between abandonment and redefinition in the Catalan Pyrenees'. *Anthropological Forum*, 25(1): 21–41.

Dematteis, G. (1975) 'Le Città alpine'. In B. Parisi (ed.), *Le città alpine. Documenti e note*. Milan: Vita e pensiero, pp. 5–103.

Dematteis, G. (2009) 'Polycentric urban regions in the Alpine space'. *Urban Research & Practice*, 2(1): 18–35.

Dematteis, M. (2010) *Mamma li turchi. Le comunità straniere delle alpi si raccontano: The Foreign Communities in the Alps Tell Their Own History*. Roccabruna: Chambra d'Òc.

Dematteis, M. and Membretti, A. (eds) (2016) *Montanari per forza. L'immigrazione straniera nelle montagne italiane, tra emergenza e inclusione sociale. Numero speciale della rivista Dislivelli*.

Available at: http://issuu.com/dislivelli/docs/64_webmagazine_febbraio16/1 (accessed 3 July 2018).

Dérioz, P., Loireau, M., Bachimon, P., Cancel, E. and Clément, D. (2014) 'What place for pastoral activities in the economic transformation of Vicdessos (Ariège Pyrenees)?' *JAR-RGA*, 102(2). Available at: https://rga.revues.org/2398 (accessed 1 August 2017).

Dessemontet, P., Kaufmann, V. and Jemelin, C. (2010) 'Switzerland as a single metropolitan area? A study of its commuting network'. *Urban Studies*, 47(13): 2785–802.

de Weck, R. (2009) *Nach der Krise. Gibt es einen anderen Kapitalismus?* München: Nagel & Kimche.

Diamond, J. (2005) *Collapse: How Societies Choose to Fail or Succeed.* New York: Viking.

Diener, R., Herzog, J., Meili, M., de Meuron, P. and Schmid, C. (2006) *Switzerland: An Urban Portrait. Vol. 1–4.* ETH Zürich Studio Basel: Birkhäuser.

Diewald, M. and Faist, T. (2011) 'Von Heterogenitäten zu Ungleichheiten: Soziale Mechanismen als Erklärungsansatz der Genese sozialer Ungleichheiten'. *Berliner Journal für Soziologie*, 21: 91–114.

Dirksmeier, P. (2010) 'Super-Gentrification und metropolitaner Habitus: eine Kritik jüngerer Entwicklungen in der britischen Gentrificationforschung'. *RuR*, 68: 447–57.

Dosi, G., Pavitt, K. and Soete, L. (1990) *The Economics of Technical Change and International Trade.* New York: New York University Press.

Duane, T. (2000) *Shaping the Sierra: Nature, Culture, and Conflict in the Changing West.* Berkeley, CA: University of California Press.

Duane, T. (2012) *The Next West.* Working Paper. Santa Cruz: University of California Press.

Duchêne-Lacroix, C. and Dick, E. (2015) 'Multilocal living in the global South and the global North: differences, convergences and universality of an underestimated phenomenon'. *Trialog*, 2(115): 4–10.

EC. (2015) *Action Plan, Accompanying the Document 'Communication from the Commission to the European Parliament, the Council, the European Economic and Social Committee and the Committee of the Regions' Concerning the European Union Strategy for the Alpine Region.* Commission Staff Working Document, 28 July. Brussels. Available at: http://ec.europa.eu/regional_policy/sources/cooperate/alpine/eusalp_action_plan.pdf (accessed 1 August 2017).

EC. (2017) *Social Innovation as a Trigger for Transformations – The Role of Research.* Eds. F. Moulaert, A. Mehmood, D. MacCallum and B. Leubolt. Bruxelles: European Commission.

Egger, T. (2010) 'Vision d'une nouvelle macrorégion alpine européenne'. *Forum du développement territorial*, 3: 61–2.

Egger, T., Stalder, U. and Wenger, A. (2003) *Brain drain in der Schweiz: Die Berggebiete verlieren ihre hochqualifizierte Bevölkerung.* Bern: SAB.

Eggerschwiler, B.D., Egli, H. and Peter, C. (2010) *Soziokulturelle und sozioökonomische Auswirkungen des Tourismusresort Andermatt.* Luzern: Erste Teilstudie.

Eisinger, A. and Schneider, M. (eds) (2003) *Urbanscape Switzerland: Topology and Regional Development in Switzerland. Investigations and Case Studies.* Basel, Boston, MA and Berlin: Birkhäuser.

Elden, S. (2004) *Understanding Henri Lefebvre: Theory and the Possible.* London and New York: Continuum.

Elmi, M. and Perlik, M. (2014) 'From tourism to multilocal residence? Unequal transformation processes in the Dolomites area'. *JAR-RGA*, 102(3). Available at: https://rga.revues.org/2608 (accessed 1 August 2017).

Engels, F. (1845) *The Condition of the Working Class in England.* German edition, Marx Engels Werke (MEW) Bd. 2 (1972). Berlin: Dietz.

Eribon, D. (2009) *Retour à Reims.* Paris: Fayard.

ESPON. (2010) *Cross-Border Polycentric Metropolitan Regions (METROBORDER)*. Final Report. Luxembourg.

Etherington, D. and Jones, M. (2009) 'City-regions: new geographies of uneven development and inequality'. *Regional Studies*, 43(2): 247–65.

Expertenkommission 'Überprüfung und Neukonzeption der Regionalpolitik'. (2003) *Neue Regionalpolitik (NRP)*. Zürich: Schlussbericht.

Fablet, G. (2013) 'Real estate development in the ski resorts of the Tarentaise valley: between cyclical variations and structural requirements'. *JAR-RGA*, 101(3). Available at: https://rga.revues.org/2196 (accessed 1 August 2017).

Fahrländer Partner. (2016) *Immobilienalmanach Schweiz 2016*. Available at: www.fpre.ch/wp-content/uploads/immobilien-almanach_schweiz_2016.pdf (accessed 1 August 2017).

FAO. (2015) *Mapping the Vulnerability of Mountain Peoples to Food Insecurity*, Eds. R. Romeo, A. Vita, R. Testolin and T. Hofer. Rome: FAO.

Faure, A. (2008) 'Social norms for population displacements caused by large dams France, 20th century: the example of the Tignes and Serre-Ponçon dams in the Alps and the Aigle and Bort-les-Orgues dams in Haute-Dordogne'. *JAR-RGA*, 96(1). Available at: https://rga.revues.org/393 (accessed 1 August 2017).

Favier, R. (1993) *Les villes du Dauphiné aux XVIIe et XVIIIe siècles*. Grenoble: PUG.

Fédération Nationale des Agences d'Urbanisme (FNAU). (2006) *Des aires urbaines {. . .} aux systèmes métropolitains*. Paris: FNAU.

Feldhoff, T. (2011) 'Retirement migration and the (re)population of vulnerable rural areas: a case study of Date City (Hokkaido, Japan)'. *Critical Planning*, 18: 32–49.

Feldhoff, T. (2013) 'Shrinking communities in Japan: community ownership of assets as a development potential for rural Japan?' *Urban Design International*, 18(1): 99–109.

Ferlaino, F. and Levi Sacerdotti, S. (2000) 'Aspetti di scenario del Verbano-Cusio-Ossola nel contesto regionale'. IRES, Working Paper no. 138/2000. Torino.

Ferrario, E. and Price, M. (2014) 'Should I stay or should I go? Alpine brain drain and brain gain: the reasons behind the choices of young mountain people'. *JAR-RGA*, 102(4). Available at: https://rga.revues.org/2381 (accessed 1 August 2017).

Ferrario, V. (2009) 'Rural/leisure landscapes and amenity-led migrations: an example in the eastern Italian Alps'. In L.A.G. Moss, R. Glorioso and A. Krause (eds), *Proc. of the Conference 'Understanding and Managing Amenity-Led Migration in Mountain Regions', May 2008*. Banff: The Banff Centre, pp. 107–17.

Flognfeldt Jr, T. (2004) 'Second homes as a part of a new rural lifestyle in Norway'. In C.M. Hall and D.K. Müller (eds), *Tourism, Mobility and Second Homes: Between Elite Landscapes and Common Ground*. Clevedon: Channel View Publications, pp. 233–43.

Florida, R. (2002) *The Rise of the Creative Class: And How It's Transforming Work, Leisure and Everyday Life*. New York: Basic Books.

Forget, M. (2015) 'Territorial trajectories within a new centre for the globalised mining industry: the Andes of northern Argentina'. *JAR-RGA*, 103(3). Available at: http://rga.revues.org/3024 (accessed 1 August 2017).

Foucault, M. (2004) *Sécurité, Territoire, Population: Cours au Collège de France 1977–1978*. Édition établie sous la direction de F. Ewald et A. Fontana par Michel Senellard. Paris: Gallimard, Hautes Études.

Fourastié, J. (1979) *Les Trente Glorieuses, ou la Révolution invisible de 1946 à 1975*. Paris: Fayard (re-edited: Hachette Pluriel).

Fourastié, J. (1989/1949) *Le grand espoir du XXe siècle. Progrès technique, progrès économique, progrès social*. Paris: PUF.

Fourny, M.-C. (1996) 'Nouveaux habitants dans un pays de moyenne montagne'. *Études Rurales*, 135–6: 83–95.

Fourny, M.-C. (2005) *Identité et dynamiques territoriales. Coopération, différenciation, temporalités. Vol 1. Rapport pour l'habilitation à diriger des recherches.* Grenoble: Université Joseph-Fourier.

Fourny, M.-C. (2006) 'Quelle spécificité des villes des Alpes? Une analyse critique des approches géographiques de la ville alpine'. In P. Leveau and B. Rémy (eds), *La ville des Alpes occidentales à l'époque romaine.* Grenoble: Cahiers du CRHIPA 13, pp. 27–47.

Fourny, M.-C. (2014) 'Périphérique, forcément périphérique? La montagne au prisme de l'analyse géographique de l'innovation'. In M. Attali, A.M. Granet-Abisset and A. Dalmasso (eds), *Innovation en territoire de montagne: le défi de l'approche interdisciplinaire.* Grenoble: PUG, pp. 135–66.

Fourny, M.-C. (ed.) (2018) *Montagnes en mouvements. Dynamiques territoriales et innovation sociale.* Grenoble: PUG.

Fourny, M.-C. and Denizot, D. (2007) 'La prospective territoriale, révélateur et outil d'une action publique territorialisée'. In R. Dodier, A. Rouyer and R. Séchet (eds), *Territoires en action et dans l'action.* Rennes: Presses Universitaires de Rennes, pp. 29–44.

Frey, R.L. (1981) *Von der Land- zur Stadtflucht.* Bern, Frankfurt: Peter Lang.

Fujita, M., Krugman, P. and Venables, A.J. (1999) *Spatial Economy: Cities, Regions, and International Trade.* Cambridge, MA: MIT Press.

Furter, R., Head-König, A.L. and Lorenzetti, L. (eds) (2015) *Des manufactures aux fabriques – Les transformations industrielles, XVIIIe – XXe siècles/Von der Manufaktur zur Fabrik. Industrieller Wandel, 18. – 20. Jahrhundert. Histoire des Alpes/Geschichte der Alpen/Storia delle Alpi 20.* Zurich: Chronos.

Fusco, G. and Scarella, F. (2011) 'Métropolisation et ségrégation socio-spatiale. Les flux de mobilité résidentielle en Provence-Alpes-Côte d'Azur'. *L'espace géographique*, 4: 319–36.

Garofoli, G. (1993) 'Economic development, organization of production and territory'. *Revue d'économie industrielle*, 64(1): 22–37.

Garofoli, G. (2009) 'Industrial districts in Europe'. In G. Becattini, M. Bellandi and L. de Propris (eds), *A Handbook of Industrial Districts.* Cheltenham: Edward Elgar Publishing, pp. 488–500.

Geoffroy, C. (2007) 'From Chamouni to Chamonix: British travellers and migrants'. In C. Geoffroy and R. Sibley (eds), *Going Abroad: Travel, Tourism and Migration. Cross-Cultural Perspectives on Mobility.* Newcastle: Cambridge Scholars Publishing, pp. 93–109.

George-Marcelpoil, E. and François, H. (2012) 'From creating to managing resorts'. *JAR-RGA*, 100(3). Available at: https://rga.revues.org/1925 (accessed 1 August 2017).

Gilly, J.P. and Pecqueur, B. (2002) 'La dimension locale de la régulation'. In R. Boyer and Y. Saillard (eds), *Théorie de la régulation – État des savoirs.* Paris: La Découverte, pp. 304–12.

Giuliani, G. (2002) *Landwirtschaftlicher Bodenmarkt und landwirtschaftliche Bodenpolitik in der Schweiz.* Diss. ETH No. 14781. Available at: http://e-collection.ethbib.ethz.ch/eserv.php?pid=eth:26182&dsID=eth-26182-02.pdf (accessed 1 August 2017).

Glasze, G., Webster, C. and Frantz, K. (eds) (2006) *Private Cities: Global and Local Perspectives.* London: Routledge.

Gloersen, E., Price, M., Aalbu, H., Schuler, M., Stucki, E., Roque, O., Perlik, M. et al. (2004) *Mountain Areas in Europe: Analysis of Mountain Areas in EU Member States, Acceding and Other European Countries.* Nordregio: Stockholm.

Glorioso, R.S. (2006) 'A bioregion in jeopardy: the strategic challenge of amenity migration in Baguio, the Philippines'. In L.A.G. Moss (ed.), *The Amenity Migrants: Seeking and Sustaining Mountains and Their Cultures.* Wallingford and Cambridge, MA: CABI, pp. 261–77.

Glorioso, R.S. and Moss, L.A.G. (2006) 'Santa Fe, a fading dream. Profile 1986 and postscript 2005'. In L.A.G. Moss (ed.), *The Amenity Migrants: Seeking and Sustaining Mountains and Their Cultures.* Wallingford and Cambridge, MA: CABI, pp. 73–93.

Glückler, J. (2007) 'Geography of reputation: the city as the locus of business opportunity'. *Regional Studies*, 41(7): 949–61.

Gosnell, H. and Abrams, J. (2011) 'Amenity migration: diverse conceptualizations of drivers, socioeconomic dimensions, and emerging challenges'. *GeoJournal*, 76. Available at: www. springerlink.com/content/9l40n2843572mm05/fulltext.pdf (accessed 26 November 2018).

Government of the Islamic Republic of Afghanistan (GoIRA). (2015) *The State of Afghan Cities 2015 Volume 1.* Kabul: GoIRA. Available at: http://unhabitat.org/books/soac2015/ (accessed 4 September 2016).

Grabher, G. (1993) 'The weakness of strong ties: the lock-in of regional developments in the Ruhr area'. In G. Grabher (ed.), *The Embedded Firm: On the Socioeconomics of Industrial Networks.* London and New York: Routledge, pp. 255–77.

Grabher, G. and Stark, D. (1997) 'Organizing diversity: evolutionary theory, network analysis, and post-socialism'. *Regional Studies*, 31(5): 533–44.

Graf, F. (2019) 'The migrants' construction of social spaces in the Alps'. In M. Perlik, G. Galera, I. Machold, and A. Membretti (eds), *Alpine Refugees. Immigration at the Core of Europe.* Cambridge: Cambridge Scholars (forthcoming).

Graham, J. and Keil, R. (1998) 'Reasserting nature: constructing urban environments after Fordism'. In B. Braun and N. Castree (eds), *Remaking Reality: Nature at the Millennium.* London and New York: Routledge, pp. 100–25.

Granovetter, M. (1973) 'The strength of weak ties'. *American Journal of Sociology*, 78(6): 1360–80.

Gravier, J.F. (1947) *Paris et le désert français.* Paris: Le Portulan.

Gray, M., Golob, E. and Markusen, A. (1996) 'Big firms, long arms, wide shoulders: the "hub-and-spoke" industrial district in the Seattle region'. *Regional Studies*, 30(7): 651–66.

Gretter, A., Machold, I., Membretti, A. and Dax, T. (2017) Pathways of immigration in the Alps and Carpathians: Social innovation and the creation of a welcoming culture. *MRD*, 37(4): 396–405.

Guérin, J.P. and Gumuchian, H. (1979) 'Ruraux et rurbains: Réflexions sur les fondements de la ruralité aujourd'hui'. *RGA*, 67(1): 89–104.

Guex, D. and Crevoisier, O. (2017) *Globalisation postindustrielle et milieux locaux: une typologie.* MAPS Working Paper 1–2017/F. Neuchâtel: Maison d'analyse des processus sociaux.

Gugger, H. and Kerschbaumer, G. (2013) 'The compact city: sustainable, or just sustaining the economy?' In *The Economic Performance of Sustainable Construction.* Berlin: Ruby Press, pp. 242–52.

Guimond, L. and Simard, M. (2010) 'Gentrification and neo-rural populations in the Québec countryside: representations of various actors'. *Journal of Rural Studies*, 26(4): 449–64.

Gunderson, R., Pinto, J. and Williams, R. (2008) 'Economic or amenity driven migration?' *Journal of Regional Analysis & Policy*, 38(3): 243–54.

Hall, C.M. and Müller, D.K. (2004) *Tourism, Mobility and Second Homes: Between Elite Landscape and Common Ground. Aspects of Tourism.* Clevedon: Channel View.

Haller, A. (2014) 'The "sowing of concrete": peri-urban smallholder perceptions of rural – urban land change in the Central Peruvian Andes'. *Land Use Policy*, 38: 239–47.

Harris, M. (1999) *Theories of Culture in Postmodern Times.* Walnut Creek, CA, London and New Delhi: AltaMira Press.

Harris, M. (2001/1979) *Cultural Materialism: The Struggle for a Science of Culture. Updated Edition.* Lanham, MD: AltaMira Press.

Harvey, D. (1973) *Social Justice and the City.* London: Arnold.

Harvey, D. (1985) *The Urbanisation of Capital: Studies in the History and Theory of Capitalist Urbanisation*. Baltimore, MD: Johns Hopkins University Press.

Harvey, D. (1989) *The Urban Experience*. Baltimore, MD: Johns Hopkins University Press.

Harvey, D. (2006/1982) *Limits to Capital*. London and New York: Verso.

Harvey, D. (2006) *Spaces of Global Capitalism: Towards a Theory of Uneven Development*. London: Verso.

Häussermann, H. and Siebel, W. (1995) *Dienstleistungsgesellschaften*. Frankfurt: Suhrkamp.

Head-König, A.L. (2011) 'Migration in the Swiss Alps and Swiss Jura from the middle ages to the mid-20th century: a brief review'. *JAR-RGA*, 99(1). Available at: https://rga.revues.org/1359 (accessed 1 August 2017).

Heeg, S. (2012) 'From the old downtown to the new downtown: the case of the South-Boston waterfront'. In I. Helbrecht and P. Dirksmeier (eds), *Planning Urbanity: Life/Work/Space in the New Downtown*. Aldershot: Ashgate, pp. 85–106.

Heinonen, J., Jalas, M., Juntunen, J.K., Ala-Mantila, S. and Junnila, S. (2013) 'Situated lifestyles: II. the impacts of urban density, housing type and motorization on the greenhouse gas emissions of the middle-income consumers in Finland'. *Environmental Research Letters*, 8(3). doi:10.1088/1748-9326/8/3/035050. Available at: http://iopscience.iop.org/article/10.1088/1748-9326/8/3/035050/pdf (accessed 1 August 2017).

Herrera, C. (2010) 'In search of the territorial land resource in mountain areas'. *JAR-RGA*, 98(2). Available at: https://rga.revues.org/1197 (accessed 1 August 2017).

Hesse, G. (1982) *Die Entstehung industrialisierter Volkswirtschaften*. Ein Beitrag zur theoretischen und empirischen Analyse der langfristigen wirtschaftlichen Entwicklung. Tübingen: J.C.B. Mohr.

Hesse, M. and Kaltenbrunner, R. (2005) 'Zerrbild "Zersiedelung": Anmerkungen zum Gebrauch und zur Dekonstruktion eines Begriffs'. *disP*, 160: 16–22.

Hilferding, R. (1982/1927) 'Die Aufgaben der Sozialdemokratie in der Republik'. In C. Stephan (ed.), *Zwischen den Stühlen oder über die Unvereinbarkeit von Theorie und Praxis. Schriften Rudolf Hilferdings 1904 bis 1940*. Bonn: Dietz, pp. 212–36.

Hirschman, A.O. (1970) *Exit, Voice and Loyalty: Responses to Decline in Firms, Organizations and States*. Cambridge, MA: Harvard University Press.

Hobsbawm, E. (1975) *The age of capital 1848-1875*. London: Weidenfeld & Nicolson.

Hobson, J.A. (2011/1902) *Imperialism: A Study*. Cambridge: Cambridge University Press. Available at: www.econlib.org/library/YPDBooks/Hobson/hbsnImp.html (accessed 24 August 2016).

Hoffmann, D. (2007) 'The Sajama national park in Bolivia: a model for cooperation among state and local authorities and the indigenous population'. *MRD*, 27(1): 11–14.

Hoffmann, D. and Requena, C. (2012) *Bolivia en un mundo 4 grados más caliente. Escenarios sociopolíticos ante el cambio climá tico para los años 2030 y 2060 en el altiplano norte*. La Paz: Instituto Boliviano de la Montaña.

Holenstein, A., Kury, P. and Schulz, K. (2018) *Schweizer Migrationsgeschichte*. Baden: Hier und Jetzt.

Horáková, H. and Boscoboinik, A. (eds) (2012) *From Production to Consumption: Transformation of Rural Communities*. Etudes d'Anthropologie Sociale de l'Université de Fribourg 35. Münster: Lit Verlag.

Huddleston B. et al. (2003) *Towards a GIS-Based Analysis of Mountain Environments and Populations*. Environment and Natural Resources Working Paper No. 10. Rome: FAO.

Huete, R., Mantecón, A. and Estévez, J. (2013) 'Challenges in lifestyle migration research: reflections and findings about the Spanish crisis'. *Mobilities*, 8(3): 331–48.

Hug, F. (2002) *Ressourcenhaushalt alpiner Regionen und deren physiologische Interaktionen mit den Tiefländern im Kontext einer nachhaltigen Entwicklung*. Diss. ETH No. 14540.

Ives, J.D. and Messerli, B. (1989) *The Himalayan Dilemma: Reconciling Development and Conservation*. London and New York: UN University and Routledge.

Jacobs, J. (1961) *The Death and Life of Great American Cities*. New York: Random House.

Jacobs, J. (1969) *The Economy of Cities*. New York: Vintage Books.

Jacobs, J. (1984) *Cities and the Wealth of Nations*. New York: Random House.

Jacobs, J. (2000) *The Nature of Economies*. New York: Modern Library.

Jacquemet, E. (2018) 'Réinventer le Khumbu: la société sherpa à l'ère du "Yak Donald's"'. In M.-C. Fourny (ed.), *Montagnes en mouvements. Dynamiques territoriales et innovation sociale*. Grenoble: PUG.

Janoschka, M. (2009) 'Contested spaces of lifestyle mobilities: regime analysis as a tool to study political claims in Latin American retirement destinations'. *Die Erde*, 140(3): 1–20.

Janoschka, M. and Haas, H. (eds) (2013) *Contested Spatialities, Lifestyle Migration and Residential Tourism*. London: Routledge.

Jedrej, C. and Nuttall, M. (1996) *White Settlers: The Impact of Rural Repopulation in Scotland*. Luxembourg: Harwood.

Jelen, I. (1996) 'Le calendrier écologique, fondement de la cohésion sociale des communautés alpines: Le cas des Slovènes des Préalpes juliennes (Vénétie occidentale)'. *Géographie et Cultures*, 18: 93–118.

Jenkins, J.S. (2016a) *Rare Earth at Bearlodge: Extractive Mineral Development, Multiple Use Management, and Socio-Ecological Values in the American West*. Electronic Theses and Dissertations, UC Santa Cruz. Available at: https://escholarship.org/uc/item/74p458q2 (accessed 6 November 2018).

Jenkins, J.S. (2016b) 'Contested terrain of extractive development in the American West: using a regional political ecology framework to understand scalar governance, biocentric values, and anthropocentric values'. In I. McKinnon and C. Hiner (eds), '(Re)considering regional political ecology?' Special Section of the *Journal of Political Ecology*, 23: 182–96.

Jessop, B. (1992) 'Fordism and post-Fordism: a critical reformulation'. In M. Storper and A. Scott (eds), *Pathways to Industrialization and Regional Development*, reprint 1996. London: Routledge, pp. 47–69.

Jessop, B. (2004) *Spatial Fixes, Temporal Fixes, and Spatio-Temporal Fixes*. Lancaster: Department of Sociology, Lancaster University. Available at: www.comp.lancs.ac.uk/sociology/papers/jessop-spatio-temporal-fixes.pdf (accessed 1 August 2017).

Jessop, B. (2014) *On the Limits of Limits to Capital*. Lancaster: Department of Sociology, Lancaster University. Available at: www.lancaster.ac.uk/fass/resources/sociology-online-papers/papers/jessop-limits-to-capital.pdf (accessed 1 August 2017).

Jessop, B. and Sum, N.L. (2006) *Beyond the Regulation Approach: Putting Capitalist Economies in Their Place*. Cheltenham. Edward Elgar Publishing.

Jones, H., Ford, N., Caird, J. and Berry, W. (1984) 'Counter-urbanization in societal context: long-distance migration to the highlands and islands of Scotland'. *Professional Geographer*, 36(4): 437–44.

Joye, D., Busset, T. and Schuler, M. (1992) 'Clivages et différenciations géographiques de la Suisse'. In P. Hugger (ed.), *Les Suisses: modes de vie, traditions, mentalités (3 vol.)*. Lausanne: Payot, pp. 661–76.

Kaltenborn, B., Andersen, O., Nellemann, C., Bjerke, T. and Thrane, C. (2008) 'Resident attitudes towards mountain second-home tourism development in Norway: the effects of environmental attitudes'. *Journal of Sustainable Tourism*, 16(6): 664–80.

Kapos, V., Rhind J., Edwards, M. and Price, M.F. (2000) 'Developing a map of the world's mountain forest'. In M.F. Price and N. Butts (eds), *Forest in Sustainable Mountain Development: A State of Knowledge Report for 2000*. Wallingford: CABI, pp. 4–18.

Karki, M. et al. (2012) *Sustainable Mountain Development 1992, 2012, and Beyond Rio+20*. Assessment Report for the Hindu Kush Himalayan Region. Kathmandu: ICIMOD, SDC and Mountain Partnership.

Kasimis, C. and Papadopoulos, A. (2013) 'Rural transformations and family farming in contemporary Greece'. In A. Moragues Faus, D. Ortiz-Miranda and E. Arnalte Alegre (eds), *Agriculture in Mediterranean Europe: Between Old and New Paradigms*. (Research in Rural Sociology and Development 19). Bingley: Emerald, pp. 263–93.

Kaufeisen, G. and Foppa, A. (2016) Gold exploration in Val Medel, Switzerland. In T. Niederberger, T. Haller, H. Gambon, M. Kobi and I. Wenk (eds), *The Open Cut: Mining, Transnational Corporations and Local Populations. Action Anthropology/Aktionsethnologie, 2*. Zurich: Lit Verlag, pp. 91–116.

Keckstein, V. (1999) 'Kleinstädte und Marktgemeinden zwischen Urbanität und Zersiedelung'. In M. Perlik and W. Bätzing (eds), *L'avenir des villes des Alpes en Europe/Die Zukunft der Alpenstädte in Europa*. GB P36/RGA, 87(2): 89–103.

Keil, R. and Lieser, P. (1992) 'Frankfurt: global city-local politics'. In M.P. Smith (ed.), *After Modernism: Global Restructuring and the Changing Boundaries of City Life (Comparative Urban and Community Research, 4)*. London: Sage, pp. 39–69.

Keller, E. (2015) *Beyond the Lens of Conservation: Malagasy and Swiss Imaginations of One Another*. New York: Berghahn.

Kemeny, T. and Storper, M. (2014) 'Is specialization good for regional economic development?' *Regional Studies*. Available at: http://luskin.ucla.edu/sites/default/files/Specializationpaperpublished.pdf (accessed 1 August 2017).

Khawas, V. (2007) 'Environmental challenges and human security in the Himalaya'. Paper at the National Seminar 'Himalayas in the New Millennium: Environment, Society, Economy and Polity', January. Centre for Himalayan Studies, North Bengal University, Darjeeling. Available at: http://lib.icimod.org/record/12968/files/526.pdf (accessed 26 November 2018).

Klagge, B., Martin, R. and Sunley, P. (2017) 'The spatial structure of the financial system and the funding of regional business: a comparison of Britain and Germany'. In R. Martin, J. Pollard (eds), *Handbook on the Geographies of Money and Finance*. Cheltenham: Edward Elgar Publishing, pp. 125–55.

Klaus, P. (2004) 'Creative and innovative microenterprises between world market and subculture'. In INURA (ed.), *The Contested Metropolis: Six Cities at the Beginning of the 21st Century*. Basel, Boston, MA and Berlin: Birkhäuser, pp. 261–8.

Klein, J.L., Laville, J.L. and Moulaert, F. (eds) (2014) *L'innovation sociale*. Toulouse: ERES.

Klepeis, P. and Laris, P. (2008) 'Hobby ranching, and Chile's land reform legacy'. *The Geographical Review*, 98(3): 372–94.

Knoepfel, P. and Gerber, D. (2008) *Institutional Landscape Regime. An Approach to the Resolution of Landscape Conflicts*. Research Report NRP 48. Zurich: vdf Hochschulverlag.

Knox, P. and Mayer, H. (2013) *Small Town Sustainability: Economic, Social, and Environmental Innovation*, 2nd edn. Basel: Birkhäuser.

Kohler, T., Balsiger, J., Rudaz, G., Debarbieux, B., Pratt, D.J. and Maselli, D. (eds) (2015) *Green Economy and Institutions for Sustainable Mountain Development: From Rio 1992 to Rio 2012 and Beyond*. Bern: CDE, SDC, University of Geneva and GB. Available at: www.fao.org/fileadmin/user_upload/mountain_partnership/docs/LOW_Global_Green_Economy_RIO20.pdf (accessed 5 November 2018).

Kohler, T. and Messerli, P. (2017) Comment on: Müller-Jentsch, D. (2017) *Strukturwandel im Schweizer Berggebiet* (in German). Available at: https://naturalsciences.ch/organisations/icas/diskussionsforum/kommentar_thomas_kohler_und_paul_messerli (accessed 1 September 2017).

Kolinjivadi, V., Van Hecken, G., Vela Almeida, D., Dupras, J. and Kosoy, N. (2017) 'Neoliberal performatives and the "making" of Payments for Ecosystem Services (PES). *Progress in Human Geography*, (November): 1–23.

Körner, C. (2015) 'Mountain future in a bioclimatic framework'. Keynote speech at the Perth III Conference 'Mountains of Our Future Earth', 4–8 October, Perth, Scotland. Available at: https://cast.switch.ch/vod/clips/7jb7mfb5o/streaming.html (accessed 1 August 2017).

Krätke, S. (2007) 'Metropolisation of the European economic territory as a consequence of increasing specialisation of urban agglomerations in the knowledge economy'. *European Planning Studies*, 15(1): 1–27.

Krätke, S. (2010) 'Creative cities and the rise of the dealer class: a critique of Richard Florida's approach to urban theory'. *International Journal of Urban and Regional Research*, 34(4): 835–53.

Kreutzmann, H. (1991) 'The Karakoram highway: impact of road construction on mountain societies'. *Modern Asian Studies*, 25(4): 711–36.

Kritzinger, S. (1989) 'Un exemple d'immigration d'alternatifs Allemands dans les Pyrénées ariégeoises'. *Revue géographique des Pyrénées et du Sud-Ouest*, 60(2): 199–222.

Kronthaler, F. (2008) *Wertschöpfung des Tourismus in den Regionen Graubündens – Stand und Entwicklung. Im Auftrag des Amtes für Wirtschaft und Tourismus Graubündens*. Final Report. Chur.

Krugman, P. (1991) *Geography and Trade*. Leuven, Cambridge, MA and London: Leuven University Press and MIT Press.

Kübler, D., Schenkel, W. and Leresche, J.P. (2002) 'Bright lights, big cities? Metropolisation, intergovernmental relations, and the new federal urban policy in Switzerland'. *Swiss Political Science Review*, 9(1): 261–82.

Kunzmann, K.R. and Wegener, M. (1991) 'The pattern of urbanisation in Western Europe 1960–1990'. Report for the Directorate General XVI of the EC, Berichte aus dem Institut für Raumplanung, Dortmund.

Lampič, B. and Mrak, I. (2012) 'Globalization and foreign amenity migrants: the case of foreign home owners in the Pomurska region of Slovenia'. *European Countryside*, 4(1): 45–56.

Läpple, D., Mückenberger, U. and Oßenbrügge, J. (2010) *Zeiten und Räume der Stadt: Theorie und Praxis*. Leverkusen: Barbara Budrich.

Lash, S. and Urry, J. (1987) *The End of Organised Capitalism*. Cambridge: Polity Press.

Leborgne, D. and Lipietz, A. (1992) 'Conceptual fallacies and open questions on post-Fordism'. In M. Storper and A. Scott (eds), *Pathways to Industrialization and Regional Development*. London: Routledge, pp. 332–98.

Lefebvre, H. (1970) *La révolution urbaine*. Paris: Gallimard. [(2003) *The Urban Revolution*. Minneapolis, MN: University of Minnesota Press].

Lefebvre, H. (1972) *La pensée marxiste et la ville*. Paris: Casterman.

Lefebvre, H. (1974) *La production de l'espace*. Paris: Anthropos. [(1991) *The Production of Space*. Oxford: Basil Blackwell].

Lehmann, B. and Messerli, P. (2007) 'The Swiss national research programme "Landscapes and Habitats of the Alpine Arc"'. *JAR-RGA*, 95(4). Available at: https://rga.revues.org/344 (accessed 1 August 2017).

Lenin, W.I. (1917) *Imperialism, the Highest Stage of Capitalism* (in Russian). English version, Lenin (1963): *Selected Works. Vol. 1*. Moscow: Progress Publishers, pp. 667–766.

Lerjen, H.P. (1998) *Vom Arbeiter- zum Freizeitbauern: sozialgeographische Annäherung an ein Oberwalliser Phänomen im Einzugsgebiet der chemischen Industrie in Visp 1970–1994*. Bern: Edition Soziothek.

Libération (1998) *L'héritage du Plan neige. En 1964, la France lançait un grand programme d'aménagement des stations. Avec quelques ratés* (issue from 29 December 1998, author: Gabrielle Serraz).

Liechti, K., Wallner, A. and Wiesmann, U. (2010) 'Linking a world heritage site to sustainable regional development: contested natures in a local negotiation process'. *Society & Natural Resources*, 23(8): 726–41.

Lipietz, A. (1977) *Le capital et son espace*. Paris: F. Maspero.

Lipietz A. (1980) 'Le tertiaire, arborescence de l'accumulation capitaliste: prolifération et polarisation'. *Critiques de l'Économie Politique*, (July–September): 17–69.

Lipietz, A. (1990) 'La trame et la chaîne et la régulation'. *Économies et sociétés, Série Théorie de la régulation*, 5: 137–74.

Lipietz, A. (2012) *Green Deal: La crise du libéral-productivisme et la réponse écologique*. Paris: La Découverte.

Löffler, R., Beismann, M., Walder, J. and Steinicke, E. (2011) 'New highlanders in traditional out-migration areas in the Alps: the example of the Friulian Alps'. *JAR-RGA*, 102(3). Available at: https://rga.revues.org/2546 (accessed 1 August 2017).

Los, B., McCann, P., Springford, J. and Thissen, M. (2017): The mismatch between local voting and the local economic consequences of Brexit. *Regional Studies*, 51(5): 786–99.

Lynch, O.J. and Maggio, G.F. (2001) *Mountain Laws and Peoples: Moving Towards Sustainable Development and Recognition of Community-Based Property Rights. A General Overview of Mountain Laws and Policies with Insights from the Mountain Forum's Electronic Conference on Mountain Policy and Law*. Available at: www.activeremedy.org/wp-content/uploads/2014/10/mountain_laws_and_peoples_1997.pdf (accessed 26 November 2018).

Marcelpoil, E. and Hugues, F. (2008) 'Les processus d'articulation des proximités dans les territoires touristiques. L'exemple des stations de montagne'. *Revue d'Économie Régionale & Urbaine*, 2: 179–91.

Marchant, C. and Rojas, F. (2015) 'Local transformations and new economic functionalities generated by amenity migration in northern Chilean Patagonia'. *JAR-RGA*, 103(3). Available at: http://rga.revues.org/2988 (accessed 1 August 2017).

Markusen, A. (1999) *Second Tier Cities*. Minneapolis, MN: University of Minnesota Press.

Markusen, A. (2000) 'Des lieux-aimants dans un espace mouvant: une typologie des districts industriels'. In G. Benko and A. Lipietz (eds), *La richesse des régions. La nouvelle géographie socioéconomique*. Paris: PUF, pp. 85–119.

Marnezy, A. (2009) 'Alpine dams: from hydroelectric power to artificial snow'. *JAR-RGA*, 96(1). Available at: https://rga.revues.org/430 (accessed 1 August 2017).

Marsden, T. (2012) 'Third natures? Reconstituting space through place-making strategies for sustainability'. *International Journal of Sociology of Agriculture and Food*, 19(2): 257–74.

Marshall, A. (1919) *Industry and Trade: A Study of Industrial Technique and Business Organization; and of Their Influences on the Condition of Various Classes and Nations*. London: Palgrave Macmillan.

Martin, N., Bourdeau, P. and Daller, J.F. (eds) (2012) *Du tourisme à l'habiter: les migrations d'agrément*. Paris: l'Harmattan, Collection Tourismes et Sociétés.

Martin, R., Berndt, C., Klagge, B. and Sunley, P. (2005) 'Spatial proximity effects and regional equity gaps in the venture capital market: evidence from Germany and the United Kingdom'. *Environment and Planning A*, 37(7): 1207–31.

Martin, R., Berndt, C., Klagge, B., Sunley, P. and Herten, S. (2003) *Regional Venture Capital Policy: UK and Germany Compared*. London: Anglo-German Foundation for the Study of

Industrial Society. Available at: www.agf.org.uk/cms/upload/pdfs/R/2003_R1346_e_regional_venture_capitalism.pdf (accessed 1 August 2017).

Martin, R. and Sunley, P. (2000) 'L'économie géographique de Paul Krugman et ses conséquences pour la théorie du développement régional: une évaluation critique'. In G. Benko and A. Lipietz (eds), *La richesse des régions. La nouvelle géographie socioéconomique*. Paris: PUF, pp. 33–84.

Martin, R. and Sunley, P. (2006) 'Path dependence and regional economic evolution'. *Journal of Economic Geography*, 6: 395–437.

Martinengo, E. (1991) 'Die Berggebietspolitik in Italien und die Schlüsselprobleme der Entwicklung des italienischen Alpenraumes'. In W. Bätzing and P. Messerli (eds), *Die Alpen im Europa der neunziger Jahre*. Bern: GB P22, pp. 205–29.

Marx, K. (1852) *The Eighteenth Brumaire of Louis Napoleon*. German version. *MEW*, 8(1977): 111–207. Berlin: Dietz.

Marx, K. (1858) *Grundrisse (Outlines of the Critique of Political Economy)*. German edition. *MEW*, 42(1983): 19–875. Berlin: Dietz.

Marx, K. (1867, 1885, 1894) *Capital: A Critique of Political Economy I – III*. German edition. *MEW*, 23–25(1977). Berlin: Dietz.

Matanle, P. and Rausch, A. (2011) *Japan's Shrinking Regions in the 21st Century: Contemporary Responses to Depopulation and Socioeconomic Decline*. London: Cambria Press.

Mathieu, J. (1998) *Geschichte der Alpen 1500–1900. Umwelt, Entwicklung, Gesellschaft*. Wien: Böhlau. [(2009) *History of the Alps, 1500–1900: Environment, Development, and Society*. Morgantown, VA: West Virginia University Press].

Mathieu, J. (2011) *The Third Dimension: A Comparative History of Mountains in the Modern Era*. Cambridge: White Horse Press.

Mattiucci, C. (2015) 'Mountain condominiums: a discussing of settlement and dwelling on the outskirts of an Alpine city'. *JAR-RGA*, 103(3). Available at: http://rga.revues.org/3089 (accessed 1 August 2017).

Mauz, I. (2006) 'La montagne comme ménagerie'. *RGA*, 94(4): 111–28.

Mayer, H. and Cortright, J. (2011) 'The role of culture, consumption and community in cluster development: the case of Portland's athletics and outdoor industry, Oregon (USA)'. *Geographica Helvetica*, 66(4): 261–70.

Maza, A. and Villaverde, J. (2010) 'European metropolitan regions: a convergence process?' *Economics Bulletin*, 30(3): 2312–20.

McIntyre, N. (2009) 'Rethinking amenity migration: integrating mobility, lifestyle and social-ecological systems'. *Die Erde*, 140(3): 229–50.

McIntyre, N., Williams, D. and McHugh, K. (2006) *Multiple Dwelling and Tourism: Negotiating Place, Home and Identity*. Wallingford and Cambridge, MA: CABI.

Meadows, D.H., Meadows, D.L., Randers, J. and Behrens III, W.W. (1972) *The Limits to Growth*. New York: Universe Books.

Meessen, H., Švajda, J., Kohler, T., Fabriciusová, V., Galvánek, D., Buraľ, M. et al. (2015) 'Protected areas in the Slovak Carpathians as a contested resource between metropolitan and mountain stakeholders'. *JAR-RGA*, 103(3). Available at: http://rga.revues.org/3055 (accessed 1 August 2017).

Meili, R. and Mayer, H. (2015) 'Zuwanderung und Unternehmensgründungen in peripheren Berggebieten in der Schweiz'. *Geographische Rundschau*, 67(9): 42–8.

Membretti, A., Lucchini, F. (2018) *Foreign Immigration and Housing Issues in Small Alpine Villages. Housing as a Pull Factor for New Highlanders*. Chapter 10, pp. 203–19. Available at www.researchgate.net/publication/324676320_FOREIGN_IMMIGRATION_AND_HOUSING_ISSUES_IN_SMALL_ALPINE_VILLAGES_Housing_as_a_Pull_Factor_for_New_Highlanders (accessed 3 July 2018).

Mercier, C. and Giovanni, S. (1983) 'Le néo-ruralisme: nouvelles approches pour un phénomène nouveau'. *RGA*, 71(3): 253–65.

Merlin, T. (1983) *Sulla pelle viva. Come si costruisce una catastrofe. Il caso del Vajont.* Milan: La Pietra.

Messerli, B. and Hurni, H. (eds) (1990) *African Mountains and Highlands; Problems and Perspectives.* Arusha: African Mountain Association.

Messerli, B. and Ives, J.D. (eds) (1997) *Mountains of the World: A Global Priority.* Carnforth and New York: Parthenon.

Messerli, P., Giger, M., Dwyer, M.B., Breu, T. and Eckert, S. (2014) 'The geography of large-scale land acquisitions: analysing socio-ecological patterns of target contexts in the global South'. *Applied Geography*, 53: 449–59.

Messerli, P., Scheurer, T. and Veit, H. (2011) 'Between longing and flight: migratory processes in mountain areas, particularly in the European Alps'. *JAR-RGA*, 99(1). Available at: http://rga.revues.org/1336 (accessed 1 August 2017).

MicroGIS (2012) 'Oui à l'initiative Stop aux résidences secondaires: le Plateau balaie les Alpes'. *Le Temps*, 12 March.

Millennium Ecosystem Assessment (MA). (2005) *Ecosystems and Human Well-Being.* Washington, DC: Island Press.

Mitscherlich, A. (1965) *Die Unwirtlichkeit unserer Städte. Thesen zur Stadt der Zukunft.* Frankfurt: Suhrkamp.

Mocarelli, L. (1997) 'La lavorazione del ferro nel Bresciano tra continuità e mutamento (1750–1914)'. In G.L. Fontana (ed.), *Le vie dell'industrializzazione europea. Sistemi a confronto.* Bologna: Il Mulino, pp. 721–60.

Morelli, M. and Rohner, D. (2013) *Resource Concentration and Civil Wars.* Working Paper 13 August, Department of Economics, University of Lausanne.

Morgan, K. (1997) 'The learning region: institutions, innovation and regional renewal'. *Regional Studies*, 31: 491–503.

Morgan, K., Marsden, T. and Murdoch, J. (2006) *Place, Power, and Provenance in the Food Chain.* Oxford: Oxford University Press.

Moriconi-Ebrard, F. (1993) *L'urbanisation du monde.* Paris: Anthropos, coll. Villes.

Moriconi-Ebrard, F., Harre, D. and Heinrigs, P. (2016) *Urbanisation Dynamics in West Africa 1950–2010. Africapolis I, 2015 Update. West African Studies.* Paris: OECD. Available at: https://read.oecd-ilibrary.org/development/urbanisation-dynamics-in-west-africa-1950-2010_9789264252233-en#page1 (accessed 6 November 2018).

Mose, I. and Jacuniak-Suda, M. (2016) 'The highlands and islands of Scotland in transition. Selected findings from empirical case studies in the Western Isles'. *Mitteilungen der Fränkischen Geographischen Gesellschaft Band*, 61–2: 1–10.

Moss, L.A.G. (ed.) (2006) *The Amenity Migrants: Seeking and Sustaining Mountains and Their Cultures.* Wallingford and Cambridge, MA: CABI.

Moss, L.A.G. and Glorioso, R.S. (eds) (2014) *Global Amenity Migration: Transforming Rural Culture, Economy and Landscape.* Kaslo, British Columbia: New Ecology Press.

Moulaert, F., MacCallum, D., Mehmood, A. and Hamdouch, A. (eds) (2013) *The International Handbook on Social Innovation. Collective Action, Social Learning and Transdisciplinary Research.* Cheltenham: Edward Elgar Publishing.

Moulaert, F. and Mehmood, A. (2010) 'Analysing regional development and policy: a structural – realist approach'. *Regional Studies*, 44(1): 103–18.

Moulaert, F. and Mehmood, A. (2015) 'Analysing regional development: from territorial innovation to path-dependent geography'. In J.B. Davis and W. Dolfsman (eds), *The Elgar Companion to Social Economics.* Cheltenham: Edward Elgar Publishing, pp. 607–31.

Moulaert, F. et al. (2000) *Globalization and Integrated Area Development in European Cities.* Oxford: Oxford University Press.

Moulaert, F., Swyngedouw, E. and Rodriguez, A. (2001) 'Large scale urban development projects and local governance: from democratic urban planning to besieged local governance'. *GZ*, 89(2–3): 71–84.

Müller-Jentsch, D. (2017) *Strukturwandel im Schweizer Berggebiet. Strategien zur Erschliessung neuer Wertschöpfungsquellen.* Zurich: Avenirsuisse. Available at: www.avenir-suisse.ch/pub lication/strukturwandel-im-berggebiet/ (accessed 1 September 2017).

MVRDV. (2005) 'What could Switzerland become?' In A. Eisinger and M. Schneider (eds), *Urbanscape Switzerland: Topology and Regional Development in Switzerland. Investigations and Case Studies.* Basel, Boston, MA and Berlin: Birkhäuser, pp. 349–403.

Myrdal, G. (1957) *Economic Theory and Underdeveloped Regions.* London: Gerald Duckworth.

Nahrath, S. and Bréthaut, C. (2016) 'Coordination between institutional resource regimes as a condition for sustainable management of Alpine touristic resources. *JAR-RGA* 104(3).

Naitthani, P. and Kainthola, S. (2015) 'Impact of conservation and development on the vicinity of Nanda Devi national park in the North India'. *JAR-RGA*, 103(3). Available at: http://rga.revues.org/3100 (accessed 29 June 2017).

Narain, V. and Singh, A.K. (2019) 'Replacement or displacement? Periurbanisation and changing water access in the Kumaon Himalaya, India'. *Land Use Policy* 82, March 2019, pp. 130–137.

Nared, J. (2009) 'Regional policy in Slovenia'. *Regions*, 276: 23–6.

Negrier, E. (2005) *La question métropolitaine.* Grenoble: PUG.

Nelson, P.B. (2006) 'Geographic perspectives on amenity migration across the USA: national, regional and local scale analysis'. In L.A.G. Moss (ed.), *The Amenity Migrants: Seeking and Sustaining Mountains and Their Cultures.* Wallingford and Cambridge, MA: CABI, pp. 55–72.

Nelson, R. and Winter, S. (1982) *An Evolutionary Theory of Economic Change.* Cambridge, MA and London: The Belknap Press of Harvard University Press.

Nepal, S.K. and Jamal, T.B. (2011) 'Resort-induced changes in small mountain communities in British Columbia, Canada'. *MRD*, 31(2): 89–101. Available at: www.bioone.org/doi/ full/10.1659/MRD-JOURNAL-D-10-00095.1 (accessed 1 August 2017).

Nepali, P.B. and Upreti, B.R. (2012) 'Land acquisition dynamics in Nepal: actors, process, and effects'. Pre-conference Proceedings International Conference on Research for Development (ICRD), University of Bern, Switzerland, 20–22 August. Session 7: Land Grabbing. Accessible at: www.north-south.ch/publications/Infosystem/On-line%20Dokumente/ Upload/WEB_Print_conference_reader.pdf (accessed 7 September 2017).

Niederberger, T., Haller, T., Gambon, H., Kobi, M. and Wenk., I. (eds) (2016) *The Open Cut: Mining, Transnational Corporations and Local Populations.* Berlin, Münster, Wien, Zürich and London: Lit Verlag.

North, D. (1990) *Institutions, Institutional Change, and Economic Performance.* Cambridge: Cambridge University Press.

Novotná, M., Preis, J., Kopp, J. and Bartoš, M. (2013) 'Changes in migration to rural regions in the Czech Republic: position and perspectives'. *Moravian Geographical Reports*, 21(3): 37–54.

Nüsser, M. (2002) 'Lesotho: water policy and management – trade-offs between mountains and downstream areas'. In Mountain Agenda (ed.), *Sustainable Development in Mountain Areas: The Need for Adequate Policies and Instruments.* Prepared for the World Summit on Sustainable Development in Johannesburg. Bern, pp. 44–5. Available at: http://boris.unibe.ch/85054/ 1/Mountains%20of%20the%20World-all_2002.pdf (accessed 26 November 2018.

Nüsser, M. (ed.) (2014) *Large Dams in Asia: Contested Environments between Technological Hydroscapes and Social Resistance.* Berlin: Springer.

Nüsser, M. and Gerwin, M. (2008) 'Diversity, complexity and dynamics: land use patterns in the Central Himalayas of Kumaon, Northern India'. In J. Löffler and J. Stadelbauer (eds), *Diversity in Mountain Systems*. Asgard: Sankt Augustin, pp. 107–19.

OECD. (2001) *Territorial Outlook*. Paris: OECD.

OECD. (2015) *In It Together: Why Less Inequality Benefits All*. Paris: OECD.

Offe, C. (1985) *Disorganized Capitalism: Contemporary Transformation of Work and Politics*. London: Polity Press.

Ono, M. (2009) 'Japanese lifestyle migration/tourism in Southeast Asia' (Special Issue: New Trends of Tourism/Migration in Japan and Beyond). *Japanese Review of Cultural Anthropology*, 10: 43–52.

Ojeda, G., Rueff, H., Rahim, I. and Maselli, D. (2012) 'Sustaining mobile pastoralists in the mountains of northern Pakistan'. *Evidence for Policy Series, Regional edition Central Asia*, no. 3, Ed. Mira Arynova. Bishkek, Kyrgyzstan: NCCR North-South.

Ostrom, E. (1990) *Governing the Commons: The Evolution of Institutions for Collective Action*. Cambridge: Cambridge University Press.

Otero, A., Nakayama, L., Marioni, S., Gallego, E., Lonac, A. and Dimitriu, A. et al. (2006) 'Amenity migration impacts on the Patagonian mountain community of San Martín de los Andes, Argentina'. In L.A.G. Moss (ed.), *The Amenity Migrants: Seeking and Sustaining Mountains and Their Cultures*. Wallingford and Cambridge, MA: CABI, pp. 200–12.

Otero, A. and Rodrigo González, C. (2011) 'The role of the state facing amenity/lifestyle mobility processes in Argentina'. 2nd International Workshop on Lifestyle Migration and Residential Tourism, Madrid, 23–25 March. Available at: www.congresos.cchs.csic.es/lifestyle-migration/sites/congresos.cchs.csic.es.lifestyle-migration/files/Paper%20Adriana%20Otero%20&%20Rodrigo%20Gonz%C3%A1lez.pdf (accessed 1 August 2017).

Overvåg, K. (2009) *Second Homes in Eastern Norway: From Marginal Land to Commodity*. Thesis, Norwegian University of Science and Technology, Faculty of Social Sciences and Technology Management, Department of Geography, Trondheim.

Pallarès-Blanch, M., Tulla, A.F. and Vera, A. (2015) 'Environmental capital and women's entrepreneurship: a sustainable local development approach'. *Carpathian Journal of Earth and Environmental Sciences*, 10(3): 133–46.

Parkinson, M. et al. (2012) *SGPTD – Second Tier Cities and Territorial Development in Europe: Performance, Policies and Prospects*. Luxembourg: ESPON.

Pecqueur, B. (1997) 'Processus cognitifs et construction des territoires économiques'. In B. Guilhon, P. Huard, M. Orillard and J.B. Zimmermann (eds), *La connaissance dans la dynamique des organisations productives*. Paris: L'Harmattan, pp. 154–76.

Pecqueur, B. (2006) 'Le tournant territorial de l'économie globale'. *Espaces et sociétés*, 124–5(2): 17–32.

Pecqueur, B. (2007) 'L'économie territoriale: une autre analyse de la globalisation'. *L'Économie politique*, 33(1): 41–52. Available at: www.cairn.info/revue-l-economie-politique-2007-1-page-41.htm (accessed 1 August 2017).

Pecqueur, B. (2009) 'De l'exténuation à la sublimation: la notion de territoire est-elle encore utile?' *Géographie, économie, société*, 11(1): 55–62. Available at: www.cairn.info/revue-geographie-economie-societe-2009-1-page-55.htm (accessed 1 August 2017).

Pecqueur, B. and Peyrache-Gadeau, V. (2010) 'Fondements interdisciplinaires et systématiques de l'approche territoriale'. *RERU*, 4: 613–23.

Pecqueur, B. and Rousier N. (2005) 'Villes technopoles et ségrégation spatiale'. In M.A. Buisson and D. Mignot (eds), *Concentration économique et ségrégation spatiale*. Paris: De Boeck, pp. 201–20.

Périsset, D., Steiner, E. and Ruppen, P. (2012) '"Gouverner, c'est prévoir": les dilemmes des responsables politiques régionaux et locaux à propos de l'évolution des régions alpines et de leurs écoles'. English Abstract. *Revue suisse des sciences de l'éducation*, 34(2): 261–83.

Perlik, M. (1999) 'Processus de périurbanisation dans les villes des Alpes'. *RGA*, 87(1): 143–51.

Perlik, M. (2001) *Alpenstädte – Zwischen Metropolisation und neuer Eigenständigkeit*. Bern: GB P38. [Perlik, M., Messerli, P. and Bätzing, W. (2001) 'Towns in the Alps'. *MRD*, 21(3): 243–52.]

Perlik, M. (2006) 'The specifics of amenity migration in the European Alps'. In L.A.G. Moss (ed.), *The Amenity Migrants: Seeking and Sustaining Mountains and Their Cultures*. Wallingford and Cambridge, MA: CABI, pp. 215–31.

Perlik, M. (2010) 'Leisure landscapes and urban agglomerations: disparities in the Alps'. In A. Borsdorf, G. Grabherr, K. Heinrich, B. Scott and J. Stötter (eds), *Challenges for Mountain Regions: Tackling Complexity*. Vienna: Böhlau, pp. 112–19.

Perlik, M. (2011) 'Alpine gentrification: the mountain village as a metropolitan neighbourhood'. *JAR-RGA*, 99(1). Available at: http://rga.revues.org/1370 (accessed 1 August 2017).

Perlik, M. (2012) *Les zones de montagne comme laboratoire en vue d'identifier les nouvelles inégalités spatiales post-fordistes*. Habilitation à diriger des recherches (HDR). Université de Grenoble.

Perlik, M. (2015) 'Mountains as global suppliers: new forms of disparities between mountain areas and metropolitan hubs – an introduction'. *JAR-RGA* 103(3). Available at: https://rga.revues.org/3142 (accessed 1 August 2017).

Perlik, M. (2018a) 'Innovations sociales en montagne: au-delà de l'ingénierie sociale, une véritable force transformatrice ?' In M.-C. Fourny (ed.), *Montagnes en mouvements. Dynamiques territoriales et innovation sociale*. Grenoble: PUG.

Perlik, M. (2018b) Less regional rhetoric, more diversity – urbanised Alps in the interest of cohesive societies. *JAR-RGA* 106(2).

Perlik, M. and Debarbieux, B. (2002) 'Les villes des Alpes entre 'métropolisation' et identité.' In CIPRA (ed.): *2ème rapport sur l'état des Alpes*. Schaan: CIPRA, pp. 86–95.

Perlik, M., Galera, G., Machold, I. and Membretti, A. (2019) *Alpine Refugees. Immigration at the Core of Europe*. Cambridge: Cambridge Scholars (forthcoming).

Perlik, M. and Kohler, T. (2015) 'Green economy and urbanisation in mountains'. In T. Kohler, J. Balsiger, G. Rudaz, B. Debarbieux, D.J. Pratt and D. Maselli (eds), *Green Economy and Institutions for Sustainable Mountain Development: From Rio 1992 to Rio 2012 and Beyond*. Bern: CDE, SDC, University of Geneva and GB, pp. 70–4.

Perlik, M. and Membretti, A. (2018) 'Migration by necessity and by force to mountain areas: an opportunity for social innovation'. *MRD*, 38(3): 250–64.

Perlik, M. and Messerli, P. (2004) 'Urbanisation in the Alps: development processes and urban strategies'. *MRD*, 24(3): 215–19.

Perlik, M., Streifeneder, T. and Weiß, M. (2013) *Planned industrial estates in Greece: a lever to boost national productivity and territorial management. Recommendations for the development of Business Parks in Greece. Result of an expert hearing, organized for the Ministry of Development, General Secretariat of Industry, Directorate of Industrial Location and Environment, Athens/Greece*. By order of the European Union, Task Force for Greece. Bolzano-Bozen: EURAC.

Perlik, M., Wissen, U. and Schuler, M. et al. (2008) *Szenarien für die nachhaltige Siedlungs- und Infrastrukturentwicklung in der Schweiz (2005–2030)*. SNSF, National Research Programme 54. Zurich: ETHZ.

Perroux, F. (1964) *L'économie du XXème siècle*, 2nd edn. Paris: PUF.

Petite, M. (2013) 'Mountain dwellers versus eco-freaks: an nth manifestation of the conflict in the context of the Weber initiative'. *JAR-RGA*, Hors série. Available at: https://rga.revues.org/1865 (accessed 1 August 2017).

Petite, M. (2014) 'Longing for the mountains?' *JAR-RGA*, 102(3). Available at: http://rga. revues.org/2625 (accessed 1 August 2017).

Petite, M. and Camenisch, M. (2012) 'Vivre à la montagne en Suisse. Trajectoires résiden- tielles, parcours de vie et identités'. In N. Martin, P. Bourdeau and J.F. Daller (eds), *Du tourisme à l'habiter: les migrations d'agrément*. Paris: l'Harmattan, Collection Tourismes et Sociétés pp. 135–50.

Pettenati, G. (2013) 'Maira valley (Piedmont): a territorial laboratory of a new moun- tain population'. *JAR-RGA*, 101(3). Available at: https://rga.revues.org/2208 (accessed 1 August 2017).

Pflieger, G. and Rozenblat, C. (2010) 'Introduction. Urban networks and network theory: the city as the connector of multiple networks'. *Urban Studies*, 47(13): 2723–35.

Piore, M.J. and Sabel, C.F. (1984) *The Second Industrial Divide*. New York: Basic Books.

Ploeg, J.D. van der and Roep, D. (2003) 'Multifunctionality and rural development: the actual situation in Europe'. In G. van Huylenbroeck and G. Durand (eds), *Multifunc- tional Agriculture: A New Paradigm for European Agriculture and Rural Development*. Farnham: Ashgate, pp. 37–53.

Poisson, C. and Bourniquel, C. (2009) 'Le rural en Midi-Pyrénées. Des territoires attractifs, inégalement équipés'. 6 pages de l'INSEE, no. 123, December 2009.

Porcellana, V., Fassio, G., Viazzo, P.P. and Zanini, R.C. (2016) Socio-demographic changes and transmission of tangible and intangible resources: Ethnographic glimpses from the Western Italian Alps. *JAR-RGA*, 104(3).

Porter, M. (1998) *The Competitive Advantage of Nations*. New York: Free Press.

Price, M.F., Jansky, L., Latsenia, A.A. (eds) (2004) *Key Issues for Mountain Areas*. Tokyo: UNU Press.

Prigge, W. (1987) *Die Materialität des Städtischen: Stadtentwicklung und Urbanität im gesell- schaftlichen Umbruch*. Basel: Birkhäuser.

Provo, J. and Jones, M. (2011) 'The challenge of reconciling development objectives in the context of demographic change: evaluating asset-based development in Appalachia'. *JAR- RGA*, 99(1). Available at: https://rga.revues.org/1339 (accessed 1 August 2017).

Pumain, D. (1997) 'Pour une théorie évolutive des villes'. *L'Espace géographique*, 97(2): 119–34.

Pumain, D. (1999) 'Quel rôle les petites et moyennes villes ont-elles encore à jouer dans les régions périphériques?' In M. Perlik and W. Bätzing (eds), *L'avenir des villes des Alpes en Europe*. Bern: GB P36, *RGA*, 87(2): 167–84.

Pumain, D. and Moriconi-Ebrard, F. (1997) 'City size distributions and metropolisation'. *GeoJournal*, 43(4): 307–14.

Puymbroeck, C. van and Reynard, R. (2010) 'Répartition géographique des emplois. Les grandes villes concentrent les fonctions intellectuelles, de gestion et de décision'. INSEE Première 1278.

Pyke, F., Becattini, G. and Sengenberger, W. (eds) (1990) *Industrial Districts and Inter-firm Cooperation in Italy. International Labour Organization*. Geneva: International Institute for Labour Studies.

Qin, D.H. (2002) *Assessment of Environment Change in Western China, Volume 2: Prediction of Environment Change in Western China*. Beijing: Science Press.

Racaud, S. (2013) *The Uporoto Mountains between Urban and Rural: Geography of Flows and Territorial Integration in Tanzania*. PhD Thesis, Toulouse.

Racine, J.B. (1999) 'Introduction – La ville alpine entre flux et lieux, entre pratiques et représentations'. *RGA*, 99(1): 111–17.

Radcliffe-Brown, A.R. (1940) 'On joking relationships'. *Journal of the International African Institute*, 13(3): 195–210.

Raffestin, C. (1980) *Pour une géographie du pouvoir*. Paris: Libraires techniques.

Raffestin, C. (1993) 'Les territorialités alpines ou les paradoxes du dialogue nature – culture'. In K. Mainzer (ed.), *Économie et Écologie dans le contexte de l'arc alpin*, S. 37–50. Bern: Schriftenreihe Institut Kurt Boesch, Bd. 1.

Rao, K.S., Maikhuri, R.K., Nautiyal, S. and Saxena, K.G. (2002) 'Crop damage and livestock depredation by wildlife: a case study from NDBR, India'. *Journal of Environmental Management*, 66: 317–27.

Rao, K.S., Nautiyal, N., Maikhuri, R.K. and Saxena, K.G. (2000) 'Management conflicts in the Nanda Devi biosphere reserve, India'. *MRD*, 20(4): 320–3.

Rasker, R., Gude, P., Gude, J. and van den Noort, J. (2009) 'The economic importance of air travel in high-amenity rural areas'. *Journal of Rural Studies*, 25(3): 343–53.

Ravazzoli, E., Puzo, Q., Streifeneder, T. and Perlik, M. (2013) *Der erweiterte Alpenraum*. *EURAC. Bolzano-Bozen*. Available at: www.eurac.edu/en/research/mountains/regdev/projects/Pages/The-extended-Alps.aspx (accessed 26 November 2018).

Région Midi-Pyrénées. (2013) *Evolution et adaptation de l'economie du tourisme et des loisirs au changement climatique dans les territoires de montagne de la région Midi-Pyrenees*. Rapport de Atout France.

Rérat, P. (2011) 'The new demographic growth of cities: the case of reurbanisation in Switzerland'. *Urban Studies*, 49: 1107–25.

Rérat, P., Söderström, O., Piguet, E. and Besson, R. (2010) 'From urban wastelands to new-build gentrification: the case of Swiss cities'. *Population, Space and Place*, 16(5): 429–42.

Revelli, N. (1977) *Il mondo dei vinti. Testimonianze di vita contadina*. Torino: Einaudi.

Ricciardi, T. (2015) *Morire a Mattmark – L'ultima tragedia dell'emigrazione italiana*. Rome: Donzelli.

Richard, F., Dellier, J. and Tommasi, G. (2014) 'Migration, environment and rural gentrification in the Limousin mountains'. *JAR-RGA*, 102(3). Available at: https://rga.revues.org/2561 (accessed 1 August 2017).

Ritter, W. (1984) Die Entstehung industrialisierter Volkswirtschaften. *Frankfurter Wirtschafts- und Sozialgeographische Schriften*, H. 46: 107–20.

Roca, Z. (ed.) (2013) *Second Home Tourism in Europe: Lifestyle Issues and Policy Responses*. Farnham: Ashgate.

Rodewald, R. and Knoepfel, P. (eds) (2005) *Institutionelle Regime für nachhaltige Landschaftsentwicklung. Régimes institutionnels pour le développement durable du paysage*. En collaboration avec A. de Fossey, J.-D. Gerber, C. Mauch. Zurich: Rüegger (série Écologie & Société, vol. 20).

Rokkan, S. and Urwin, D.W. (1983) *Economy, Territory, Identity: Politics of West European Peripheries*. London: Sage.

Rolshoven, J. (2001) 'Depopulation and reterritorialisation in peripheral regions: new social spaces in the south of France'. In *Mobility and Social Change/Mobilität und sozialer Wandel. A Choice of Texts 2001–2006*, pp. 2–9. Available at: https://static.uni-graz.at/fileadmin/_Persoenliche_Webseite/rolshoven_johanna/Dokumente/jr_textauswahl.pdf (accessed 25 August 2017).

Romero, H., Méndez, M. and Smith, P. (2012) 'Mining development and environmental injustice in the Atacama desert of northern Chile'. *Environmental Justice*, 5(2): 70–6.

Romero, H. and Órdenes, F. (2004) 'Emerging urbanisation in the Southern Andes: environmental impacts of urban sprawl in Santiago de Chile on the Andean Piedmont'. *MRD*, 24(3): 195–9.

Rosenberg, H.G. (1988) *A Negotiated World: Three Centuries of Change in a French Alpine Community*. Toronto: University of Toronto Press.

Roth, C. (1996) *La séparation des sexes au Burkina Faso*. Paris: L'Harmattan.

Roth, C. (2010) 'Intergenerational relationships under pressure in Burkina Faso'. *Autrepart*, 53: 95–110.

Roth, C. (2014) 'The strength of badenya ties: siblings and social security in old age – the case of urban Burkina Faso'. *American Ethnologist*, 41(3): 547–63.

Roth, C. (2018) *Urban Dreams: Transformations of Family Life in Burkina Faso*. Eds. W. de Jong, M. Perlik, N. Steuer and H. Znoj. New York: Berghahn.

Rousselot, Y. (2015) 'Upstream flows of water: from the Lesotho highlands to metropolitan South Africa'. *JAR-RGA*, 103(3). Available at: http://rga.revues.org/3023 (accessed 1 August 2017).

Roux, C. (1996) *Histoire de Veynes*. Gap: Société d'Etudes des Hautes Alpes.

Rozenblat, C. (2010) 'Opening the black box of agglomeration economies for measuring cities' competitiveness through international firm networks'. *Urban Studies*, 47(13): 2841–65.

Rudaz, G. (2011) 'The cause of mountains: the politics of promoting a global agenda'. *Global Environmental Politics*, 11(4): 43–65. Available at: http://dx.doi.org/10.1162/GLEP_a_00083 (accessed 26 November 2018).

Rudaz, G. and Debarbieux, B. (2013) *La montagne Suisse en politique*. Lausanne: Presses polytechniques et universitaires romandes.

Rudzitis, G. (2009) 'Amenity development in the American West: tonic or slow poison?' In L.A.G. Moss, R. Glorioso and A. Krause (eds), *Proc. of the Conference 'Understanding and Managing Amenity-Led Migration in Mountain Regions', May 2008*. Banff: The Banff Centre, pp. 84–90.

Rudzitis, G. (2011) *Amenity Migration and a Radical Theory of Place Rough Draft*. Available at: www.congresos.cchs.csic.es/lifestyle-migration/sites/congresos.cchs.csic.es.lifestyle-migration/files/Paper%20Gundars%20Rudzitis.pdf (accessed 1 August 2017).

Ruppert, R. (1987) 'Klima und die Entstehung industrialisierter Volkswirtschaften'. *Zeitschrift für Wirtschaftsgeographie*, 31(1): 1–11.

SAB. (2010, 2016, 2017) *Les régions de montagne suisses 2010. Faits et chiffres*. Groupement suisse pour les régions de montagne, Bern: SAB. Available at: www.sab.ch/fileadmin/user_upload/customers/sab/Dokumente/Publikationen_SAB/Schweizer_Berggebiet_2016_Internet.pdf (accessed 3 July 2018).

Sacareau, I. (2017) Mountains and mountain dwellers of the global South and the globalisation of tourism: Imaginaries and practices. *JAR-RGA*, 105(3).

Sassen, S. (1991) *The Global City*. Princeton, NJ: Princeton Paperbacks.

Savage, M. (2011) 'The lost urban sociology of Pierre Bourdieu'. In G. Bridge and S. Watson (eds), *The New Blackwell Companion to the City*. Oxford: Blackwell, pp. 511–20.

Savage, M., Bagnall, G. and Longhurst, B. (2005) *Globalization and Belonging*. London: Sage.

Saxinger, G. (2016) *Unterwegs. Mobiles Leben in der Erdgas-und Erdölindustrie in Russlands Arktis/Mobil'nyy obraz zhizni vakhtovykh rabochikh neftegazovoy promyshlennosti na Russkom Kraynem Severe/Lives on the Move–Long-distance Commuting in the Northern Russian Petroleum Industry*. Vienna, Weimar, Cologne: Böhlau.

Sayer, A. (1992) *Method in Social Science: A Realist Approach*. London: Routledge.

Sayre, N. (2009) 'Commentary: scale, rent, and symbolic capital – political economy and emerging rural landscapes'. *GeoJournal*. Available at: www.springerlink.com/content/d21u3186w6757411/fulltext.pdf (accessed 26 November 2018).

Schaaf, T. (2006) 'UNESCO's role in the conservation of mountain resources and sustainable development'. *Global Environmental Research*, 10(1): 117–23.

Schad, H., Hilti, N., Hugentobler, M. and Duchêne-Lacroix, C. (2014) 'Multilokales Wohnen in der Schweiz – erste Einschätzungen zum Aufkommen und zu den Ausprägungen'. In *Mobil und doppelt sesshaft. Studien zur residenziellen Multilokalität*. Abhandlungen zur

Geographie und Regionalforschung 17. Wien: Institut für Geographie und Regional-forschung, pp. 176–201.

Schaltegger, S. and Gmünder, M. (1999) 'Private Kommunen. Funktionsweise und Entwicklung in der Praxis'. *Die Außenwirtschaft*, 54(2): 209–24.

Scheurer, T. and Küpfer, I. (1997) 'Was können Schutzgebiete im Alpenraum zur regional-wirtschaftlichen Entwicklung beitragen?' *RGA*, 85(2): 113–30.

Schmid, C. (2006) 'Theory'. In R. Diener, J. Herzog, M. Meili, P. de Meuron and C. Schmid (eds), *Switzerland: An Urban Portrait. Vol. 1–4.* ETH Zürich Studio Basel: Birkhäuser, pp. 163–223.

Schmid, C. (2012) 'Henri Lefebvre, the right to the city, and the new metropolitan mainstream'. In N. Brenner et al. (eds), *Cities for People, Not for Profit: Critical Urban Theory, and the Right to the City.* London: Routledge, pp. 42–62.

Schmidt, M. (2004) 'Interdependencies and reciprocity of private and common property resources in the central Karakorum'. *Erdkunde*, 58: 316–30.

Schneider, F. (2015) 'Exploring sustainability through stakeholders' perspectives and hybrid water in the Swiss Alps'. *Water Alternatives*, 8(2): 280–96.

Schuler, M. (2012) *Siedlungs- und Bevölkerungsgeschichte seit dem 18. Jahrhundert. Die Geschichte des Kantons Schwyz,* vol. 5. Schwyz: Historischer Verein des Kantons Schwyz, pp. 33–73.

Schuler, M. and Dessemontet, P. (2013) 'The Swiss vote on limiting second homes'. *JAR-RGA*. Hors série.

Schuler, M. and Dessemontet, P. et al. (2007) *Atlas des mutations spatiales de la Suisse.* Zürich: OfS. Neuchâtel, NZZ.

Schuler, M and Perlik, M. (2011) 'Regionale Disparitäten'. In R. Schneider-Sliwa (ed.), *Schweiz – Geographie, Geschichte, Wirtschaft, Politik.* Darmstadt: WBG, pp. 240–55.

Schuler, M., Perlik, M. and Pasche, N. (2004) *Non urbain, campagne ou périphérie – où se trouve l'espace rural aujourd'hui?* Ed. Federal Office for Spatial Development. Bern: ARE.

Schuler, M., Dessemontet, P., Joye, D. and Perlik, M. (2005) *Recensement fédéral de la population 2000 – Les niveaux géographiques de la Suisse.* Neuchâtel: OfS.

Schuler, M., Dessemontet, P. and Perlik, M. (2012) 'Le territoire suisse et ses transformations depuis 1848'. In A. Plata and O. Mazzoleni (eds), *Le fédéralisme face aux nouveaux défis territoriaux: institutions, économie et identité.* Actes de la 3 ème Conférence nationale sur le fédéralisme, Mendrisio, 26–27 May 2011. Bellinzona: Salvioni.

Schumpeter, J.A. (1975/1942) *Capitalism, Socialism and Democracy.* New York: Harper.

Schütz, M. (2010) *Die Alp als Ort der Gegenkultur.* Licentiate thesis, University of Basel, Cultural Studies/European Ethnology. Available at: www.zalp.ch/aktuell/suppen/suppe_2011_09_01/bilder/Die_Alp_als_Ort_der_Gegenkultur.pdf. (accessed 20 February 2018).

Schweizer, R. (2013) 'Accessibility, equity and the sharing of water resources: a critical analysis of community governance models based on a case study of the irrigation channels of the Valais'. *JAR-RGA*, 101(3). Available at: https://rga.revues.org/2238 (accessed 1 August 2017).

Scott, A.J. (1988) *Metropolis: From the Division of Labour to Urban Form.* Berkeley, CA: University of California Press.

Scott, A.J. and Storper, M. (2003) 'Regions, globalization, development'. *Regional Studies*, 41(S1): 191–205.

Sega, R. (2018) *Nuove ecologie alpine: Industrializzazione e costruzione della città-territorio.* Lausanne: EPFL.

Sega, R. (2018b) 'Towards a Productive Mesh of the European City-Territory'. In *The horizontal metropolis between urbanism and urbanization.* New York, NY: Springer Berlin Heidelberg, pp. 313–320.

Segessemann, A. (2016) *De la production à la consommation: Le rôle de l'économie résidentielle dans le développement régional.* Thèse de doctorat. Groupe de recherche en économie territoriale (GRET), Institut de Sociologie. Université de Neuchâtel. Available at: http://doc.rero.ch/record/258842/files/00002517.pdf (accessed 1 August 2017).

Segessemann, A. and Crevoisier, O. (2015) 'Beyond economic base theory: the role of the residential economy in attracting income to Swiss regions'. *Regional Studies.* Available at: www.tandfonline.com/doi/full/10.1080/00343404.2015.1018882 (accessed 1 August 2017).

Sencébé, Y. (2004) 'Etre ici, être d'ici. Formes d'appartenance dans le Diois (Drôme)'. *Ethnologie française,* 34(1): 23–9.

Serroi, B., Besancenot, F., Brégard, P., Hanus, G. and Hobléa, F. (2015) 'Water in the Chartreuse, a mirror reflecting a renewal of relationships between mountains areas and their surrounding towns'. *JAR-RGA,* 103(3). Available at: http://rga.revues.org/3173 (accessed 1 August 2017).

Sharma, P. and Pratap, T. (1994) *Population, Poverty, and Development Issues in the Hindu Kush Himalayas, Development of Poor Mountain Areas.* Kathmandu: ICIMOD.

Siegrist, D. (2017) *Comment on: Müller-Jentsch, D. (2017) Strukturwandel im Schweizer Berggebiet* (in German). Available at: https://naturalsciences.ch/organisations/icas/diskussions forum/kommentar_dominik_siegrist (accessed 1 September 2017).

Simard, M. and Guimond, L. *La migration de la ville vers la campagne au Québec? Portrait sociodémographique et économique de deux MRC contrastées et de leurs nouveaux résidents.* Institut de la statistique du Québec. Available at: www.bdso.gouv.qc.ca/docs-ken/multimedia/PB01629FR_pano_regions2010A00F02.pdf (accessed 1 August 2017).

Simmen, H., Marti, M., Osterwald, S. and Walter, F. (2005) *Die Alpen und der Rest der Schweiz: wer zahlt – wer profitiert?* Synthesis of the ALPAYS project 'Alpine landscapes: payments and spillovers' in the frame of the National Research Programme 48 'Landscapes and Habitats of the Alps' of the SNSF. Zürich: vdf Hochschulverlag.

Smeral, E. (2000) 'Some clarifications on the Tourism Growth Puzzle'. Paper presented at the 2nd Tourism Summit, Geneva/Chamonix-Mont-Blanc, December. Available at: www.wifo.ac.at.egon.smeral/tourism_summit_chamonix_12_2000.htm (accessed 1 August 2017).

Smith, N. (1996) *The New Urban Frontier.* London: Routledge.

Smith, N. (2007) 'Nature as accumulation strategy'. *Socialist Register,* 43: 16–41.

Smith, N. (2008/1984) *Uneven Development: Nature, Capital and the Production of Space,* 3rd edn. Athens, GA and London: University of Georgia Press.

SNSF. (n.d.) National Research Programme (NRP) 42+ 'Relations between Switzerland and South Africa' available at: www.snf.ch/SiteCollectionDocuments/nfp/nfp42p/nfp42p_portrait.pdf (accessed 24 February 2018).

Soja, E. (2000) *Postmetropolis.* Oxford: Blackwell.

Soja, E. (2010) *Seeking Spatial Justice.* Minneapolis, MN: University of Minnesota Press.

Solé, A., Solana, M. and Mendizábal, E. (2014) 'Integration and international migration in a mountain area: the Catalan Pyrenees'. *JAR-RGA,* 102(3). Available at: https://rga.revues.org/2484 (accessed 1 August 2017).

Sonderegger R. (2014) *Zweitwohnungen im Alpenraum.* Saarbrücken: Südwestdeutscher Verlag für Hochschulschriften.

Sonderegger, R. and Bätzing, W. (2013) 'Second homes in the Alpine region: on the interplay between leisure, tourism, outmigration and second homes in the Alps'. *JAR-RGA.* Hors-Série. Available at: https://rga.revues.org/2511 (accessed 1 August 2017).

Sorrell, S. and Dimitropoulos, J. (2008) 'The rebound effect: microeconomic definitions, limitations and extensions'. *Ecological Economics,* 65(3): 636–49.

Spindler, K. (2003) 'Transhumanz'. *Preistoria Alpina,* 39: 219–25.

Stanek, Ł., Schmid, C. and Moravánsky, Á. (eds) (2015) *Urban Revolution Now: Henri Lefebvre in Social Research and Architecture*. Farnham: Ashgate.

Steinicke, E., Čede, P. and Fliesser, U. (2010) 'Development patterns of rural depopulation areas. Demographic impacts of amenity migration on Italian peripheral regions'. *Mitteilungen der Österreichischen Geographischen Gesellschaft*, 151: 195–214.

Steinicke, E. and Neuburger, M. (2014) 'Fair distribution of revenues from tourism in the Mount Kenya National Park'. In B. Debarbieux, M. Oiry Varacca, G. Rudaz, D. Maselli, T. Kohler and M. Jurek (eds), *Tourism in Mountain Regions: Hopes, Fears and Realities*. Geneva: University of Geneva, pp. 50–1.

Stephen, L. (1871) *The Playground of Europe*. London: Longmans, Green & Co.

Storper, M. (1995) 'The resurgence of regional economies, ten years later: the region as a nexus of untraded interdependencies'. *European Urban and Regional Studies*, 2(3): 191–221.

Storper, M. (1997a) *The Regional World: Territorial Development in a Global Economy*. New York: Guilford Press.

Storper, M. (1997b) 'Beautiful cities, ugly cities: urban form as convention'. In M. Benedikt (ed.), *Center: Architecture and Design in America. Vol. 10: Value*. Austin, TX: University of Texas Press, pp. 106–23.

Storper, M. and Harrison, B. (1991) 'Flexibility, hierarchy and regional development: the changing structure of industrial production systems and their forms of governance in the 1990s'. *Research Policy*, 20(5): 407–22.

Storper, M. and Manville, M. (2006) 'Behavior, preferences and cities: urban theory and urban resurgence'. *Urban Studies*, 43: 1247–74.

Storper, M. and Scott, A.J. (eds) (1996) *Pathways to Industrialization and Regional Development*. London: Routledge.

Storper, M. and Scott, A.J. (2009) 'Rethinking human capital, creativity and human growth'. *Journal of Economic Geography*, 9: 147–67.

Storper, M. and Walker, R. (1989) *The Capitalist Imperative*. New York and Oxford: Basil Blackwell.

Strabo. (1903) *The Geography of Strabo*. Literally translated, with notes, in three volumes. London: George Bell & Sons.

Streckeisen, P. (2014) *Soziologische Kapitaltheorie*. Bielefeld: Transcript.

Stucki, E.W., Roque, O., Schuler, M. and Perlik, M. (2004) 'Contents and impacts of mountain policies, Switzerland'. National report for the study 'Analysis of Mountain Areas in the European Union and in the Applicant Countries'. Bern: Federal Department of Economic Affairs.

Sud-Ouest Européen and Revue Géographique des Pyrénéés et du Sud-Ouest. (2011) *Récompositions récentes dans le périurbain toulousain*. Toulouse: Presse Universaires du Mirail.

Swyngedouw, E. (2004) 'Scaled geographies: nature, place, and the politics of scale'. In E. Sheppard and R.B. McMaster (eds), *Scale and Geographic Inquiry: Nature, Society, and Method*. Oxford: Blackwell, pp. 129–53.

Swyngedouw, E. and Kaika, M. (2000) 'The environment of the city... or the urbanisation of nature'. In G. Bridge and S. Watson (eds), *A Companion to the City*. Oxford: Blackwell, pp. 567–80.

Talandier, M. (2012) 'Geographie et impacts socioeconomiques des migrations d'agrément dans les espaces ruraux français'. In N. Martin, P. Bourdeau and J.F. Daller (eds), *Migrations d'agrément: du tourisme à l'habiter*. Paris: L'Harmattan, pp. 182–205.

Taut, B. (1919) *Alpine Architektur*. Hagen i.W.: Folkwang.

Tejada, L. (2015) *Large-scale land acquisitions in Peru: Land (re)-concentration, agrarian change and reactions from rural communities*. Congreso Internacional de Americanistas. San Salvador, El Salvador, 12–17 July.

Therrien, C. (2014) 'Quest migrants: French people in Morocco searching for "elsewhere-ness"'. In M. Janoschka and H. Haas (eds), *Contested Spatialities, Lifestyle Migration and Residential Tourism*. London and New York: Routledge, pp. 108–23.

Thierstein, A. and Wulfhorst, G. et al. (2016) *Living, Working and Mobility: The Future of the Metropolitan Area Munich*. Munich: Technical University of Munich.

Thomson, K., Vellinga, N., Slee, B. and Ibiyemi, A. (2014) 'Mapping socio-economic performance in rural Scotland'. *Scottish Geographical Journal*, 130(1): 1–21.

Thünen, J.H. von (1826) *Der isolirte Staat in Beziehung auf Landwirtschaft und Nationalökonomie, oder Untersuchungen über den Einfluß, den die Getreidepreise, der Reichthum des Bodens und die Abgaben auf den Ackerbau ausüben*. Hamburg: Perthes.

Tiwari, P.C. and Joshi, B. (2016) *Rapid urban growth in mountainous regions: the case of Nainital, India*. Urbanization and Global Environmental Change Project (UGEC). UGEC Viewpoints. Avaialble at: https://ugecviewpoints.wordpress.com/2016/03/29/rapid-urban-growth-in-mountainous-regions-the-case-of-nainital-india/ (accessed 26 November 2018).

Torricelli, G.P. (1993) 'La ville dans les Alpes: Zone grise ou laboratoire pour les transports de demain?' *RGA*, 81(4): 37–62.

Torricelli, G.P. (2003) 'Networks and borders: a comparative approach to the study of mobility in the mountain areas of the Western Alps and Southern Andes'. *RGA*, 91(3): 83–100.

Torricelli, G.P. (2009) *Potere e spazio pubblico urbano. Dall'agorà alla baraccopoli*. Milano: Academia Universa Press.

Ullman, E. (1954) 'Amenities as a factor in regional growth'. *Geographical Review*, 44: 119–32.

UNEP and DEWA Europe. (2007) *'Carpathians Environment Outlook. Chapter 2: Socio-Economic Driving Forces'*. Chatelaine, CH.

United Nations Department of Economic and Social Affairs, Population Division (UN-DESA-PD). (2012) *World Urbanisation Prospects: The 2011 Revision*. New York: United Nations.

United Nations Human Settlements Programme (UN-HABITAT). (2010) *The State of Asian Cities 2010/11*. Fukuoka: Regional Office for Asia and the Pacific. Available at: https://unhabitat.org/books/the-state-of-asian-cities-201011/ (accessed 1 August 2017).

Vaccaro, I. (2016) 'Theorizing impending peripheries: postindustrial landscapes at the edge of hyper-modernity's collapse'. *Journal of International and Global Studies*, 8(1): 22–44.

Vaccaro, I. and Beltràn, O. (2009) 'L'espace montagnard comme objet de consommation'. *RGA*, 97(3). Available at: http://rga.revues.org/index1081.html (accessed 1 August 2017).

Vaccaro, I. and Beltràn, O. (eds) (2010) *Social and Ecological History of the Pyrenees: State, Market and Landscape*. Walnut Creek, CA: Left Coast Press.

Vandermotten, C., Halbert, L., Roelandts, M. and Cornut, P. (2008) 'European planning and the polycentric consensus: wishful thinking?' *Regional Studies*, (42)8: 1205–17.

Vanier, M., Meunier, I. and Davezies, L. (2010) *Étude prospective sur l'avenir de l'économie résidentielle en Région Provence Alpes Côte d'Azur. Le Rapport de la phase 1 de l'étude*. Available at: https://www.maregionsud.fr/it/etudesregionales/detail-etudes-regionales/article/etude-etude-prospective-sur-lavenir-de-leconomie-residentielle-en-region-provence-alpes-cote-2.html (accessed 26 November 2018).

Varone, F., Nahrath, S. and Gerber, J.D. (2008) 'Régimes institutionnels de ressources et théorie de la régulation'. *Revue de la régulation*, 2. Available at: http://regulation.revues.org/2623 (accessed 26 November 2018).

Varotto, M. and Lodatti, L. (2014) 'New family farmers for abandoned lands: the adoption of terraces in the Italian Alps (Brenta Valley)'. *MRD*, 34(4): 315–25.

Veblen, T. (1994/1899) *The Theory of the Leisure Class*. New York: Penguin Books.

Veltz, P. (2017) *La société hyper-industrielle. Le nouveau capitalisme productif*. Paris: Seuil.

Veyret, P., Veyret, G. and Armand, G. (1967) 'L'organisation de l'espace urbain dans les Alpes du Nord: Contribution à l'étude des problèmes de régionalisation'. *RGA*, 55(1): 5–71.

Viazzo, P.P. and Zanini, R.C. (2014) '"Taking advantage of emptiness"? Anthropological perspectives on mountain repopulation and spaces of cultural creativity in the Alpine area'. *JAR-RGA*, 102(3). Available at: https://rga.revues.org/2478 (accessed 1 August 2017).

Vlès, V. (2012) 'Ski resorts in crisis and territorial construction in French Catalonia'. *JAR-RGA*, 100(2). Available at: https://rga.revues.org/1824 (accessed 1 August 2017).

Vogt, L. (2008) *Regionalentwicklung peripherer Räume mit Tourismus? Eine akteur- und handlungsorientierte Untersuchung am Beispiel des Trekkingprojekts Grande Traversata delle Alpi. Erlanger Geographische Arbeiten 38.* Erlangen: Fränkische Geographische Gesellschaft.

Vollmar, A., Zumbühl, J. and Rau, M. (2016) 'The Marlin gold-silver mine in San Marcos, Guatemala'. In T. Niederberger, T. Haller, H. Gambon, M. Kobi, and I. Wenk (eds) *The Open Cut: Mining, Transnational Corporations and Local Populations. Action Anthropology/Aktionsethnologie,* 2. Zurich: Lit Verlag, pp. 251–71.

Walker, P. (2009) 'Commentary for special issue of GeoJournal on amenity migration, exurbia, and emerging rural landscapes'. *GeoJournal.* Available at: www.springerlink.com/content/261801664v5567680/fulltext.pdf (accessed 26 November 2018).

Wallimann, A, (2016) 'The Las Bambas copper mine project in Apurimac, Peru'. In T. Niederberger, T. Haller, H. Gambon, M. Kobi and I. Wenk (eds) *The Open Cut: Mining, Transnational Corporations and Local Populations. Action Anthropology/Aktionsethnologie,* 2. Zurich: Lit Verlag, pp. 271–300.

Wang, Y., Wu, N., Kunze, C., Long, R., Perlik, M. et al. (2019) 'Drivers of change to mountain sustainability in the Hindu Kush Himalaya'. In P. Wester, A. Mishra, A. Mukherji, and A.B. Shrestha (eds), *The Hindu Kush Himalaya Assessment – Mountains, Climate Change, Sustainability and People.* Dordrecht: Springer Nature.

Wehler, H.U. (1974) 'Der Aufstieg des organisierten Kapitalismus und Interventionsstaates in Deutschland'. In H.A. Winkler (ed.), *Organisierter Kapitalismus. Voraussetzungen und Anfänge.* Göttingen: Vandenhoeck & Ruprecht, pp. 36–57.

Weichhart, P. (2015) 'Residential multi-locality: in search of theoretical frameworks'. *Tijdschrift voor economische en sociale geografie,* 106(4): 378–91.

Werthmann, K. (2000) 'Gold rush in West Africa: the appropriation of "natural" resources – non-industrial gold mining in Burkina Faso'. *Sociologus,* 50(1): 90–104.

Wester, P., Mishra, A., Mukherji, A. and Shrestha, A.B. (eds) (2019) *The Hindu Kush Himalaya Assessment – Mountains, Climate Change, Sustainability and People.* Dordrecht: Springer Nature.

Wiesinger, G. (2007) 'The importance of social capital in rural development, networking and decision-making in rural areas'. *JAR-RGA,* 95(4). Available at: https://rga.revues.org/354 (accessed 1 August 2017).

WIFO. (2011) *Eine wirtschaftlich-soziale und demografische Analyse Südtiroler Gemeinden.* On behalf of Handels-, Industrie-, Handwerks- und Landwirtschaftskammer Bozen. Bolzano-Bozen.

Wittfogel, K.A. (1957) *Oriental Despotism: A Comparative Study of Total Power.* New Haven, CT: Yale University Press.

Witzens, U. (2000) *Kritik der Thesen Karl A. Wittfogels über den hydraulischen Despotismus mit besonderer Berücksichtigung des historischen singhalesischen Theravāda-Buddhismus.* Dissertation, University of Heidelberg. Available at: http://d-nb.info/963951270/34 (accessed 1 August 2017).

Wolf, E. (1972) 'Ownership and political ecology'. In G. Berthoud (ed.), Special issue: Dynamics of ownership in the circum-Alpine area. *Anthropological Quarterly,* 45(3): 201–5.

Wolf, E. (2001) *Pathways of Power: Building an Anthropology of the Modern World*. Berkeley, CA: University of California Press.

Woods, M. (2009) 'The local politics of the global countryside: boosterism, aspirational ruralism and the contested reconstitution of Queenstown, New Zealand'. *GeoJournal*. Available at: www.springerlink.com/content/y96382w162502025/fulltext.pdf (accessed 26 November 2018).

World Commission on Dams (WCD). (2000) *Dams and Development: A New Framework for Decision-Making*. London and Sterling, VA: Earthscan.

Wozniak, M. (2002) 'Les stations de ski: quelles représentations des clientèles pour quel cadre bâti?'. *RGA*, 90(4): 18–31.

Zanini, R.C. (2013) 'Dynamics of the population and dynamics of the memory of an alpine community on the border'. *JAR-RGA*, 101(3). Available at: https://rga.revues.org/2254 (accessed 1 August 2017).

Zeller, C. (2001) *Globalisierungsstrategien – Der Weg von Novartis*. Berlin and Heidelberg: Springer.

Zeller, C. and Messerli, P. (2010) 'The pharma-biotech complex and interconnected regional innovation arenas'. *Urban Studies*, 47(13): 2867–94

Index

Page numbers in *italics* indicate figures and in **bold** indicate tables.

For Product Safety Concerns and Information please contact our EU
representative GPSR@taylorandfrancis.com Taylor & Francis Verlag GmbH,
Kaufingerstraße 24, 80331 München, Germany

Printed and bound by CPI Group (UK) Ltd, Croydon, CR0 4YY
01/05/2025
01858416-0005